T0258196

The CISO Evolution

The CISO Evolution

Business Knowledge for Cybersecurity Executives

MATTHEW K. SHARP

KYRIAKOS P. LAMBROS

WILEY

Published by John Wiley & Sons, Inc., Hoboken, New Jersey.
Published simultaneously in Canada.

For general information on our other products and services or for technical support, please contact our Customer Care Department within the United States at (800) 762-2974, outside the United States at (317) 572-3993 or fax (317) 572-4002.

Wiley also publishes its books in a variety of electronic formats. Some content that appears in print may not be available in electronic formats. For more information about Wiley products, visit our web site at www.wiley.com.

Library of Congress Cataloging-in-Publication Data

Names: Sharp, Matthew K., author. | Lambros, Kyriakos P., author.
Title: The CISO evolution : business knowledge for cybersecurity executives
  / Matthew K. Sharp, Kyriakos P. Lambros.
Description: Hoboken, New Jersey : Wiley, [2022] | Includes index.
Identifiers: LCCN 2021044404 (print) | LCCN 2021044405 (ebook) | ISBN
  9781119782483 (hardback) | ISBN 9781119782506 (adobe pdf) | ISBN
  9781119782490 (epub)
Subjects: LCSH: Chief information officers. | Computer security. |
  Management information systems—Security measures.
Classification: LCC HD30.2 .S5325 2022 (print) | LCC HD30.2 (ebook) | DDC
  658.4/038011—dc23
LC record available at https://lccn.loc.gov/2021044404
LC ebook record available at https://lccn.loc.gov/2021044405

Cover Design: Wiley
Cover Image: © Wahyu Hermawan and Mark John N. Madriaga of 99Designs

SKY10085491_091924

This book is dedicated to:

Matt's wife and son, Luz and Aleco
Rock's wife, Mary
They provided us with unlimited love and support in this journey.

Contents

Foreword   ix

Preface   xi

Acknowledgments   xv

Introduction   1

PART I   Foundational Business Knowledge   7

CHAPTER 1   Financial Principles   9

CHAPTER 2   Business Strategy Tools   29

CHAPTER 3   Business Decisions   55

CHAPTER 4   Value Creation   91

CHAPTER 5   Articulating the Business Case   129

PART II   Communication and Education   167

CHAPTER 6   Cybersecurity: A Concern of the Business,
                Not Just IT   169

CHAPTER 7   Translating Cyber Risk into Business Risk   197

CHAPTER 8   Communication – You Do It Every Day
                (or Do You?)   239

PART III   Cybersecurity Leadership   **273**

CHAPTER 9   Relationship Management   275

CHAPTER 10   Recruiting and Leading High Performing Teams   307

CHAPTER 11   Managing Human Capital   339

CHAPTER 12   Negotiation   367

Conclusion   383
Index   385

Foreword

Welcome to an incredible period of change in cybersecurity – what an amazing time to be in this field!

In the chapters that follow, two of the industry's leading critical thinkers divulge the skills and knowledge a cybersecurity leader must acquire to successfully build a modern-day cybersecurity program. To get the job done they combine personal stories, practical knowledge, and intimate case studies.

My colleagues Rock Lambros and Matthew Sharp will challenge us to think about cybersecurity on a new level. They encourage us to contemplate managing our cybersecurity programs differently, through a business lens. What's more, they offer us the tools to make that transition a reality.

With 40 years combined industry experience across many verticals, I'm confident you'll find the following pages rich with key insights about building, sustaining, and maintaining your cybersecurity program. I can't think of two more qualified practitioners to lead the charge in shaping how we must evolve our approach to aligning cybersecurity programs with business objectives.

Rock and Matt offer profound insights into how organizations should design, adapt, and embrace cybersecurity best practices to ensure business alignment. Gone are the days of selling your security program through Fear, Uncertainty, or Doubt (FUD). The era of digital business will require executive presence to claim your seat at the table.

The success that has brought you to your current role is a good start. I'd like to disrupt your assumptions and inspire a deliberate review of what you need to survive in the middle of the cybersecurity jungle. I would encourage you to consult this timeless, universally applicable reference in your journey forward.

The *CISO Evolution: Business Knowledge for Cybersecurity Executives* is not only your survival guide – it's a blueprint for the aspiring cybersecurity leaders of tomorrow. The concepts in this book are proven through multiple industries. As life learners, Rock and Matt hope to ignite a spark in you; meanwhile, their courage coupled with their commitment to give back to our community was the driving force that led to this seminal work.

The only constant with our field is change, and the rate of change continues to intensify. If you think you've seen it all so far; I'm here to tell you we've not seen anything yet. The future holds boundless uncertainty!

How do we stay current? More importantly, how do we embrace this change while ensuring alignment with the business?

The answer is *The CISO Evolution: Business Knowledge for Cybersecurity Executives*.

As you read this book, please keep in mind that most businesses are trying to move at the speed of innovation. We need something radically different. Rock and Matt are the industry experts prying open a new door to an unexplored path that will make us think differently about our cybersecurity programs.

Demetrios Lazarikos (Laz)
3x CISO, 30+ Year Security Veteran
Business and Technical Advisor
Co-Founder, Blue Lava

Preface

To know and not to do, is really not to know.
                                        —Stephen R. Covey

Go to enough conferences, and a clear pattern emerges. A few industry leaders have the courage and presence to impart wisdom. Yet, most of the industry is an echo chamber of platitudes. Maybe you've heard a hollow statement from a so-called expert. These throwaway phrases reveal nothing, yet our colleagues masquerade behind them as thought leaders. The most insipid example, "Speak to the business in business terms." For too long we have allowed one another to nod in agreement while behind the scenes we consistently fail to apply this wisdom and execute. This book provides a roadmap so that you can start asking the right questions, making the right investments, and delivering outcomes that matter.

The first generation of CISOs learned that with confidence you can cast cybersecurity as a black art that cannot be measured. Eventually, the anecdotes and hopeful statements weren't enough. Business leaders soon learned that cybersecurity knowledge is only part of the job. So, we have arrived at an inflection point. We can do better. We must do better. It's time to evolve.

The challenges of information sharing in our field are known, along with the talent crunch. To cultivate the future leaders of our profession we must exhibit the courage to be vulnerable, as people. Cryptocurrencies, IoT, and the public cloud will accelerate the demand for safe computing. Future economies will rise in cyberspace. The wars of the information age will be fought and won digitally. Competition is no longer about company versus company. Instead, bundles of services and the most effective supply chains dictate the winners and losers of commerce. Courage is the path forward. It won't be easy; it will require that we circumnavigate the legal constraints, licensing restrictions, fear, and self-preservation that has prevented the requisite knowledge sharing and talent development. We fought back each of these dragons in the process of publishing this book.

With the stakes higher than they have ever been, Rock and I hope to share our experience as builders, operators, and consultants. We are both experienced CISOs and MBA graduates. We have supported leaders who failed to convince their businesses of the importance of cybersecurity risk. We have lived these symptoms:

- Failure to garner trust from executive leadership
- Misaligned expectations around risk appetite and capital allocation
- Misperception of cybersecurity's role in business
- Demoralization of your team in the face of cyber risk acceptance
- Increased stress and anxiety from managing an underfunded program

As authors, we see the world through different lenses. We disagree in our politics, our management styles are varied, and we think this phase shift in values and approach will benefit you as the reader. Path dependence is when the decisions presented to people are dependent on historical experiences. So, we complement each other in the diversity of our experience and the order of our career transitions. Rock was an operator for years before starting his own consultancy. In contrast, I spent years in consulting before I was entrusted with the responsibility of operating a security program. Indeed, the world looks different from the vantage of a vendor versus that of an end user. You are treated differently, welcomed or not into circles of peers, and so the lessons you learn, the relationships you build, and soft skills you hone are a product of your path dependence.

With this book, we created a streamlined business reference that is tailored to cybersecurity professionals. It will equip you with insights curated to develop your business acumen, communication, and leadership skills. The chapters expand upon the content often delivered in MBA programs. Each of these capabilities is required by the modern CISO.

We provide you with the tools you need to evolve from a technical leader into an effective cybersecurity executive. Each chapter is packed full of specific, practical advice and real-life stories to help you communicate with business leaders, establish an executive presence, secure cybersecurity budgets, protect what matters, and not only enable, but also accelerate business outcomes.

By contributing our mistakes and experience, we hope to fuel your success and stimulate more forthright dialogue in our industry. If you find value in this book, we'd love to hear from you. And if you disagree, take issue, or find room for us to improve, we'd love to hear from you too!

You can find us at www.CISOEvolution.com, or on LinkedIn:

- Matthew K Sharp – https://www.linkedin.com/in/ciso-mba/
- Kyriakos "Rock" Lambros – https://www.linkedin.com/in/rock lambros/

Acknowledgments

We are grateful to all the people who helped us bring this project to life.

We thank our families that encouraged us and took on responsibilities we could not in the early mornings, long nights, and weekends spent to realize this book. Thank you for reviewing our early drafts, providing your guidance on the logo and cover, and creating space week after week. Thank you for your empathy through the challenges we faced and the mounting stress as the deadline for our final manuscript approached. Thank you for your reassuring words, patience, and believing in this book as we conquered each new surprise. Most of all, thank you for your hugs and for your loving support. Without them, this book would not have been possible.

We thank the many individuals who invested their time to help review and refine the manuscript. The perspectives gained from CEOs, equity investors, industry analysts, consultants, MBA professors, and the many CISOs and cybersecurity professionals who contributed surely improved the accuracy and relevance of our content.

We want to express specific gratitude to Kenneth Ziegler, Brian Ahern, and Lisa Xu, who helped in reviewing various chapters, offering revisions and insights and examining content from a CEO's perspective. Karan Saberwal, Shaun Gordon, and Michael Lee were generous in extending their expertise as equity investors. Paul Proctor has been an inspiration for years. His work at Gartner continues to push the industry forward, and we were lucky enough to benefit from his passion and commitment to emphasize the most important ideas in our text. Timothy Galpin added his perspective with years in M&A consulting and more recently in academia as a professor and academic director. Dave Hannigan and Caroline Wong were reviewers of our book proposal as we pursued a publisher and later contributed as valued reviewers. Their perspectives as cloud and application security pioneers, experienced operators, and mentors have been invaluable. Malcolm Harkins's expertise as a successful Fortune 50 CISO and later entrepreneur has been a beacon, especially during our formative years in the profession. Marilyn Daly for her support in considering the impact of our words from a variety of unique perspectives. Demetrios Lazarikos for his generous time writing the foreword and being a dedicated mentor in cybersecurity and entrepreneurship. The Lean CISO group not already mentioned here: Philip Beyer, Russell Eubanks, Alex Kreilein, Sean Martin, and Jasper Ossentjuk for their friendship and for supporting physical and mental health throughout an unprecedented year.

We thank them all for their guidance and the time each individual invested as it doubtlessly improved our book.

We thank those who gave us permission to quote them, contributed graphics, extended our professional networks, and encouraged our work. Chris and Kristine Laping, Tage Tracy, Craig Fletcher, Stefan Peter Roos, Steven Martano, and Ryan Freilino: we thank you for your willingness to support this project.

We thank the authors and experts who came before us. In many cases, we merely extended their theories, research, and formulated thoughts or shared our experience putting their ideas to work throughout our careers. In most cases, we are bridging other's content into the world of cybersecurity. The Notes section at the end of each chapter does a great job capturing the people who inspired us in this regard. Without their deliberate contributions this body of work would not have been possible.

Finally, we thank Richard Seiersen for his introduction to our publisher. And we thank our team at John Wiley & Sons for seeing the potential of this project: Susan Cerra, Sheck Cho, Samantha Enders, Michael Isralewitz, Beula Jaculin, and the countless others behind the scenes.

Introduction

In the foreword and preface we got aligned on the challenges our industry faces, our motivations for writing the book, and a bit about the authors. To help you use this book as reference in your day-to-day experience, we'll now review the structure of the book and offer a summary of each chapter.

First note that the book has three parts. So, if you plan to read the book front-to-back the flow is natural and the content is cumulative. Chapters at the back of the book assume you are capable of financial analysis, business cases, and other topics covered early on.

In our view, it was important to first establish requisite Foundational Business Knowledge in Part I. That is where you will learn key vocabulary, basic financial formulas, and business strategy tools. We will also review business decision models, valuation methodologies, and business case development. Each chapter (or class) includes one or more case studies to apply the knowledge you've learned. That's true throughout the book, and also true in any MBA program as well. What is different here is that our case studies are developed through the lens of the CISO, rather than a strict business perspective that surfaces in MBA curricula.

Equipped with a common foundation of business knowledge and clear examples of how to apply the core concepts we move on to Part II – Communication and Education. Here you can expect a review of how to leverage COSO, an enterprise risk management framework, to ensure cybersecurity risk fits into the broader context of business risk management. Remember, cybersecurity risk is another risk that needs to be addressed along with financial, operational, strategic, legal, and compliance risk. Just as market, credit, and liquidity risks are types of financial risk, there are subcategories of cyber risk too. So, Part II is the connective tissue that ensures cybersecurity risk is properly framed and prioritized.

Finally, assuming a foundation of business concepts and the proper governance structures for treating cybersecurity risk are in place, you need to lead a team and execute according to the priorities you have established and the projects you have funded. In Part III – Cybersecurity Leadership we review techniques for attracting and retaining talent, and finally negotiation skills that will help you navigate interactions with your employees, colleagues, investors, regulators, and outside vendors.

Now that you know how the book is structured, it's also important to understand how the chapters are structured throughout the book. Through personal stories we outline the opportunities we feel are most relevant at the very beginning of each chapter. Then we introduce theory or research in the *Principle* section. Next, each chapter extends theory with an *Application* section that features one or more illustrative case studies. In some cases, the names or details were adapted to protect the innocent. Finally, each chapter is summarized with a *Key Insights* section that draws out the salient lessons we hope you learn. There is also a Notes section provided at the end of each chapter that outlines supporting research and reference materials.

We recommend that before you read a chapter, you read the Key Insights and examine the Table of Contents. Since we cover many high-level frameworks quickly, this approach will be helpful to keep you oriented in the chapter and book. It's also a speed-reading technique. The following paragraphs provide a summary of each chapter.

Part I – Foundational Business Knowledge

Chapter 1 – Financial Principles. This chapter builds your knowledge of financial statements, reviews connections between each statement, offers free resources for further study, and features two case studies that relate cybersecurity operations to accounting rules and financial statements. Read this chapter to solidify your understanding of EBITDA, CapEx, OpEx, Retained Earnings, and Net Income along with other fundamental vocabulary and accounting concepts.

Chapter 2 – Business Strategy Tools. In the second chapter, we introduce business models, KPIs, and value chains. Other topics include board composition and systems theory. We provide a case study to demonstrate the use of the business model canvas. There are two additional case studies that feature value chain linkages to create competitive advantage. One case study features optimization while the second focuses on coordination. Read this chapter for tools that will help you dissect your business's strategy, understand the supply and demand dynamics of your company operations, connect to primary business measures, and optimally position cybersecurity as a source of competitive advantage.

Chapter 3 – Business Decisions. Our third chapter explores how business decisions are made. Decision-making can be improved with an awareness of the biases and noise that commonly afflict us as human beings. We cover a lightweight application of the scientific method to enhance learning. From there, we dive into decision science and choice architecture frameworks. We briefly examine the use of an influence model, and then we finish the chapter with two case studies. The first case study examines various applications of the decision science framework in the context of a hypothetical new CISO scenario. In the second case study we apply choice architecture to phishing defense.

Chapter 4 – Value Creation. The fourth chapter is all about business valuation. We naturally start by defining what we mean by *value*. Then, we examine the critical attributes of value. Next, we explore how those attributes surface in determining business valuations. Additionally, we examine investor types, means of return, valuation methodologies, and common value drivers. The application section covers the core concepts in a case study that applies security strategy in the context of business valuation for a hypothetical beverage manufacturer.

Chapter 5 – Articulating the Business Case. To get the fifth chapter started, we review several important cost concepts including incremental, opportunity, and sunk cost. From there we explore a communication framework, and two financial analysis methods: cost benefit analysis and net present value. Finally, we close out the chapter with three case studies. The first examines a successful budget request for password management, and the second applies cost benefit analysis to the same project. The final case study leverages a Monte Carlo simulation to examine possible net present value outcomes of a revenue-generating opportunity resulting from delivery of security services.

Part II – Communication and Education

Chapter 6 – Cybersecurity: A Concern of the Business, Not Just IT. In Part II, we will build upon Part I and introduce additional tools that transform cyber risk issues into enterprise risk dialogue. This chapter starts to break down the COSO framework. It lays the foundation for elevating cyber risk conversations to enterprise risk by focusing on the first two guiding principles of COSO:

- *Governance and Culture*
- *Strategy and Objective Setting*

At the end of this chapter, the case study relives one of the author's greatest regrets and warns of the consequences of failing to establish a robust governance structure.

Chapter 7 – Translating Cyber Risk into Business Risk. Chapter 6 discussed establishing a cyber risk management program's foundation using COSO's first two guiding principles. This chapter expands upon those foundations and focuses on executing the cyber risk program and rolling up cyber risk into a portfolio view of enterprise risk that executive leaders, and the board, can use to make business decisions. To do this, we will align with the final three risk management components of COSO:

- *Performance*
- *Review and Revision*
- *Information, Communication, and Reporting*

The case study reveals how the author helped an organization align its cybersecurity program to its enterprise risk management efforts. This ultimately highlighted previously unknown risks and secured additional funding from its board of directors.

Chapter 8 – Communication – You Do It Every Day (or Do You?). This chapter challenges you to examine how you communicate. It provides a structure to improve communication for the explicit purpose of advancing a cybersecurity program. We close this chapter by expanding upon the case study in Chapter 7. We take you into the boardroom to eavesdrop on the conversation between the author and the board of directors.

Part III – Cybersecurity Leadership

Chapter 9 – Relationship Management. You cannot operate in a vacuum. A robust cybersecurity program relies on individual technical skills and interpersonal relationships. Read this chapter to master the four key skills of relationship management: maintaining trust, indirect influence, managing through conflict, and professional networking. We conclude with two case studies. The first demonstrates how some humble pie is the remedy to establishing greater trust. The second case study shows the importance of a professional network as the author transitioned from being an operator to an entrepreneur.

Chapter 10 – Recruiting and Leading High Performing Teams. The cybersecurity skills gap is well documented yet hotly debated. However, as a leader, you must ensure you have the right people in the right roles at the right time. This chapter will dive into methodologies we utilized to attract, retain, and lead high-performing teams. The case study walks through the perils of combining a bureaucratic hiring process with an inability to implement the hiring practices we advocate for in this chapter. The same case study then walks through what it was like to get "baptized by fire" in servant leadership.

Chapter 11 – Managing Human Capital. Read this chapter for specific tools to baseline strengths, critical considerations in managing a multigenerational workforce, the importance of training, the criticality of diversity, and cognitive biases to be aware of that may rear themselves in our day-to-day jobs. The case study brings to bear a cost-benefit analysis technique outlined in Chapter 5 to demonstrate the actual value of training and the true cost of eliminating it from a constrained budget.

Chapter 12 – Negotiation. In this penultimate chapter, we focus on adapting the skills from Chris Voss (a former FBI hostage negotiator) as featured in his book *Never Split the Difference: Negotiating As If Your Life Depended On It*. There are countless negotiations you perform every day. If you can be successful in your negotiations while preserving your relationships, you have what it takes to generate cultural change. The chapter concludes with a case study on building security culture and application security using the negotiation techniques introduced.

Conclusion. We conclude the book with a heartfelt note of gratitude and an optimistic eye toward a brighter future. Engage us online at www.CISOEvolution.com

PART I

Foundational Business Knowledge

CHAPTER 1

Financial Principles

Embrace Reality and Deal with It.

— Ray Dalio

Opportunity

It's easy to get distracted by how you think things should be. Yet, it is critical to understand how they really are. Early in my career, I often identified ways that would make my work more efficient. When there was a dependency on resources I didn't have, I usually stewed in frustration about how stupid the people were who designed such a flawed system in the first place.

It wasn't until years later that I learned optimizing all parts of a system does *not* necessarily optimize the system itself. You see, every organization has a mission and limited resources. Today, nearly all organizations in the modern economy deliver value through technology. However, not all organizations and leaders agree upon the importance of cybersecurity.

As a cybersecurity leader, it's your job to educate, build consensus, and secure necessary resources. Organizational mission and cybersecurity goals must be aligned. I think Malcolm Harkins said it best: "We provide protection that enables information to flow through the organization, our partners, and our customers. We protect the technology that our organizations create to provide new experiences and opportunities for our customers."[1]

Now, imagine for a moment you are on vacation and you've decided to travel internationally. The country you're visiting speaks another language. You've done your part to learn a few keywords before your arrival, so you have the basic vocabulary. You can count to 10, you can ask about the time, and you know different words that indicate modes of transportation.

There you sit in the terminal at the bus station, and the time comes for your bus to leave. You make your way to the platform and discover – no bus. Of course, you don't know if you missed the bus, if it is late, or if they simply changed the platform. When you turn to ask a passerby, they don't speak your language. You go back to the information desk and ask for help. The attendant offers hints at what to do through gestures, but you remain a bit uncertain. The attendant tells you what you can only make out to mean "The bus will come 8."

What does that mean? Bus #8, platform 8, at 8 p.m., in 8 minutes – there's no way to be sure because neither of you possesses adequate language.

It is precisely this experience that happens worldwide as companies decide how much they should invest in cybersecurity. Without a foundational understanding of accounting and financial principles you are unlikely to succeed in securing the appropriate resources required so that you may effectively protect and enable your organization.

What is also true is that business leaders speak the language of business. They are dependent upon you to communicate about your topic of expertise, cybersecurity, in a language they can understand.

This concept isn't new – we've been hearing about it for several decades now. You'll encounter the phrase "speak in business language" in professional journals and conferences alike. Yet, there seems to be very little information available to outline the critical vocabulary and concepts that cybersecurity practitioners need to secure their "seat at the table."

Principle

The focus of this first chapter is to establish critical vocabulary and fundamental business knowledge. We will briefly overview several terms only to the extent required to understand their application. Naturally, these terms have been covered in detail elsewhere. When possible, we will point to our favorite resources. These resources emphasize cheap or free, easy to consume, and available in a convenient format. That should help you dig into various topics that pique your interest or prove weak points in your knowledge base. We think you'll pick up a few of the most valuable nuggets right here in this very first chapter, so resist your temptation to skip forward.

To get you started, I'll share the approach I used to structure my pursuit of business acumen. At the time, I was a consultant, and a high percentage of my work weeks included commuting by plane to a customer site.

That's where I learned about Josh Kaufman's *The Personal MBA* (https://personalmba.com/), which touts "A world-class business education in a single volume." Since I am perhaps the slowest reader in the world, I decided to expedite my knowledge acquisition by leveraging getAbstract (https://www.getabstract.com/), which as of this writing, claims to contain "the key insights of 20,000+ nonfiction books summarized into compelling 10-minute reads." These were a great start, but ultimately, I obtained an MBA because I wasn't confident that my cursory review was sufficient. We hope this book can be an alternative, serving as a shortcut to the long nights and imbalance that a master's degree can impose on your personal life.

Conceptually there are relatively few things you need to master from this chapter. You need to know a handful of vocabulary words, how to read and understand financial statements, and how to apply them to your role as a cybersecurity leader. The good news is – that's it – from an accounting and finance perspective!

It is worth mentioning that later in the book, we'll continue to infuse these foundational business concepts with other topics intended to develop more complete business acumen, including Part II – Communication and Education and Part III – Cyber Security Leadership. So let's dive in with our first topic.

Financial Statements

There are three financial statements. The *Income Statement* offers a window into profit performance on a specific date. The *Balance Sheet* describes the financial position comprised of assets, liabilities, and equity at a particular point in time. And finally, the *Statement of Cash Flows* describes what cash came into the business and what went out in a given period (typically a quarter or a year).

Income Statement

As with any complex topic, it can be helpful to start at a very high level and then pursue a more nuanced understanding. To get started, we're going to review the critical elements of an income statement:

- Revenue
- Cost of Goods Sold (COGS) / Cost of Revenue
- Gross Profit (GP)
- Sales, General and Administrative (SG&A) Expenses
- Earnings Before Interest, Taxes, Depreciation, and Amortization (EBITDA)
- Depreciation Expense
- Amortization Expense
- Earnings Before Interest and Taxes (EBIT)
- Interest Expense
- Income Tax Expense
- Net Income (Bottom Line)

The order of each item conveys a story. A few items appear in gray. They are not required and, therefore, may not be present in all income statements. However, you can always calculate them from the information available. The elements in gray often serve as metrics that have a significant influence on behaviors in business. Let's cover each of the items and reveal the story they tell.

Revenue

First, we start with revenue, which can often be called the *top line*. Revenue is essentially the amount of money that the company received for the sale of its product or services. Without revenue, you can't pay for any of the expenses that follow, so this is a great place to start. Some companies focus on Net Revenue. You can calculate it by subtracting discounts, returns, and allowances from revenue.

Depending upon your business model and perhaps the economic sector, there are often compelling arguments that a cybersecurity leader can make about how their team contributes to enhancing revenue acquisition. Accelerating revenue is especially true for software or SaaS companies serving highly regulated industries, as their customers undoubtedly have significant compliance obligations. One good indicator is if your cybersecurity team is helping sales complete diligence questionnaires for your customers and prospects. If so, then you are certainly part of the sales cycle and serve as an advocate of revenue acquisition. Third-party risk management (TPRM) is undoubtedly a complicated endeavor that may seem duplicative and, at times, even unproductive. Do not fall prey to the trap.

Instead, embrace your role here. More sales activity means more revenue to fund operations – including cybersecurity operations. TPRM also gives you a view into revenue sources, what types of customers you will soon serve, and what value expectations exist. These insights can help you anticipate demands on other areas of your security program.

Cost of Goods Sold/Cost of Revenue

Next, we see the term *COGS*, which only makes sense in a company that produces a physical product. In a services (or software) business, you are more likely to see the term *cost of revenue*. It means the same thing, but the terminology is a bit different. There are all kinds of nuanced language with financial statements that mostly get us to the same outcome. Start with what your customers paid you, subtract the costs, and determine what remains for retained earnings, future investment, or dividends.

Suffice it to say that there are generally accepted accounting principles that specify what expenses you must group and where they must appear in the financial statements. COGS / cost of revenue includes raw materials, shipping costs, sales commission, and direct labor costs.

If your business is not primarily in the delivery of cybersecurity services or software, you probably don't have a role to play in this line item. However, you may be able to augment funding sources or support the cybersecurity program by partnering with other business stakeholders with a heavy COGS expense concentration. It may be easier to obtain security champions in other teams that perhaps establish a dotted line reporting structure. Partnering in this way can be a great source of operational leverage by ensuring more consistent security outcomes but requiring less of your direct managerial attention.

GROSS PROFIT

Gross profit (GP) is the profit a company makes after removing the costs associated with manufacturing and selling its products or delivering its services. You calculate GP by subtracting the COGS from revenue.

$$\text{Gross Profit} = \text{Revenue} - \text{COGS}$$

Note that gross margin is a commonly used and very similar term. Frequently people (incorrectly) use it interchangeably with GP. In short, gross margin is a percentage value, while GP is a monetary value. They both represent the resources available to invest in your business and accelerate growth after you have directly delivered upon your commitment to your customers.

To calculate gross margin:

$$\text{Gross Margin} = \left(\text{Net Revenue} - \text{COGS}\right) / \text{Net Revenue}$$

Margin profile can be a value gate in deriving a company's worth. That is to say, some business models anticipate a high gross margin (SaaS, professional services, etc.) while others will not (such as an electronic components distributor, value-added reseller, airline, etc.). Either way, you want to be clear on gross margin expectations. Ask your financial planning and analysis (FP&A) team if you don't already know.

SALES, GENERAL, AND ADMINISTRATIVE EXPENSES

Some costs can be difficult, if not impossible, to assign to specific revenue-generating activities directly. These are things like rent, phone, utilities, and salaries for shared services such as Legal, IT, and Cybersecurity. They all frequently fall into the category of Sales, General, and Administrative (SG&A) expenses, and this is why cyber-security is often a "cost center." For now, just know that no enterprise cost reduction or transformation effort is complete without some consideration of SG&A expenses. Note that SG&A may also appear under the title *operating expenses*.

EBITDA

One way to calculate Earnings Before Interest, Taxes, Depreciation, and Amortization (EBITDA) is by building up from the bottom of the income statement. Starting with Net Income, we'll add each item to derive our final value, or we can start with the top line and subtract.

$$EBITDA = Net\ Income + Interest + Taxes + Depreciation + Amortization$$

OR

$$EBITDA = Net\ Revenue - Cost\ of\ Goods\ Sold\,(COGS) - Operating\ Expenses + Depreciation + Amortization$$

We'll go into business valuation in much more detail in Chapter 4 – Value Creation. For now, it's essential to know that using an EBITDA multiple is one of the most common methods for valuing a company. EBITDA is particularly useful to investors as it provides a more transparent view of financial results. Unfortunately, accounting methods selected (for depreciation in particular) can enhance profits artificially. Using EBITDA helps expose the underlying cash generating profile of the business. In any given year, there are one-time expenses that may impact EBITDA. The goal is not to make you an expert in calculating EBITDA (leave that to your accounting and finance departments). Instead, the purpose of reviewing the formulas is to offer you an awareness of the relationship each of the income statement line items has with the metrics your company executives care about most.

DEPRECIATION AND AMORTIZATION

In the course of operating a business, assets wear down or become obsolete. Obsolescence applies to both tangible and intangible assets. For example, servers may break down over time, and a company can only legally enforce intellectual property rights, such as patents, for a limited number of years. Because assets have useful lives that frequently last longer than one accounting period, accountants reduce the value of these assets over their estimated service lives. The term *depreciation* applies when the asset is tangible, such as furniture or computers. Similarly, accountants use *amortization* when an asset is intangible.

EBIT

Earnings Before Interest and Taxes (EBIT) is similar to EBITDA. In this case, we pull the depreciation and amortization expenses back into the picture. *Operating profit* considers the Capital Expenditures that span more than one accounting period and reflect the profit or loss resulting from operations more accurately. Investors examine operating profit to separate a company's operational performance from the costs of the capital structure and tax expenses.

$$EBIT = Net\ Income + Interest + Taxes$$

OR

$$EBIT = Net\ Revenue - Cost\ of\ Goods\ Sold\,(COGS)$$
$$- Operating\ Expenses$$

INTEREST EXPENSE

Interest expense reflects the payable liability resulting from any borrowing management has done to fund operations. It is often evaluated outside the operational analysis and is called a nonoperating expense. Interest expense includes loans, lines of credit, bonds, and any type of convertible debt. There is often very little that cybersecurity teams can do to affect the interest expense.

INCOME TAX EXPENSE

The government collects taxes to finance public services or national programs. One source of funding that contributes to these services is income tax. So, a tax expense is a liability owed to the government. Again, cybersecurity teams cannot impact the tax expense materially.

NET INCOME

Net income is what you have left after you have subtracted away everything you spent. For that reason, it is also known as the bottom line. As you will see, net income connects to retained earnings, which is the cash a company keeps to finance further operations. The relationship becomes much more apparent in the Connections Between the Financial Statements section later in this chapter.

If by this point you are feeling pretty good, then, by all means, keep reading. If you're feeling a little uncertain or unsettled about your mastery of the materials, spend some time settling in with these concepts. Here are several great resources to help you close the knowledge gap:

- http://www.responsive.net/Accounting.skills.html
- http://www.accountingcoach.com/
- http://accountingexplained.com/financial/introduction/

Balance Sheet

A balance sheet offers a view into the capital structure or how an organization finances its assets through a combination of debt and equity. A simple formula summarizes the information contained on the balance sheet:

$$Assets = Liabilities + Equity$$

The financial condition includes ensuring that the company has enough cash and controlling liabilities relative to assets and revenues. The financial state is primarily a Chief Financial Officer (CFO) responsibility.

One standard financial ratio on the balance sheet is the Debt-to-Equity (D/E) ratio. A heavily leveraged company will have a relatively high D/E ratio. Meaning, the company has borrowed a lot to finance operations. Typically, analysts compare a D/E ratio of one company to another company competing in the same or similar industry.

That is to say, comparing the debt-to-equity (D/E) ratio of a high-growth SaaS technology company to an energy company wouldn't be an informative analysis. The risk profile, stability of revenue, equipment required to operate, and borrowing costs will be very different given the risk to lenders for each of these very different business models. In my experience, the only time I ever considered any of these balance sheet topics was in deciding to take the job or not. Even then, the issue surfaced indirectly via a line of questioning: "Do I have a budget? How is it funded? What control do I have over it?"[2]

While the balance sheet is essential to company managers, it is not typically a driving force in conversations outside of one key element that appears indirectly on the balance sheet – Capital Expenditures.

CAPITAL EXPENDITURES

Capital Expenditures (CapEx) are expenses that a company capitalizes. That means it records expenses on its balance sheet as an investment rather than on its income statement as an expenditure. This process was touched upon briefly in the Depreciation and Amortization section. Again, for clarity, assets have useful lives that last longer than a given accounting period. So, accountants reduce the value of these assets over their estimated service lives. This value appears as a depreciation or amortization expense, which is a fraction of the actual cost in most cases.

CapEx becomes particularly crucial in a business where Enterprise Value (EV), or what the company is worth to investors, is determined by an EBITDA multiple. Notice that EBITDA, the value driver of the business, does not include depreciation and amortization expense.

In some cases, CapEx may include capitalized labor associated with the development of intangible assets – such as software, intellectual property, and patents. There are several cybersecurity activities in the new cloud era you can consider capitalizing.[3]

Additionally, consider the Productive Asset Investment Ratio (PAIR). If capital expenditures exceed annual depreciation, the business is likely expanding as more fixed assets are added than have depreciated over the same time. This ratio can be a clear indicator of a company's willingness to maintain its current level of investment. If the value is below 1.0, the business may have accounting or operational challenges. Companies with a value greater than 1.0 have more valuable earnings (because they aren't delaying capital expenditures to boost their profits).

Statement of Cash Flows

Cash flow statements show the change in cash over the accounting period. Cashflow statements are structured to demonstrate how the cash balance was affected by Operating, Investing, and Financing activities.

Operating activities may include selling, collecting payments and interest, building or purchasing inventory, paying salaries, and contracting third-party suppliers and service providers. Investing may comprise buying and selling noncurrent assets, typically termed Property, Plant, and Equipment (PPE). Finally, Financing activities include paying down debts, issuing equity and dividends, borrowing funds, and even repurchasing stock.

There is value in clarifying: the statement of cash flow tells you **nothing** of profit. That is to say, your cash balance can, and often does, go down during profitable growth. Also, it is equally probable for cash to increase while a business operates in the red (unprofitably).

The relationship between cash and profit is perhaps one of the most common points of confusion. At the heart of the difficulty is accrual accounting. Accrual accounting matches revenue and expenses at the time of a transaction, rather than when payment is received or made. This matching simplifies accounting in practice but conceptually results in some very unintuitive implications for managers.

For example, if you outsourced your third-party risk management (TPRM), you may pay an annual subscription fee upfront, say on January 1. However, to consummate the transaction, the partner must deliver the service in full. So, if there was a $120,000 subscription for the year, your expenses may accrue $10,000 per month throughout the year. In this example, you paid the TPRM vendor in January, but the service must be delivered to complete the transaction. Now imagine, in this case, that your TPRM vendor heavily discounted the sale to a point where providing the service was not profitable. On January 1, you paid the service in full, but the business proceeded to operate unprofitably, and your vendor realized a loss by the end of the year. Indeed, cash flow is not profit.

You may be wondering, "Then what good is cash flow, and why should we care?" Simply stated, it's the inflows and outflows of cash for a business. To operate a business, you have to pay your debts when they come due. If you cannot, you may be declared insolvent. Cash flow and balance sheet insolvency tests are the two ways of determining insolvency.[4]

As a cybersecurity leader, managing operating activities is likely the most significant lever you have to impact insolvency, for example, by negotiating extended payables when you contract with third-party providers. There are assuredly prescriptive procurement processes in larger companies that ensure your contracting practices align with company standards. Otherwise, you can try requesting Net 45 rather than Net 30 in your terms and conditions. That just means payment is due 45 days after the invoice date rather than the typical 30. Everyone recognizes it takes time to make a payment. While that time passes, essentially, one company is "financing" the amount for the other. Let's be honest; the payment terms on cybersecurity consulting engagements aren't likely to make a sizable difference for the business. But your finance department will at least appreciate awareness of the issue. Also, tactically conceding terms like this helps create reciprocity when negotiating a contract. More on negotiating in Chapter 12 – Negotiation.

Now, let's briefly contrast insolvency with bankruptcy. An organization may declare bankruptcy if its only option to resolve a distressed financial position cannot be addressed by selling off all assets to clear its total debt. At this point, the courts initiate a legal process to resolve the debt. The court decides how the bankrupt company will repay debts. Debt repayment plans may include selling tangible and intangible assets.

While your ability to impact insolvency is low, your ability to protect against bankruptcy is more pronounced. Some examples where cybersecurity failures led directly to bankruptcy include (Dante, 2019):[5]

- Intellectual-property loss (Westinghouse Nuclear, Nortel Networks, SolarWorld)
- Loss of cash resulting from cryptocurrency exchange compromise (Mt. Gox, YouBit)
- Wire transfer fraud (Little and King, LLC)
- Lost revenue from contract termination (Altegrity Risk International)
- Ransomware (Colorado Timberline)
- Other extortion (Code Space)

In many businesses, cash is king. To successfully navigate the political landscape, you must know what figures business managers are looking to optimize either for their benefit or the company as a whole. Next, we'll examine the best resource I know of to empower your understanding of how financial statements impact behaviors and decisions.

Connections Between the Financial Statements

How to Read a Financial Report: Wringing Vital Signs Out of the Numbers by John A. Tracy is one of the most profoundly productive resources presented during my MBA. In particular, he offers an exhibit that provides a visual overview of the connections between the three financial statements (see Figure 1.1).

Throughout this chapter, I mentioned we would pull together a few concepts in this section, including:

- Net Income and Retained Earnings
- CapEx and EBITDA
- Cash and Profit

NET INCOME AND RETAINED EARNINGS

As you can see in Figure 1.1, the balance sheet features retained earnings. Retained earnings are the cash that a company decides to keep at the end of an accounting period. But notice that in this example, retained earnings are less than net income. Where did the rest of the cash go? Follow the arrows, and you quickly discover a Cash Dividend from Profit paid to owners.

Retained Earnings = Net Income – Cash Dividend from Profit

CapEx AND EBITDA

Again, using Figure 1.1, it is easy to connect the relevant elements in the financial statements. In this case, the Accumulated Depreciation contra account on the balance sheet relates to the Depreciation Expense on the income statement. Ironically, because depreciation is a noncash expense, it is added back to the cash flow statement in the operating activities section, alongside other expenses such as amortization. This accounting trick keeps the books balanced but tends to be conceptually very difficult.

The point is only to clarify relationships in the figure. It's worth noting that long-term equity investors will prefer another value, Free Cash Flow, which we will discuss further in Chapter 4 – Value Creation. This preference is that EBITDA ignores CapEx, which is an issue to be considered in capital-intensive industries.

Dollar Amounts in Thousands

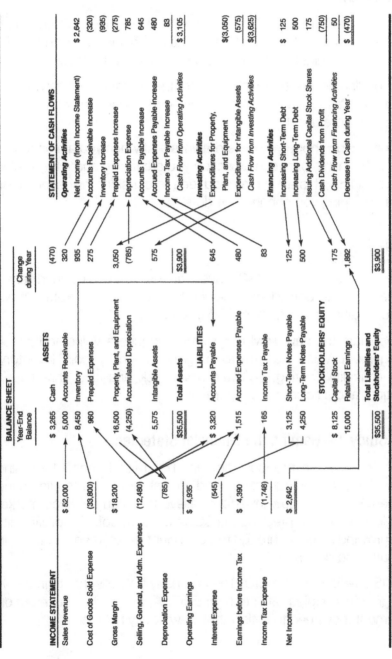

FIGURE 1.1 Connections Between Three Financial Statements

Source: J. A. Tracy and J. Wiley (2013). *How to Read a Financial Report: Wringing Vital Signs Out of the Numbers* (7th ed.). John Wiley & Sons. Reproduced with permission of John Wiley & Sons.

Cash and Profit

Finally, in this example, it's evident that the Decrease in Cash during Year on the Statement of Cash Flows has nothing to do with the Net Income (bottom line) of the company on the Income Statement.

Tracy dedicates an entire chapter to the *Impact on Growth and Decline on Cash Flow* if you're interested in understanding this relationship in more detail.

The conclusion I hope you have drawn is that when you are uncertain of the relationship between an action you are taking and a key metric in the business, it is always a good idea to consider this resource as an aid in helping you connect the dots.

Application

Imagine there are two CISOs hired at the same time in different companies. They both identify the need to create and operate a threat and vulnerability management (TVM) program.

You estimate the new TVM program will require a Vulnerability Risk Management (VRM) platform to integrate scanning tools, inventory, asset criticality scoring, software-driven risk analytics, threat feed ingestion, and efficient ticket operations.

Case Study 1 – Gaming the Financial Statements

In this first case, a product company has raised capital by selling equity. They are a publicly traded global product manufacturing company, and their new investors believe they can enhance market capitalization by compressing the SG&A costs to optimize profitability while growing revenue through more efficient deployment of capital in the marketing department.

The CISO reports to the CIO. The company believes that higher revenue growth, coupled with stronger EBITDA, will provide the return on investment they need to satisfy their new equity holders.

What are the key challenges you see in this situation? What actions might you recommend?

In this case, likely, the CISO budget primarily comprises SG&A. This account is already a target for cost reduction, so you can anticipate more scrutiny before you begin.

Unfortunately, "One size fits all" targets are all too common when performing cost reduction.[6] Deloitte reports that "it is common for companies to tackle SG&A cost reductions by implementing across-the-board cuts without fully understanding the potential impact on their business. A company may use an opportunity assessment and a high-level business case to identify optimal savings and improvements. Targeted restructuring or cost reductions may be better suited to optimize growth strategies."[7]

While it's not clear how your company will behave, one approach to consider is to capitalize the program build-out while noting in the future you will eventually need an operational budget to manage and maintain the program.[8] There are accounting rules that guide what can be capitalized, so if there's any confusion, a quick conversation with your accounting team will provide the clarity you need.

By capitalizing costs in the first year, you can move the expense from SG&A to a much smaller depreciation expense by spreading the investment over several years. For example, a purchase of $1M can be expensed equally over four years of its useful life, implying an annual expense of $250K. The yearly impact on EBITDA is only $250K. Your employer's FP&A can advise you on the threshold over which specific amounts are capitalized, as well as timeframes for useful lives.

Case Study 2 – Proper Team Structure and Tooling Enables Value Creation

The other business is a professional services firm. The CISO reports up through Legal and to the Board of Directors via the Audit Committee. The company recently hired a new CTO to transform the business by bringing new digital platforms online to support more efficient operations and innovative new service offerings for customers. The company's focus is on building an agile and more entrepreneurial business by encouraging the rapid adoption of state-of-the-art technologies in the public cloud.

Also, the company plans to test and iterate through various technology platforms rapidly. As such, you don't want to make any large investments with significant implementation timelines where incorrect assumptions could lead to poorly tooled security operations.

Knowing your company's key financial metrics helps you better structure your budget and potential investments. In this case, the company's focus is on growing revenue and market share.

By now, you should be thinking about how the business will consider OpEx. Yes, your CTO will favor an approach that heavily leans into cloud-native technologies and augments that with additional independent software vendors (ISVs) that play well in a multi-cloud environment.

There will be a much larger appetite for you to hire team members with skills that help guide DevOps teams. By collaborating to implement best practices that are architecturally sound and congruent with rapid development, you might even consider placing budget and staff outside the security team directly under the control and supervision of the CTO. Expensive scanning tools that integrate into traditional endpoint and SIEM solutions might be great for the existing technology stack and security operations. However, be conscious of the need to accommodate new requirements stemming from emerging technology such as Amazon Machine Images (AMIs), Kubernetes (k8s) Clusters, Docker Images, and serverless approaches. Suppose the technology you select and integrate does not have a flexible pricing model. In that case, you might inadvertently commit your mid- to long-term security roadmap to a set of technologies that your company isn't using in a few short months! Instead, consider the following as reported by CSO Online:

- CISOs could depart for their organization suffering a damaging breach, but could leave too in the event of failing to spot or report a bug, poor purchasing decisions, or because of disagreements with senior management.

- One head of information governance, previously working in the US media sector, tells me that there were two occasions she saw her CISO asked to leave. Both dismissals, she said, "mostly centered about [an] inability to address risk to a satisfactory state and in an economical manner."

- Other sources, speaking to me anonymously, recall occasions where their firm's CISO was dismissed for poor reporting, exceeding their budget, not following business strategies, or even spreading FUD (Fear, Uncertainty, and Doubt) rather than delivering practical solutions to these same problems. It was, as one CIO remarked, a case of the CISO "talking the talk, but not walking the walk."[9]

Certainly, exceeding budgets, poor purchasing decisions, and impractical solutions likely stem from a poor understanding of the business. So talk to your finance department. No, really, go send out the invite!

Key Insights

- Align to critical business activities: Depending upon your business model and perhaps the economic sector, there are often compelling arguments that a cybersecurity leader can make about how their team contributes to enhancing revenue acquisition. More sales activity means more revenue to fund operations – including cybersecurity operations.

- Leverage insights that help you plan your future security program: Third-party risk management (TPRM) gives you a view into revenue sources, what types of customers you will soon serve, and what expectations of value exist. These insights can help you anticipate demands on other areas of your security program.

- Know which financial metrics derive your company's valuation:
  - Revenue
  - Enterprise Value
  - EBITDA

- - Debt-to-Equity (D/E) ratio
  - Productive Asset Investment Ratio (PAIR)
  - Etc.
- Understand the role CapEx plays in your business: A $1M capital expenditure can be spread over a useful life of four years, leading to a run rate of $250K per year. Understand how this can impact valuation metrics like EBITDA.
- Place security champions in other teams to keep your CFO happy (depending upon your business model).
- Know how cybersecurity failures can lead directly to bankruptcy.
- Don't commit your mid- to long-term security roadmap to a set of technologies that your company isn't using in a few short months.

Notes

1. Harkins, M.W., *Managing Risk and Information Security: Protect to Enable*, Apress Open, 2016, 6.
2. Hayslip, G., "Questions to Ask Before Accepting That CISO Job Offer," LinkedIn, October 21, 2018. https://www.linkedin.com/pulse/questions-ask-before-accepting-ciso-job-offer-gary-hayslip-cissp-/.
3. Scaled Agile Framework, "CapEx and OpEx," October 2, 2018. https://www.scaledagileframework.com/capex-and-opex/.
4. Udofia, K., "Establishing Corporate Insolvency: The Balance Sheet Insolvency Test," July 2, 2019. https://blogs.harvard.edu/bankruptcyroundtable/tag/cash-flow-insolvency-test/.
5. Dante, E., "Cybersecurity Breach Bankruptcy: It Does Happen – Virtual CISO," January 23, 2019. https://fractionalciso.com/cybersecurity-breach-bankruptcy/.
6. Hawke, K. et al., "Reset and Reallocate: SG&A in the New Normal," June 10, 2020, McKinsey. https://www.mckinsey.com/business-functions/operations/our-insights/reset-and-reallocate-sga-in-the-next-normal.
7. Elliott, D., Kruger, L., Babu, A., and Grobicki, A., "Selling, General and Administration (SG&A) Cost Reduction Focus: A Systematic Approach: The Opportunity Assessment and the Business Case for Improvements," Deloitte, 2016.
8. Golden, B., "IT Moves from SGA to COGS," CIO, March 17, 2016. https://www.cio.com/article/3045279/it-moves-from-sga-to-cogs.html.
9. Drinkwater, D., "These CISOs Explain Why They Got Fired," CSO Online, April 20, 2016. https://www.csoonline.com/article/3057243/these-cisos-explain-why-they-got-fired.html.

CHAPTER 2

Business Strategy Tools

*Everything around you that you call life was made up by
people that were no smarter than you.
And you can change it, you can influence it. . . Once you learn
that, you'll never be the same again.*

— Steve Jobs

Opportunity

Chapter 1 established foundational vocabulary and connected you to
the business's scoreboard, the financial statements. The financial
statements are how the outside world judges your CEO and Board of
Directors. However, most employees never see complete financial
statements. Even in a publicly traded company where the financial
statements are readily available for download, you are unlikely to have
your manager speak directly to the Annual Report, much less distribute it for your review. Instead, operators of the business focus on how
to create, deliver, and capture value.

To ease into the concept of value as a black box, let's begin with an
analogy. Shortly after I graduated from college, I accidentally stumbled into a penetration testing role. I loved it. Breaking stuff was fun!

A successful penetration (pen) tester must understand foundational technologies to be effective. Without knowledge of how database queries or serialization languages function, a pen tester may fail to identify a bug. Further, without understanding the functional and non-functional requirements of an application, coding defects will likely remain undiscovered.[1]

In short, pen testers may emulate specific tactics, techniques, and procedures (TTP) to evaluate an application. Mastery of the pen testing discipline requires that you move beyond guessing what's in the black box. You have to combine TTP **and** organizational context to thrive. You must understand how your target contributes to the organizational flywheel and if you can disrupt the flywheel – people care.[2]

As a leader, the knowledge you use evolves from technical specifics such as SQL, XML, and JSON to business knowledge and influence skill. Mastery of development frameworks, coding methodology, and encoding techniques are no longer the primary predictors of your effectiveness.

Instead, your tool belt looks quite different. Most security professionals fail to capture the elusive opportunity to inject security into executive dialogue and decision-making processes. This chapter will review foundational tools that will enable you to decompose any business from several different perspectives. Without the understanding that these tools provide, you are the management equivalent of a script kiddie. That said, reckless application of these tools can be as dangerous as Metasploit in the hands of a teenager.

So, this chapter will get you pointed in the right direction. Later, in Part II – Communication and Education and Part III – Cyber Security Leadership, we will expand upon the tools covered in this chapter by offering guidance on how to secure budgets, navigate bureaucracies, steer technology decisions, and modify behaviors throughout the business.[3]

Principle

The most fundamental goal of any business is to serve its customers profitably. This section will overview essential tools that intimately connect you to the heart of a company. Specifically, you will learn about business models, company performance metrics, value chains, systems theory, and risk-adjusted measurement. These tools will enable you to:

- Identify key value drivers
- Understand which measures likely influence peer behavior
- Clarify your (cybersecurity) role in the value chain
- Avoid pitfalls revealed by system theory
- Report risk measures in the context of business performance

No doubt, equipped with these requisite tools, your future exploits on the internal battlefield will produce better results. Let's begin with the business model.

Business Model

The business model describes the rationale of how an organization creates, delivers, and captures value. Meanwhile, The Business Model Canvas (the canvas) offers a shared language for describing, visualizing, assessing, and changing business models. The canvas comprises nine basic building blocks, including customer segments, value propositions, channels, customer relationships, revenue streams, key resources, key activities, key partnerships, and cost structure.[4]

Figure 2.1 presents the canvas visually:

As a new or incoming security leader, I suggest building a canvas to solidify your early understanding of the business. Produce the canvas as a formal deliverable of your systematic approach to learning in the first 90 days of employment.[5] Do this business analysis before you get

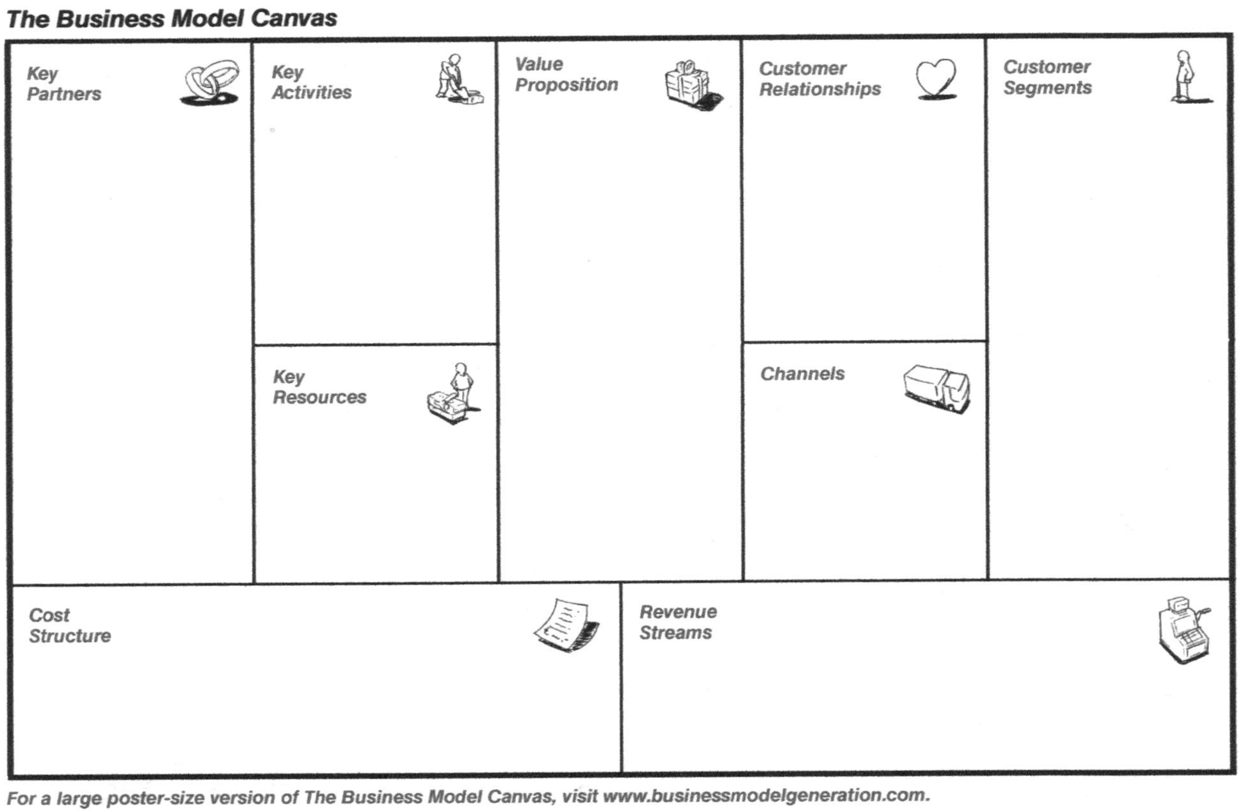

The Business Model Canvas

Key Partners	Key Activities	Value Proposition	Customer Relationships	Customer Segments
	Key Resources		Channels	
Cost Structure			Revenue Streams	

For a large poster-size version of The Business Model Canvas, visit www.businessmodelgeneration.com.

FIGURE 2.1 The Business Model Canvas

Source: Osterwalder, A., and Pigneur, Y., *Business Model Generation: A Handbook for Visionaries, Game Changers, and Challengers*, John Wiley, 2010. Reproduced with permission of John Wiley & Sons
Note that you can use online tools such as the canvanizer (https://next.canvanizer.com/demo/business-model-canvas) to map out your business.

recent audit reports, pen test results, or a systems inventory. Now, if you've been with a company for quite some time, you will also benefit from new insights by completing the mapping exercise. In the Application section of this chapter, we will construct a sample canvas and offer a few examples of how the canvas has proven helpful in driving change within a services business.

Company Performance Measures

One cannot deploy security countermeasures successfully while lacking a solid understanding of the business, its risks, and its compliance obligations.[6] After achieving clarity on the business model, the logical next step in understanding how a business derives value for its customers and equity holders is to dissect its key performance indicators (KPIs).

In most companies, success or failure depends upon a small set of executive KPIs. This streamlined set of metrics often impacts returns for shareholders and compensation for teams/individuals.

Personally, both times that I built and led a security function, the commitment to adding a security leader came immediately following an infusion of capital from a Private Equity (PE) transaction. I have learned that it can be beneficial to understand your Board's makeup, including those who are Independent Directors vs. Controlling Shareholders. Understanding Board composition is helpful even if you don't interact with the Board directly.

There are many types of investors. Each investor has a strategy that will guide the types of investments made. Frequently the investment strategy is derived from a unique ability to enhance the performance of the target investment.

For example, PE investors say they place a heavy emphasis on adding value to their portfolio companies, both before and after they invest. The sources of that added value, in order of importance, are increasing revenue, improving incentives and governance, facilitating a high-value exit or sale, making additional acquisitions, replacing management, and reducing costs.[7]

That is to say, knowing about investors can clarify what types of value creation activities will be most important. The metrics investors commonly care about most include Revenue, Gross Profit, EBITDA, and Free Cash Flow. The relative priority of these metrics will be determined in large part by how investors realize gains. More on this in Chapter 4 – Value Creation.

Ironically, in high-performing teams, these numbers are not usually the focus of individual managers outside of the executive leadership team. To understand why, we need to discuss lead and lag measures. A lead measure tells you if you are likely to reach the goal, while a lag measure tells you if you've achieved it. All the metrics above are lag measures. To illustrate, consider W. Edwards Deming's comments that managing a company by looking at financial data, which are lag measures, is like "driving a car by looking in the rearview mirror."

Considering the lead measures that directly affect the Key Activities, Value Propositions, Cost Structure, and Revenue Streams is an ideal starting place. Once you are clear about which numbers drive your organization's value, you can begin to connect security using the concept of value chains.

Cybersecurity: Part of the Value Chain

For most companies, strategic planning usually starts as a cross-functional off-site exercise for executive teams. Once complete, with organizational targets set, teams break off to organize themselves and execute accordingly. This pattern usually results in cascaded goals, objectives, and measures. Unfortunately, teams optimize within their department, often unaware of the interdependent processes affected by their efforts.

As we all know, operating in silos causes many vexing cultural and performance challenges for middle managers in particular. More than 35 years ago, Michael Porter wrote a book titled *Competitive Advantage: Creating and Sustaining Superior Performance*. In his book, he outlines The Generic Value Chain.

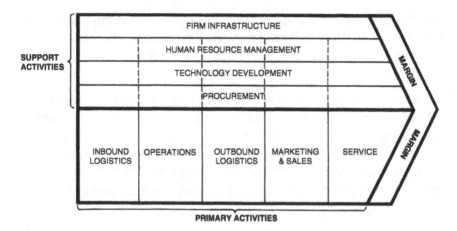

FIGURE 2.2 The Generic Value Chain

Source: Porter, M.E. *Competitive Advantage: Creating and Sustaining Superior Performance*, The Free Press, 1985. Copyright © 1985 by Michael E. Porter. Reprinted with the permission of The Free Press, a division of Simon & Schuster, Inc. All rights reserved.

Using the value chain model, we can examine the discrete building blocks of competitive advantage. He explains that "Firm infrastructure consists of many activities, including general management, planning, finance, accounting, legal, government affairs, and quality management." As seen in Figure 2.2, infrastructure, unlike other support activities, usually supports the entire chain and not individual activities.[8]

Given this definition, cybersecurity can be considered *firm infrastructure* in the context of the value chain model. Per Porter's admission, firm infrastructure is sometimes viewed only as "overhead" but can be a powerful source of competitive advantage. He goes on to explain, "firms have often gained a competitive advantage by redefining the roles of traditional activities."

But we're not done with the model yet. We can go beyond the simple rosy statement that cybersecurity teams can add value in unconventional ways. "Although value activities are the building blocks of competitive advantage, the value chain is not a collection of independent activities but a system of interdependent activities. Linkages within the value chain relate value activities. Linkages are relationships between the way one value activity is performed and the cost or performance of another. Competitive advantage frequently derives from linkages among activities just as it does from the individual activities themselves."

"Though linkages within the value chain are crucial to competitive advantage, they are often subtle and go unrecognized." Indeed, "exploiting linkages also frequently requires optimization or coordination that cuts across conventional organizational lines." And finally, we observe that "given the difficulty of recognizing and managing linkages, the ability to do so often yields a *sustainable* source of competitive advantage."

Porter explains that there are two basic types of competitive advantage: cost leadership and differentiation. Considering his model from the vantage point of cybersecurity yields critical and empowering insights:

- There is ample room for a company to leverage cybersecurity as a competitive advantage.
- A cybersecurity teams' unique position and skill permit it to identify what Porter terms "proprietary learning," a primary source of sustainable differentiation.
- While other parts of a company have a cross-functional supporting role, most of these functions, such as finance, legal, and quality, lack the technical expertise or technology operations intimacy to offer the insights cybersecurity teams naturally surface. These insights are increasingly valuable in the age of "digital transformation."

If this is all true, what should we as security practitioners be looking for given our unique vantage point?

Linkages can lead to competitive advantage in two ways: optimization and coordination.

To begin with, we can start inside our teams. We can model the changes we hope to observe in our broader organization, not by optimizing our own performance alone but instead by serving as a supporting function designed to create competitive advantages for the firm.

Malcolm Harkins got it right when he said, "Security teams need to be the risk-takers, to be at the forefront so they can shape the path." Manage the risk instead of being the ones always saying no. "If you're the one experimenting with it, you can be the one to figure out how to manage the risk before everybody else gets there." Further, "you have to show how, as technology spending grows, you're going to ask for a smaller percentage of that spend, with lower friction on the business and the user experience with lower liability."[9]

In the application section, we'll review an example of optimization and another of coordination.

Apply Systems Theory to Avoid the Trap

There is an increasing focus on Security Performance Management (SPM). This trend, no doubt, correlates with business leaders allocating material budgets to security teams, in addition to pervasive cyber-security board reporting. As with any new term, SPM means different things to different people. For our purposes, I reference SPM only to highlight cybersecurity teams are beginning to optimize in various ways. But don't fall for the trap.

As we just discussed, it is common for business leaders to optimize the performance of their team's processes. All too often we see security teams working hard to optimize security operations or security engineering processes. In contrast, the real target should be to maximize business performance as a whole. Stated differently, optimize the system.

Why is the distinction between system and process so important? The answer lies in one of the fundamental assumptions of systems theory: the whole is not equal to the sum of its parts. The assumption that it is originates in a fundamental algebraic axiom. Unfortunately, however, complex systems are anything but mathematically precise. The improper allocation of the algebraic axiom to the management of organizations would sound like this:

> - *If we break down our system into its components, maximize the efficiency of each one, then reassemble the parts, we'll have the most efficient systems.*
>
> *It's been said that elegant theories are often slain by ugly inconvenient facts. That's the case here. The mathematical or analytical approach to system improvement is one of those victims. It's also been said that the "devil is in the details." Where complex systems are concerned, those details make up many of the aforementioned ugly, inconvenient facts. And they are often in the linkages between system components, not the components (links) themselves. Yet organizations continue to blithely polish the efficiency of these links, blissfully ignorant of the real location of the most vexing contributors to less-than-desirable system performance: the interfaces among components.*[10]

Let me contrast for a moment. I am advocating that you optimize your security function. Further, I am explicitly saying you should **NOT** do so at the expense of business performance. It is necessary to remember that you play a supporting role. In that role, you should actively seek ways to protect important things. How you achieve this needs to consider company performance as a whole.

Vulnerability reporting is a straightforward example. Often, security teams report findings aggregated by the vulnerability. They are tossed over the fence in a spreadsheet format for operations teams to sort through. It is rarely the case that a single group owns all systems impacted by a particular vulnerability. Vulnerability-oriented reporting may result in a lot of effort for other teams. Before they can begin to drive resolution, they must triage and assign tickets to the appropriate team members. In a dynamic environment, it can be very challenging even to get started.

Another typical example is the drag that robust static code analysis can put on a continuous integration/continuous deployment (CI/CD) pipeline used by developers to accelerate organizational learning and enhance market responsiveness. There's no need for pandering to developers or eradicating static code analysis. There are more efficient and operationally friendly ways to balance security outcomes in the context of business performance.

For example, DJ Schleen worked to implement a "fail intelligently" approach by having security scanning tools simply tag a software build with an annotation indicating it can never be released to production because of the vulnerabilities it contains. In this scenario a message is returned to the developer with the warning, and a work item is created for the developer who checked in the code.[11] This is a great example of applying The Three Ways.[12] It serves to increase flow, decrease waste, and balance security in the process. This can be directly associated with primary business outcomes.

Now let's take that concept – security performance wrapped up in a business context – one step further by considering risk-adjusted measurement.

Measure Business Performance Relative to Risk

To illustrate the concept of risk-adjusted measurement, let's briefly examine Modern Portfolio Theory (MPT). Then we'll extend the idea into the world of cybersecurity.

The Sharpe ratio is a widely used method to determine a portfolio's risk-adjusted return.[13] By using the Sharpe Ratio, you can optimize the return of an investment relative to its risk. A portfolio manager may build a diversified portfolio of stocks that have low correlations to decrease portfolio risk. An important lesson here is that it is possible to reduce portfolio risk *without affecting returns*.

Generally, the greater the value of the Sharpe ratio, the more attractive the risk-adjusted return. Here, we see again that *a system operates best when its parts work together rather than when the pieces are all optimized as individual components, or even worse, by simply ignoring the risk altogether*.

Now, the concept of risk-adjusted measurement has the potential to connect security operations to business outcomes. So how does this risk-adjusted measurement work?

You need to start with leading performance indicators since they are things you can control. Lead measures are prime candidates to scrutinize when attempting to integrate a risk perspective into business performance measurement.

Don't be surprised if most of your executive KPIs are lag measures. You may have to dig into the metrics of other teams. Prying open metrics can be a sensitive topic for inexperienced, insecure, or underperforming leaders. Be transparent about what you are attempting to achieve and why.

I suggest you target the metrics that have an apparent causal impact on business performance. The key here is to identify Vital Behaviors, which are typically limited to one or two things that will yield a disproportionate influence on your success.[14] Apply the 80/20 rule made famous by the Pareto Principle. Be careful to avoid the false cause logical fallacy, meaning correlation is not causation.

Paul Proctor at Gartner developed a Risk-adjusted Value Model (RVM) several years ago that applied risk-adjustments to business metrics as a way of communicating risk and supporting risk decisions in a business context. In 2020, the RVM work evolved into outcome-driven metrics (ODM) and risk, value, cost (RVC) maps. The ODMs measure risk outcomes that have a dependency relationship to business outcomes, so they behave as leading indicators. The RVC maps plot business outcomes by risk, value, and cost, which creates a richer analysis than the original risk-adjusted business metrics. ODM and RVC are discussed more thoroughly in Chapter 4.

Application

Okay, so let's spend some time practically applying this content to a real business. In this case, my employer at the time of this writing.

Case Study 1 – Cybersecurity via the Business Model Canvas

Using the canvanizer, I gradually built out the following business model canvas. We indeed transformed the business over several years, so not all the executives I interviewed in 2017 were relevant or even

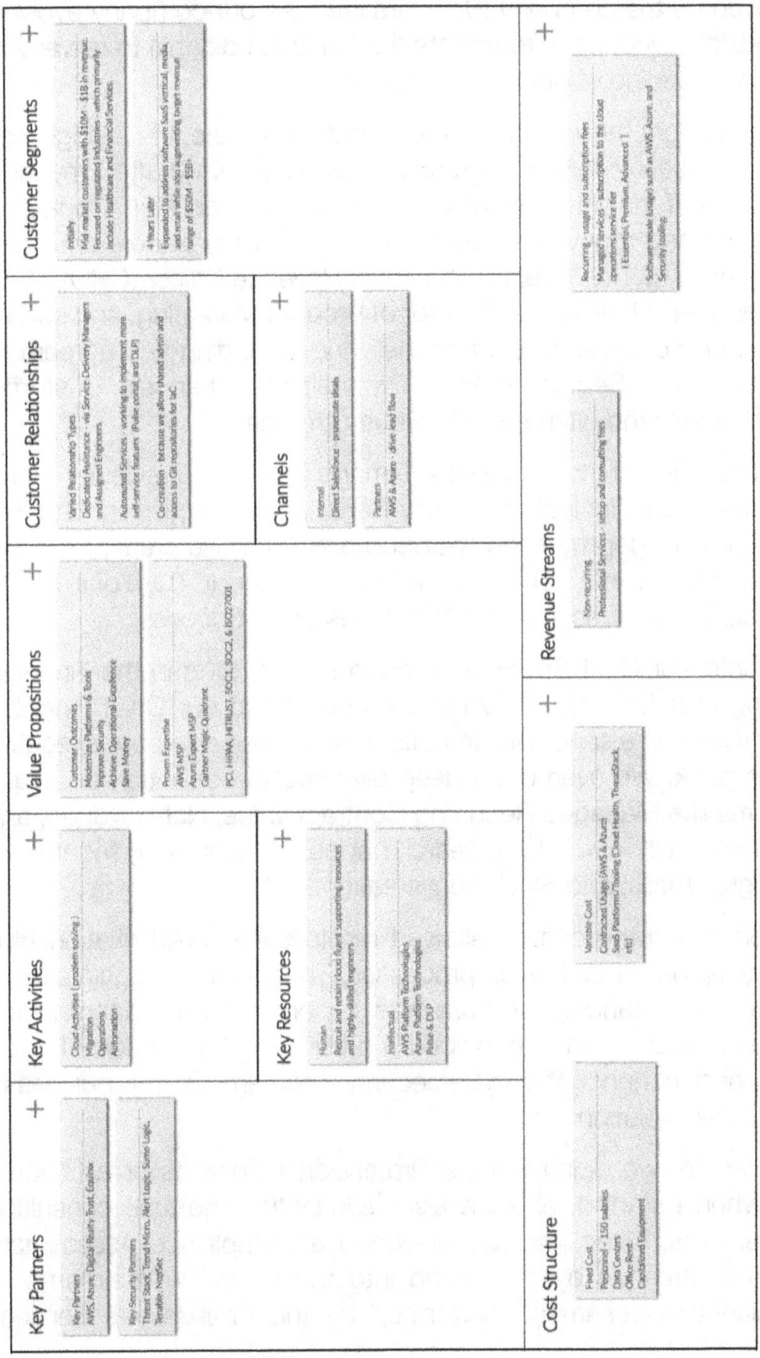

Key Partners

Key Partners
AWS, Azure, Digital Realty Trust, Equinix

Key Security Partners
Threat Stack, Trend Micro, Alert Logic, Sumo Logic, Tenable, HashiCorp

Key Activities

Cloud Activities (problem solving)
Migration
Operations
Automation

Value Propositions

Customer Outcomes
Maximize Platform & Tools
Improve Security
Achieve Operational Excellence
Save Money

Proven Expertise
AWS MSP
Azure Expert MSP
Gartner Magic Quadrant

PCI, HIPAA, HITRUST, SOC1, SOC2, & ISO27001

Customer Relationships

Varied Relationship Types
Dedicated Assistance – via Service Delivery Managers and Assigned Engineers

Automated Services – working to implement more self-service features (Puller portal, and DLP)

Co-creation – because we allow shared admin and access to Git repositories for IaC

Customer Segments

Initially
Mid market customers with $10M - $1B in revenue, focused on regulated industries – which primarily include Healthcare and Financial Services.

4 Years Later
Expanded to address software by vertical, media, and retail while also segmenting target revenue range of $50M - $5B.

Key Resources

Human
Recruit and retain cloud fluent supporting resources and highly-skilled engineers

Intellectual
AWS Platform Technologies
Azure Platform Technologies
Pulse & DLP

Channels

Internal
Direct Sales force - prosecute deals

Partners
AWS & Azure - drive lead flow

Cost Structure

Fixed Cost
Personnel – 150 salaries
Data Centers
Office Rent
Capitalized Equipment

Variable Cost
Contracted Usage (AWS & Azure)
SaaS Platforms/Tooling (Cloud Health, ThousandEyes, etc)

Revenue Streams

Non-recurring
Professional Services - setup and consulting fees

Recurring - usage and subscription fees
Managed services – subscription to the cloud operations service tier (Essential, Premium, Advanced)

Software resale (usage) such as AWS, Azure, and Security tooling

FIGURE 2.3 Logicworks' Business Model Canvas

employed by the company five years later. As our company evolved, I periodically went back to update the canvas. I did this to re-validate my understanding of our business model.

Now, you might think I just sat down and filled this out in a single setting. That doesn't reflect the reality at all. In truth, I drafted my initial impression of the business utilizing the canvas, and then I took it on the road. I had many conversations to solidify my understanding of our business model. I went to our Chief Revenue Officer (CRO), VP of Marketing, VP of Alliances, Director of Product Marketing, and several regional VPs of Sales to confirm their understanding and agreement of the Customer Segments, Value Propositions, Channels, Customer Relationships, and ultimately, Revenue Streams.

Once I completed my business's demand generation review, I examined other areas, including the Key Partners, Key Activities, and Key Resources. To get my head wrapped around those areas, I ran this document past our Chief Technology Officer (CTO), our VP of Professional Services, and our VP of Customer Success.

To dig into our Cost Structure, I found several folks in the Financial Planning and Analysis (FP&A) team reporting to our Chief Financial Officer (CFO). In a series of interactions, we pulled apart our executive metrics pack. We even did a deep dive into the definition of unique measures like Managed Recurring Contract Value, Net Revenue, and Pro-forma Cash Flow. This research happened over many months via meetings, emails, and Slack conversations.

Early on, using the canvas allowed me to safely build relationships and inquire into other teams' processes. That helped me gain a more intimate understanding of what was important to my peers in the business. Later, the model helped me build my knowledge of value chains and connect the cybersecurity program to our business's growth and evolution.

For example, we didn't have a Professional Services or a Product team when I started, and we also didn't offer one-time consulting engagements. Over time, we designed a Compliance Assessment (Revenue Streams) by integrating into these new workstreams. A Compliance Assessment, performed by the Professional Services team, combines tool output with best-practice interviews and results in a stylish report that offers clients insight into adherence to regulatory frameworks for their cloud operations. Later we evolved our offerings to include application modernization. This helped our business expand our capabilities and capture a broader set of customers. To support these changes, the InfoSec team had to adapt to accommodate an evolution in our business model, as well as operational adjustments, and new technology risks.

Similarly, Logicworks designed and built software including a Data Loss Prevention (DLP) product, a patch management system, and a multistage image bakery pipeline that included CIS benchmark hardening and agent installation for A/V, FIM, and other tooling. All these integrated products leveraged cloud-native tools and worked to classify, secure, report, and actively alert customers if their data was at risk (Key Activities). These new offerings enhanced our differentiation in the marketplace (Value Proposition), elevated our enterprise value by enriching our intellectual property (Key Resources), and made my job more manageable in the long run (Cost Structure).

All this progress happened over several years. My cybersecurity team wasn't required to scale in line with the rest of the business. This is because we had strong commitment from other teams to ensure that security was part of everyone's job.

Not long after we expanded our product portfolio, the business began to attract more enterprise prospects and capture larger, more complex deals (Customer Segments). This adjustment meant more sophisticated prospects would perform an increasingly thorough analysis of our security program before signing multi-year contracts. Because of our role in the sales cycle, I recognized this early and prepared for the inevitability.

We secured funding for each of the foundational pieces that comprise our Zero Trust model through contracting with various customers. Eventually, we integrated Single Sign-on, Multi-factor Authentication, Unified Endpoint Management, and Digital Certificates to perform intelligent decisions around access. This allowed efficient, scalable access in a multi-tenant, multi-cloud, multi-account environment.

Luckily, enough of this happened before the COVID-19 pandemic swept the globe and pushed our operations teams to work remotely.

One recent *Win Wire*, a celebratory email that our CRO sends to the organization, offered this explanation for why we were able to secure a Fortune 500 client:

> Our newest client is, without a doubt, the most diligent prospect I've worked with in the last seven years. As such, I don't hesitate to say that without Matt and his team's proactive approach to driving improvements to Logicworks' security and compliance posture, we would have been disqualified from this deal, full stop. Mid-negotiation, they hit us with demanding requirements for IAM strategy, BCP/DR plans, and foundational technology and processes such as UEM. None of which were met by Logicworks in the distant past. However, since the InfoSec team had proactively initiated workstreams in this domain, we met their requirements and moved the deal forward.[15]

Other significant achievements include changing our primary security vendor and obtaining ISO27001 certification. The vendor swap affected *everyone* in the business. It required cross-functional collaboration to alter marketing events, sales training, SKUs in Salesforce, data ingestion pipelines, alerting, runbooks, and agent deployment. It required SAML integration and revisions to multi-tenant access methods for clients. We even revised the procurement, invoicing, contracting, and pricing processes. It took more than a year. In Chapter 5 – Articulating the Business Case, we'll discuss the Monte Carlo analysis completed to evaluate the possible and probable outcomes of such a broad-sweeping change for our business. The latter, ISO27001 certification, was achieved in an unprecedented 90 days.

> Admittedly, being able to directly create value is nice, but the day job of security is to balance the needs to protect with the needs to run the business. Although we did influence a few interesting products for our customers, the real value we provided in completing projects such as ISO certification, zero

trust, and business continuity was to remove obstacles that otherwise prevented our business from:

- accepting new lead flow from partners,
- securing wins with up-market customers,
- expanding product and service offerings,
- delivering increased value through secure software and automation,
- attracting and retaining high-quality talent, and
- rationalizing our costs to deliver managed cloud operations services.

Each of these activities are measured in the form of leading indicators that other teams in our business use to direct their actions. See Table 2.1:

It's fair to say, there are plenty of things in cybersecurity that can distract you from the truly important. It is my conviction that the greatest value we add to our business stems from a foundational understanding of our business model, clarity on

TABLE 2.1 Mapping of InfoSec Projects to Leading Measures and Business Goals

Business Goal	Leading Measure	Enabling Project
Accept New Leads	Sales Accepted Leads + Win Rate → Bookings	BCP/DR Maturity
Address New Markets	Up-market Customer Bookings → Revenue	ISO27001:2013 + Zero Trust
Product Feature Innovation	Compliant Customer Contractual Obligations → Net Retention	CI/CD Maturity
Service Expansion	Application Re-factoring → Revenue	3rd Party Risk + New Access Architecture
Talent Retention	Toll[16] → EBITDA	Vulnerability Management
Efficient Delivery	Engineering Hours / Instance → EBITDA + Pro Forma Cash Flow	Patching Automation

the value streams, and direct alignment to the leading perfor-mance indicators in our business. Without that clarity we might have deployed our resources less efficiently or become lost in "thick of thin things."[17]

Now, recall that earlier in the chapter, we described the two means (optimization and coordination) to drive either of the competitive advantages (cost leadership or differentiation). The next two case studies will explore one example of optimization and another of coordination.

Case Study 2 – Competitive Advantage via Optimization

Recall, in systems theory, you may intentionally be less efficient in support activities to optimize the performance of primary activities. Further, Porter explains that "Sometimes exploiting a linkage requires that a supplier's cost go up to achieve a more than compensating fall in a firm's costs, however. A firm must be prepared to raise the price it gives suppliers in such cases to make exploiting the linkage worthwhile. The opposite case is also possible, and the firm must be prepared to elevate its own internal cost if the supplier offers a more-than-compensating price cut."

In this case, I partnered with our audit firm, Coalfire, to build a Consolidated Audit Program. During this period, my company refined our target customer segments, which eventually led to an increased set of compliance obligations.

We reached a point where pursuing certifications one after the other forced our business into persistent audit mode with all the additional audits. Conducting a series of audits presented several challenges. First, requests for evidence and meeting participation bombarded our teams all year long. Next, because we had to drive improvements and remediation throughout the year in addition to completing our audit cycles, it also meant that our teams were context-switching way too frequently.

No matter what time of year, we had an audit right in front of us. Audits can be disruptive to operations teams, and we felt it would be better to reduce the context switching by consolidating our audits. By compressing our audit calendar, Coalfire played a much more significant role in coordinating the assessments. Increasing their responsibility meant that our team received fewer information requests. They cross-walked requests in advance, so we knew which evidence would apply to each audit. The result was fewer tickets for the operations teams.

Further, multiple auditors were present for each set of interviews. That ensured that a single interview session addressed numerous compliance frameworks. Rather than interviewing the Network team ten times per year (approximately two interviews per framework), we reduced the workload to one discussion and a follow-up. We repeated this pattern for development, architecture, platform, engineering, security, and management. Since each of these interviews often included preparation and evidence gathering – the savings were appreciable.

Indeed, our audit team had to be diligent in coordinating who led each interview. Our auditors had to prepare clarifying questions to evaluate unique requirements per framework. Because they were committed to the partnership and the goals were clear, they also identified savings we didn't contemplate, such as structuring the interview schedule to dismiss some auditors early and minimize travel expenses.

In summary, we saved a ½ FTE and $20,000 in travel (which was significant given our team size), reduced the context switching challenges impacting our engineering team, and improved customer retention while flattening the cost curve. In the process, we also got higher project throughput from other groups as they helped us execute against the security roadmap.

Figure 2.4 is a copy of the key visual we presented to secure funding for the updated audit calendar:

Coordinated assessment: 3-year overview

Benefits to Logicworks

	2018	2019	2020	Total
Separate assessments – HIPAA/HITRUST*, SOC 1, SOC 2, PCI				
Logicworks resource costs (est. 450 hours/year @ $100/hour)	$45,000	$45,000	$45,000	$135,000
Coalfire assessment fees	$163,000	$219,000	$165,000	$547,000
	$208,000	$264,000	$210,000	$682,000
Coordinated assessments				
Logicworks resource costs (est. 195 hours/year @ $100/hour)	$19,500	$19,500	$19,500	$58,500
Coalfire assessment fees	$208,000	$237,000	$183,000	$628,000
	$227,500¹	$256,500	$202,500	$686,500
Three-year benefits: 765 internal resource hours saved; onsite visits reduced from 9 to 3				

C ⊘ A L F I R E.

* Per the HITRUST framework, 2018 and 2020 will be interim HITRUST assessments and 2019 will be a full HITRUST assessment. Based on current scope and controls requirements, the 2019 assessment is estimated at $105k-$120k with final pricing dependent on annual scoping.
1) includes $27,500 for initial invoices of the additional 2018 PCI assessment to align PCI timing with the other frameworks

FIGURE 2.4 Three-Year ROI for Consolidated Audit Program

Source: Coalfire Systems Inc. Used with permission.

Case Study 3 – Competitive Advantage via Coordination

In 2017 the WannaCry ransomware attack spread across the globe. For many, this was a wake-up call to the perils of ransomware. For some, it was a catalyst to further enhance existing patching practices.

No question, patching is tricky. That's exactly why so many companies struggle to do it well. Year after year the FBI espouses the wisdom of getting patching and configuration hardening right. There are so many reasons why something that sounds easy, turns out to be very difficult. Further, doing it at scale is a complex undertaking for anyone. In our services model, any manual activity equates to expense. So naturally, it's safe to say that patching could be a sizable expense when supporting a client's cloud infrastructure if it wasn't highly automated. A customer that isn't patched may become upset and leave. No doubt, profitable operations, customer satisfaction, and retention are things any business would want to optimize!

Now, Porter explains in his book: "To identify a new value chain, a firm must examine everything it does, as well as its competitors' value chains, in search of creative options to do things differently. A firm should ask questions including 'How can the activity be performed differently or even eliminated?'"

Competitive Value Chains

When we looked at competitive value chains, here's what we found. Most of our competitors were focused on point-in-time fixed-fee project work to migrate their clients to the cloud. They didn't own a long-term relationship as we did. When you own cloud operations in the long term, you care much more about the readability of Infrastructure as Code (IaC) and you have a lot more opinions about the tools you layer into the technology stack. As a result, platform approaches to identify and correct configuration drift were also not part of our competitors' services. During the early days in the cloud, some prospects and customers were not equipped to examine or appreciate the more subtle differences in the level of service we offered. Over time, customers came to love the attention our team applied to these details that made our cloud deployments far more sustainable and manageable.

Perform the Activity in a New Way

Looking back, we had performed a detailed analysis considering the top patch management vendors according to the analysts and referrals from friends and their value-added resellers. There was only one commercially supported solution we surfaced that had coverage for all the operating systems required. That solution was seemingly price prohibitive.

Shortly after the alleged North Korean hackers weaponized the NSA-developed EternalBlue exploit, I co-opted a small cross-functional group of engineers and experimented with patching automation. A few months later, we conducted a demo of our "patching product." It leveraged cloud-native AWS System Manager (SSM) and AWS Step Functions. "Step Functions offer a serverless orchestration service that lets you easily coordinate multiple Lambda functions into flexible workflows."[18] We formulated a rough set of patching templates for the demo, a supporting instance tag structure, and several spreadsheets that would eventually help our service delivery team identify patch groups and establish patch schedules with our clients.

The use of SSM gave us other benefits such as the potential to establish software inventory, perform cross-account sync, and enable the use of services, including Amazon Athena or Amazon QuickSight. Leveraging a fast, cloud-powered business intelligence service would later allow our team to deliver insights quickly. Of course, we figured that it would also enhance our vulnerability management.

I wasn't a fan of the build option, and I preferred the buy or partner options because we had a few key engineers who commonly created engineering throughput constraints. Nevertheless, there were too many tangential benefits to ignore the potential upside. After all, the SSM agent was free! And I thought the buy-in of those creating the solution would outweigh the energy I would have to invest in selling another product. The following year, I added *% managed AWS instances with the current SSM agent* as one of the very few Key Performance Indicators for our team. It was a leading measure that would set the stage for both patching and enhanced operational telemetry. Two years later, we would eventually leverage these foundational investments to evaluate and enforce the configuration of AWS resources automatically, including:

- Install agents following the desired state
- Ensure compliance
- Validate agent health
- Provide real-time reporting on an entire fleet of systems

The leverage our business gained from our unconventional approach to patching and the pressure we placed on our organization to ubiquitously install SSM created operational leverage. Further, we set the stage for some intellectual property that will enhance company valuation when we exit. Through coordination, patch management became a competitive advantage.

Key Insights

- Understand Board composition: This will impact the value creation agenda of your company.
- Understand your business model: This serves as the context in which you will determine daily priorities and investments in security.
- Apply systems theory: To optimize a system, it is not necessarily true that you can simply optimize each of its parts independently.
- Leverage your vantage point: Cybersecurity can contribute to sustainable competitive advantage (cost leadership and differentiation) through proprietary learning. Typically, opportunities to improve company-wide performance surface in the form of coordination and optimization activities that serve as the connective tissue between silos in your company.
- Connect your activities directly to the business: This is done by understanding valuation and other KPIs. Then determine what your business feels are leading indicators of business success. Finally clarify what you can do to support and protect business value creation. Consider risk-adjusted value metrics and outcome-driven metrics to measure and report your progress in business terms.

Notes

1. Armerding, T., "Security Flaws and Bugs: Both Bad, but in Different Ways," Synopsys, July 29, 2020. Accessed September 3, 2020. https://www.synopsys.com/blogs/software-security/security-flaws-vs-bugs/.

2. Collins, J., *Good to Great: Why Some Companies Make the Leap and Others Don't*, HarperCollins Publishers Inc., 2001.

3. Harkins, M.W., *Managing Risk and Information Security: Protect to Enable*, 2016.

4. Osterwalder, A., and Pigneur, Y., *Business Model Generation: A Handbook for Visionaries, Game Changers, and Challengers*, John Wiley & Sons, 2010.

5. Watkins, M., *The First 90 Days: Critical Success Strategies for New Leaders at All Levels*. Harvard Business Review Press, 2003.

6. Fey, M., Kenyon, B., Reardon K., Rogers, B., and Ross, C. *Security Battleground: An Executive Field Manual*, Intel Press, 2012.

7. Gompers, P., Kaplan, S.N., and Mukharlyamov, V., *What Do Private Equity Firms Say They Do?*, 2015. Accessed September 8, 2020. https://www.hbs.edu/faculty/Publication Files/15-081_9baffe73-8ec2-404f-9d62-ee0d825ca5b5.pdf.

8. Porter, M.E., *Competitive Advantage: Creating and Sustaining Superior Performance*, The Free Press, 1985.

9. Lewis, J., "The CISO as a Choice Architect: A Conversation with Malcolm Harkins," Rain Capital, August 13, 2020. Accessed September 3, 2020. https://www.raincapital.vc/blog/2020/8/13/the-ciso-as-a-choice-architect-a-conversation-with-malcolm-harkins.

10. Dettmer, H.W., *The Logical Thinking Process: A Systems Approach to Complex Problem Solving*, ASQ Quality Press, 2007.

11. Stearn, A. et al., *Epic Failures in DevSecOps: Volume 1*, 2018.

12. Kim, G., Humble, J., Debois, P., and Willis, J., *The DevOps Handbook: How to Create World-Class Agility, Reliability, & Security in Technology Organizations*, IT Revolution Press, 2016.

13. Sharpe, W.F., "The Sharpe Ratio," *Journal of Portfolio Management* (Fall 1994). Accessed September 10, 2020. http://web.stanford.edu/~wfsharpe/art/sr/sr.htm.

14. Grenny, J., Patterson, K., Maxfield, D., McMillian, R., and Switzler, A., *Influencer: The New Science of Leading Change*, McGraw-Hill Education, 2013.

15. Freilino, R., "Logicworks Win Announcement," 2020.

16. Harvieux, E., "Identifying and Tracking Toil Using SRE Principles," 2020. https://cloud.google.com/blog/products/management-tools/ identifying-and-tracking-toil-using-sre-principles.

17. Covey, S.R., *The 7 Habits of Highly Effective People: Powerful Lessons in Personal Change*, Simon & Schuster, 1989.

18. AWS, "Create a Serverless Workflow with AWS Step Functions." Accessed September 27, 2020. https://aws.amazon.com/getting-started/hands-on/ create-a-serverless-workflow-step-functions-lambda/.

CHAPTER 3

Business Decisions

*Courage is willingness to take the risk once you know the odds.
Optimistic overconfidence means you are taking the risk
because you don't know the odds. It's a big difference.*
— Daniel Kahneman

Opportunity

I took a Mayan Studies class in college, where I learned about ancient archaeological sites throughout Mexico and South America. I began dreaming of a self-powered tour of the Yucatán Peninsula by bike. Soon, I recruited a classmate who later became my wife. After graduating from college, we flew into Cancun Airport. We pedaled south to Tulum and then set course for Coba, Chichen Itza, and Merida.

I remember how I anticipated riding my bike, isolated in the seldom-visited parts of the Mayan Riviera. At that time, I couldn't stomach wasting money to purchase a mattress, much less a bedframe. On the floor at night, I lay staring at the ceiling, envisioning a casual morning ride that gradually revealed historic monuments shrouded in the clearing mist. In my dreams, the majestic Mayan ruins were covered in the cold morning dew, cresting just beyond my evaporating sight-line, still silent save for the chirping local fauna.

Just after graduating, we made the trip. Later I secured a great job, we bought a house, and eventually we got married in Tulum. But I was still hungry for adventure. In my naïve view, the only way to replicate the euphoria of travel was more travel. I thought it was the only thing that would ever make me feel happy.

About that time, the article "Happiness Is Love – and $75,000" surfaced on the web, referencing research from Dr. Angus Deaton and Dr. Daniel Kahneman. They had determined that happiness results from the fulfillment of two abstract psychological states – emotional well-being and life evaluation.[1]

From a life evaluation perspective, I had accomplished the goals I had set. I was financially secure, and in a sense, emotionally fulfilled. I was living a fast-paced corporate life while producing strong results at work. I was a Hilton Diamond member, Emerald Club, United Premier, and Southwest A-list. The travel status gave me a false sense of self-importance.

Meanwhile, I strained my relationships, traveling 80% of the year. My stress levels were through the roof. I had not seen a friend in months, and I rarely exercised. In all my success at work, I was lonely and unhappy.

I began to search for happiness, which resulted in a case for more adventure travel. I eventually concluded that a career break would reduce my stress, boost creativity, amplify life satisfaction, and ulti-mately increase my productivity. I was unwilling to consider that this move could be a taboo career mistake. I compiled a convincing mountain of evidence and resolved an unwavering commitment to travel once more.

And so, more than a decade ago, my wife and I decided to embark upon a round-the-world (RTW) trip. Usually, when we tell the story, it goes something like this: "We sold everything that didn't fit in a small travel suitcase and hit the road." Only, that is not how it happened.

We debated for years. Then we started saving money, albeit mis-aligned on why we were saving in the first place. We might have been saving for a down payment on a new home, or to enroll in graduate school, or for retirement. Eventually, we sold our home and rented a single room in a small trailer park in Westminster, Colorado. We reduced our monthly costs and strained our marriage to the brink of divorce. Eventually, we hit the road, but we did so with an agreement that we would evaluate whether or not we should continue in marriage after the first month on the road.

In hindsight, we decided to travel out of optimistic overconfidence more so than courage. We did the best we could, but our thinking and decision processes were flawed. In the end, I'm confident the RTW decision was the right decision for us. However, the process we followed to make the decision was a painful experience. It's fair to say we lacked the emotional skills to navigate the conflict we experienced during our decision. We faltered in thinking through or communicating basic financial concepts such as cash-based budgeting, sunk cost, and opportunity cost. I looked extensively for information that justified a decision to travel and entirely neglected any opposing views.

On the one hand, we learned that American culture sets a default path through life that many will follow. On the other hand, we also learned that there are several things you can do to improve choice architecture and decision processes. All these insights apply equally to your role as a cybersecurity leader and business decision-maker.

"I have heard CISOs frequently exclaim, they have enormous accountability and responsibility, but they lack the authority to get things done. It comes down to architecting the choices your business makes by blending perspectives enough to get the best outcome."[2]

To improve your ability to integrate cybersecurity perspectives into business decisions, we will explore the scientific method, consider decision science, and identify strategies to strengthen choice architecture. Then, in the Application section of the chapter, we will apply these tools to real-world decisions that every CISO must make. Finally, in Part II – Communication and Education and Part III – Cybersecurity Leadership, we'll explore how cybersecurity teams can play a positive role in forming business culture and decisions.

Principle

Yogi Berra once said, "In theory, there is no difference between theory and practice. In practice, there is." The quote is both funny and true. I mention the quote now because we're starting with a brief discussion on the scientific method. Rest assured, I have no illusion that the scientific method is more theory than practice for most business managers. I believe that Eric Reis got it right in his book *The Lean Startup*. The key is small-batch thinking – where you use the scientific method to iterate through and refine your hypothesis. The point is not perfect science but instead **expedited learning**. Once you have the basics down, you can execute the process in just a few minutes. Done right, you will find a balance between complete analysis and the application of your new learnings. Done wrong, you can find yourself making quick irreversible decisions that have a very high cost. In modern lexicon, this is essentially "fail fast, fail often."

Scientific Method

According to professional decision-maker Ray Dalio, "most of the processes that go into everyday decision making are subconscious and more complex than is widely understood." Here, we have intentionally set aside the sub-conscious and emotional components of decision-making. We'll address those elements under the heading of Decision Science below. Instead, this section presents the scientific method, which is a structured approach to *learning*.

To place the scientific method in the context of decision-making, consider Ray Dalio's perspective that "while there is no one best way to make decisions, there are some universal rules for good decision making. They start with recognizing: 1) the biggest threat to good decision making is harmful emotions, and 2) decision making is a two-step process (first learning, and then deciding)."[3]

Indeed, the scientific method is "a process for experimentation used to explore observations and answer questions. . .The goal is to discover cause and effect relationships by asking questions, carefully gathering and examining the evidence, and combining the available information into a logical answer."[4] Figure 3.1 illustrates the scientific method[5]:

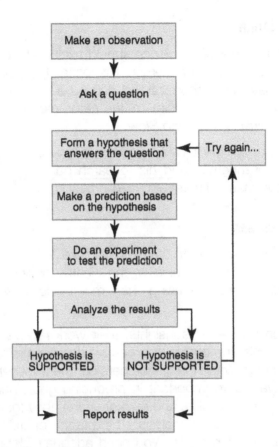

FIGURE 3.1 Flowchart of The Scientific Method

Source: Rice University / CC BY 4.0.

Business decisions rarely follow such a structured approach. Even resource-rich companies, flush with cash and surrounded by data, may skip the rigor required to establish and test a hypothesis. Further, it is all too common that confirmation bias corrupts the analysis phase. As discussed in Chapter 1 – Financial Principles, technical, statistical, or business comprehension issues affect both the presenter and the audience.

Nevertheless, you can control your role in the decision process by keeping the scientific method present as you apply discipline and diligence to an objective and structured learning methodology.

Decision Science

No discussion of decision science should exclude Nobel Prize–winning psychologist Daniel Kahneman. His research supplied the foundation of behavioral economics and derived a new way of thinking about human error. At a minimum, we recommend a review of his 2011 work, *Thinking, Fast and Slow*.

If you are not up for the full read, you are in luck! Conveniently, many findings from Kahneman and his research partner, Amos Tversky, have been summarized here: https://yourbias.is/.

Decision Processes

This section mirrors the structure of *Decisive*, a book authored by Chip and Dan Heath. In *Decisive*, the Heaths outline strategies to improve decision-making using their mnemonic *WRAP*, summarized below.

Building upon Kahneman's insights, their work reveals that despite thorough analysis, the quality of executive decisions is often lacking. More importantly, "when the researchers compared whether process or analysis was more important in producing good decisions (that increased revenues, profits, and market share), they found that 'process mattered more than analysis – by a factor of six.'"[6] Indeed, to improve your decision quality, you need adequate data and robust analysis, but the process is paramount. That is to say; a robust process makes a world of difference.

If you think about a normal decision process, it usually proceeds in four steps. The book *Decisive* explains that there is a villain that afflicts each of these steps, as follows:

- "You encounter a choice. But narrow framing makes you miss options.
- You analyze your options. But the confirmation bias leads you to gather self-serving information.
- You make a choice. But short-term emotion will often tempt you to make the wrong one.
- Then you live with your choice. But you'll often be overconfident about how the future will unfold."[7]

At this point, we have enumerated the primary decision-making stumbling blocks. As any tenured cybersecurity pro knows, the natural companion to a gap analysis is a remediation roadmap. Here are the questions we can ask to improve upon the decision-making process:

- "Widen Your Options. How can you expand your set of choices?
- Reality-Test Your Assumptions. How can you get outside your head and collect information that you can trust?
- Attain Distance Before Deciding. How can you overcome short-term emotions and conflicted feelings to make the best choice?
- Prepare to Be Wrong. How can we plan for an uncertain future so that we give our decisions the best chance to succeed?"[8]

Many of the challenges we face in cybersecurity programs stem from a failure of imagination, diligent research, or a willingness to acknowledge the human element. Individual behavior is ultimately an accumulation of choice. Naturally, there is a difference between split-second judgment and deliberate thinking, as Kahneman points out. Regardless, we must recognize and leverage both intuitive and intentional thinking patterns to our advantage.

Employ the tactics below to engage your cognitive self, confront your biases, and consciously decide. Doing so will dramatically improve the odds that you make wise decisions. Further, identifying when others fall victim to cognitive biases and nudging them in a positive direction will go a long way to alleviate common points of contention that often plague cybersecurity leaders.

WIDEN YOUR OPTIONS

Here are a few things you can do to avoid selecting from a narrow set of options:

- Blend Prevention and Promotion for a wiser decision. "Psychologists have identified two contrasting mindsets that affect our motivation and our receptiveness to new opportunities: a 'prevention focus,' which orients us toward avoiding negative outcomes, and a 'promotion focus,' which orients us toward pursuing positive outcomes."[9] No doubt, professional risk managers will lean towards preventative thinking. Still, it is essential to use both when considering your interaction with the business.

- Be wary of "whether or not" decisions. For example, don't be limited to deciding whether or not to allow the business to migrate data to the cloud. *Perhaps some alternatives are smaller in risk and investment, such as beginning to build your cloud expertise on low-risk workloads.* Further, research shows that selecting from two options yields significantly stronger business outcomes.
- Avoid faux options. As a complement to avoiding whether or not decisions, you must be aware of fake alternatives. Often a decision is between one good option and one poor alternative. Reject these imposter options. For example, *We can either implement DLP or completely lose control of all data in our data warehouse.*
- Remove options. Force yourself to remove the options available and consider what you might do despite the limited options. What would I do if forced to operate an entire security program with no additional hires? (Here, we eliminate hiring as an option.) By removing the obvious choices, you must consider alternatives. Are there ways to recruit additional support from other executives in the business? Can you reframe responsibilities? Is there an option to outsource fractional components of your program? Would you be able to hire unpaid interns, develop skills in existing staff, or stop performing an activity altogether?
- Consider Opportunity Cost. Opportunity cost is the loss of gain from other options by selecting the one at hand. Note that a security initiative that goes unfunded faces a preferred opportunity cost more often than not. By choosing a platform technology, I may lock myself in from accessing best-of-breed tooling. By hiring a security engineer, a business cannot hire another sales professional, make additional investments in operations support, or fund a new initiative.
- Explore multiple options in parallel, not in serial. Using the multi-track method avoids ego issues because no one identifies their ego with a solution they worked to develop. You often learn the shape of the problem, and it offers a built-in fallback plan. For example, hire two firms to design your IAM program's Phase

I architecture. Then observe where their approaches converge and what differences exist. Select the best ideas. I detest Request for Proposal (RFP) processes in most cases, but they can serve as a method to multi-track a solution. I caution that a rigid process may limit opportunities for firms to differentiate.

- Push for "this AND that" rather than "this or that." It's possible to find a third alternative that satisfies both sides of an argument more often than you think. Often the key is to clarify what you want and separate that from the chosen strategy to achieve it. "We need two more app sec pros, and a Static Application Security Testing (SAST) tool" is really about ensuring secure code. The secure code outcome may come by other means. For example, perhaps the DevOps team integrates four mutually approved lightweight open-source tools into the DevOps toolchain and agrees to use an inherently more secure development framework rather than adopting an SAST tool. Additionally, they commit to respond within a defined service level objective to Dynamic Application Security Testing (DAST) performed on a subset of sensitive code modules. If defect density is reduced, but you don't get the tooling or staff you want – does it matter? I say it does not.
- Find someone who has already solved your problem. If your company is large, there might be someone else who has already solved your issue. Look for internal bright spots. Perhaps the software development group resolves vulnerabilities much more efficiently than your infrastructure team. Why is that? Alternatively, explore solutions in other businesses by visiting industry groups, Information Sharing and Analysis Centers (ISACs), public slack channels, meetup groups or otherwise. Still at a loss? Consider exploring adjacent disciplines (legal, human resources, etc.). For example, others have encountered and navigated making decisions in the face of uncertainty, achieving business alignment, and establishing strong executive accountability. Design flaws and user adoption are no stranger to our counterparts in the IT organization. Marketing our capabilities and services to our organizations can benefit from engaging – no surprise here – our Marketing teams. Another example is reviewing literature on

leadership during World War II. I found a surprising number of instructive lessons about leadership and communication. Dwight D. Eisenhower made greater use of press conferences than any previous president, and Winston Churchill exploited words to achieve a great many things. So frequency of communication and precise, simple language can be a powerful combination.

REALITY-TEST YOUR ASSUMPTIONS

Once you have explored a broad set of options, you need to choose between the alternatives. Before you do, it's essential to identify the tendency toward confirmation bias and challenge your thinking. After all, "open-mindedness is motivated by the genuine worry that you might not be seeing your choices optimally. It is the ability to effectively explore different points of view and different possibilities without letting your ego or your blind spots get in your way. It requires you to replace your attachment to always being right with the joy of learning what's true."[10] One way to ensure you are in pursuit of the truth is to spark constructive disagreement intentionally. Here are a few other ideas:

- Gather more trustworthy information with disconfirming questions. When we implemented our Unified Endpoint Management platform, I asked the salesman plenty of questions about the platform's ability to restrict specific executables, report upon patch levels, perform zero-touch hardware deployments, and validate USB blocks. Of course, the answer was 'Yes, we can do that.' I took their word because they were in the top right quadrant in analyst reports. But I should have asked better questions like "Can this be managed with a team of one? If so, can you put me in touch with a reference customer?" or "What problems or challenges during implementation do customers typically encounter?" *Research shows that specific penetrating questions are much more likely to receive honest answers. However, if there is a power differential or an apparent discrepancy in levels of expertise, you need to tread lightly. As an executive team member, you likely wield a degree of authority. In cases where there is an apparent power dynamic, you are better off asking open-ended questions.*

- Consider the opposite.[11] Once you have drawn a conclusion, stop and ask yourself what would have to be true to invalidate this decision? This technique aims to shift your pattern of thinking from a defensive mindset to one of problem-solving. It "is particularly useful in organizations where dissent is unwelcome, where people who challenge the prevailing ideas are accused of failing to be 'team players.'"[12] For example, I took a stance that a particular tooling suite was not optimal to protect our organization. There were many business and nontechnical reasons this position was contentious. Before we were willing to replace the tooling, we collectively needed to convince ourselves that we were not the cause of the challenges we had encountered. So, I championed an excellence program rather than immediately replacing the platform. After exerting a diligent effort to make our partnership work, our entire business hesitantly decided to find an alternative.

- Construct small experiments. You can construct micro experiments to test your assumptions. Rapidly improve your hypothesis by applying the scientific method to the smallest scope available. Don't let waterfall thinking or perfection be your enemy. Consider Kickstarter, a site that allows creators to validate the value hypothesis of their creative work. In many cases, a complete product isn't available, but instead, Kickstarter requires projects to show backers a prototype of what they're making. If there's a community of users who value the new creation, the project will likely get funded.[13]

ATTAIN DISTANCE BEFORE DECIDING

Now that you have broadly explored alternatives and embraced the joy of learning what is true, it's essential to quiet short-term emotion, gain some perspective, and validate alignment with core priorities. Here are a few techniques to do just that:

- 10/10/10 is a strategy developed by Suzy Welch to keep short-term emotions in check. It's simple, just ask yourself, "How will this decision impact me in ten minutes, ten days, and ten years?"

Adding this temporal component to decision-making can help manage the overactive short-term emotional impact of a decision.

- Advise Your Best Friend. A quick shift in perspective can work wonders. By taking a moment to gain an observer's perspective, you may simplify your decision. Attaining distance can make you see the core issues and help you clear the fog of loss-aversion or mere-exposure phenomena that commonly lead to status-quo bias. In 2014 I interviewed at an insurance company in Nevada that still hadn't permitted wireless networks in their corporate office. Suffice it to say, status-quo can play an influential role in both adopting new cybersecurity controls as well as in shedding them.

- Honor Your Core Priorities. Clarifying core priorities can help you navigate challenging decisions in a leadership role. Are you committed to continuous improvement or fortified defenses? Does your business have a culture that favors failing forward, or is the risk appetite too small for that type of experimentation? Is a small step in the right direction enough for today, knowing there's more to come, or are you fighting for complete control? For example, is your business prepared to accept the risks of operating applications on top of Kubernetes clusters and Docker container images? Should your business's digital transformation slow down and wait for the cybersecurity team to learn these technologies, identify, adopt, and operationalize security products? In most cases, you can take these questions back to the leaders pressing to adopt new technology and frame their decisions in a context that considers the company's risk appetite or priorities. In Chapter 12 – Negotiations, we'll talk about adapting SRE error budgets to security paradigms or leveraging calibrated "How" questions to recruit others into the problem solving.

Prepare to Be Wrong

Preparing to be wrong when considering a range of outcomes can help you explore a broader set of possibilities, overcome your overconfidence, and stack the deck in your favor. There are several specific techniques to consider. Doing so will help you anticipate and respond to both good and bad outcomes. Finally, it's worth having a clear understanding of when to reconsider a previous decision. Techniques that can help you respond to uncertainty include:

- Limit Test. My experience in becoming a calibrated subject matter expert, following the practices of quantitative risk management promoted by Hubbard Decision Research (https://hubbardre-search.com/) and the FAIR Institute (https://www.fairinstitute .org/), validates the research that overconfidence is the norm. Considering a range of outcomes that includes the worst case and the best case can significantly improve forecast ability. Following this pattern expands our thinking and places our best guess on a continuum of possibilities. This examination of outer bounds helps us avoid anchoring, recency bias, framing, and overconfidence. Naturally, considering upside and downside risks is an integral part of a cybersecurity leader's job.
- Premortem. Prospective hindsight is when you assume a particular outcome and then explore why it might be right. For example, it's two years later, and your attempt to implement privileged access management has failed. Why did it fail? Asking this question in advance is a different way to manage the risks of a project. Had we done so in our attempt to roll out a password management tool, we would likely have paid much closer attention to user adoption and culture within our engineering teams.
- Preparade. Naturally, you also need to consider the opposite of a failed program or project. What if your efforts are wildly successful? We'll see more on this in the application section of the chapter.
- Set a Trigger. At some point, grit becomes stupidity. Persistence is certainly a valued trait in leadership, but don't let your commitment to a decision prevent you from confronting the brutal facts. Having an objective trigger to reconsider a decision forces a level of awareness. When you first consider adding Identity Governance and Administration (IGA), you might learn that the return on investment (ROI) only makes sense with 500 or more users. Set a trigger to reconsider investment in IGA when you can justify an ROI.

Ideally, you can establish the threshold in a broader governance forum such as the Risk Committee, Audit Committee, or Executive Leadership Team. That way, you are sure to plan for an investment before your identity challenges become too complicated. Meanwhile, dust off your python and PowerShell skills and prepare for some intense spreadsheet manipulation!

Choice Architecture

The section above offers techniques to mitigate the well-researched phenomenon of loss aversion, status quo, confirmation, and other biases in the process of decision making. Equipped with these strategies and an awareness of decision-making pitfalls, we turn our attention to choice architecture. This section will lean heavily on the work *Nudge* by Richard H. Thaler and Cass R. Sunstein. As they define a few terms, "A choice architect has the responsibility for organizing the context in which people make decisions. Further, a nudge, as we will use the term, is any aspect of choice architecture that alters people's behavior in a predictable way without forbidding any options or significantly changing their economic incentives."[14]

My experience with implementing cybersecurity across several organizations matches the following description. Most people want to do the right thing. Yet, they might forget or avoid implementing security if it is too complicated or otherwise feel pressed for time. When given adequate encouragement and support, most people will gladly comply with security requirements. So, when are nudges helpful, and what are the most beneficial ways CISOs structure choices and nudge their organizations?

According to Thaler and Sunstein, nudges can be most helpful when making a decision that offers benefits now and costs later. Often people (and organizations) struggle with self-control and accountability. As the time between a choice and its consequences increases, so does the accountability gap. Further, when the frequency of action is low, the complexity of a decision is high, or the feedback offered along the way is limited, a nudge might help. Finally, look to nudge when the relationship between a choice and the experience that follows is ambiguous.

To understand how this all applies to the CISO, let's use the mnemonic tool NUDGES in a cybersecurity context:

- i<u>N</u>centives
- <u>U</u>nderstand mappings
- <u>D</u>efaults
- <u>G</u>ive feedback
- <u>E</u>xpect error
- <u>S</u>tructure of complex choices

iNCENTIVES

To explore incentives in a structured way, let's consider the *six sources of influence* model published by Vital Smarts. Motivation and ability are the foundation of the model. They subdivide these domains into three distinct categories: personal, social, and structural, which in turn reflect separate and highly developed bodies of literature: psychology, sociology, and organizational theory.

"The first two domains, Personal Motivation and Ability, relate to sources of influence within an individual (motives and abilities) that determine their behavioral choices. The next two, Social Motivation and Ability, relate to how other people affect an individual's choices. The final two, Structural Motivation and Ability, encompass the role of non-human factors, such as compensation systems, space, and technology."[15]

Figure 3.2 presents the entire model:

The authors of *Influencer* found in their research that successful influencers increased their chances of success tenfold by combining strategies from all Six Sources of Influence. However, the point here is that incentives are a necessary but insufficient source of influence required to modify behaviors. Next, we can explore personal, social, and structural motivations with a choice architect perspective.

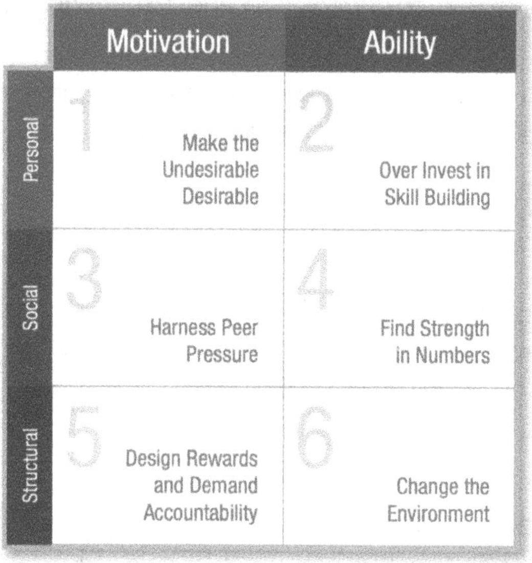

FIGURE 3.2 The Six Sources of Influence

Source: Grenny, J., Maxfield, D., and Shimberg, A., *How to 10X Your Influence.* Used with permission.

PERSONAL INCENTIVES – MAKE THE UNDESIRABLE DESIRABLE

In my estimation, the personal category of the motivation domain contains several components. The first is how much you enjoy the task. Making all aspects of security enjoyable seems unlikely. A close alternative, however, is to make it easy to perform. The people in your organization will opt for the path of least resistance. Simple, intuitive processes are best. An example of this approach is the emerging trend toward passwordless login methods.

Additional strategies the Vital Smarts framework surfaces include:

1. Allow for choice – replace judgment with empathy and lectures with questions. Ask thought-provoking questions and listen, allowing others to discover on their own what they must do.
2. Create direct experiences – this can remove the fear of the unknown, reinforce understanding, and improve compassion.

3. Tell meaningful stories – help people understand the consequences of their actions vicariously.
4. Make it a game – identify a scoreboard that reflects the individual's direct actions and make the score visible.

SOCIAL INCENTIVES – HARNESS PEER PRESSURE

There are several things that cybersecurity leaders can do to overdetermine success. One of those things is to harness the power of peer pressure. Some examples:

- Minor tweaks in language can have an outsized impact on your success. For example, rather than telling people what to do, describe for them what others are doing. Psychologists call this practice positive injunctive norming. To get users to take annual security training and secure code training, we used to send reminder emails weekly. Now, we send fewer reminders phrased like this "*Please join the majority (78%) of your peers who have already completed the secure code training.*" We also publish the metrics in aggregate and share them with multiple department managers at once to encourage friendly competition.
- Offer guidance on scheduling and include visuals or links to prime people with cues and make their choice easier. In our reminders, we've started adding content such as this: *Don't wait till the last minute. Schedule 1 hour in your calendar this week to be sure you have completed the training well before the 10/31 completion date. Click here to get started.*
- "The 'mere-measurement effect' refers to the finding that when people are asked what they intend to do, they become more likely to act in accordance with their answers. This finding can be found in many contexts. If people are asked whether they intend to eat certain foods, to diet, or to exercise, their answers to the questions will affect their behavior."[16] This year, we added a few free-text answer boxes in the Security Awareness quiz to ask users how they intend to support the security program in the coming year. We hope to prompt our colleagues to describe when and

how they plan to do it and expect this will further establish a personal commitment to the security initiatives this year.

- Recruiting thought leaders as security champions can be an excellent method for changing culture and reinforcing the desired behavior. The right security champions align social incentives to encourage positive norms in the workplace.
- Finally, don't confuse (or miss) Dr. Cialdini's Principles of Persuasion if you want to dig deeper (https://www.influenceatwork.com/principles-of-persuasion/).

Structural Incentives – Design Rewards and Demand Accountability

Today most businesses include incentive-based pay and management by objective approaches. When you examine more traditional literature on managing human capital, you might conclude that incentives play a huge role in corporate performance or successful transformation.

However, as outlined in *Influencer*, "in a well-balanced change effort, rewards come *third*. Influencers first ensure that vital behaviors connect to intrinsic satisfaction. Next, they line up social support. They double-check both of these areas before they finally choose extrinsic rewards to motivate behavior." Expanding upon this, the authors explain it is best not to "use incentives to compensate for your failure to engage personal and social motivation." Instead, "ensure that the rewards come soon, are gratifying, and are clearly tied to vital behaviors. When you do so, even small rewards can be used to help people overcome some of the most profound and persistent problems."[17]

Indeed, new management theories, such as those presented by Daniel Pink in his book *Drive,* bring purely economic incentives into question. Pink postulates that it is better to motivate teams intrinsically using three key factors: Autonomy, Mastery, and Purpose.

Understand Mappings

To help people make better decisions, we must make information on their options more comprehensible. That means we need to create a tighter relationship between choice and experience where it is ambiguous. The Risk-Adjusted Value Model described in Chapter 2 – Business Strategy Tools serves this purpose.

Rather than describing the technical risk of failing to patch timely, you can relate patch failures to the probability of an outage, which leads to lost revenue on an e-commerce website. Instead of describing the failure of a SOC2 control, you can explain the probable impact on revenue. In that way, executives can decide if they want to take the 30% risk of lost revenue resulting from unpatched systems or an 80% chance that the team will attract three fewer clients because of adverse audit findings.

This decision is much easier to make than resolving the need for more staff to have 1,000 critical vulnerabilities instead of 2,000 on our production website.

DEFAULTS

As we all know, it is preferred to set the best possible defaults. In the world of technology, the question is who determines the definition of "best"? For years, we've accommodated insecure defaults from operating system vendors who felt that their products' easy and rapid adoption was the highest priority. That is in stark contrast to the security viewpoint. The good news is that the future looks bright. For instance, we can easily default to new approaches, including Center for Internet Security (CIS – https://www.cisecurity.org/) hardened images in both the Amazon and Microsoft Azure Marketplace.

I know what you are thinking. We still have to address the cloud management plane, containers, APIs, and other attack surfaces, but hey – cheap, available, hardened images is a start! The other thing you might have rightfully objected to is that we don't have any reason to believe all developers will immediately decide on their own to use these readily available images. And you are right. That's where forcing functions come in!

No one is immune to post-completion errors. Have you ever sent a beautifully crafted email only to have forgotten the attachment or left your gas cap at the gas station after filling the fuel tank of your car? These are common mistakes resulting from failing to complete a secondary task after completing the primary. A forcing function mitigates this type of human error. Now, email platforms prompt the user when no attachment is present, and car manufacturers have attached the gas cap to the car. As choice architects, we can implement forcing functions.

A large part of digital transformation is automation. With more robust continuous integration/continuous deployment (CI/CD) pipelines implemented, dozens of opportunities to place forcing functions to avoid security control omissions arise. An alternative to using CIS hardened images is to run a lightweight hardening script such as the DevSec Hardening Framework (https://github.com/dev-sec) to prevent deployment of unhardened systems.

Indeed, moving fast in a DevOps world is far more rewarding for developers and can produce healthier outcomes for security teams as well. Pipeline enhancement is just one example of how we can properly align incentives. When we cannot start with the best possible defaults, we can always lean on a forcing function.

Give Feedback

One of the foundational assumptions in a strong security culture is that the cybersecurity team doesn't own the risk. The business does. Institutionalize this by providing feedback to business managers on how their teams are performing. You must indicate good or bad and empower the team with the necessary information to pinpoint how to make improvements where they are needed.

Vulnerability Management Index

Let's compare two alternative dashboards from NopSec that you might provide to a manager.[18] In Figure 3.3, you get a clear indication of the overall picture, but you don't have any supporting details. In this case, if I am a product manager with a resource-constrained team, I might decide to delay remediation for any of the vulnerabilities detected until a future sprint. After all, my boss will be okay with a B or C in security if my end users are happy and benefiting from the timely release of new features.

FIGURE 3.3 Letter Grade

Source: Xu, L., "NopSec Unified VRM." Used with permission.

Infrastructure Vulnerabilities Summary

Risk per NopSec Prioritization
Total # current open vulns with **NopSec** risk grade

Urgent	Critical	High	Medium	Low	None	Total
14	**113**	**129**	**135**	**96**	**196**	**683**
vulnerabilities	vulnerabilities	vulnerabilities	vulnerabilities	vulnerabilities	vulnerabilities	vulnerabilities

FIGURE 3.4 Vulnerability Details

Source: Xu, L., "NopSec Unified VRM." Used with permission.

In contrast, Figure 3.4 gives vulnerability counts but doesn't put them in the context of any expectations. Are 14 urgent vulnerabilities acceptable or not? How quickly do I need to remediate these? What happens if I don't?

SECURITY CULTURE INDEX

Occasionally, unhealthy team subcultures can create challenges for security programs. Resistant subcultures are common for new security leaders inheriting contentious programs built under former leadership. If you find yourself in this position, you can rely upon other forms of feedback to cut through the politics. For example, you could distribute a security culture metric to help managers understand the prevalence of security tool adoption in their team and the broader organization. Documenting the frequency of policy exceptions can also illuminate conflict lurking in subcultures.

Here's a sample of what you might include in such a measure, but don't be afraid to use your imagination and improve upon this list:

- Password Manager active user? { Yes / No }
- Phishing program contributor/active user? { Yes / No }
- Security Awareness completed on-time? { Yes / No }
- Secure Code Training completed on-time? { Yes / No }
- Anti-virus exceptions required/requested { Yes / No }
- Encryption exception required { Yes / No }
- Patching exception required { Yes / No }
- Firewall custom rules required { Yes / No }

Expect Error

It can be helpful to try to empathize with those you hope to influence. Doing so can help establish stimulus-response compatibility. In most cases, when stimulus-response compatibility challenges arise, the root cause is a design failure. Endless security prompts for insecure websites or out-of-date certificates can make users numb to alerts. Similarly, accusing people of intentionally undermining the security program will make them defensive and resistant to other security enhancements you propose.

Users have come to expect that firewalls are the problem, anti-virus programs slow down their machines, and all security is painful. Overcoming these biases is not easy and requires attention to human-centered design. Security teams often fail to empathize with colleagues, but a little empathy when designing controls yields collaborative relationships and willing participants that you need to shift culture.

Structure Complex Choices

"As the choices become more numerous and vary on more dimensions, people are more likely to adopt simplifying strategies." Therefore, "as alternatives become more numerous and more complex, choice architects have more to think about and more work to do, and are much more likely to influence choices (for better or for worse)."[19]

Helping people decompose a challenge or place realistic brackets around the range of possible outcomes can improve their decisions. The advantage of serving in this capacity is that you frame the analysis and set an anchor. Don't underestimate the impact of structuring complex choices.

That means you can help remind people that a risk of a breach might have a more significant range of potential impact on the business or a higher probability of occurring than they think. If you have run a calibration exercise, you can usually remind people of their calibration training experience.

Technical teams are often overconfident in the underestimated timelines required to apply security after the fact. Helping them anchor on more realistic or even slightly conservative estimates will ensure they are successfully delivering secure computing without compromising their delivery timelines.

"In many domains, the evidence shows that, within reason, the more you ask for, the more you tend to get. Lawyers who sue cigarette companies often win astronomical amounts, in part because they have successfully induced juries to anchor on multimillion-dollar figures. Clever negotiators often get amazing deals for their clients by producing an opening offer that makes their adversary thrilled to pay half of the very high amount."[20]

Application

Up to this point in the chapter, we have covered a lot of material. Let's quickly summarize and then begin to examine a few practical examples. So far, you have learned that:

- the Scientific Method provides a structured approach to learning,
- the WRAP framework improves decision-making processes,
- WRAP also enhances your ability to guide others as they navigate complex decisions,
- the Six Sources of Influence model offers a structured view into incentives and reveals other essential points of leverage in building influence strategies, and
- as a choice architect, you can use the NUDGES framework to encourage a security-friendly organizational culture.

Case Study 1 – Decision Science

In my experience, staffing strategy plays a crucial role in determining how cybersecurity teams interact with an organization. When first sizing up the staffing approach, you need to consider several factors. The most impactful considerations include the capabilities you intend to build (or continue to support), the scope in which you will apply those capabilities, and the distribution of the responsibilities between the cybersecurity team and the other parts of your organization.

Assume for a moment that you inherit a new team. There are two existing technical cybersecurity engineers managing a program primarily comprised of vulnerability scanning and security logging. The existing management team would like a more structured and mature approach that will permit them to offer assurances to their new Board of Directors that cybersecurity risk is a properly managed risk.

After a structured learning effort during the first three months of employment, you have analyzed the business using a framework of your choosing. Presumably, the framework you selected is relevant to your industry. You now have in your hands a maturity mapping and gap analysis. What you learn is that the most needed capabilities are nascent. What's more, many of the foundational processes that typically support information assurance practices are missing. For example, general vendor management and procurement procedures lack definition, change management is weak, business continuity is a paper tiger, and centralized inventory is nonexistent. Further, there is no Enterprise Risk Management function, internal audit, or privacy officer.

You suggest to your CFO that you will need significant investment to be successful. He advises you that the current three-year forecast doesn't contemplate significant staffing increases, especially for a non-revenue generating function. The expectation is that SG&A costs will *decrease* in the next two years.

What might you do in this scenario? Stop for a moment, and attempt to answer the question.

Let's apply the WRAP framework and see where we end.

First, we are going to explore the options available by using some techniques to *Widen the Options*.

You might consider *whether or not* you should remain with the company. You may have even told yourself that you'd never end up in that scenario because you are careful to ask specific questions in the interview process. Admittedly, "abandon ship" might be a first emotional response, but we hope you'll persist. It is not unusual for a new security leader to stretch into their first leadership role. Assume you just moved across the country or find yourself in a down economy and have to make the best of the situation. Now what?

Don't let sham options dominate your thinking. Your alternatives are much broader than to quit or begrudgingly stay in a hopeless situation. Once you realize the expansive list of options available, I'm confident you will be intrinsically motivated to find a path to success.

You can start by exploring a combination of prevention and promotion thinking. Is there a way that your efforts could save the business money and at the same time capture some of those savings to further fund your initiatives? I've used Information Governance processes to identify significant savings in legal hold and data backup expenditures in the past. On a separate occasion, I successfully framed a security remediation initiative in the name of tech debt reduction that resulted in dozens of decommissioned systems. The project had licensing, storage, operational, staffing, and security implications. Imagine the delight of my business as we realized the cost optimization benefits while we reduced our risk!

As options vanish, you force greater creativity. Earlier, we suggested finding ways to ensure the broader organization takes a more prominent role in fulfilling the security mission. While convincing other teams to take ownership of security outcomes is slower, the cultural shift yields more resilient business processes. Pause to consider the projects you can execute with existing staff that enable other managers and business executives to become the primary owners of security and compliance outcomes. One specific strategy is to draft and socialize a cybersecurity program charter. Explain the three lines of defense, and articulate who will own essential security engineering or operations activities.

Expand your business knowledge, take your concerns back to your CFO, and ask for help understanding the reasoning behind the rejection of your funding request. What alternatives is she evaluating? Why is cash allocation better applied elsewhere? With an improved understanding, perhaps you can improve cost performance or add business value in other ways. For example, you might offer to help implement cloud deployment guardrails that restrict instance types, explaining the positive impact this can have on cost engineering efforts performed by FinOps in a cloud environment.

Maybe you decide to define vendor management and procurement procedures, taking the opportunity to add a few security checks into the process. That way, you maintain awareness of purchases happening around the business and insert the security perspective needed to balance risk and reward. If intellectual property is a vital part of your enterprise value, perhaps you can help explain the need to ensure open-source licenses are carefully considered as your product teams develop software. An early investment in tooling to aid with open-source software governance makes sense to guarantee you avoid surprises during M&A diligence later on. The last thing your CFO or CTO wants to discover is an open-source license such as AGPL, or GPL 3.0, was integrated into your intellectual property requiring re-work or forcing you to release your code under the same license.[21]

The varied approaches discussed help you push for "this and that." If none of this works, reach out to your network and seek out someone who has already solved this problem. You might discover the challenges you are facing are surprisingly common. Maybe a little empathy will help diffuse your frustration and expand your perspective.

By now, we can assume you've decided to stay, and you've identified a couple of opportunities to align your program with business objectives. You've built some goodwill and enhanced relationships in the process of widening your options. You may even be pleasantly surprised by the commitment of resources other than cash that might be available to help your efforts.

In setting up your roadmap for the next year, you identify a set of projects you think will benefit the business most, and now you must *Reality-test Your Assumptions* before moving forward. To do so, you head out to actively gather information about your proposed roadmap by asking disconfirming questions. You discover that the engineering teams are not ready to support your aggressive plans because they thought you would reduce the amount of work they had to do, not increase it! They suggest you should anticipate making less progress given their staffing constraints.

Now it's your turn to consider their feedback carefully. Remember that someone has the unenviable responsibility of deciding to accept the risk of *not* doing what you suggest. It's your responsibility to facilitate an informed decision, and keep in mind that it might very well be in the shareholders' best interest to do less than you recommend! Security practitioners provide one point of view, but it's essential to place yourself in a decision-maker position and consider other demands. Considering the opposite is one of the most productive moments of validation to this point in your journey.

You feel confident that you should make progress and that perhaps you overestimated what you might accomplish in the first year on the job. Finance and engineering seem to validate what lies ahead. Cross-functional feedback is causing a sense of frustration and hopelessness. You begin to question the motivations for hiring you in the first place. Are you there to make a difference or just to serve as a scapegoat?

It's time to *attain distance* before deciding upon your next move. So, to put short-term emotion into perspective, you apply 10/10/10. It becomes clear that quitting in a dramatic style would probably make you feel vindicated in the near term. But in 10 days, you will be out on the job market, and what will you say in the interview process about your exceedingly short time with your employer? Certainly, omitting the role from your resume would be unethical. You decide that in 10 years you will be better off having identified a way forward, despite the complications, than if you evacuate every time the going gets tough.

You've been in the workforce long enough to know that no matter what happens, it's not likely that your projections of the future are 100% accurate. To acknowledge this fact, you decide to boundary test the possible outcomes. You imagine a worst-case and best-case scenario. Worst case, you stay way too long, and you are miserable for it. Best case, you learn a lot about yourself, business practices, and your ability to connect with a deep and meaningful personal purpose in a more intimate way than you ever thought possible.

You set a trigger to reevaluate your situation in 12 months. In the end, it turns out you make more progress than you thought, and you are glad you took the time to WRAP your head around the decision.

Case Study 2 – Choice Architecture

As time goes on, it appears that attackers become increasingly efficient and lean more toward attacks such as phishing and credential theft.[22] To help, many cybersecurity teams empower all employees to report phishing in more convenient and automated ways. Of course, this improves phishing defenses beyond what purely technological approaches can accomplish.

This section will explore how security leaders can serve as choice architects to defend against one of the most prevalent attack patterns, phishing. To do so we will employ the NUDGES framework.

i**N**centives

Attackers know that sending unsolicited emails with clickbait to our end users is an effective way to steal credentials. Indeed, data breaches often stem from phishing. In this case, we can determine the vital behavior, clicking on links or opening attachments from unsolicited senders, and measure it using a simulated phishing program. The following sections describe the application of the six sources model to the challenge of behavioral change in support of phishing defense as summarized Table 3.1.

Personal

Before phishing reporter tools were broadly available, it was challenging for users to report phishing attempts. Sending the necessary information and including key header and attachment artifacts is not intuitive. So, the first step in driving a successful phishing response is to make it easy to report suspected phishing.

Beyond enabling people with tools, we must consider how to make phishing defense more desirable. We can provide opportunities for direct experience by sending simulation emails. People get additional training when they fail to avoid phishing tests, and they experience all the emotions that accompany clicking an untrusted link. Perhaps they feel fear or shame, which is not the point. They must confront the fact that, as individuals, we are all vulnerable to phishing.

With your organization's support, you can take the direct experience one step further by including social engineering and phishing as part of penetration testing. As a leader, I have called for unrestricted "gloves-off" testing. I have also made the timing of the testing blind to our security organization as much as possible. No target is off-limits, not even our CEO. When phishing is successful, pen testers are permitted to pivot and attack further. Some employees benefit from the

TABLE 3.1 The Six Sources of Influence Applied to Phishing Defense

	Motivation	Ability
Personal	Direct Experience & Gamification	Phishing Reporter Tool
Social	Reset Norms – Un-discussible becomes Discussible	Social Accountability
Structural	Gift Certificates	n/a

experience of having their email accounts compromised. They get to observe how clever the attack patterns in the wild appear. They learn first-hand how attackers send modified versions of their own office documents embedding malicious macros to attack their colleagues. For those who don't experience the attack directly, we've invited affected team members to tell their story during our Annual Security Awareness Training, extending a vicarious experience to a broader audience in our organization.

Many modern phishing simulation tools can show who in the company was the first to report the phishing. In my current role, we've gamified reporting a periodic phishing simulation email. The user who reports the phish in the least amount of time wins a small reward. These days, most simulations get reported in less than 20 seconds, and our employees have taken to bragging rights for those with the fastest time.

SOCIAL

Embedding the program into our social fabric has dramatically improved performance. One of the first phishing simulations we performed was entirely believable. We only leveraged information readily available on the internet. We even included the photograph of one of our employees and invited the company to his Halloween party. Over 30% of the company clicked the link. I was horrified but later realized that the very personal nature and high failure rate inspired the transition of phishing defense from an undiscussed topic to a very openly discussed issue.

During the idle chat before one executive session, a key executive described how the fake spa invite from "Your Special Admirer" had come just a few days before his wedding anniversary. He clicked, expecting a cool gift from his spouse only to find out that it was a security training exercise. As an opinion leader in the company, he vowed that would be the first and only time the InfoSec department would "get him" with the phishing simulation.

This open conversation and commitment to do better has proved valuable across his team and the broader organization. Most sales organizations perform poorly in my experience, but our entire

Go-To-Market team is often the first to spot and report a phish and frequently has a very low click rate.

STRUCTURAL

A year or so after starting our program, confident that we had connected vital behaviors to intrinsic satisfaction, we augmented our practices to include awarding the fastest phishing reporter each month with a $25 Amazon Gift Card. People love it!

Understand Mappings

The lack of a phishing program dramatically increases the probability that your organization will experience a data breach. However, describing attack probabilities to our CFO isn't what secured investment in this new capability.

Holistically, we needed to improve spam and malware detection in our email systems. We also required staff and tooling to enhance our phishing response. To obtain funding, I asked, *"How many deals are we willing to lose or customers are we ready to churn as a result of failing to manage phishing risk?"* In that way, the decision wasn't about reducing the number of phishing emails, the safety of links and attachments in email, or encouraging widespread organizational behavior change. We simply focused on explaining how this new capability would protect critical value creation activities in our business. The added angle of loss aversion resulting from the precise format of the question was no accident.

Defaults

Of course, we equip all new employees with pre-installed software, including the phishing reporter. We have also taken up the practice of actively inviting all new employees to a Slack channel where we answer cybersecurity policy questions and provide other updates. More than 75% of the organization remains in the Slack channel, and a large number of team members engage in answering questions about the policy, program capabilities, and best practices. The engagement takes workload from my team and helps institutionalize the knowledge of our organization. Before we had the phishing reporter tools installed and configured, we encouraged people to report suspected phishing in the slack channel.

Give Feedback

Today, we publish click rates and other vital behavior measures to the entire organization every month. To continue to harness the power of social influence, we are now exploring additional means to encourage accountability, including publishing reporter metrics by team and issuing a challenge to those teams with lower security culture engagement. Simultaneously, we are contemplating aggregate click reporting to elevate awareness of poor-performing teams with higher click rates or repeat offenders.

Expect Error

As we implemented our simulated phishing program, we delayed deploying an easy method to report phishing. When we finally released the button, we had cultivated a skeptical, click-wary culture eager to ensure the attachments and links they opened were safe. As a result, we experienced an overwhelming volume of reported emails. Over time, click rates were down, but reporting was so high we were forced to implement automation and supplement our team with outsourcing.

We learned that if we didn't respond to the reporting of phishing emails that our user community did not engage. However, as we built the capability to respond to every reported email, engagement rose precipitously.

Structure of Complex Choices

When choices are numerous or complex, we look to simplify. To help our employees, we've authored a few rhyming rules of thumb to streamline phishing identification:

- Be wary of urgent and scary.
- Sender unknown, leave it alone.
- Stop and think about attachments and links.
- When in doubt, report and wait it out.
- Don't dig in your trash – if it's in your spam filter, there's a reason.

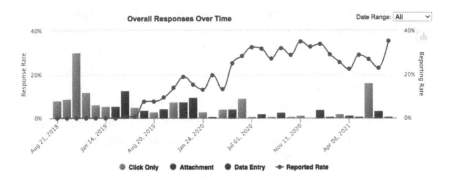

FIGURE 3.5 Overall Phishing Responses Over Time

Source: Cofense Phishing Detection and Response Platform. Used with permission.

In summary, you can see the cumulative impact of investments in our phishing influence plan over time reflected in our Cofense Phishing Detection and Response Platform (Figure 3.5).[23] Using the NUDGES model and the Six Sources of Influence framework, our organizations' ability to identify and respond to phishing has markedly improved. Indeed, benchmarks indicate our employees exhibit world-class phishing awareness. You can see inflection points in our metrics as we improved our influence strategy over time. Movement in the data matches the timing of when we implemented the many tactics discussed above.

Key Insights

- Decision-making is a two-step process that starts with learning and ends with a decision.
- Use the Scientific Method to enhance learning: begin with a problem statement, document a hypothesis, establish a learning plan, clarify your assumptions, and finally state your conclusion and provide a concise recommendation.
- Decision process is *more* important than complete analysis: have a defined process such as WRAP to ensure you do not fall victim to common cognitive errors that afflict us as humans.

- As a leader you can also refer to the WRAP framework to guide others in making complex decisions.
- Vary your sources of influence: the Six Sources of Influence model offers a structured view into incentives and reveals other essential points of leverage in building influence strategies.
- As a choice architect, you can use the NUDGES framework to encourage a security-friendly organizational culture. By architecting choices, you will ensure your company makes incrementally smarter decisions that build up over time.

Notes

1. Robison, J., "Happiness Is Love – and $75,000," Gallup, 2011. Accessed November 14, 2020. https://news.gallup.com/businessjournal/150671/happiness-is-love-and-75k.aspx.
2. Lewis, J., "The CISO as a Choice Architect: A Conversation with Malcolm Harkins," Rain Capital, August 13, 2020. Accessed September 3, 2020. https://www.raincapital.vc/blog/2020/8/13/the-ciso-as-a-choice-architect-a-conversation-with-malcolm-harkins.
3. Dalio, R., *Principles*. Simon & Schuster, 2017.
4. Science Buddies, "Steps of the Scientific Method." Accessed October 8, 2020. https://www.sciencebuddies.org/science-fair-projects/science-fair/steps-of-the-scientific-method.
5. OpenStax, "The Process of Science," 2021. http://cnx.org/contents/443e8445-8894-4d58-a72d-43a5cc541fc4@13.
6. Heath, C., and Heath, D., *Decisive*. Crown Publishing Group, a division of Penguin Random House LLC, 2013.
7. Heath, C., and Heath, D., *Decisive*.
8. Heath, C., and Heath, D., *Decisive*.
9. Heath, C., and Heath, D., *Decisive*.
10. Dalio, R., *Principles*.
11. Venables, P., "The Most Important Mental Models for CISOs – Simple Steps for Outsize Effects," Risk & Cybersecurity – Thoughts from the Field, September 27, 2020. Accessed November 14, 2020. https://www.philvenables.com/post/the-most-important-mental-models-for-cisos-simple-steps-for-outsize-effects.
12. Heath, C., and Heath, D., *Decisive*.

13. Kickstarter, "Our Rules – Kickstarter." Accessed November 14, 2020. https://www.kickstarter.com/rules?ref=learn_faq.

14. Thaler, R.H., and Sunstein, C.R., *Nudge: Improving Decisions About Health, Wealth, and Happiness*, Yale University Press, 2008.

15. Grenny, J., Maxfield, D., and Shimberg, A., *How to 10X Your Influence*, Vital Smarts, 2013.

16. Thaler R.H., and Sunstein, C.R., *Nudge: Improving Decisions About Health, Wealth, and Happiness*.

17. Grenny, J., Patterson, K., Maxfield, D., McMillian, R., and Switzler A., *Influencer: The New Science of Leading Change*, McGraw-Hill Education, 2013.

18. Xu, L., "NopSec Unified VRM," 2020.

19. Thaler R.H., and Sunstein, C.R., *Nudge: Improving Decisions About Health, Wealth, and Happiness*.

20. Thaler R.H., and Sunstein, C.R., *Nudge: Improving Decisions About Health, Wealth, and Happiness*.

21. Synopsys Editorial Team, "Top Open Source Licenses and Legal Risk," Synopsys, October 21, 2019. Accessed November 14, 2020. https://www.synopsys.com/blogs/software-security/top-open-source-licenses/.

22. *Data Breach Investigations Report*, 2020. https://enterprise.verizon.com/resources/reports/2020-data-breach-investigations-report.pdf.

23. Cofense Phishing Detection and Response Platform, 2020.

CHAPTER 4

Value Creation

Nowadays, people know the price of everything and the value of nothing.

— Oscar Wilde

Opportunity

Until your organization can relate cybersecurity activities directly to the value they preserve or create, your budget will be a function of compliance. Business executives need to know that you are thinking about value the way they do. As CISO, it isn't your job to determine the value of the business. In fact, quite the opposite. Determining business value should come from other offices. However, CISOs should use the knowledge presented below to ensure they understand what other execs say about business value. My goal here is to establish a foundation that enables you to immerse yourself in your own company's value creation engines. Then you should leverage that knowledge to drive cybersecurity priorities and investments.

By the time you finish this chapter, I hope you are equipped to more easily:

- Structure and align your thinking to the business,
- Engage others in your company to fully understand the unique ways your company creates value, and
- Identify additional resources that can help you quickly and continuously align your cybersecurity program with the primary value drivers in your business.

We start with an analogy. Real estate is often the most significant investment most individuals make. Likewise, it is through real estate that I have learned the most about value. Early in my life, there were several transitions, each featuring real estate. When I was 11 years old, my parents bought a new home. I recall there was an eight-foot-high basketball hoop. I imagined slam dunking on my friends. There was a backyard overgrown with weeds that held the potential to become a beautiful garden. My brother, sisters, and I hoped to play soccer, splash on a slip 'n' slide, and have water fights with super-soakers in that yard. At 11 years old, I assembled my own story about what the property meant to me, and my parents had their accounts too.

Later, I learned that this home's value and banks' willingness to provide cash-out refinancing funded my childhood. Our bikes, vacations, and large screen televisions were all purchased on credit cards. My parents then rolled those debts into our home's refinancing with an adjustable-rate mortgage (ARM). They gradually extracted the equity value through this process, over time, until there was none.

Transitioning from college, I struggled to find a job and returned home to live in that same house for another six months or more. I was a terrible interviewer. I didn't know that I could easily prepare to answer a set of predictable questions. I didn't know how to research a company. I wasn't aware of the need to tailor my experiences or skills to match the job description, company culture, or interviewer. Instead, I figured my skills and resume spoke for themselves. I had completed several internships and held a competitive grade point average when compared to my peers. I eventually watched all my friends get jobs before I was hired as a web developer. Writing code was the *last* thing I wanted to do!

Before I got that technical role, I became so discouraged that I decided to pursue a real estate license, which I eventually obtained but never activated. In the early 2000s, sites like Zillow didn't exist. Pricing residential real estate was a manual exercise your real estate agent did by searching the Multiple Listing Service (MLS) and finding comparable properties. Then they evaluated the differences to derive a target price. In theory, the methodology for establishing the price played into the eventual price negotiation.

Now, we have access to tons of information about real estate. There are photos and virtual tours, information about the surrounding neighborhood, nearby schools, restaurants, and even tools that use machine learning to offer suggested pricing ranges and appreciation rates. Today, rather than sourcing information you don't have, your real estate agent emphasizes what information you should prioritize.

They also find alternative ways to add value to your purchasing process. One of the first things they do is establish credibility and trust with their clients. To add value, they may listen with empathy, provide references, demonstrate real estate domain proficiency, orchestrate the sales process, lead price negotiations, and connect you with supporting resources such as mortgage brokers, lawyers, inspectors, appraisers, etc.

Ironically, I failed to recognize that becoming a real estate agent only amplified the need for all the soft skills impeding my technical job search progress. However, becoming a licensed agent wasn't a total loss because I acquired the knowledge to buy real estate confidently. So, in Q4 2007, I purchased a small condominium in Westminster, Colorado.

By that time, I had indirectly benefited from both the long- and short-term debt cycles. I didn't even consider that property values could go down! But then those adjustable-rate mortgages from my childhood came due for my parents and many others. These defaulted mortgages ultimately led us into a global financial crisis. In the end, we lost about 10% of our home's value when we sold it in Q2 of 2011.

All the lessons I learned from real estate over the years have influenced my decisions as a CISO. Looking closer now, I can identify the salient concepts as follows:

- Value varies by context. The value of a real estate agent putting you at ease during a significant financial transaction is quite different from the value a real estate agent adds when negotiating the price of your home.
- Value varies by audience. Moderate differences in your home's listing value may significantly affect the time and effort required to sell it. At the same time, these changes result in a negligible increase in a real estate agent's compensation. What may be worth tens of thousands of dollars to you may only be worth hundreds of dollars to your real estate agent. The incremental value to you is significant. Meanwhile, your real estate agent might not gain much at all given the increased effort and expense to secure that value on your behalf.
- Macroeconomic and geopolitical conditions. The broader economy impacts supply and demand and thus value.
- Timing is critical. Increasing home equity plus available credit helped finance my childhood. However, poor timing also led to a loss on the sale of our first home.
- Stories matter. The homes we buy tend to be a combination of the future we imagine plus the value we can afford. What is affordable is governed by rules of thumb loosely agreed upon by bankers, appraisers, brokers, agents, and lawyers. And so, stories are essential to decisions we make and have an outsized influence on the jobs we secure, the budgets we control, and the teams we lead. We'll discuss this in more detail in Chapter 8 – Communication – You Do It Every Day (or Do You?).

In the Principle section, we will become more intimate with value. We will decompose the concept using the Five W's + H (who, what, where, when, why, and how) framework. In the process, we will bridge the gap between property value and enterprise value and introduce standard business valuation methods at a high level.

Then, once we know more about business valuation, we can use that lens to examine decisions inside a cybersecurity program. Aligning your cybersecurity program with your business's primary value drivers is the focus of this chapter's Application section.

Principle

My goal is not to convert you into a Chartered Financial Analyst® charter holder. However, to be an effective business operator, you need to know how alternative strategies will affect shareholder value. Further, as a cybersecurity leader, you should supply your Board of Directors with an appropriate set of levers to manipulate the cost, value, and risk your program facilitates. After all, if you don't possess a clear understanding of value, how can you optimize your program to preserve and create it?

To examine value in more detail, we will ask the following questions:

- Who determines value?
- What delivers value to investors?
- Where is value created?
- When is value created?
- Why is value so important?
- How is value determined?

Who Determines Value?

As I learned in my journey with real estate, *stories matter,* and *value varies by audience.* Interviewing for a job or selling a home involves telling a story. Either you intentionally control the narrative or simply present facts and let someone else fill in the gaps. As a CISO utilizes storytelling to add value inside a business, it is important to tailor each story for the audience, just as you would highlight unique features of your experience in a job interview.

"Your business story may not be the same when you are talking to different stakeholders (employees, customers, or potential investors) because each has a different interest in the story. While employees may share your enthusiasm for the success of the business, they are just as interested or perhaps more so in how you plan to share that success with them and the personal risks they face from failure. Customers are more interested in your products than in your profits and want to hear the part of your story in which you explain how your product or service will meet their needs and what they will have to pay in return. **Investors want to know about these same products and services, but generally from the perspective of how you plan to convert potential into revenues and value.** Even among investors there can be big differences in time horizon (short term vs. long term) and how they expect to generate their returns (cash return vs. growth in value), and your story may succeed with one while failing with the other."[1]

This chapter will focus on the investor or shareholder perspective, noting the strong relationships among customer benefit, employee satisfaction, and shareholder value.

Just because we are looking at business value from the investor perspective doesn't mean we have enough information to understand what might create value for the investor. We can consider two investor personas: The Financial Investor and the Strategic. Each invests with a unique perspective and varied skills and resources to enhance an acquired business's value.

The following list describes the generic differences, although the specifics will vary by investor:[2]

- Financial Buyers
  - They are usually long-term investors interested in the return that they can get by buying a well-managed company. Some financial buyers are willing to invest in earlier stages and help companies become best in class/well managed, and others expect their investments to have mature operations already. As you might guess, the maturity of an operation will affect a company's valuation.
  - Look to generate cash flow by boosting revenue, cutting costs, or creating economies of scale by buying similar companies.

- They are also focused on what exit strategies they can build, such as private market methodologies (sale to other financial buyer or strategic buyer), structural methodologies (redemptions/dividends/conversions), or public market methodologies (IPO or merger with SPAC).

- Strategic Buyers
  - They are more interested in how a potential acquisition fits into their own long-term goals.
  - They are often more prominent companies that are well-capitalized, spend more, and are less interested in whether a company can generate quick cash flow.
  - They care about cultural fit more than financial buyers because they will probably be integrating the acquired company with an existing business.

Another way to stratify the investment community is by considering the differences between venture capital, private equity (PE), and hedge funds. The type of investor and age of the fund can give clues to the intended time horizon of an investment, in addition to the control and impact an investor may have on management, operations, or other methods.

The following list offers a generic summary of each type of investor, but there are always exceptions:

- Venture Capital Firms
  - Focus on investing in early-stage startups that cannot otherwise secure bank financing due to the inherently high-risk nature of entrepreneurship.
  - Usually invest in 50% or less of the company equity.
  - Operate a fund on a 7- to 10-year cycle.
  - Dedicate the first 1 to 3 years of the fund to finding investments.
  - Direct energy in the later years toward portfolio management and seeking a successful exit of each portfolio company to provide a return to investors.
  - Exit their investment via the sale of their equity position, complete acquisition, or an initial public offering (IPO).

- Private Equity Firms
  - Focus on either growth stage $10 million, or more mature companies targeting investments of $100 million or more.
  - Secure controlling interest in the firm. This is generally via majority ownership, except for growth equity–focused private equity firms.
  - Often execute a leveraged buyout (LBO), and plan to add value in one of three ways:[3]
    - Reengineering the firm – many PE firms have experienced former executives that share their expertise and contacts with portfolio firm managers.
    - Helping obtain debt financing on more advantageous terms.
    - PE ownership can focus on long-term performance because they are not facing pressure from public market shareholders and sell-side analysts.
  - The investment horizon tends to be 5 to 7 years.

- Hedge Funds – although some hedge funds have a flexible mandate and can be "hybrid" doing public equities with some private deals, the following is generally applicable:
  - Investments happen all at once
  - Tend to be very liquid
  - Invest in many things, not just the equity of companies
  - Tend to be riskier investments attempting to make large profits on shortened timelines

Table 4.1 provides an excellent summary of factors by investor type.

In summary, most companies in the early venture capital funding stages don't already have a CISO. Hedge funds tend to be more liquid, and so the terms of their deals are less likely to include control

TABLE 4.1 Factors by Investor Type

Investor Type	Target Return	Time Horizon	Risk Tolerance
Venture Capital	25%–30%	3–7 Years	Very High
Private Equity	20%–25%	4–10 Years	High
Hedge Fund	8%–10%	Liquid Assets	Very High

mechanisms that put them in direct control of the day-to-day management. However, PE firms play an active role in adding value through financial contributions, better access to capital, and a more hands-on steering approach that includes placing Board Directors and executives within the company.

As a final note, Chris Castaldo has done a great job walking founders through how to Start-up Secure. In his book, he describes how to integrate cybersecurity into a business during the key stages of company formation, validation, and growth.

What Delivers Value to Investors?

Remember, we are focused on the investor perspective. So, another way to ask this question is – How does an investor get paid?

There are three basic ways that investors get a return on their investment.

1. Dividends
2. Redemptions
3. Capital appreciation

Dividends are regular distributions of profits to shareholders – typically, on a yearly or quarterly basis. Then you have instruments of debt and equity used to raise capital. Redemptions are essentially a loan for a business. Usually, they include regular interest payments (cash or Payment-In-Kind), voluntary or nonvoluntary prepayments, conversions, or at-maturity redemption. Finally, capital appreciation occurs when the equity an investor holds appreciates.

As a final note, remember that *value varies by context*. Your board of directors may appreciate a well-formed metrics program and a transparent methodology for risk management and capital allocation. Indeed, a robust cybersecurity program can help an individual board director limit her liability and fulfill her fiduciary duties to shareholders. But be careful to avoid confusion when mere appreciation diverges from enterprise value.

Where Is Value Created?

In every business, there are value levers, just as there are cost drivers. Suppose your business delivers value primarily through profitable operations. In that case, at least a portion of the value your company provides to investors likely comes from the dividend they receive. Stocks that commonly pay dividends are more established companies that don't need to reinvest their profits. For example, more than 84% of companies in the S&P 500 currently pay dividends.[4]

If your business delivers value to investors via capital gains, you need to be clear on how investors determine your business's value. Traditionally there are three common ways that investors determine the value of a company (see Figure 4.1):

- Asset Based: Calculate the assets of a company in case of dissolution, replacement, or liquidation.
- Market-Based: Utilize relative pricing models that compare features of one business to another business or set of similar companies. Note: This is analogous to the real estate comparable sales pricing method.
- Discounted Cashflow: Commonly, discounted cash flow (DCF) methods attempt to project future cash flow discounted to a current value. You can estimate the future revenues and expenses of a business and apply a formula to calculate the present value of future cash flows. Discounting is used because a dollar today is worth less than a dollar tomorrow, assuming inflation. Other considerations, such as execution risk, control premiums, and marketability, also come into play.

For now, suffice it to say that investors assign value to a company typically with some objective metric. "When pricing companies, it is not your place or mine to determine what investors should be using to price companies, but what they actually are using. Thus, if the metric investors focus on when pricing social media companies is the number of users these companies have, you should focus on that metric in pricing your company."[5]

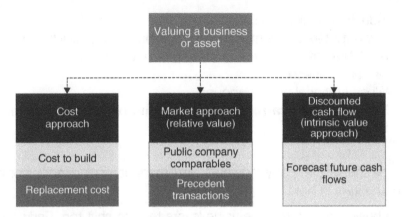

FIGURE 4.1 Valuation Methods

Source: Corporate Finance Institute, "Valuation Methods," 2021. https://corporate-financeinstitute.com/resources/knowledge/valuation/valuation-methods/. Used with permission.

When Are Gains Realized?

Equity investors may have a long-term or short-term view on their investment depending upon the fund's type and cycle. They can obtain a return on their investment in many ways, including dividends, profit sharing, operating and monitoring fees, and capital gains upon exit. Investors realize capital gains by selling an asset for more than they paid for it. Nevertheless, equity investors have many other paths within the law to realize profits.

The macroeconomic environment is vital to consider when realizing gains. When the broader economy is thriving, there is more confidence in the continued growth and availability of capital. When the market sentiment is optimistic, companies and individuals are likely to spend more freely. Valuations will tend to be larger when markets are thriving and investors are confident about growth. The maximum valuation (or, in reality, range of values) at a point in time is a function of numerous factors, including:[6]

- Conditions in the stock market
- The level of interest rates and the availability of financing
- Conditions in the relevant economic markets (national, regional, local)

- Industry conditions
- Current interest of competing strategic buyers in similar businesses
- Availability of investment funds in private equity funds focused on similar businesses
- When irrational buyers abound
- **The level of earnings and conditions in the business being sold**

Notice that a company's owners and management directly control only the item in bold.

As a business matures, the value levers tend to shift too. Early on, a company will focus on revenue growth, later operating margins, and once in decline, cash flow is the determinant value lever. This evolution of maturity is termed the *company life cycle*.

As a final comment on the timing of realized gains, awareness of a fund's life cycle can be helpful. A fund manager operating a fund in its later stages will have less appetite for an extended investment horizon and will be eager to see high growth or large profits.

Why Is Value So Important?

The decisions you make about structuring your team, the controls you implement, the architectures you choose, and the partners you leverage need to be congruent with your company's value agenda. The things you prioritize and protect, the risks you accept, and the stories you tell must also align with the value agenda.

It doesn't matter if the value agenda comprises evolving your business model, streamlining your operating costs, heavy M&A activity, or finding ways to maximize an EBITDA multiple. Cybersecurity leaders need to be aware of the value agenda, and they need to be able to design programs that support and accelerate it. In short, cybersecurity operations that impede the value agenda are doomed.

As a side note, understanding how these dynamics affect decisions in your business will make a difference in the executive visibility you are permitted. Failure to understand the value agenda will limit what resources you obtain and form your perspective on resource allocations, the organizational support you garner and thus determine satisfaction in your role (see Figure 4.2).[7]

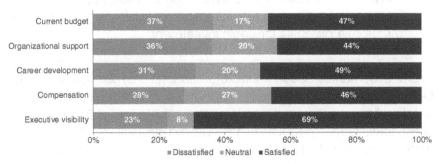

Drivers of satisfaction for CISOs

How would you rate the underlying drivers of satisfaction?

FIGURE 4.2 Drivers of CISO Satisfaction

Source: IANS Research, *2020 CISO Compensation and Budget Study*, 2020. Used with permission.

How Is Value Determined?

Value comes in many forms. Previously we reviewed three methods to determine value. They are asset-based, market-based, and discounted cash flow. Because the asset-based approach leaves little room for the CISO to influence, we'll only address the market-based and DCF methods in this text.

The valuation process involves the following steps:[8]

1. *Understanding the business.* Industry and competitive analysis, together with an analysis of financial statements and other company disclosures, provides a basis for forecasting company performance.
2. *Forecasting company performance.* Forecasts of sales, earnings, dividends, and financial position (pro forma analysis) provide the inputs for most valuation models.
3. *Selecting the appropriate valuation model.* Depending on the characteristics of the company and the context of valuation, some valuation models will be more appropriate than others.

4. *Converting forecasts to a valuation*. Beyond mechanically obtaining the "output" of valuation models, estimating value involves judgment.
5. *Applying the valuation conclusions*. Depending on the purpose, an analyst may use the valuation conclusions to make an investment recommendation about a particular stock, provide an opinion about the price of a transaction, or evaluate the economic merits of a potential strategic investment.

In practice, market-based (multiple) valuations are more common, but DCF is still genuinely relevant. The valuation methods most widely used by Morgan Stanley Dean Witter's analysts for valuing European companies place the DCF in fifth behind several different multiple methods such as PER, EV/EBITDA, and EV/EG (see Figure 4.3).[9]

It's worth noting that the above valuation methods apply to public stocks and public markets. Generally, VC and PE funds do not invest in the public markets. I'll assume you have done your homework to understand your business, using the tools of Chapter 1 – Financial Principles and Chapter 2 – Business Strategy Tools. Trust that your

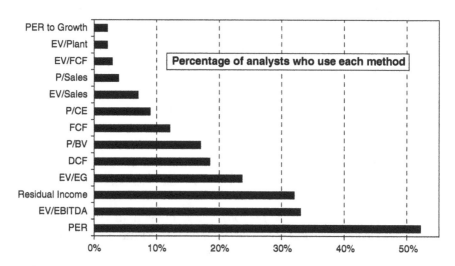

FIGURE 4.3 Common Valuation Methods

Source: Fernandez, P., *Valuation Methods and Shareholder Value Creation*, 1st ed. Reproduced with permission of Elsevier.

Finance team will know how you are valued, and rest assured it's likely either of these:

- Multiples Valuation Model
- Discounted Cash Flow on Free Cash Flow to the Firm Valuation Model

Multiples Valuation Model

To perform a relative valuation using a multiple, you must select a set of comparable companies and decide upon a metric. Then you examine each asset's characteristics and decide if the differences justify the variation in value relative to one another. The sector in which you operate will determine the metric you use, and with good reason. These multiples tend to be more highly correlated with the actual value engines that power the sector or business model.

As with real estate, the comparable assets you select will significantly impact the value you derive. You could have picked the S&P 500, Russell 3000, or any other grouping to perform your analysis. However, the most common approach used by investors is to find a similar industry or industries with which to compare the target company. Investors also use recent comparable transactions. Bankers will have similar data about how privately held companies are valued.

"Multiples almost always have a broad dispersion, which is why valuations performed using multiples are always highly debatable."[10] Further, asset characteristics will play a significant role. For example, in real estate, how do you adjust the value for square footage, a mountain view, being just inside a "good" school district, etc.? It turns out there are agreed-upon ways to handle these differences, and those same subjective methods exist when determining enterprise value as well.

Let's examine a hypothetical example to make this more concrete. Select all the publicly traded companies in your industry. Look up the price-to-earnings ratio (PER) for each. There are plenty of places to source this data. I typically just reference https://finance.yahoo.com/ or https://www.morningstar.com/.

Then compute the average PER for all companies in the industry. Now tell a story about your company relative to the competition. One common way to collect and analyze the varied factors that influence your business is to perform an analysis using *Porter's Five Forces* (https://hbr.org/1979/03/how-competitive-forces-shape-strategy) framework. We review Porter's Five Forces in more detail in Chapter 6 – Cybersecurity: A Concern of the Business, Not Just IT.

According to Ken Ziegler, if you have four of the following six items present in your comps, your business is going to be valued favorably:

- Growth
- Revenue Model
- Margins
- Scale
- Supply vs. Demand
- Differentiation

Cyber-professionals can do a ton to contribute to many of these. To be effective, you have to be able to answer questions like:

- Are you able to out-innovate, and do you anticipate gaining market share?
- What is unique about your business model? Are there networking effects, recurring revenue implications, or first-mover advantages that enhance your value?
- Are you better positioned to acquire talent because of your brand?
- Do economies of scale permit you to operate more efficiently?
- What about your intellectual property impacts the value story?
- Are there barriers to entry in your industry, or do market forces make your business different or scarce?

Whatever story your business projects, it must be grounded in the numbers on your financial statements. Investors will look to validate the story by examining performance. They will evaluate things such as: What is your cumulative annual growth rate in the last three years? Is your capital structure heavily biased with debt? How much cash are you generating each year? What percent of your revenues can be dependably accounted for because they are already under contract? What does your operating margin look like compared to your competitors? Do you have a history of paying a dividend? Depending upon how aligned your story is with the objective answers to these questions, you might justify a higher multiple.

Likewise, suppose you anticipate a significant patent infringement ruling that will impact your revenue growth or material regulatory enforcement fines. Investors might decide the average PER is an overvaluation of your firm.

Discounted Cash Flow on Free Cash Flow to the Firm Valuation Model

The DCF model leverages a forecast of future cash flow to the firm (FCFF). Once calculated, the model discounts FCFF to present value using a discount rate. Thus, every valuation starts with a story, and the business forecast is born from the story.

It's simple in concept. Over time, you learn the value drivers that have the most considerable effect on the terminal value in a DCF model are growth, profit, risk, and interest rates. So, these will tend to be the things to consider as you set a strategy for your cybersecurity program. As you can see in Figure 4.4, many other considerations may also play a factor depending upon your specific scenario:

Notice that risk plays a material role in valuation. The primary risks considered are operating risk and financial risk. A data breach impacts both, so in theory, cybersecurity should play a role in the company's valuation.

Areas where cybersecurity risk could affect the valuation of a company are:[11]

- The discount rate through the company-specific risk premium that is adjusted for cybersecurity risk
- The cash flow that is adjusted to account for losses due to cybersecurity breaches
- A direct adjustment to the value of the company

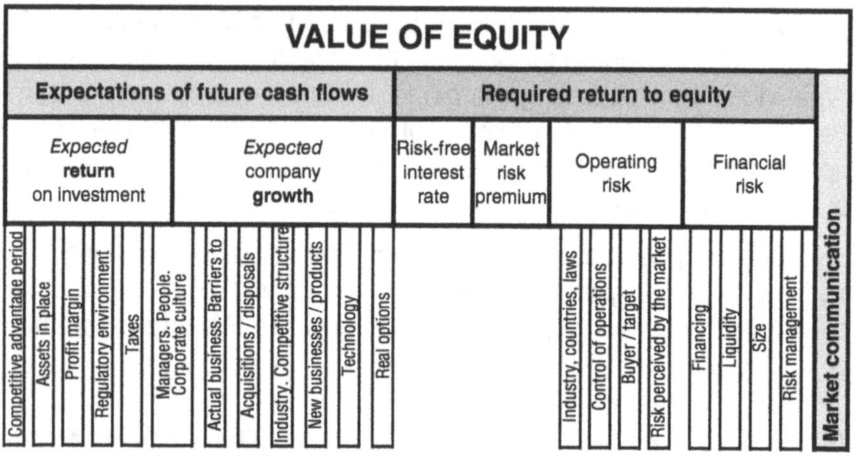

VALUE OF EQUITY					
Expectations of future cash flows		**Required return to equity**			
Expected **return** on investment	*Expected* company **growth**	Risk-free interest rate	Market risk premium	Operating risk	Financial risk

Column labels under "Expected return on investment": Competitive advantage period · Assets in place · Profit margin · Regulatory environment · Taxes

Column labels under "Expected company growth": Managers. People. Corporate culture · Actual business. Barriers to · Acquisitions / disposals · Industry. Competitive structure · New businesses / products · Technology · Real options

Column labels under "Operating risk": Industry, countries, laws · Control of operations · Buyer / target · Risk perceived by the market

Column labels under "Financial risk": Financing · Liquidity · Size · Risk management

Right-side vertical label: **Market communication**

FIGURE 4.4 Equity Value Drivers

Source: Fernandez, P., *Valuation Methods and Shareholder Value Creation*. Reproduced with permission of Elsevier.

In practice, most risk disclosures for public companies have converged on common language. Therefore, the chances of cybersecurity posture impacting a discount rate (or multiple) in an analyst valuation report are low. So long as you can demonstrate adequate security diligence and cyber liability insurance and have a reasonable degree of confidence that there are no ongoing cybersecurity incidents, the DCF terminal value is not likely to be affected.

As a cybersecurity leader, your business's narrative, supporting assumptions, and the resulting forecasts in your business are not your responsibility. Typically, your CEO, CFO, and CRO lead those efforts. However, understanding the story and the key metrics that impact valuation is absolutely a part of your job. For now, it's enough to know that there are many nuances to selecting the discount rate and a precise formula to calculate FCFF.

Let's review to close the real estate analogy. Business value is affected by many variables, including:

- Context: investor vs. employee vs. customer
- Audience: investor type, such as VC vs. PE vs. hedge fund, and financial vs. strategic
- Macroeconomic conditions: capital markets, sector, and industry performance, etc.

- Timing: the company life cycle and stage of the investment fund
- Stories: set the stage for forecasting, which informs valuation

Now that you know the driving forces and influencing factors of value in a business, figure out who in your company serves in the Financial Planning and Analysis (FP&A) function. Have a conversation with them and clarify how the variables above appear in your business.

If you can already answer the questions posed below, then validate your understanding with your CFO. If you are in a publicly traded company, you MUST listen to the earnings calls first. In my experience, there's a good chance you might learn something subtle about your business that you didn't already know by validating your understanding.

On earnings calls, corporate executives will tend to describe their business very differently than they do when speaking to employees at an all-hands meeting. For example, I once observed company leadership speak very frankly in an earnings call about the number of retail stores that would be closed in the coming months. Then, the next day, there was no mention of closing stores in our company all-hands meeting. Instead, the conversation focused on all the positive benefits employees should anticipate.

Essential questions to understand value drivers in your business include:

- Who are the primary investors? Do they have seats on our board?
- What value do our investors add to our company? How?
- Have our investors played a role in placing any executives in the company?
- Which fund are we part of, and where are we in the fund life cycle? Does that influence how the Board views or business or how our executive team makes decisions?
- What is our hurdle rate, internal rate of return, or the average cost of capital?
- What type of exit is likely? What story are we likely to tell investors about our business to enhance our valuation?

For a complete overview of financial valuation techniques, consult any of these brief courses:

- https://courses.corporatefinanceinstitute.com/courses/business-valuation-fundamentals-certificate-course
- https://execed.stern.nyu.edu/products/advanced-valuation-with-aswath-damodaran
- https://future.aicpa.org/cpe-learning/course/introduction-to-business-valuation

Application

This section will put the concepts shared so far to practical use by exploring the value agenda for a beverage manufacturer. Specifically, we'll examine the business and demonstrate how to place competing priorities relative to one another in the context of business value. With a complete picture, you can help your business balance investment and risk with the need to achieve desired business outcomes. From a cost perspective, the business may spend more, spend less, or real-locate spending to achieve the appropriate level of risk for a particular business initiative.

Case Study – Beverage Manufacturer with Competing Priorities

Imagine you are the new CISO for a large soft drink manufacturer. The quarterly earnings call was last night, and you decided to tune in and see what information you might glean. You learn that although your company is not a growth company, you continue to see single-digit revenue growth numbers that outpace inflation and competition. You note that growth seems important. Further, your primary business of carbonated beverages is declining, and you have managed to diversify revenues by acquiring snack brands and developing healthier drinks. Also, increased marketing spend has translated to better consumer brand recognition and more shelf space from retailers. Finally, as a business, you are also finding ways to take your sales direct to customers, omitting retailers from the equation.

The next day in the lunchroom, you find yourself seated next to a colleague from the Finance department, and you gather that you have a long-established history of paying dividends. Then a week later, you hear from your CIO that combined with your modest top-line growth, the business continues to find ways to compress company expenses. He will support this cost reduction effort by implementing warehouse and distribution center robotics automation. Ideally, this will result in more profits for the company.

In a relatively short period, you have just learned several critical business priorities. Naturally, you may want to seek to be involved in these initiatives. Unfortunately, you haven't been invited by others to participate.

Before you set out on crashing meetings, initiating security tool proofs of concept, or crafting job descriptions, you decide to ensure you fully understand the value agenda.

You begin by asking yourself some basic questions (featured earlier in the chapter), and here's what you come up with:

- **Who determines value?** Investors in the NYSE.
- **What delivers value to investors?** Dividends + Capital Appreciation – not sure which is more important.
- **Where is value created?** Market-Based or DCF – not sure which one.
- **When is value created?** Quarterly dividends and upon sale of equity.
- **How is value determined?** Earnings per Share (EPS) or Price to Earnings (PER) – not sure.

You are confident in some of your answers. Meanwhile, other questions have you feeling a bit uncertain. For example, you know you have a stock ticker symbol, so the stock market determines your market capitalization. You know that you are dividend stock, and based on the general tone of conversations, you decide that profit is a significant focus for the company. Some quick research on the internet reveals that the markets regard your company as an "Established dividend payer with a mediocre balance sheet." In other words, you deliver value to investors via both dividends and capital appreciation. You assume the market utilizes a multiple-based valuation of your company, but in truth, you don't necessarily know which multiple.

You figure it behooves you to understand which multiple the analysts are using to value your company and calculate the multiple. Maybe once you determine that, you can examine the business's various activities that directly impact the metric. You also identify that you might not be as aware of the macroeconomic conditions that affect your industry, so you resolve to seek out a source of information that can help you get up to speed on these factors.

The Multiple

To get started, you find an analyst in your FP&A team. She advises you that the market, and most importantly a small number of institutional investors that own a large percentage of shares, values the company on an EV/EBITDA ratio (in reality, it's probably PER, typical of cyclical manufacturing, but indulge in the scenario). She also reinforces that the market considers your company "an established dividend payer with a mediocre balance sheet." Given this primary determinant of value, you decide to decompose the formulas and assumptions used to calculate the ratio.

In the numerator of the ratio, you have EV:

$$EV = \text{Market Capitalization} + \text{Market Value of Debt} - \text{Cash and Equivalents}$$

And in the denominator, EBITDA can be calculated as follows (review EBITDA formulas in Chapter 1):

$$EBITDA = \text{Net Income} + \text{Interest} + \text{Taxes} + \text{Depreciation} + \text{Amortization}$$

OR

$$EBITDA = \text{Operating Income} + \text{Depreciation} + \text{Amortization}$$

Where

$$\text{Operating Income} = \text{Net Revenue} - \text{Cost of Goods Sold}\,(\text{COGS})$$
$$- \text{Operating Expenses}$$

In your conversation with Finance later that week, you discover that pressure from analysts and shareholders has influenced some past managers in the business to focus on short-term results while pursuing a long-term strategy. You note that quick wins for new executives will be necessary. In particular, during the research you did to prepare for your interviews, you noticed that your Chief Marketing Officer was recently promoted from within the organization.

Armed with the multiple, you wonder – is a large or small ratio good? You reason that this depends upon the perspective of your audience. As an employee, you want your EV/EBITDA to be large, assuming restricted stock units (RSUs) comprise part of your compensation. You believe correctly that your incentives align with those of the shareholders in the stock market. In contrast, your customers would no doubt be happy to pay less for your product in exchange for you realizing lower profits.

You conclude that mathematically, you want to either make EV (the numerator) larger or make EBITDA (the denominator) smaller. In reality, no one is pursuing a strategy for less EBITDA. Since the market determines EV, which stems directly from your business story, you make a note to examine the role you might play in that narrative.

You notice how the calculations seem to exclude depreciation and amortization from the valuation calculation (if needed, see the section on Capex and EBITDA from Chapter 1 for a refresher on what this means). Next, EBITDA has several formulas above. You quickly observe that you don't play a role in determining interest or taxes. You also recall that you may be able to take advantage of depreciation or amortization in funding your program in the short term. You finish your assessment with some more clarity, given that the only natural area in the first formula to focus on is *net income*. Unsurprisingly, that means more revenue and less cost.

The Value Agenda

As a CISO, you can now examine the role you play in each value agenda component. You have a limited budget, time is scarce, and you already know that talent acquisition will be a challenge. So, you need to know what to prioritize and how to spend the dollars you have available. If you can't quite achieve what is necessary for the business to be successful, you need to outline what limitations you face and *how that will impact the broader value agenda*. You decide to build a picture that will help your C-suite optimize cost and risk while pursuing an increased market cap.

Gartner has a model that uses risk, value, and cost (RVC) to put cybersecurity priorities and investments in a business context (see Figure 4.5).[12] The bubbles are business outcomes, the vertical axis is business value, the horizontal axis is risk posture, and the size of the bubbles are relative costs to maintain the desired risk posture. We will use this model to show how all the concepts presented in this chapter can be consolidated into a single representation to engage your executives and drive security investment.

Logically, to increase net income, you either increase revenues or reduce expenses. Naturally, your business story will give you a feeling about where to focus. In this case, you decide that the earnings call seems to indicate as a business; you are pursuing both. Better marketing and diversification should drive top-line growth. Increased automation in factories and distribution centers and a direct-to-consumer strategy should result in cost reductions.

To cozy up to the value agenda, you now decide you need to explore each of the four key initiatives to more intimately understand how those initiatives impact individuals, teams, and the performance of the company overall. These initiatives will represent the business unit bubbles in our RVC diagram in Figure 4.5. Later we'll add the risk perspective. For now, you take solace in your belief that risk is ultimately a choice related to investments and priorities. To get started, you schedule four meetings, each holding one of the following meeting titles:

- Marketing
- Diversification

- Warehouse and Distribution Center Automation
- Direct-to-Consumer

Here's what you learn in each meeting respectively:

MARKETING

Anticipating the meeting, you think to yourself that cybersecurity teams often play no role until there is a significant cybersecurity incident when it comes to market communication. Even then, the CISO isn't likely to speak with the press or analysts unless legal and PR teams have coached that message. So, you expect that there's a real chance your marketing team hasn't given much thought to cybersecurity. It's even less likely that your new CMO actively concerns himself with cyber risk.

To prepare for the meeting, you craft a few questions you hope to explore, as follows:

- Where is your marketing team funneling increased spending?
  - Better market segmentation
  - Improved targeting
  - Enhanced differentiation
  - Adapted positioning
- How is the marketing team measured? What are key goals related to variable compensation plans, raises, or recognition for individuals or the department as a whole?
- Does the initiative mentioned in the earnings call include new technologies such as AI Marketing platforms? (They are currently "in vogue".)
- Does this innovative platform cause any concerns about preserving consumer privacy as required by GDPR?
- How does cybersecurity impact the four P's of marketing: product, price, place, and promotion? (See MindTools – https://www.mindtools.com/pages/videos/4ps-transcript.htm.)
- What role does cybersecurity play in differentiation and positioning?

Leaving the meeting, you now know that AI/ML technologies will touch customer data directly to enhance segmentation and targeting.

You confirm that in the beverage business and the consumer-packaged goods (CPG) industry in general, cybersecurity isn't likely going to feature as a prominent point of differentiation. There's no interest in pursuing that discussion further.

You also get an education on overall marketing strategy, which doesn't follow the four P's of marketing you learned in your MBA class. Your CMO appreciated the initiative in preparing for the meeting and corrected your attempt to describe the value his department delivers. Your CMO excitedly declares his initiatives are a "game changer" that will undoubtedly catapult revenues forward, but it will take time. He also assures you it isn't any singular thing he has planned, but instead how they all play together. He declares attribution is difficult, and you think to yourself how true that is in cybersecurity, too!

Then, your CMO reveals that, in truth, this is the first time he's ever spoken to a CISO and wasn't aware of the privacy implications that you raised concerning customer analytics. Nevertheless, he agrees that you should partner to explore that in a bit more detail to make sure everything is on the up and up. You agree to set a follow-up meeting in 30 days as a touchpoint to reengage.

Diversification

As you have been getting to know your team, you validated that you already have a robust third-party risk management (TPRM) program. However, while speaking with your Corporate Development (corp-dev) team, you learn that the business is not yet taking advantage of that program. In fact, the corp-dev team was hesitant in accepting a meeting with you and rescheduled several times before you met in person. You offer that InfoSec participation might help to create a more risk-aware transaction during the M&A diligence process. You comment you are surprised the capability isn't being used, recalling for everyone that after Yahoo disclosed two massive breaches in recent years, Verizon cut its offer by $350 million, or about 7% of the original price. Also, the part of Yahoo that wasn't sold to Verizon agreed to assume 50% liability from any future lawsuits related to the data breaches.[13]

The corp-dev team explains that once they have completed an acquisition, there is a post-merger integration (PMI) process. You decide that your team needs to play an active role despite the corp-dev team's apparent disinterest. In thinking about how to structure a proposal, you ask your TPRM team to evaluate how they might fit into the 10 critical work streams of PMI and instruct them to map that to the existing corp-dev playbooks:

1. Executive leadership roles and responsibilities
2. Business integration planning and implementation
3. Internal and external communications
4. Organization structure and staffing
5. Retention of key customers
6. Retention and re-recruitment of key talent
7. Cultural integration
8. Human resources integration
9. Measurement and feedback
10. Integration program management[14]

You think it's essential to have an active role in the M&A process, but you realize getting started with visibility might be enough at first. You can't shake the feeling that there is something unusual about the corp-dev team's less than inviting treatment.

WAREHOUSE AND DISTRIBUTION CENTER AUTOMATION

You decide to speak with your CIO on this one since it seems more likely that the technology team leads the charge rather than the operations group. It turns out that there are many automated warehouse robotics investments that your business is likely to explore. In this case, the decision has been made to start with pick-to-light systems to help enable the emerging direct-to-consumer strategy. However, the vision is much larger, including potential sortation systems and, perhaps eventually, drones.

In the discussion, you identify that there's likely a need to answer a few basic questions, but perhaps a threat model might be in order for each new technology. You explain that you minimally should be considering questions such as:

- What robots are being tested or considered for purchase?
- How are they connected to your networks?
- What data is being produced and processed?
- Are you leveraging cloud-based technologies to enhance robot decision-making capabilities?
- What are specific processes in the warehouses and distribution centers affected?

You note that your CIO is very excited about the potential of these investments. He's convinced that he may be able to automate away labor costs on the order of 1–2% of revenue. He quips, at that scale of return, we would offset a decent percentage of the entire cost of IT.

Direct-to-Consumer

Direct-to-consumer strategies can vary by company, but in this case, you learn that the investments will include mobile and web applications and engage customers via social media. These are new motions for your business. They will require entirely new processes, tools, and skills in many teams across the enterprise.

Interestingly, you thought this initiative was about cost reduction, but it is not. It's going to be an expensive endeavor, and the investment goals are almost exclusively about revenue growth. In the end, it will provide your product to customers at a lower cost. In the first few years, the expenses your company saves by removing the middle-man will fund the new capabilities. The company already has teams working on web and mobile projects. However, as a growing practice, some structural changes for the cybersecurity team will need to be made to fit into the modern DevOps processes introduced. You note that your CIO is less energetic about these projects but thinks building technology competence will be a fun endeavor.

Now you have a clearer picture of the value agenda, but it's far from perfect. To place each initiative in context, you create the following table (see Table 4.2). The value of each initiative sets the value of our business outcomes in the vertical dimension of the RVC diagram (Figure 4.5).

Security Strategy

As a skilled choice architect, you are conscious of utilizing the WRAP and NUDGES frameworks in preparing your presentation and framing of the issues. Having completed a study of the value agenda, you recognize that you need to overlay the risk and mitigation costs into a single picture. If you can pull this off, you are confident your executive team will appreciate the holistic view. More so, you recognize that they are the best-equipped decision-makers in the business to strike a balance between risk and the associated means to achieve business outcomes. By the time you are done, you hope to have all stakeholders aligned on the relative importance and defensibility of how you have selected the allocation of resources.

To layer in the cost and risk perspective, you dig into each initiative, this time utilizing the more familiar lens of people, process, and technology via the risk management perspective. Aligning cyber risk management with enterprise risk management practices to form a holistic

TABLE 4.2 Relative Comparison of Strategic Initiative Value

Strategic Initiative	Value	Notes
Marketing (Business Unit C)	Moderate	Suspect CMO is hyperbolic in expectations. The strategy seems sound but admittedly experimental.
Diversification (Business Unit A)	High	It is proven to be helping to outpace the competition and expand customer reach.
Warehouse and Distribution Center Automation (Business Unit D)	High	Realistic opportunity to reduce 1–2% of overall company revenue in labor costs.
Direct-to-Consumer (Business Unit F)	Low	D2C initiative seems experimental.

view of risk is covered in depth in Chapters 6 and 7. The goal is only to establish relative ratings of risk and cost for each initiative.

MARKETING

People – Naturally, you want to consider the value agenda when constructing your team. Your team comprises full-time employees, contractors, and partners. You can also work with other executives to ensure that their teams are staffed and trained to help you achieve security and compliance objectives.

The broader macroeconomic environment is also important to keep in mind. Cybersecurity talent in the marketplace is limited. Finding data security and privacy experts with cloud-relevant skills may be challenging, so this is an area to consider building a center of excellence. Interdepartmental partnerships and cross-training are also good options.

Process – Process areas to consider are software development, data privacy, and how projects get funded. The initiative is the first step in digital transformation for this department, so it is essential to consider how your team structure integrates with the more agile software delivery cadence that is likely to emerge. Until you see things stabilize, you surmise that having a consultant in the short term is a good option.

Next, it certainly makes sense to consider how the security implementation of Privacy protections will work. You decide it's also time to engage your legal team to evaluate your approach and solicit buy-in. It's an excellent opportunity for you to examine whether they already have resources or initiatives underway that you could readily leverage.

Finally, you note that it may be possible to capitalize some of this work, which would be in line with the company's focus on EBITDA. To be sure, you plan to check with accounting to see if this is possible or desirable.

Technology – Securing a data warehouse, enabling the use of emerging AI/ML pipeline tools, and ensuring privacy are incremental investments for your team. You will no doubt have pressure to contain labor costs and keep pace.

You aren't sure how it will work out. Still, if the timing of these investments precedes the broader market adoption of such technologies, you will not likely be able to rely upon traditional security companies. Although conventional players are making strides in certain areas, and many are pursuing an M&A approach to maintain relevance, your best bet is to survey the startup landscape to see if you can find support from innovators building new companies. This ability to survey cybersecurity innovators may be a new capability or network you need to develop.

In the end, you decide that it's not fair to assign all these costs to this initiative alone since you will get leverage out of the investments in other areas of the business as well. You note that upon initial review, the Marketing initiative has these properties:

- **Risk:** High
- **Cost:** Moderate-High

DIVERSIFICATION

People – Luckily, you already have a core team prepared to conduct third-party diligence. Depending upon the deal pipeline, you may need a slight increase in staff.

Process – Although you are collecting all the necessary data as part of your third-party risk management program, there's a good chance that you need to put energy into developing a new deliverable format to present the data to a new audience, that of the M&A team.

For example, as a buyer in an M&A transaction, your report could be translated into a representation or warranty as part of the deal consummation. If your diligence was primarily driven by interviews and questionnaires, without detailed testing of evidence and artifacts, having a deliverable that is detailed and establishes the sellers' assertions of the state of their cybersecurity could be important in settling any post-closing disputes. Although not a customary practice, cybersecurity could also be considered in break fees or reverse fees, which are deal protections where one party agrees to pay a fee to another party if the transaction fails.

Consider your audience, the structure of your diligence process, and the application of the report in your deal structure.

Technology – In our example, no technology investment is necessary to integrate into the Diversification value stream.

You note that upon initial review, the Diversification initiative has these properties:

- **Risk:** High
- **Cost:** Low

WAREHOUSE AND DISTRIBUTION CENTER AUTOMATION

Your team proposes to start with a functional threat model for new or evolving technology investments. From there, you agree that you can determine the skills required for your team. Once the trust boundaries and risks are understood, you will devise a plan to secure the designated technology investments.

You push the team towards using free and open-source methodologies and tools to enable your threat model practices:

- https://owasp.org/www-project-threat-dragon/
- https://www.microsoft.com/en-us/securityengineering/sdl/threatmodeling

Based upon your early exposure, it's clear the team might benefit from some immediate training in these methodologies.

Finally, you note that upon initial review, the Warehouse and Distribution Center Automation initiative has these properties:

- **Risk:** Moderate
- **Cost:** Moderate

DIRECT-TO-CONSUMER

People – The D2C website is leveraging Docker containers on Kubernetes (k8s), and this is the first time your business will allow containerized deployments. It is time to consider new tools and evaluate if you have the demand for your team to find and keep a full-time application security expert with container expertise.

Further, it's essential to consider the orchestration engine and how to secure it. The skills and knowledge will vary depending on your choice of k8s variants such as Azure Kubernetes Service (AKS) or Amazon Elastic Kubernetes Service (EKS).

Whatever configuration you start with will certainly not be where your development team ends as they look for the optimized application deployment model and build their code deployment pipeline. So, attracting talent that is continually willing to tackle the accelerating learning curve is undoubtedly a cultural consideration.

Process – Given the introduction of many new DevOps principles, it is time for you to examine your team structure to ensure that you are congruent with the faster, iterative development of applications that rely upon cloud-driven business processes.

Technology – You will want to dive into the four C's of Cloud-Native Security and ensure you have a clear understanding of how you will secure technology investments to address the cloud, cluster, container, and code.[15]

You note that upon initial review, the Direct-to-Consumer initiative has these properties:

- **Risk:** Low
- **Cost:** High

Based upon what you know, you craft Table 4.3, hoping to capture a picture of how the investments sit relative to one another. The risk scoring of the business outcome sets the position on the horizontal axis (risk posture) of the RVC diagram. The cost to mitigate sets the relative size of the bubble in the RVC diagram for each business outcome (see Figure 4.5).

TABLE 4.3 Relative Comparison of Strategic Initiatives

Strategic Initiative	Value	Risk	Cost to Mitigate
Marketing (Business Unit C)	Moderate	High	Moderate
Diversification (Business Unit A)	High	High	Low
Warehouse and Distribution Center Automation (Business Unit D)	High	Moderate	Moderate
Direct-to-Consumer (Business Unit F)	Low	Low	High

Shortly after that, you translate the table into Figure 4.5.

At your next Quarterly Risk Committee Meeting, you introduce the model and ask the executives to confirm that you have properly assessed the relative value from the executives' perspective. The power of the RVC diagram is to show the executives what security looks like in a business context to support business decision-making in security investment. You can now use the assessment to develop a prioritized list of investments.

From there, you propose that you can redeploy resources currently allocated to the Direct-to-Consumer initiative and apply those to the

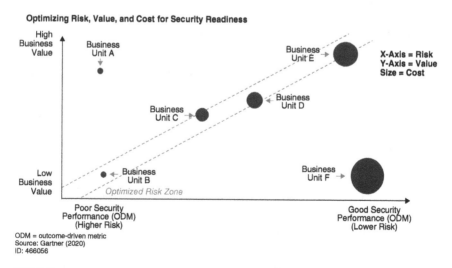

FIGURE 4.5 Optimizing Risk, Value, and Cost for Security Readiness

Source: Gartner, "Optimize Risk, Value and Cost in Cybersecurity and Technology Risk." Used with permission.

Diversification initiative. Even though you initially had push back from the corp-dev team, in this context, it's hard to argue that the application of more resources to such a high-value and high-risk initiative is anything but diligent. You explain that it leaves your team fully utilized and that you'll need help to address the additional marketing initiative. You suggest that one option is to bring in a skilled cloud partner to help mitigate the risks. Perhaps you can define additional support in the form of outcome-driven measurement, and SLAs embedded into the contract with the technology partner marketing intends to leverage.

The meeting adjourns, and you have a feeling of accomplishment. Although there's still work to do, you have engaged the executive team in a meaningful discussion that resulted in a credible and defensible series of decisions that balance cyber risk with a desire to grow revenue and cut costs. Your diverse audience has aligned on value and context. You have demonstrated you understand the value agenda. Your conversation focused on business issues, and you now share a common story that includes the macro-economic realities of your situation.

As a follow-up, you have agreed that you will establish a much tighter plan that articulates a direct line of sight between security capability measures and risk to business outcomes. Work breakdown structures, more precise budget estimates, and outcome-driven metrics illuminate the path forward for you, your team, and your business.

Key Insights

- Lessons from real estate highlight unique elements that affect value, including the importance of context, audience, macroeconomic and geopolitical conditions, timing, and stories.
- It is crucial to understand investor personas and the expected drivers behind their actions.
- You should understand the three methods for valuing a company. You should also know the common multiples and fundamentals of deriving a discounted cash flow terminal value.
- You may appreciate a real estate agents' friendly, accommodating approach, but in the end, the price you pay for a new home is the primary source of value. Similarly, shareholders may appreciate

the assurance of robust security operations, but in the end, protecting value, as determined by the investor community (often in the form of market-based multiples or DCF calculations), is what matters.

■ It is possible to combine the value agenda, the risk to business outcomes, and the cost to mitigate those risks to obtain stakeholder alignment. Once aligned, it is much easier for executives to weigh the trade-offs of their decisions and take ownership of their selected outcomes.

Notes

1. Damodaran, A., *Narrative and Numbers: The Value of Stories in Business*, Columbia University Press, 2017.

2. Twin, A., "Financial Buyer," *Investopedia*, August 30, 2019. Accessed January 16, 2021. https://www.investopedia.com/terms/f/financial-buyer.asp.

3. *2012 CFA Level II Book 4: Alternative Investments and Fixed Income*, Kaplan Schweser, 2011.

4. Marquit, M., "What Is a Dividend?" Forbes Advisor, December 16, 2020. Accessed January 16, 2021. https://www.forbes.com/advisor/investing/what-is-dividend/.

5. Damodaran, A., *Narrative and Numbers: The Value of Stories in Business*.

6. Mercer, C., "How to Maximize Business Value: Focus on Increasing EBITDA and Not the Multiple," chrismercer.net, February 15, 2019. Accessed January 16, 2021. https://chrismercer.net/how-to-maximize-business-value-focus-on-increasing-ebitda-and-not-the-multiple/.

7. IANS Research, *2020 CISO Compensation and Budget Study*, 2020. Accessed January 17, 2021. https://www.iansresearch.com/ciso-comp-study.

8. *Equity Level II, 2012 (CFA Program Curriculum)*, vol 4, Pearson, 2012.

9. Fernandez, P., *Valuation Methods and Shareholder Value Creation*, 1st ed. Academic Press, 2002.

10. Fernandez, P., *Valuation Methods and Shareholder Value Creation*.

11. Ekeu, A., "Impact of Cybersecurity Risk on the Valuation of Businesses," The Washington Valuation Group, October 8, 2019. Accessed January 17, 2021. https://www.washingtonvaluation.com/post/2019/10/08/impact-of-cybersecurity-risk-on-the-valuation-of-businesses.

12. Gartner, "Optimize Risk, Value and Cost in Cybersecurity and Technology Risk," February 12, 2020. Accessed May 27, 2021. https://www.gartner.com/document/3980889?ref=solrAll&refval=292102879.

13. Moldenhauer, C., Potter, J., Cunning, M., Falciani, L., and George, J., "When Cyber Threatens M&A," PwC, 2018. Accessed January 16, 2021. https://www.pwc.com/us/en/deals/publications/assets/pwc-when-cyber-threatens-m-and-a.pdf.

14. Galpin, T., *Winning at the Acquisition Game: Tools, Templates, and Best Practices Across the M&A Process*, Oxford University Press, 2020. https://books.google.de/books?id=D3%5C_4DwAAQBAJ.

15. Kubernetes, "Overview of Cloud Native Security," December 13, 2020. Accessed January 16, 2021. https://kubernetes.io/docs/concepts/security/overview/.

CHAPTER 5

Articulating the Business Case

*Effective people are not problem-minded; they're opportunity-minded.
They feed opportunities and starve problems.*

— Stephen R. Covey

Opportunity

This chapter marks the end of Part I of the book. Up to this point, we have reviewed how to read a financial report and equipped you with essential knowledge and vocabulary. We have explored several business strategy tools. Specifically, we reviewed frameworks that decompose a business by examining its business model and value streams. We learned that business decisions often involve uncertainty and are not entirely rational because many psychological factors affect deliberate and snap decisions. Further, we looked at several methods for valuing a business (asset-based, market-based, and discounted cashflow) to help you directly connect the activities you perform inside your cybersecurity program to the value engines of your business. In the process, we showed how important it is to tell compelling stories.

There are a few outstanding concepts we would be remiss to omit. We'll burnish Part I of the book with a review of several cost concepts. Then, we'll illustrate these concepts via the business case. Building a business case is the final, essential skill that will serve as a natural capstone for our discussion on the first pillar of *The CISO Evolution*, Foundational Business Knowledge.

As I'm writing this, CVE-2021-3156 recently surfaced. If you are not familiar, a heap-based buffer overflow was discovered in the sudo binary, allowing privilege escalation to root. There is exploit code available, and some product vendors have not yet released a fix. As usual, it's a big deal.

Now, assuming you have the correct instrumentation to find which systems are affected, you have a choice. In some cases, you might be able to simply update the sudo library to the latest version. Between the release of the CVE and patch availability, you could declare a change freeze, disable sudo in all environments, enhance monitoring on Linux servers, etc. Or, you could do nothing and wait for vendors to implement a fix. Additionally, you might consider moving to a new method of privileged access management, such as pbrun.

The point is, with every vulnerability, you face risk at the tactical level. You decide upon a remediation strategy informed by the speed and complexity to implement a fix, the impact on operations, ongoing maintenance costs, and other factors.

While these discussions are not likely to be elevated to the board-room, the concepts present certainly do surface in executive decision-making every day. Look closer and you'll find opportunities to discuss the incremental, opportunity, and sunk cost. Even with such tactical decisions, you are performing a cost-benefit analysis in addition to a risk assessment. Dig further, and you will uncloak cost savings and cost avoidance guarded behind the mist of your risk analysis. In my experience, most cybersecurity leaders fail to integrate these critical business concepts into the discussion.

As a result, some of the symptoms below (which we'll continue to revisit throughout this book) have the appearance of being "just part of the job" when in fact we can do better. Much better. Symptoms include:

- Failure to garner trust from executive leadership
- Misaligned expectations around risk appetite and capital allocation
- Misperception of cybersecurity's role in business
- Demoralization of your team in the face of cyber risk acceptance
- Increased stress and anxiety from managing an under-funded program

Principle

First, we'll review several key cost concepts, and then we'll decompose the elements of a business case with a focus on early messaging and financial analysis. Later, in the Application section of this chapter, we'll review several bona fide business cases to illustrate the presence of cost concepts and the use of these powerful tools.

Cost Concepts

Here we'll briefly review incremental, opportunity, and sunk cost. Further, we'll review the differences between cost savings and cost avoidance. Familiarity with all of these cost concepts will improve your ability to explain the investments you are proposing and making every day.

Incremental Cost

Incremental cost is the change in cost from one alternative to another. The value is comparative and usually positive. For example, above, we considered several alternatives to treating the risk presented by CVE-2021-3156 as follows:

- Option 1: Declare a change freeze, disable sudo in all environments, and enhance monitoring on Linux servers. Eventually patch as usual.

- Option 2: Do nothing and wait for vendors to implement a fix. Eventually patch as usual.
- Option 3: Move to a new method of privileged access management, such as pbrun.

Adding a new control has an incremental cost. Note that often there are economies of scale that may play a role. So, moving from monitoring 10 instances to 100 instances may cost less per instance than increasing from 101 instances to 500 instances, etc., as shown in Figure 5.1.

Imagine that you have decided to monitor 10 more instances as a stopgap in this scenario per Option 1. To calculate the incremental cost, you need to know how many instances you are already licensed to monitor. In this example, we'll suppose that we are increasing from 400 instances to 410 instances. That means that the *marginal cost* or extra cost incurred per added unit (per added instance) is $40. Further, the incremental cost when comparing monitoring costs in Option 1 vs. Option 2 is $40/instance * 10 instances = $400.

You might be thinking, "Wait! you neglected the labor to install, tune, and respond to these new logs," and you would be correct in contemplating a complete incremental cost. To keep the example simple, we'll exclude those added costs for now.

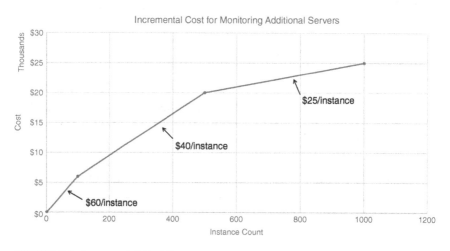

FIGURE 5.1 Incremental Cost Curve

Opportunity Cost

An opportunity cost is the potential benefit given up where the choice of one action precludes the choice of another. Recall, we discussed opportunity cost briefly in Chapter 3 – Business Decisions.

There is an opportunity cost in everything you do. Looking inside your security program, you might find areas where you are securing an application or process that provides relatively low value to the business and otherwise not protecting something very valuable.[1] Immature programs often over-secure easily defended targets. The energy to over-secure comes at the opportunity cost of developing new skills or improving processes where teams lack sufficient knowledge. An imbalanced focus on the familiar is also prevalent during digital transformation, where leaders may introduce substantial changes very quickly.

As we have discussed in earlier chapters, a well-run business will continuously adapt to optimize value. Naturally, digital transformation initiatives focus on the highest value technology investments. Modern technology such as containers and serverless patterns enable transformation. These technologies improve the overall simplicity, agility, and speed of a business.

Often, businesses adopt modern technology before they have established a robust protection paradigm. Sometimes, innovative technology teams fail to include cybersecurity teams while formulating the adoption of new technology or practices. This omission only ensures a broader disconnect between the two groups. As Chris Laping says, "If people don't ask you to get involved, there's one of two reasons. Reason #1 is that they didn't know you could help. Reason #2 is that they knew you could help but don't like working with you. And the kind truth is, you control both."[2] We'll address reason #1 in Part II – Communication and Education, specifically in Chapter 9 – Relationship Management. In thinking about reason #2, at least part of the rationale for excluding cybersecurity leaders from innovation decisions is control friction.

The 9 Box of Controls is a risk framework that considers control friction.[3] As seen in Figure 5.2, using semiautomated methods to detect the change in an environment is far less performant than automating preventive controls. In the context of containers and serverless patterns, it's common for security teams to first attempt to extend the use of existing tools and processes to the practices of agile application development and the use of public clouds. This incremental growth pattern flows as a natural evolution but predictably produces poor outcomes.

Instead, combining tools like the 9 Box of Controls with the Value Chain Mapping exercise we saw in Chapter 2 – Business Strategy Tools can create the clarity needed when considering opportunity costs. Through these mental frameworks, it becomes evident that protecting the company's core value engines requires keeping pace with technology innovation. In a resource-constrained reality, that may even come at the expense of operating existing controls. Force ranking priorities and intentionally managing your calendar is a terrific way to use the concept of opportunity cost. There are only 24 hours each day. You must focus on less, to accomplish more.

For example, redirecting funding for staffing that currently executes manual efforts to respond to incidents in your SIEM to instead fund improvements to the CI pipeline may dramatically improve your ability

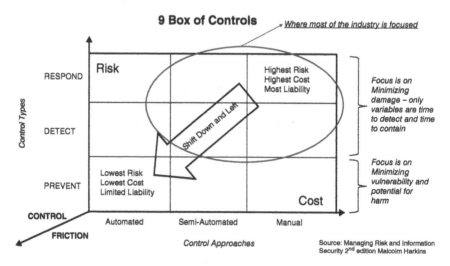

FIGURE 5.2 9 Box of Controls

Source: Harkins, M.W., *Managing Risk and Information Security: Protect to Enable.* Used with permission.

to focus on securing innovations. Further, the skills needed to automate improvements in software deployment apply to SOAR platforms and their interaction with various public clouds.

As a reminder, one of the symptoms mentioned above is misaligned expectations around risk appetite and capital allocation. Using the concept of opportunity cost more broadly in your business can help you understand the unenviable decision someone else has to make:

Do we spend more on security, or do we tackle this other value-creating activity?

In summary, incremental change, inertia, and comfort in the familiar prevent us from addressing the truly important. If you find yourself in a position where some important things might not get done, you need to elevate your efficiency, delegate, or secure additional resources. Applying the concept of opportunity cost helps keep you focused on the most critical items in your control.

Reference Tools:

- https://www.mindtools.com/pages/article/zero-base-budgeting.htm
- https://evernote.com/blog/getting-started-with-gtd-templates/
- https://fullfocusplanner.com/system/
- https://kanbanize.com/kanban-resources/getting-started/what-is-kanban
- https://gettingthingsdone.com/

Sunk Cost

Sunk Costs are costs incurred in the past that cannot be altered by any current or future decision. Common sayings related to sunk cost are "That's water under the bridge" and "Don't cry over spilled milk." When thinking about sunk cost, you need to just let it go – but that's not always easy.

In my experience, politics and ego are two reasons that sunk costs get ignored or miscategorized. Sometimes the political capital required to change direction or kill an initiative is so significant that a project may progress toward failure far too long. In other cases, individuals attach their self-worth to the value of a project or idea. If these individuals are in positions of power or influence, they may fiercely object to reversing or changing course as they defend a sense of self-worth.

If you are the executive sponsor of an initiative and have already spent $1M implementing a solution that isn't working, you may hesitate to call the project off. Even so, there may be a better solution that could be more easily implemented at less cost today than completing the work you have already initiated. If this is true, don't throw good money after bad. Find the humility needed to change course.

Common projects in cybersecurity that have sunk costs include DLP, IAM, and endpoint. Many DLP projects are only successful in narrow use cases and do not deliver the entire value proposition initially expected. Similarly, IAM practices have struggled for years, with Single Sign-On yielding a reduced number of logins but never reducing access to a single username and password. Passwordless initiatives have reduced the number of passwords but have yet to end the need for password management infrastructure. Finally, endpoint protection is a typical rip-and-replace project for new CISOs, and in many cases the incremental benefits are not the most impactful enhancements available.

While the initial work on these projects can supply many benefits, these initiatives tend to consume far too many resources while trying to be all things to all people. Be wary of sunk costs and their influence on decision-making, especially in the face of complex and highly visible projects where politics and ego are likely to surface.

Cost Avoidance vs. Cost Savings

Cost Savings and Cost Avoidance are also relative terms, meaning they compare one outcome to another. So, what's the difference? Generally, cost savings have to do with reducing spending that is already taking place, while cost avoidance is reducing spending that likely would have taken place in the future.[4]

For example, cutting existing staffing is an easy demonstration of cost savings. In contrast, implementing a SOAR solution to reduce the need for added SOC analysts one to two years into the future is cost avoidance. While you may feel the growth in staff is inevitable, your CFO may have other thoughts. As a result, any time you are making a business case based upon cost avoidance, you are on shaky ground until you have confirmed that all decision-makers agree that the future costs in question are inevitable.

Business Cases

The business case will enable you to secure adequate resources. Generally, a business case will do the following:

- Provide a concise summary of the business needs.
- Enumerate relevant assumptions, risks, and objections.
- Outline anticipated implementation costs.
- Examine the cost of ongoing management of the proposed investment.
- Describe the primary direct and indirect benefits.
- Document a financial analysis of the investment, including future cash flows, etc.
- Establish a timeline and payback period (if applicable).
- Offer an analysis of various alternatives (often including the status quo).

There are plenty of business case development templates on the internet. Your company may even have a prescribed format. For that reason, I'd like to review several different tools to improve your ability to leverage any business case template effectively. First, we'll look at getting your messaging right using a combination of stakeholder analysis, influence maps, and the SCI-PAB® Thinking & Messaging Tool. Then, we'll examine two primary financial analysis approaches, namely Cost-Benefit Analysis (CBA) and Net Present Value (NPV).

In my experience, if you get the messaging and financial analysis correct in a business case, mistakes in other elements of your business case are more readily forgiven and forgotten.

Business Case Messaging

For many years I viewed sales as a necessary evil, but now I know that selling can be a great educator. There are plenty of reasons why many people coming from a technical background are skeptical or distrusting of sales professionals. The justification is usually straightforward and goes something like this: "Salespeople are unscrupulous, morally flexible people that inevitably do anything just to line their pockets." Before I had the opportunity to help with the sales process during my time as a consultant, I believed that the sales profession did little to add value and often weakened the fabric of trust between people and businesses. While it is true that some salespeople fit this stereotype, it is not true of most salespeople. Further, I strongly feel that you must also be an excellent salesperson to be an effective cybersecurity leader.

At the heart of sales is empathy or the ability to understand and share someone else's feelings. Often when presenting a business case, the most relevant question you can ask is, "What emotion do I hope to evoke in each audience member?"

Initially, I believed that presenting different facts, or emphasizing additional data depending upon my audience, was ultimately a failure of integrity. Earlier, we learned there is an opportunity cost for every investment. So, it is essential to have the ability to consistently empathize with your colleagues and articulate how cybersecurity projects impact the things that are significant to them. I now know that presenting the same topic in different ways to varied audiences is essential.

STAKEHOLDER ANALYSIS

Taking the time to identify and prioritize stakeholders is a great place to start. Common stakeholders are listed in Figure 5.3.

Now that you have a concise list of the people affected by your project, invest some time to understand their perspectives. Questions that can help you understand your stakeholders include:[5]

Your boss	Shareholders	Government
Senior executives	Alliance partners	Trade associations
Your co-workers	Suppliers	The press
Your team	Lenders	Interest groups
Customers	Analysts	The public
Prospective customers	Future recruits	The community
Your family	Key contributors	Key advisers

FIGURE 5.3 Common Stakeholders

Source: MindTools Content Team, "Stakeholder Analysis: Winning Support for Your Projects." Used with permission.

- What financial or emotional interest do they have in the outcome of your work? Is it positive or negative?
- What motivates them most of all?
- What information do they want from you, and what is the best way of communicating with them?
- What is their current opinion of your work? Is it based on good information?
- Who influences their opinions generally, and who influences their view of you? Do some of these influencers, therefore, become important stakeholders in their own right?
- If they aren't likely to be positive, what will win them around to support your project?
- If you don't think that you'll be able to win them around, how will you manage their opposition?
- Who else might be influenced by their opinions? Do these people become stakeholders in their own right?

INFLUENCE MAPPING

It can be constructive to understand that the normal chain of command is just one way to advance your objectives. Like defense in depth, having a multilayered approach is always a more resilient mode of operating when considering the many internal battlefield objections you may face. Knowing who the real influencers are can help you determine where you should put your effort if you want to succeed. Discovering all your project's stakeholders (not just the obvious ones) and the influence relationships present is what influence mapping is all about. Influence maps help you target the key influencers to win the resources and support you need to reach your goal.

An influence map is a visual model showing the people who influence and make decisions about your project. The map helps you understand how stakeholders relate to one another so that you can quickly see how influence flows.

Remember that even the most powerful people rarely act alone. Top executives and other people in authority rely on advisers. Find out who the advisers are and understand how they operate. This clarity can be vital to your project's success.

There are three primary considerations when you construct an influence map:

1. The importance or weight of a stakeholder's overall influence (represented by the size of the circle representing that stakeholder)
2. The relationships between stakeholders (represented by the presence of lines or arrows between them)
3. The influence stakeholders have on others (represented by the heaviness of the lines drawn between them)

Your completed influence map shows the stakeholders with the most influence as individuals with the most prominent circles. Lines (arrows) drawn to other stakeholders show the presence and strength of influence.[6]

SCI-PAB® THINKING & MESSAGING TOOL

You need to build a concise message that considers all the information you have gathered in your Stakeholder Analysis and Influence Mapping exercises. Note that creating these resources once allows

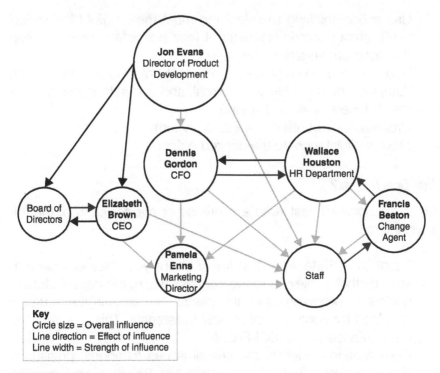

FIGURE 5.4 Hypothetical Influence Map

Source: MindTools Content Team, "Influence Maps: Uncovering Where the Power Lies in Your Projects." Used with permission.

you to complete this type of analysis efficiently or even intuitively for future projects.

WHAT IS SCI-PAB® [SIGH-PAB]?

SITUATION→COMPLICATION→IMPLICATION→POSITION→ ACTION→ BENEFIT®[7]

With amazingly little time needed, this thinking tool helps business communicators to:

- Think efficiently and insightfully about the content they want to communicate from the perspective of their listeners' unique interests, needs, wants, and priorities.

- Use critical thinking to select the most meaningful ("the critical few") listener-centric elements of their possible content to keep their listeners engaged and open
- Structure the communicators' content (information, ideas, and data) into the most efficient, logical, and understandable flow for their listeners' style and setting
- Organize their content flow into story form
- Move their listeners to the desired outcome

How Does It Work?

It's straightforward; just write a sentence or two for each of the following items:

- Situation – State what you know about your listener's circumstances that is relevant to the discussion (e.g. the current state of business, technology, industry, plans). The facts in the Situation shouldn't be controversial or new to listeners. This is always the first sentence in your SCI-PAB®.
- Complication – Identify the critical issues (changes, pressures, demands, etc.) that are impacting the Situation and creating problems or opportunities. Often, the most effective Complication statement provides new, thought-provoking information.
- Implication – Show the personal or business consequences of not acting on the problems or opportunities described in the Complication. The Implication provides a logical transition and adds urgency to your recommendations.
- Position – State clearly and confidently your opinion about what needs to be done to solve your listener's problem. Communicate this at a high level; this isn't the tactical Action step that follows, but rather a strategic statement about your point of view on the issues(s). Keep it short.
- Action – Help your listener understand the role you want them to play or the questions you'd like them to consider during your presentation or conversation. Use action words like consider, discuss, explore, and understand.
- Benefit – Describe how your recommended Position/Action will address listeners' needs. State the results clearly and quantifiably.

The benefits you describe should differentiate you and be meaningful to your listeners.[8]

Now that you know all the stakeholders and influencers and you have tailored a meaningful message to help them frame a discussion topic, let's round out your skills by delving into the Financial Analysis tooling that will support any business case presentation.

Business Case Financial Analysis

In this section, we will review both Cost-Benefit Analysis and Net Present Value. In both types of financial analysis, you outline the benefits a project will deliver, how, at what cost, and how long it will take. Each approach has limitations, and we'll review those, too.

COST-BENEFIT ANALYSIS

Traditional cost-benefit analysis (CBA) is a process where you consider all the costs of executing a project and then examine the benefits. CBA, at first, feels a lot like the Pros vs. Cons analysis that Benjamin Franklin did so many years ago. When conducting a cost-benefit analysis, it makes sense to assign a monetary value to everything you can. Because the CBA is often used to make quick and simple decisions, it is suited for most cybersecurity decisions.

Follow these steps to perform Cost-Benefit Analysis:[9]

1. Brainstorm Costs and Benefits
2. Assign a Monetary Value to the Costs
3. Assign a Monetary Value to Benefits
4. Compare Costs and Benefits

BRAINSTORM COSTS AND BENEFITS

First, take time to brainstorm all the costs associated with the project and list them. Then, do the same for all the benefits of the project. You should be particularly diligent in exploring unexpected costs. Also, don't be afraid to capture any benefits that you may not have initially anticipated. Remember from Chapter 3 – Business Decisions, we need to work hard to overcome the pitfalls of confirmation bias.

The School of Thought offers several great resources, such as a Creative Thinking Cards Deck (https://thethinkingshop.org/collections/products/ products/creative-thinking-cards-deck), that are worthwhile investments. There are a series of cards for each category below that contemplate unique approaches for stimulating your creative prowess:

- Perspective Shifts
- Idea Generation
- Provocation
- Other Mental Models that can be useful at this stage

ASSIGN A MONETARY VALUE TO THE COSTS

Costs include the costs of physical resources needed and the cost of software and labor involved in all phases of a project. Costs are often relatively easy to estimate (compared with revenues). Remember to consider both the impact on your department and the impact on other departments or business units.

When you develop a list of costs, think about the lifetime of the project. Adding a temporal dimension to your thinking will help you consider maintenance costs, tech debt, renewal licensing, incremental staffing, and perhaps control friction. Don't forget about training, context switching, and lost productivity. Also, remember to include opportunity costs in this list.

Ideally, the project will optimize the business and not just your departmental operation. Remember, from the Phoenix Project and the Theory of Constraints, you mustn't introduce a new system-level constraint. Again, a slower process doesn't necessarily produce a lower overall output for a system. Lean tools designed to *Exploit the Constraint* like Andon, Standardized Work, and Kaizen are excellent indicators of how impactful a change is to the overall system. Further, applying lean tools like Kaizen can be helpful to *Subordinate to the Constraint* if that scenario arises.[10]

Assign a Monetary Value to Benefits

Usually, the list of benefits is far more subjective and intangible or "soft." Revenue forecasting is challenging and often not a core competency of cybersecurity professionals. Further, things like the value of reduced risk or meeting regulatory compliance are difficult to quantify. That's also true of other investments in a business. For example, it is easy to measure the cost of offering a $500/employee stipend for home office equipment during a global pandemic, but what are the benefits? Morale, productivity, loyalty, etc., are all difficult to quantify and likely to be met with skepticism when presenting a business case.

Compare Costs and Benefits

As a final step, compare costs and benefits and decide upon the best course of action. At this stage, it's essential to consider the payback time to find out how long it will take for you to reach the breakeven point or the point in time at which the benefits have just repaid the costs.

For simple examples where the same benefits are received each period, you can calculate the payback period by dividing the projected total cost of the project by the projected total revenues:

$$\text{Total cost/total revenue (or benefits)}$$
$$= \text{length of time (payback period)}$$

Flaws of Cost-Benefit Analysis

For all its advantages, CBA has several limitations. The most relevant limitations for cybersecurity leaders to consider include:

- Revenue forecasts and the value of intangible benefits are very subjective.
- CBA does not gracefully handle a project that has positive cash flow over time, especially when those cash flows vary (which is true in most cases).
- Often the framing of CBA leads to whether-or-not decisions that we learned to be wary of in Chapter 3 – Business Decisions.

Note that the time value of money can make quite a difference in deciding to go ahead with a proposed project. In these cases, consider Net Present Value (NPV) and Internal Rate of Return (IRR) calculations as an alternative to CBA. We'll look at these analysis methods more closely in the following section.

NET PRESENT VALUE (AND IRR)

First, let's examine Net Present Value. Then we can progress to the concept of IRR. You can quickly decompose NPV into two separate concepts:

1. The time value of money.
2. The final gain or loss.

PRESENT VALUE

Here's how I think about this:

EXAMPLE 5.1

If you were offered $100K today, or $100K in 10 years, which would you prefer? You'd likely take the money now even if you weren't going to spend it. Why? Because if you have the money today, you can put it in an interest-bearing account and make a few extra dollars between now and the 10-year time horizon. In contrast, if the money didn't grow, but the overall economy experienced inflation, you will end up with less buying power in the future than you have today.

But what exactly is the difference in value? Selecting a discount rate can be subjective. However, in this example, we'll use 6% each year. Personally, that's a conservative assumption for how I expect my investment portfolio to grow on average over an extended period.

So,

$$\text{Present Value} = \text{Future Value} / (1 + \text{rate})^{\wedge}(n\,\text{periods})$$

In other words, the present value of $100K in 10 years assuming a 6% portfolio return (discount rate) is worth less today because you wouldn't get the benefit of that interest over 10 years:

$$\text{Present Value} = \$100K / (1 + .06)^{\wedge} 10 = \$55,839.48$$

I know no one would prefer to receive $56K over $100K today, but this type of thinking is common in our industry.

Present Value of a Multi-Year Project

EXAMPLE 5.2

To secure a contract with a new customer, you must implement additional security tooling to secure the cloud management plane in your SaaS offering. You would otherwise never do such a thing.

Suppose you had to invest an incremental:

- $20K cloud security posture management software
- $25K consulting costs to implement
- $10K internal resources

Then in years 2 and 3, you had to:

- Renew software maintenance at $2K/year
- Invest $5K internal labor to operate and respond to the software each year

(continued)

(continued)

Additionally, your prospective customer is at the end of the year, and they would like to spend some cash to retain their budget for next year. So, they ask to pay for the entire contract now.

You want to offer a fair price for the entire expense required to implement and maintain this solution over the contract term. Because it's a competitive bid, you want to keep your costs on this undifferentiated obligation as aggressive as possible without losing margin on the overall deal.

What is the most aggressive price you can offer while maintaining a 30% margin for the engagement, assuming a 15% discount rate?

In this case,

$$\text{Present Value} = \Sigma\left(\text{Cost} / (1+\text{rate}) \wedge \text{period t}\right)$$

$$= (20K + 25K + 10K) / (1+15\%) \wedge 0$$
$$+ 7K / (1+15\%) \wedge 1 + 7K / (1+15\%) \wedge 2$$

$$= \$55K + \$6.09K + \$5.29K$$

$$= \$66.38K$$

Now add 30%:

$$\text{Present Value} + 30\% \text{ margin} = \$66.38K * 130\% = \$86.29K$$

Compare this to simply adding the costs and then augmenting that with a 30% margin:

$$\text{Sum of Costs} + 30\% \text{ margin} = \$69K * 130\% = \$89.70K$$

The difference is $3.4K or 4% when comparing these different approaches. At this scale, the differences are most likely inconsequential. However, as the term of the contract extends, the discount rate grows, or the size of the investment scales – these subtle differences can become material (see Table 5.1).

TABLE 5.1 Impact of Variations by Term & Discount Rate

Term	Discount Rate	Difference	Percent Difference
3 Years	15%	$3.4K	4%
3 Years	30%	5.8K	7%
5 Years	15%	$10.4K	11%
5 Years	30%	$16.7K	18%

It can be helpful to keep the impact of these variables in mind when negotiating multi-year contracts for outsourced operations or software renewals.

FUTURE VALUE

Let's go back to our example of $100K now vs. in ten years. Let's look at it from the perspective of Future Value.

EXAMPLE 5.3

Suppose you invest $100K today and receive 6% interest each year for 10 years. What would you receive in 10 years?

$$\$100K = \text{Future Value} / (1+.06)^{\wedge}10$$

$$\$100K * (1.06)^{\wedge}10 = \text{Future Value}$$

$$179,084.77 = \text{Future Value}$$

Again, everyone would rather have $179K as compared to $100K in 10 years.

NET

Now that you understand Present Value, we need to add the concept of Net before we arrive at our final destination: Net Present Value.

So how do we "net it out"? Simple. Subtract expenses from the present value of the project. Let's review with an example.

EXAMPLE 5.4

Suppose that to receive $100K in 10 years, you'd have to spend $60K in software and labor today.

Recall,

$$\text{Net Present Value} = \text{Present Value} - \text{Cost of Investment}$$

So,

$$\text{Net Present Value} = \$55,839.48 - \$60K = -\$4,160.52$$

Here we see that this is a terrible investment. You would actually lose money. It is generally not wise to make a decision that produces a negative NPV. Naturally, you want to favor projects that deliver the highest NPV. Note how important the discount rate is in this calculation.

EXAMPLE 5.5

Integrate the concept of opportunity cost by considering the Best Alternative to a Negotiated Agreement (BATNA). We can now easily calculate that $60K invested today with a 6% growth rate will produce $107,450.86 in 10 years.

So, we could reasonably conclude that any investment of $60K today certainly needs to produce a positive NPV, and the Future Value (in 10 years) had better exceed our BATNA ($107,450.86).

As we saw in Chapter 2 – Business Strategy, you should seek to optimize the return of an investment relative to its risk. In this example, you can put the money in a traditional diversified investment portfolio and avoid liquidity risks we might otherwise incur.

INTERNAL RATE OF RETURN (IRR)

Another way to think about opportunity cost is by utilizing the Internal Rate of Return (IRR). To find the IRR, identify solutions for the discount rate where NPV = $0.

EXAMPLE 5.6

Weighted Average Cost of Capital (WACC) is the average rate a company pays to finance its assets. Consider a business that has a WACC and hurdle rate of 20%. For this example, the finance team requires all significant investments to exceed this rate of return.

NOTE: You can ask your finance department for this figure if you are interested. It also wouldn't hurt to inquire if they set the hurdle rate at or above WACC.

You propose spending $60K today to receive $200K in three years. Does this project get approved?

Set NPV = $0,

$$\text{Net Present Value} = \$0 = \text{Present Value} - \text{Cost of Investment}$$

Substitute the formula for Present Value,

$$\$0 = \left[\text{Future Value} / (1 + \text{rate}) \wedge (n \, \text{periods}) \right] - \text{Cost of Investment}$$

(continued)

(continued)

Plug in values,

$$\$0 = \left[\$200K / (1 + \text{rate}) ^ (3)\right] - \$60K$$

Solve for the rate,

$$\$60K = \left[\$200K / (1 + \text{rate}) ^ (3)\right]$$

$$\$60K * \left[(1 + \text{rate}) ^ (3)\right] = \$200K$$

$$(1 + \text{rate}) ^ (3) = \$200K / \$60K$$

$$1 + \text{rate} = \sqrt[3]{(\$200K / \$60K)}$$

$$\text{rate} = \sqrt[3]{(3.33)} - 1$$

$$\text{rate} = 49.38\%$$

Certainly, 49.38% exceeds the hurdle rate of 20%. So, the project is eligible to be contrasted with other opportunities that may be more beneficial.

In practice, you are unlikely to perform these calculations. Recognizing the concepts and understanding the terms can help you in navigating the internal battlefield. It's far more likely that by adding security costs at the end of a project, the actual gain or loss of a project changes.

Suppose a project was close to the hurdle rate without security costs involved. In that case, the project sponsor may propose the effort, obtain approval, and then add security after the fact. Many corporate leaders are willing to ask for forgiveness rather than waiting for permission, especially in a consensus-driven culture.

EXAMPLE 5.7

If security requirements slow the delivery of a project, the timeline to realize benefits can be affected. What is the impact on your rate if you add six months to the project above?

$$\$60K = \left[\$200K / (1 + \text{rate})^{\wedge}(3.5) \right]$$

Solve for the rate,

$$\text{rate} = 41.02\%$$

Just the time cost of money pulls 8% off the rate of return. Imagine if the delays also result in additional labor (six months of team coordination and status updates, added executive visibility, and mind share, etc.).

You can see why being the department of "No" is career limiting. It destroys value.

Application

This section will use two scenarios from my experience to highlight concepts featured in the chapter. First, we will use the SCI-PAB® Thinking & Messaging Tool to introduce a Password Management business case presentation. Then I will apply CBA to present a business case for Password Management. Finally, I will present the business case utilized for Threat Stack, Inc. that applies Monte Carlo analysis to NPV for the project. Put on your safety belt, this gets pretty advanced.

Case Study 1 – SCI-PAB® to Present a Business Case for Password Management

When I started at the company, I performed a gap analysis. For expedience, my information came almost exclusively from interviews. As a result, my assessment suffered from selection bias and, in hindsight, was undoubtedly optimistic.

As the first CISO, I was naturally working to establish a positive presence in the business. I wanted to dispel the false narrative that security is always inconvenient. I was also working to highlight the difference between security-driven culture and compliance-driven culture.

As I conducted interviews, what became apparent is that there were many strong security-related practices. Still, the underlying beliefs that grounded why and how my colleagues performed these activities were often only partially correct.

Most companies leverage compensating controls and feature deviations from standard best practices. Here too, there were architectural limitations that hinted at excessive privilege and shared accounts. As an auditor, I frequently found people will store passwords on sticky notes. As I toured the office in my new company after hours, I eventually found pockets of this behavior. Luckily all the passwords were for noncritical systems.

I was starting to think about quick wins and some of the longer, more challenging projects required to burn down the risks present in the environment. About that time, I saw the post in Figure 5.5 on LinkedIn:

 Mike Johnson   ▪▪▪
CISO at Lyft
2d

Want to both improve the security of your environment /and/ delight your workforce? Deploy a password manager enterprise wide. Off the top of my head, I can't think of any better win/win out there for security. Both 1Password and Lastpass are great options here with good enterprise management capabilities. If you haven't done this yet, take a look at it as your next investment.

Side note: this is a fine example of where compliance does not mean security. There's not a single compliance framework out there that requires password managers.

452 Likes · 162 Comments

FIGURE 5.5 Social Media Post from Industry Thought Leader
Source: Mike Johnson.

As a new CISO, often nothing you want in the first year is budgeted. So, the need for a business case was born.

I decided to follow the sage advice and extend the benefits of a Password Manager to my colleagues. My gap analysis revealed that there was a lot of work to be done, and I wasn't going to be able to address single sign-on or privileged access management immediately. However, a password manager seemed like a great starting point. This is what I presented to our Executive Leadership Team (ELT):

- **Situation** – Everyone in the business is actively managing dozens of passwords.
- **Complication** – As we scale the business, we will add new SaaS platforms to satisfy unforeseen business requirements. We will increase the volume of staff, which will, in turn, necessitate more complex networks of collaboration and communication. We will add the complexity of supporting additional public cloud platforms. That will require more complex authentication and authorization schemas. And we will need to separate Administrative and Standard user accounts to satisfy the evolution of our compliance obligations.
- **Implication** – All of this will require exponential growth in the number of passwords each employee will have to manage. And suppose we fail to solve this problem. In that case, our revenues and employee morale will dip, competitors will encroach, and we'll face audit findings or adverse audit opinions that can deter prospective clients from joining our platform.
- **Position** – We must act now to ensure our colleagues can continue to perform their jobs with ease and enjoyment. We must ensure that our revenues continue up and to the right. We must not distract our engineers with the burden of clumsy password management.
- We can solve these problems with a small investment in software and a dedicated project team to mobilize rapid adoption. There are already several employees taking advantage of free software that solves this problem. I believe we can do better, and we should.

- **Action** – With your permission, I'd like to organize a small team of senior engineers, purchase the software, and make it available to everyone by the end of this year.
- **Benefits** – With your support, we can simplify every employee's experience and ensure the growing complexity and quantity of accounts doesn't expose us to lost revenue, plummeting morale, or qualified audit reports.

I was successful in obtaining funding and initially received approval from the leadership team to proceed with the purchase and implementation. Note that I was successful in adapting the SCI-PAB® framework from Mandel Communications. While they have permitted me to present their communication tool above, they do not endorse its use in the example. Nonetheless, it served in capturing approval and funding for the project.

Case Study 2 – Cost-Benefit Analysis

The previous section establishes early messaging for this business case. Now, let's begin to examine the supporting data and presentation that complemented the introductory content. Note that this process gathered all the information that produced the messaging above. It wasn't the reverse.

Summary of Costs and Benefits

Below we consider quantitative and qualitative costs and benefits of implementing a password manager. As with most cybersecurity business cases, it's the storytelling that secures funding. Keep an eye open for the presence of incremental and opportunity costs.

We wanted something likely to achieve high user adoption and very compatible with DevOps and Site Reliability Engineering best practices. Specifically, we needed to ensure any solution we selected would extend itself to enhanced automation opportunities in the future. We had a stated preference for a SaaS solution, and we wanted to ensure at least feature parity with our existing solution.

First, we conducted a competitive analysis of eight solutions available on the market. Figure 5.6 presents the first level of diligence performed by our DevOps team in narrowing the list of solutions that might be suitable:

From there we reduced the number of vendors considered to just two finalists. Armed with a shortlist, we brainstormed the costs and benefits and assigned a monetary value to each. Table 5.2 gives a summary of the primary expenses of the two finalist solutions:

Then we summarized the benefits for our favored solution as shown in Table 5.3:

Requirement	Secureauth	Thyotic Secret Server Professional	Duo	LastPass Enterprise	CyberArk Enterprise Password Vault	1password for Teams Pro	Vault	Dashlane
Provides minimum functionality to replace PMP	❌ not a shared credential manager	❓	❌	✓	✓	✓	❌ No UI with OSS version	(NA) No API or CLI
SaaS solution	(NA)	⚠ Secret Server primary offering is a self hosted solution. They do have a new SaaS offering.	(NA)	✓	❌ self hosted only, they have marketplace (Windows ®) AMIs	✓	(NA)	✓
'Break the glass' access to selected creds	(NA)	(NA)	(NA)	❌	❌ Can request approval for cred access though	❌	(NA)	(NA)
AD integration (user login, groups determining roles, etc...)	(NA)	⚠ yes, but syncs x times/day	(NA)	✓ Vast set of rules/permissions that can be set at user and group level.	✓	❌ feature coming early 2018, asked for more info	(NA)	(NA)
Activity log levels are acceptable	(NA)	(NA)	(NA)	✓	✓	✓	(NA)	(NA)
Alerting (or logs can feed into suitable alerting mechanisms)	(NA)	(NA)	(NA)	⚠ Alerting can be configured, forwarding only supported to Splunk. API can return event records.	✓ syslog forwarding	✓	(NA)	(NA)
Has API for service users to retrieve creds where roles are not applicable	(NA)	✓	(NA)	⚠ CLI application can get/put records	✓	⚠ op CLI application can retrieve records, app outputs JSON	✓	❌
Has native or integrates with MFA for administrative (or all?) changes	(NA)	✓ native	(NA)	✓ Duo, among many others	✓ Duo	✓ Duo	(NA)	(NA)

FIGURE 5.6 Password Management Solution Comparison

TABLE 5.2 Summary of Costs

Category	Details	LastPass Year 1 Cost	Competitor Year 1 Cost
Software	There is a licensing cost for the software or subscription fee for the hosted SaaS platform.	$7.2K (incremental)	$100.3K (incremental)
Internal Labor – Implementation	We will require a Project Manager, DevOps engineer, and Sr. Engineer familiar with the existing solution. PM – 40 hours DevOps – 40 Eng – 40 hours	120 hours @ $120/hour = $14.4K	$14.4K
Professional Services	Consulting services to support the implementation.	$0	$15K (incremental)
Training	Training Preparation – 8 hours Deliver Training to 150 Employees – 1 hour each = 150 Employees	158 hours @ $100/hour = $15.8K	$15.8K
Internal Labor – Ongoing Maintenance	Password resets, answering questions, configuration, audit support, etc. Corporate IT – 50 hours *SaaS vs. On-prem differences – patching, etc. For on-prem is required.* Corporate IT – Monthly Application Software Updates and Testing – 24 Hours NOC – Monthly Patching (OS) – 24 hours NOC – Hardening and Vulnerability Management – 24 hours	$5K $0 $0 $0	$5K $2.4K $2.4K $2.4K
	INCREMENTAL COST	$7.2K	$115.3K
	TOTAL COST	$42.4K	$157.7K

TABLE 5.3 Summary of Benefits

Benefit	Benefit Within 12 Months
More efficient operations – estimate saving 6 mins/day/engineer ■ 6 mins/day ■ 80 engineers ■ 260 working days Savings of 2,080 Hours/year or 1 FTE.	~$200K Reduced Operating Expense
Hours saved by moving to a SaaS solution – 72 hours	$7.2K Reduced Operating Expense
Without a tool like LastPass, the inherent risk of data loss and destructive attack is HIGH. Adding a tool to our operations reduces risk significantly.	Reduced Risk
Without a Password Manager that integrates into browsers, users are likely to continue to utilize sticky notes and other cleartext storage methods that may lead to a data breach or audit findings.	Improved Audit Performance
As we increase the volume of platforms, identities, and passwords, people are likely to get frustrated and may choose alternative employment.	Improved Morale + Employee Retention
Keeping engineers focused on their primary value activities will help ensure that we maintain our differentiation in the market.	Sustained Competitive Advantage
TOTAL BENEFIT	~$207.2K

The cost benefit analysis summary concludes that even 25% of the benefits (25% * $207.2K = $51.8K savings vs. $42.4K costs) will leave the business better off than before.

Assumptions and Risks

With every business case, you are likely to identify other essential topics. In this case, several of the key discussion points included:

■ **Revenue Impact:** We should carefully consider the potential impact on sales and customer retention. We may have obligations for disclosures, or the use of such a tool may surface in security diligence, influencing renewal decisions and customer acquisition rates.

- **Adjacent Market Pursuit Limitations:** Utilizing LastPass will exclude us from achieving FedRAMP certification in the immediate future.
- **Legal Liability:** By using such a solution, we do not avail ourselves of the inherent liabilities.
- **History:** Hackers have compromised both LastPass and OneLogin/Team Viewer previously. All solutions of this nature will remain high on the target list for foreign adversaries and organized crime.

Case Study 3 – Net Present Value

In some business models, a CISO can participate in revenue generation. When that is true, the use of NPV and IRR are applicable. One typical pattern that is likely to emerge is SaaS-based providers that charge a base fee for their services and offer an up-charge for additional security services surrounding their infrastructure or applications.

In this case, Logicworks was in a long-standing partnership with a Managed Security Services Provider (MSSP) that offered host-based intrusion detection, log aggregation, and log review services. Over time, the technology and services became less competitive and no longer met the needs of our changing target market segments. Although the company continued to innovate, migrating to the new platform was just as labor intensive as moving to a new platform altogether. So, we decided to explore alternatives in the market, hoping to identify an easier to manage solution that offered improved security outcomes, a more competitive licensing model, and a more attractive price.

Because these add-on security features complemented our Managed Cloud Operations offerings, it was easy to identify many of the costs associated with operating and upgrading the existing features. As a business, our FP&A team had established a revenue forecast and targets for new customer acquisition. Using descriptive statistics features in Excel, we were able to identify our mean instance count per customer, as well as the standard deviation. This provided us a range of potential costs and established with high confidence that the actual outcome would land in a favorable range.

We were also able to garner information from sales like the average deal term and information from our operations team, including customer growth and churn rates. Further, as container adoption increases, the growth of compute instances will slow, and we were able to capture these assumptions in a financial model. This information was important because we were working to identify a marginal cost/instance utilizing an incremental cost curve like the one featured earlier in the chapter.

In the end, we carved out our cost categories as shown in Table 5.4 (note that a nondisclosure agreement prevents us from disclosing bulk pricing information).

Without revealing the core assumptions and actual calculations, we offer a summary of the final business case in Table 5.5.

After a fair bit of discussion, it was clear to all that there was an entire range of potential outcomes that any number of factors could alter. We wanted to dispel any confusion that these variables offered a significantly different result that would change a decision to proceed with a new partnership. We used Monte Carlo analysis, a simulation model that generates many scenarios, to help us gain confidence in our decision. Note that this topic will come up again in Chapter 7 – Translating Cyber Risk into Business Risk.

First, we constructed an NPV calculator and changed from static variables to a set of variables that ranged from very aggressive assumptions to very conservative given the many factors (see Table 5.6).

TABLE 5.4 Summary of Costs

Category	Details
Licensing	More competitive licensing terms and economies of scale will play a role in pricing the total cost to operate.
Efficiency Savings Incident Investigation Time	The information, enrichment, user interface, and customer support influence the amount of time it takes to triage, root cause, and respond or escalate to a customer.
Transition Migration Costs	There will need to be a comprehensive customer transition plan that includes: ■ Customer Outreach ■ Customer outage coordination ■ New legal efforts, which may include development of Service Orders & Contracts ■ Customer education on a new platform ■ Updates to Professional Services onboarding check-lists, project plans, etc. ■ Removal of the old solution ■ Installation of the new solution ■ Testing to ensure the new solution doesn't interfere with customer applications
Transition Training Costs	The entire organization has training needs. For example: ■ We must educate sales and marketing on the industry and market landscape ■ Technical sales needs to understand the detection and alerting mechanisms and limitations ■ Sales and financial operations teams must connect SKUs, terms of service, and other elements to profitability models, forecasts, revenue reports, etc. ■ We must partner with finance to determine how to calculate and generate invoices ■ Technical teams need to understand how to implement and troubleshoot the technology ■ Cloud operations teams need to build runbooks and understand how to communicate with customers ■ Customer service teams need to know how to provide meaningful summaries of the monthly outcomes achieved
Incremental Margin Contribution	The new vendor is more proactive in the sales cycle and can help bring us leads in our target market.

TABLE 5.5 Summary of Costs and Benefits

	Year 1	Year 2	Year 3	Total 3-Year
Licensing	$ 277,848.00	$ 326,005.02	$ 334,916.39	$ 938,769.41
Efficiency Savings	$155,664.00	$155,664.00	$155,664.00	$ 466,992.00
Transition Costs	$ (73,090.00)	0	0	$ (73,090.00)
Incremental Margin Contribution (New Security)	$ 57,204.00	$ 141,048.60	$ 219,773.40	$ 418,026.00
Net Savings/ (Cost)	$ 417,626.00	$ 622,717.62	$ 710,353.79	$ 1,750,697.41

Finally, we decided to eliminate Incremental Margin from our business case so we are not dependent upon customer growth assumptions (something we cannot control). Instead, we wanted to show only outcomes that are wholly in our control.

Using a pseudo-random number generator, we were able to execute 5,000 simulations for the NPV of the model. Figure 5.7 shows a histogram of resulting values from our simulation.

In the figure, you can see that our NPV is positive and ranges from ~½ million to ~1.3 million. Even though the NPV is positive, other opportunity costs in the business outweighed this investment initially. Nonetheless, I'm happy to say that we did establish a partnership and continue to grow joint revenues as of the date of this writing.

TABLE 5.6 Net Present Value Calculator

Trial ID: 10
Enter the formula for an inverse uniform in the Random Sample column.

Input Variables		Random Sample	Min.	Max.	Variable ID	Time ID
Licensing	Year 1	$ 286,566	$ 277,848	$ 327,186	1	1
	Year 2	$ 341,682	$ 337,813	$ 422,762		2
	Year 3	$ 461,112	$ 368,098	$ 473,809		3
Efficiency Savings	Year 1	$ (30,575)	$ (95,880)	$ 191,760	2	1
	Year 2	$ 82,736	$ (95,880)	$ 191,760		2
	Year 3	$ (30,135)	$ (95,880)	$ 191,760		3
Transition Costs	Year 1	$ 156,539	$ 73,090	$ 181,470	3	
	Year 2	$ -				
	Year 3	$ -				
Incremental Margin		$ 0	$ 0	$ 0	4	
WACC		9.52%	5.00%	15.00%	5	

Cash Flow

	2020	2021	2022
Total costs	$ 156,539	0	0
Total benefits	$ 255,991	$ 424,418	$ 430,977
Net benefit	**$ 99,452**	**$ 424,418**	**$ 430,977**

Results

Net Present Value	**$ 772,669**

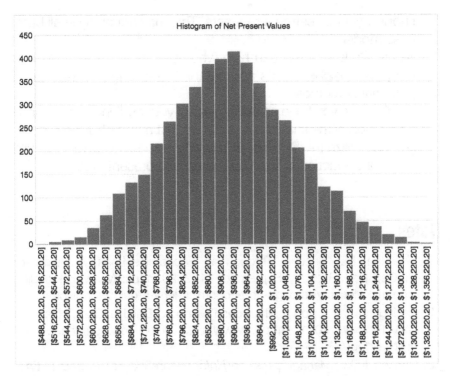

FIGURE 5.7 Summary of Costs and Benefits

Key Insights

- Familiarity with incremental, opportunity, and sunk cost concepts is critical in presenting business cases.
- Empathy with your audience is essential when presenting business cases. You can leverage Stakeholder Analysis, and Influence Maps to gain a more intimate understanding of the people who will be critical to your success.
- Utilize Cost Benefit Analysis, Net Present Value, and Internal Rates of Return in order to support the business value of proposed investments.
- Cost Benefit Analysis can be used to establish a business case for most cybersecurity investments.
- When positive cash flows result from your initiative, consider utilizing Net Present Value or Internal Rate of Return calculations to

support your investment requests. This may not apply in all business models.

- Monte Carlo analysis can help when you must consider a wide range of possible inputs and establish the range of associated potential outcomes.
- Finally, once you have an awareness of your audience, and a solid foundation of the financial parameters that affect a business case, you can utilize the SCI-PAB® Thinking & Messaging Tool to build a tight introduction to your business case presentation.

Notes

1. Sheridan, K., "Security Through an Economics Lens: A Guide for CISOs," Dark Reading, September 14, 2020. https://www.darkreading .com/risk/security-through-an-economics-lens-a-guide-for-cisos.

2. Laping, C., "If Opportunity Doesn't Knock, Build a Door," National CIO Review, 2021. https://www.nationalcioreview.com/leadership/ build-a-door/.

3. Harkins, M.W., *Managing Risk and Information Security: Protect to Enable*, Apress, 2016.

4. Schmidt, M., "How to Legitimize Avoided Cost and Opportunity in the Business Case." https://www.business-case-analysis.com/avoided-cost.html.

5. MindTools Content Team, "Stakeholder Analysis: Winning Support for Your Projects," MindTools, 2021. Accessed May 22, 2021. https://www .mindtools.com/pages/article/newPPM_07.htm.

6. MindTools Content Team, "Influence Maps: Uncovering Where the Power Lies in Your Projects," MindTools, 2021. Accessed May 22, 2021. https://www.mindtools.com/pages/article/newPPM_83.htm

7. Mandel Communications, "The SCI-PAB® Thinking & Messaging Tool." https://www.mandel.com/landing-pages/scipab-prompt.

8. Mandel Communications, "The SCI-PAB® Thinking & Messaging Tool."

9. MindTools Content Team, "Cost Benefit Analysis: Deciding, Quantitatively, Whether to Go Ahead," MindTools, 2021. Accessed May 22, 2021. https://www.mindtools.com/pages/article/newTED_08.htm.

10. Lean Production, "Focus Improvement on the Manufacturing Constraint." Accessed May 22, 2021. https://www.leanproduction.com/theory-of-constraints.html.

PART II

Communication and Education

CHAPTER 6

Cybersecurity: A Concern of the Business, Not Just IT

Knowledge will forever govern ignorance; and a people who mean to be their own governors must arm themselves with the power which knowledge gives.

– James Madison

Opportunity

In Part I, we gave you tools to bolster your foundational knowledge of how businesses operate and make decisions. We wrapped up Part I by providing you with different business case methods and templates you can use to put your foundational knowledge together and formulate business cases to secure funding for components of your cybersecurity program. In Part II, we will build upon Part I and introduce additional tools that transform common topics regarding cyber risk into enterprise risk dialogue.

Let's just come out and say it, and you already know it, organizations *must* treat cybersecurity as an enterprise risk rather than relegating it to simply an IT issue that "those tech guys" will handle.

169

Due to high-profile cybersecurity incidents such as those affecting Home Depot, Target, and Equifax, the Securities and Exchange Commission (SEC) established a cyber unit in the Enforcement Division. In the last few years, the SEC has also published numerous documents offering guidance to board directors. The new guidance covers disclosure obligations relating to cybersecurity risks and cyber incidents, as well as *Cybersecurity and Resiliency Observations* offered by the Office of Compliance Inspections and Examinations (OCIE).

More recently, domestic and global privacy regulations have come into law, including the General Data Protection Regulation and the California Consumer Protection Act. These new laws have active enforcement bodies that will not hesitate to issue material penalties for failure to comply. Presidential Executive Order on improving cybersecurity within the United States (EO 14028) is in direct response to more recent incidents such as the ones that impacted Solarwinds, Colonial Pipeline, and, later, Kaseya.

Now more than ever before, companies of all sizes have come to recognize cyber risk as a business issue. Research from the University of California at Berkeley concludes that boards deem cybersecurity risk an "existential threat," yet they are not confident they can provide effective governance and oversight. Board members mostly agree they are just now wrapping their arms around cybersecurity and believe the cyber risk environment will not stabilize predictably over the next few years. At the same time, boards are struggling with difficult questions, including whether to address cyber-risk as a central part of overall business strategy discussions and whether it should be prominently featured in board-level investment or merger-and-acquisition decisions.[1]

The National Association of Corporate Directors (NACD) is attempting to educate board directors, yet acknowledges that "many directors don't feel comfortable talking about emerging technologies, cybersecurity, and other complex topics." The NACD continues to recognize that only a small percentage of directors believe their board has a "high" level of comprehension of cyber risks or that information security reporting meets their expectations. Less than half of organizations believe their board and executive management have a sufficient understanding of cybersecurity to properly evaluate security controls.

When NACD asked public company directors to rank the quality of the information provided by senior management, cybersecurity information quality was rated the lowest. Nearly a quarter of public-company directors reported that they were dissatisfied with the quality of cybersecurity information provided by management. Only 15% said that they were very satisfied with the quality of the information they received.[2] Meanwhile, over 65% of CISOs now report to their boards at least two to four times each year, and their audience is increasingly the full board rather than a separate subcommittee.[3]

Principle

The internet has allowed organizations to integrate business with technology. Technology has been the driver for exponential economic growth since the 1950s. As technology has evolved and as organizations have become more agile in adopting technology, mainly through the use of cloud-based applications, the attack surface has increased. Just pull up your favorite media website, or log into Twitter on any given day, and you will see a new cybersecurity incident in the headlines. Protecting all data all the time is impractical, especially considering the constantly evolving threat landscape and dynamic nature of organizational strategy. The odds of success are exceedingly low, and the cost is infeasibly high. The odds of winning the multistate lottery, Powerball, grand prize jackpot is 1 in 292,201,338.00.[4] The cost of a single Powerball ticket is $2. For that price, you may say, "Sure, I'll take a chance at it," but what if the cost per ticket were $200, $2,000, or $20,000? This is the complex decision facing the executive leadership teams and boards of directors every day. How do you balance investment in risk mitigation with the business opportunity? When does the cost to mitigate risk become wasteful?

There is a better way forward. Cybersecurity risk should be integrated into the overall enterprise risk management (ERM) program to address the challenge of security and privacy in the face of data sprawl. ERM is the process of evaluating risks to identify both threats to an organization's financial well-being and opportunities in the market. The goal of ERM is to understand an organization's tolerance for risk and then identify, articulate, and manage risk according to that tolerance. Without an ERM program, organizations struggle to understand the impact of cyber risk on the business. Many organizations do not have a formal ERM program, but someone is undoubtedly responsible for enterprise risk. This may be the general counsel or the chief financial officer (CFO). Make them your friend. They have likely wanted to form a formal ERM program. Volunteering to help them do so is a golden opportunity to ensure that cybersecurity risk is integrated into overall enterprise risk. For the purposes of this book, we are going to refer to this function as the "ERM program" or the "ERM group." Although there may not be a formal group at your organization, the principles discussed in this chapter and throughout the book still apply.

The value and benefits of integrating cybersecurity risk into an overall ERM program are multifold. So, where do you start? Boards of directors love "best-practices" vs. "making it up as you go," even though what you come up with may be "better." Corporate directors want to know that you aligned the security program to established best practices. A defined framework also provides a level of "top cover" for the organization in case it ever has to defend its stance on cybersecurity. Make sure to take due care in understanding the size, complexity, and industry of your organization. Benchmark the cybersecurity program's maturity, compared to the organization's peers using the framework you selected. The board will want to know how you stack up against your peers in the industry, and it will use this benchmark to inform the organization's risk appetite. The reason is not because they do not like risk or are afraid to experiment or innovate. Corporate directors tend to avoid "invent and chose your own adventure" for a reason. The reason is because tried and-true best-practices are defensible in the worst-case scenario that a cyber incident suffered by your organization leads to litigation in the courts.

Throughout my career, I have found that COSO is an excellent place to start. In 2017, the Committee of Sponsoring Organizations of the Treadway Commission (COSO) released an update to their ERM framework. Many of the revisions are designed to absorb cyber risk as yet another business risk, but a deeper discussion surrounding precisely how to do so is warranted, and this is exactly what we will do in the next two chapters. Some benefits of using COSO to integrate cybersecurity risk into the ERM program include:[5]

- Securing the involvement of senior leadership and the board in cybersecurity initiatives
- Better alignment of cybersecurity with strategic business objectives
- Raising cybersecurity's profile within the organization ensures that enterprise risk is more accurate
- A tailored risk profile that reflects specific threats to the organization and the industry as a whole
- Increased visibility and transparency that drives better identification and treatment of risk
- More cost-efficient risk treatment

The COSO ERM framework asserts guiding principles that are grouped into five components of risk management:

1. Governance and culture
2. Strategy and objective-setting
3. Performance
4. Review and revision
5. Information, communication, and reporting

In this chapter, we will focus on the first two management components, *governance and culture* and *strategy and objective-setting,* as these establish the foundation of an ERM program and, by extension, a cyber risk management program. We will cover *performance, review and revision*, and *information, communication, and reporting* in Chapter 7 – Translating Cyber Risk into Business Risk as they focus on the actual execution of an ERM program and, again by extension, a cyber risk management program.

Governance and Culture

What the data shows is clear. Now more than ever, boards need quality information that helps them govern. While they continue to grapple with the learning curve required, and the composition of boards continues to evolve, cybersecurity leaders must also rise to the occasion.

We must find ways to bridge the knowledge and communication gap. To do so will require a solid understanding of the activities that comprise governance. Further, it will require an empathetic view of the audiences we serve. Closing these gaps is a large reason why we wrote this book. There's not a minute to waste, so let's get started.

Governance and culture are foundational to an ERM program as they establish oversight and the cybersecurity risk tolerance for the organization. The treatment of risk starts here, and only after establishing ERM can you begin to treat cybersecurity risk strategically vs. tactically (a.k.a. – fighting fires). The five COSO principles for building Governance and Culture are:

1. Exercise board risk oversight
2. Establish operating structures
3. Define desired culture
4. Demonstrate commitment to core values
5. Attract, develop, and retain capable individuals

Exercise Board Risk Oversight

Board-level governance over cybersecurity risk entails keeping tabs on the organization's cybersecurity program, strategy, and performance. As you are aware, this is nontrivial. Corporate boards worry about adequately disclosing cyber risk. They are even more concerned with cyber incidents that may have a material impact on the value a company provides to its shareholders. Further, it has become clear that each director carries a fiduciary duty and a personal liability associated with how they govern cyber risk within the companies they serve. In recent years, directors have started asking more informed questions like "Are we secure enough?" However, such a seemingly simple question is surprisingly difficult to answer. What's worse, a thorough answer may require a nuanced technical discussion that is difficult for many boards to fully comprehend. Nevertheless, boards are eager to adequately oversee their organization's cybersecurity initiatives.

Corporate boards have long been composed of "old white guys"; however, there are signs that some diversity has begun to enrich dialogue in the boardroom. On the flip-side, the boardroom isn't getting any younger as the average age of a corporate director continues to increase.[6] At the time of this writing, we, the authors, are in our forties. We specialize in cybersecurity, *and we grew up during the rise of the internet*. Yet, it's fair to suggest that we are challenged to continuously educate ourselves on the latest technology innovation and keep pace with the changing threat landscape. In response to this, many corporate boards have chosen to engage external advisers to help "bridge the gap"; however, there is no reason why *you* cannot bridge that gap by applying some of these key activities to your organization. In fact, common frameworks and regulations, such as SOC2, ISO27001, and NYDFS, *require* board involvement and oversight, so you can leverage those requirements in the framework or regulation applicable to your organization to engage your board.

Establish Operating Structures

For cybersecurity risk to be treated as an enterprise risk rather than an IT risk, cybersecurity teams cannot operate in a vacuum. Establishing a cybersecurity steering committee is nonnegotiable. In fact, do whatever you can to *fight* for it. We will talk later about a use case where I did not fight for establishing one and the cascading effect that it had.

The cybersecurity steering committee should consist of a representative from each department. This includes, but is not limited to, executive leadership, IT, finance, legal, HR, accounting, sales, marketing, operations, and so on. The committee should be chaired by the CISO (or equivalent) to provide a forum for two-way communication between the various business units and cybersecurity. The cybersecurity team can gain an understanding of the critical data or processes that must be protected for each business unit, solicit input from the business when proposing new security controls, and review new and existing risks and their treatments.

Establishing a working draft of your risk appetite is a great project to tackle with this team if you don't have that already documented. You should also plan to update the committee on the evolving threat landscape and work to translate what that means to the organization.

Implementing and enforcing security controls is much more effective when cybersecurity is done *with* the business and not *to* the business. Consider sharing the business model canvas, value chain mappings, and risk-adjusted value metrics that you produced using Chapter 2 – Business Strategy Tools. Better yet, involve the committee in reviewing and updating these working documents.

A vital benefit of the cybersecurity steering committee is bringing diversity of thought into various security issues. Via the steering committee, the cybersecurity team can be a business enabler instead of posing as a roadblock. For example, the sales team may bring up the fact that they cannot easily access customer records in the customer relationship management (CRM) system while traveling. IT may then propose moving to an SaaS solution or to enabling a mobile solution via mobile application management (MAM). The cybersecurity team can discuss what investments will be required to secure the proposed solutions consistent with the corporate risk appetite, and executive leadership can approve the investment required to implement a complete solution.

Define Desired Culture and Demonstrate Commitment to Core Values

These two COSO guiding principles go hand-in-hand. Do a quick Google search on recent cybersecurity incidents, and you will see that the root cause of just about all of them involved the weakest link in a cybersecurity program – people. Another excellent resource for curated cybersecurity news is www.TruKno.com (no, I am not a paid spokesman). We often talk of people, process, and technology. Notice how *people* comes first. Let's face it: as cybersecurity professionals, we generally shy away from squishy topics like people and culture. There is a misconception that we are a bunch of black-hoodie-wearing introverts who cannot or choose not to engage in even basic conversation. However, soft skills and personal interaction are required for a thriving security culture. Security culture requires intentional effort. "Culture eats strategy for breakfast" is a famous quote from legendary management consultant and writer Peter Drucker, However, like a child, culture requires constant nurture and nourishment.

Your organization's core values should consist of a strong cybersecurity culture, and your cybersecurity culture should align with your organization's core values. Your organization's core values are defined by the board of directors and the executive leadership team. When the top of the organization drives a strong cybersecurity culture, and when your cybersecurity policies, awareness training, employee accountability, etc., emphasize your organization's core values, it is relatively easy to inspire employee commitment to cyber hygiene.

There is no singular definition of a strong cybersecurity culture. Nor is there universal agreement upon what elements must be present. Nevertheless, my experience is that strong security cultures exhibit these essential elements:

- **Security culture is not a thing you do as an organization.** Security culture is a thing you *are* as an organization. Ben Horowitz, a co-founder of Andreessen Horowitz, states, "Your culture is how your company makes decisions when you're not there. It's the set of assumptions your employees use to resolve the problems they face every day. It's how they behave when no one is looking. If you don't methodically set your culture, then two-thirds of it will end up being accidental, and the rest will be a mistake."[7] This core concept is set by the board of directors and the executive leadership team. Security culture is emphasized and embedded into every technology and process decision.
- **Trust.** There is a high level of trust between employees from the executive level to the individual contributor. This trust is typically built upon transparency, honesty, and follow-through on commitments. Stephen Covey defines the "4 Cores of Credibility" as: (1) Integrity, (2) Intent, (3) Capabilities, and (4) Results.[8] Strive to establish and maintain trust within your immediate team in addition to promoting the importance of trust between your team and the rest of the organization. Remember the adage, "Trust takes years to build, seconds to break, and forever to repair."
- **Awareness, awareness, and more awareness.** How can people be held accountable for their actions if they are not aware of what is required of them? Security newsletters and annual training videos are not enough. Successful security cultures elevate security training to the levels of the organization's safety and ethics training. Consider bringing in people with backgrounds in marketing and education to develop and manage your cybersecurity

awareness and training programs to deliver engaging content that employees will be less likely to ignore. Of course, use simplicity as a guiding principle.

- **Cybersecurity champions.** Who are the security champions across your organization? Can you name some? If not, then encourage the development of a cybersecurity champions program. Much like the cybersecurity steering committee, a good champions program develops key individuals organization-wide to evangelize the importance of your organization's cybersecurity strategy, goals, and challenges. It also allows you to gain valuable feedback from "the front lines" about the performance and obstacles that policy and controls are having on how people are executing their job responsibilities. Gain executive support for the cybersecurity champions program by building a business case around how the program will contribute to your organization's business goals. A good cybersecurity champions program will have a substantial force-multiplier effect for your undoubtedly constrained cybersecurity team.
- **Make it fun and rewarding.** Taking a novel approach may invalidate or disrupt long held beliefs about security. Stimulating and delightful new experiences in this context can invigorate curiosity and passion. Surprises can inspire a "sticky" security culture. I am not a psychologist, but I don't need a PhD to know that engaging content is more memorable. Positive reinforcement is likely to go much further than punishment, shame, or guilt. A monthly prize for the "champion of the month" or for the person who reported the "coolest" phishing email are cost effective means to make security fun.

Attract, Develop, and Retain Capable Individuals

The notion that there is a colossal cybersecurity talent gap has been beaten into us through various studies and publications. One example comes from (ISC)², the world's largest nonprofit membership association of certified cybersecurity professionals. You may recognize them from the popular CISSP certification. In that study, (ISC)² estimated that the cybersecurity workforce at the time consisted of 2.8 million professionals but that an additional 4.07 million professionals were needed to close the skills gap.[9] Another study that was released around the same time by Cybersecurity Ventures estimates that there will be 3.5 million unfilled cybersecurity jobs globally by 2021, up from one million positions in 2014.[10] The numbers between the two studies differ a bit but suffice it to say that there is a *huge* talent shortage facing our industry.

The cyber threat landscape evolves daily and even hourly in some cases. Attackers seem to get smarter and more efficient through increasingly simple yet sophisticated attacks. How do we keep up? The reality is that your organization is unlikely to have the budget and resources to keep up with it all. Therefore, you should consider a mix of both in-house and outsourced talent. For example, you may decide to keep your governance, risk, and compliance (GRC) functions in-house but outsource security operations and incident response to a managed services security provider.

Above all, invest in your people. This seems obvious, but a report conducted by the Enterprise Strategy Group and the Information Security Systems Association (ISSA) called *The Life and Times of Cybersecurity Professionals 2020* found that there is a continuous lack of training, career development, and long-term planning for cybersecurity talent within organizations. The findings noted that "cybersecurity professionals often muddle through their careers with little direction, jumping from job to job and enhancing their skill sets on the fly rather than in any systematic way. This, combined with the continued cybersecurity skills shortage, has stalled cybersecurity progress."[11] Help correct this disturbing trend by creating a plan to encourage continuous learning. That can be part of formal training, like a SANS Institute course (although we're increasingly discouraged by the exorbitant pricing models they exhibit) or a certification bootcamp. It can also involve a paid subscription to an online platform like Cybint, Pluralsight, or Cybrary. Additionally, it can leverage education reimbursement to a college or university. Some of the accountability for continuous learning lands on the employee, and the rest resides with the employer. Do not disincentivize an employee from investing in themselves by not providing them with a path to do so. Daniel Pink outlines a framework to do so through autonomy, mastery, and purpose.[12] Hint: intrinsic motivation tends to have a greater effect than extrinsic motivation. In other words, learning, growth, and job satisfaction outweigh pay in motivating employees of the 21st century.

Don't be afraid to get creative and stretch your team's skills. Python for Managers, Crucial Conversations, communication training, and project management skills are every bit as relevant and perhaps more valuable than simply producing another Offensive Security Certified Professional. Whatever mix of in-house vs. outsourced talent you choose, it is vital to have a strategy to attract, develop, and retain the talent that is right for your organization. Doing so will require an investment in time and money, so it is crucial to create a business case around how your strategy around cybersecurity talent supports your organization's goals. Chapter 5 – Articulating the Business Case gives you tools to help you create a successful business case.

Strategy and Objective-Setting

Strategy and objective-setting work together to complement a risk management program. Organizational risk tolerance is defined and aligned to strategy. Business objectives reflect risk tolerance and strategy, laying the foundation for identifying, assessing, and treating risk. Aligning your cybersecurity risk management program in the same manner helps you align cyber risk tolerance to organizational risk tolerance. It also allows your ERM group to more easily evaluate cyber risk within the context of the overall risks that the organization faces. The case study in the Application section of Chapter 4 – Value Creation walks you through how to identify cyber risks and to use those risks to align security strategy and objectives for a fictional beverage manufacturer with competing priorities. The four COSO principles for building governance and culture are:

1. Analyzes business context
2. Defines risk appetite
3. Evaluates alternative strategies
4. Formulates business objectives

Analyzes Business Context

Things change. Constantly. As we've discussed in previous chapters, market dynamics can change the way you approach developing a business case, and market dynamics can certainly change business valuation. Since its publication in 1979, the Porter's Five Forces model has become one of the world's most highly regarded and widely utilized business strategy tools, and we are going to use the model to dive into industry dynamics below. The model was created to analyze likelihood of profit when entering an industry. Over many years, it has been adapted to analyze how an organization is positioned in the current market and how an organization can adjust its strategy to adapt. The five forces are listed below, and each sub-bullet lists a cybersecurity analogy that you can employ to strengthen your organization's position in the model:[13]

1. The industry (competitive rivalry – Trend Micro vs. McAfee)
   a. Standardization can lead to agility. Do certifications, such as ISO 27001, SOC2, or FedRAMP, differentiate your organization in the market?
   b. If not careful, standardization can also lead to bureaucracy and a lack of agility. How do McAfee vs. Symantec differentiate themselves from each other? That's right, they don't.
2. Threat of new entrants (SentinelOne and Crowdstrike)
   a. New entrants such as SentinelOne and Crowdstrike have leveraged the unsatisfaction of "traditional antivirus" to create new solutions with better automation to enter the anti-malware market. In fact, they have created a new endpoint detection and response market that has surpassed the capabilities of the de facto stalwarts in the industry.
   b. Can you use cybersecurity to become a new entrant in a market that is adjacent to your organization's current market? Can you use your organization's current investment in cybersecurity to drive down costs and increase speed to market?
3. Bargaining power of customers
   a. Demand from customers may require your organization to focus more on the cybersecurity program. Again, do any frameworks or certifications allow you to provide a solid attestation of your security program to customers?
   b. As customers, can we raise the cybersecurity bar by refusing to purchase insecure commercial-off-the-shelf software, or rejecting proposals to leverage insecure third parties and subcontractors?

4. Bargaining power of suppliers
   a. Same as 3a, but from a supplier/partner perspective. Take for example Amazon Web Services. They are large enough where they dictate business associate agreement terms, and they refuse to participate in third-party diligence questionnaires. They are careful to even avoid disclosure of the locations of their data centers.
5. Threat of substitutes
   a. Can an increased focus on the cybersecurity program incentivize customers to stay with your organization's product or service? Can the standardization of security policies and procedures allow your organization to bring a new product or service to market quickly in order to better compete with the substitute?
   b. As customers, you may evaluate Orca Side Scanning as an alternative to traditional vulnerability scanners, or you may consider developing your own SOAR solution using AWS Lamda functions vs. purchasing a traditional SOAR solution.

Each of the examples above highlight the impact of industry dynamics on our evolving role as stewards of value. In short, strategy changes. ERM, and by extension, cyber risk management, need to keep up. As strategies and business objectives change, they should also take into consideration the IT applications, networks, systems, data, and so on that are required to accomplish current and future objectives. Is your organization in crunch mode where its primary goal is to survive a downturn in the market or is your organization in a high-growth phase during a booming economy? The business objectives to deliver on these strategies may require different technologies and information to be successful. As such, different technologies and information will likely introduce other vulnerabilities. That, in conjunction with the changing cyber threat landscape, means that new and changing cyber risks are introduced to your organization.

Staying ahead, or at least alongside of the changing industry dynamics and business objectives listed above is much easier said than done. We probably would not be writing this book if it were easy. As companies become increasingly reliant upon software, there is an "emerging" concept termed Security by Design (SbD). In truth, SbD is not emerging at all. We have been screaming it since at least 2006 as evidenced by various OWASP projects, Building Security in Maturity Model (www.BSIMM.com), and the like. Nonetheless, SbD features more prominently as organizational practices become more agile. At its core, SbD is applied from the heights of strategic planning to the implementation tactical security controls. The value and the benefits are apparent and mirror the lessons we learned about the costs associated with fixing defects in software. SbD allows you to find ways to use cybersecurity as a market differentiator for your organization.

Since SbD sounds like such a no-brainer (oh, but it's not), let's examine five key activities you can undertake to start implementing the concept at your organization.

- **Project managers should engage a cybersecurity representative at the beginning of every project.** A cybersecurity champions program allows you to scale to meet this demand. Early engagement provides defined security requirements and controls at the beginning of development to most effectively reduce risk. Include cybersecurity validation during designated phases of development. Validation could come in various forms, such as manual architecture reviews or automated lightweight pre-commit code scans that are performed before code is ever checked into the code repository.
- **Awareness (there is that word, again).** Create an awareness campaign, or even specialized training, for developers around the types of threats and common vulnerabilities for software they develop. The Open Web Application Security Project (OWASP. org) is a great place to start and has a ton of free resources available. One example may be creating a series of lunch-and-learns around the OWASP Top 10 (https://owasp.org/www-project-top-ten/) and the OWASP Mobile Top 10 (https://owasp.org/www-project-mobile-top-10/).
- **Automation.** The more you can automate code checks, the better. Provide instant feedback to the developer, and do not allow the code to be committed until it passes the required security checks. These scans can use static application security testing

(SAST), dynamic application security testing (DAST), or a hybrid of both using interactive application security testing (IAST), depending on your needs and circumstances. It is important to note that manual checks are still necessary because humans are better at detecting flaws in the application logic that can be exploited.

- **SbD also enables "Privacy by Design."** Privacy concerns have become increasingly front of mind over the past several years, with lawmakers passing regulations such as the Global Data Protection Regulation (European Union) and the California Consumer Privacy Act. Consider adding Privacy by Design to your overall program, depending on the type of data the system will be handling.
- **Continuous improvement.** Take an inventory of the applications your organization has developed and prioritize them from a risk perspective. If you have not already implemented SbD in those applications, go back and evaluate them for vulnerabilities. If you have already implemented SbD, fantastic; however, keep in mind that the security posture is only good until the next code release. Make sure to consistently execute on your Security by Design practices and continuously strive to improve them and make them more efficient.

Defines Risk Appetite

COSO defines risk appetite as "The types and amount of risk, on a board level, an organization is willing to accept in pursuit of value."[14] Sounds simple enough, but I cannot begin to tell you how many times I have been asked about how an organization goes about defining their risk appetite and, more importantly, their cyber risk appetite. It seems to be an elusive magical purple unicorn because most organizations do not actually codify their risk appetite. Defining a risk appetite is fundamental to risk management and how organizations communicate and react to risk. Managing risk within the boundaries of risk appetite should be consistently shared and addressed throughout the organization as it provides the guardrails against which to manage risk.

We often interchange the terms risk appetite and risk tolerance, but they are distinctly different. Risk appetite is only part of the overall approach to managing risk. Risk appetite needs to cascade throughout the business as risk decisions must be made at different levels or business units. Each individual level or unit may have different risk tolerances around the risk appetite. While risk appetite refers to how much risk an organization is willing to accept, risk tolerance refers to the boundaries of acceptable variation in performance relative to the business objective. Risk tolerance is a performance metric. Figure 6.1 outlines some of the differences.

You may think of indicators and triggers in this context as the individual risks themselves, and the metrics used to measure them (e.g., key risk indicators). A *key risk indicator* (KRI) is a measurement of how risky an activity is. It differs from a key performance indicator (KPI) because a KPI is a leading metric while a KRI is a lagging metric. For instance, a KPI may be expressed as "We have patch coverage of

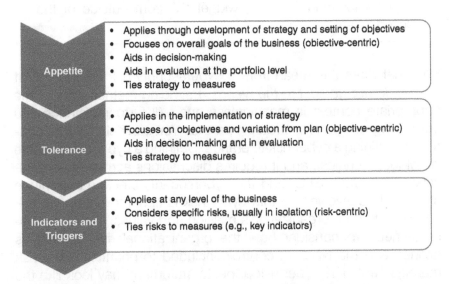

FIGURE 6.1 Risk Appetite, Risk Tolerance, Limits, and Triggers

Source: COSO (2017). Enterprise Risk Management – Integrating with Strategy and Performance. Committee of Sponsoring Organizations of the Treadway Commission (COSO). All rights reserved.

86%," while a KRI may be expressed as "When patch coverage falls below 80%, confirmed incidents rise by 60% month-over-month."

An organization may express its risk appetite as:

Brand is critical for our organization. As such, we have a low-risk appetite for negatively impacting our brand and brand loyalty. We will not make decisions that factor cost above our core beliefs, quality, or component choice. We value sustainability above revenue and growth. We will innovate within these parameters to develop products that meet market demands and have a moderate risk appetite to attain this goal.

The same organization may express one risk tolerance metric as:

We will not procure more than 10% of the critical components required for manufacturing widget "X" from outside of the United States.

So, what does this mean from a cybersecurity risk standpoint? It means *do not get lost in the weeds*. Providing metrics without the appropriate context is meaningless and will further distance you from being viewed as a strategic partner. You can help set that context by defining a cyber risk tolerance. Defining a cyber risk appetite is not just technical, and it requires discussions across the organization. The CEO, CFO, and the cybersecurity steering committee should all be involved so that cyber risk is tied into enterprise risk and reflects your organization's mission and values. These discussions need to consider how the organizational risk appetite is defined and the types of controls included to prioritize cyber risk management. The cyber risk appetite statement may look like the following when taking into account the example of organizational risk appetite:

It is essential that the cybersecurity risk management program is aligned with the enterprise risk management program and allows the organization to achieve its business goals in a method that complies with applicable laws and regulations. Our organization has defined that it has a low-risk appetite relating to impacts to brand and brand loyalty and moderate risk in sustainably achieving business objectives.

In support of the above, the organization has a low-risk appetite for the loss or breach of its intellectual property and consumer data. Information assets will be classified and protected with the commensurate security controls outlined in the Data Classification and Protection Policy (e.g., restricted, confidential, internal, or public). The organization has a low-risk appetite for a failure of access controls. All access to systems storing or processing data classified as "internal" or above will be controlled via multifactor authentication as outlined in the organization's Access Control policy.

While risk appetite is strategic and broad, risk tolerance is tactical and focused; however, they are closely linked. Per COSO, risk tolerance is the acceptable variation in performance.[15] It describes the range of acceptable risk outcomes related to achieving a specific business objective to ensure the organization continues to operate within its defined risk appetite (depicted by the dotted lines in Figure 6.2). In other words, it helps management determine if a risk is acceptable or unacceptable. A specific risk target does not typically exceed where risk profile intersects risk appetite ("A" in Figure 6.2).

Risk tolerance does not focus on specific risks. Instead, risk tolerance focuses on business objectives and performance. As such, risk tolerance should be aligned, measured, and communicated in terms of business objectives. For example, risk tolerance may be lower for business objectives that are critical to achieving the organization's strategy and higher or less critical business objectives. The organization's existing risk profile is the current level and distribution of risks across the organization.

Risk capacity is the total amount of risk that the organization can absorb in pursuit of its objectives. Risk profile, risk capacity, and risk tolerance all inform an organization's risk appetite determination.

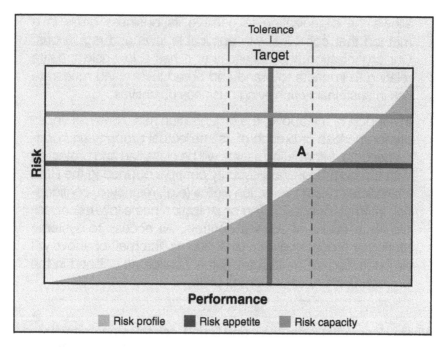

FIGURE 6.2 Risk Profile Showing Tolerance

Source: COSO (2017). Enterprise Risk Management – Integrating with Strategy and Performance. Committee of Sponsoring Organizations of the Treadway Commission (COSO). All rights reserved.

Evaluates Alternative Strategies

In COSO, an organization must evaluate alternative strategies as part of defining strategy and assess each option's risk and opportunities in conjunction with the organization's resources and ability to create, preserve, and realize value. ERM involves evaluating strategy from two perspectives:[16]

1. The possibility that the strategy does not align with the mission, vision, and core values of the organization
2. The implication from the chosen strategy

In cybersecurity, this translates to defining a set of frameworks to oversee the cybersecurity risk management program. Several cyber-security frameworks such as the NIST Cybersecurity Framework, the

International Organization for Standardization (ISO) 27001, and the Payment Card Industry Data Security Standard (PCI DSS) have been developed to help organizations establish and report on the effectiveness of their cybersecurity program. This selection and mapping of these frameworks to technical security controls and risk management processes are often also referred to as the organization's information security management system (ISMS). Organizations must determine which cybersecurity framework to build their ISMS by considering which is the best fit based on their business operations, current control structure, and various factors, such as capital, technologies, and resources.

Formulates Business Objectives

Just as an organization must develop business objectives that are specific, measurable, attainable, relevant, and timely (SMART), so must a cybersecurity risk management program. Defining business objectives makes business strategy actionable. Determining risk tolerance makes risk appetite actionable. You must define metrics against which to measure your cybersecurity program to ensure the organization is working within its specified risk tolerances. Techniques such as The Open Group's FAIR (Factor Analysis of Information Risk) can help quantify risk and derive values for risk tolerance; however, cybersecurity is not an exact science. You will most likely use a combination of quantitative and qualitative metrics. Metrics provide three primary benefits:[17]

1. Measurement provides visibility.
2. Measurement educates and provides a common language for understanding the cybersecurity program.
3. Measurement allows for improvement by enabling efficient management, investment planning, and decision-making and by driving necessary change throughout the organization.

Your organization will likely have a different risk appetite for various business units or systems (e.g., mission-critical vs. non-mission-critical or storing sensitive information vs. publicly accessible information). This means that risk tolerances may differ for different systems or assets; therefore, metrics may change or have different meanings depending on the context.

Application

I believe that failure is the greatest teacher. So, I am going to discuss a time where I *failed* to apply the principles outlined in this chapter. Don't worry; I will indulge in the successful application of the principles in the following chapter.

Case Study – A Failure to Govern

For this case study, let me set the stage. I had recently started a new role at a publicly traded company, and I was responsible for building a cybersecurity program. At the time, it was all the rage for public companies to initiate formalized investments in cybersecurity. As some readers may be experiencing today, my organization did not have a formal security function before my arrival. There was no decomposition of IT Risk. Instead, cybersecurity risk was buried deep in the annals of IT Risk. So, there it stood, a solitary item on the company's enterprise risk register.

It was my job to establish the program's framework. I was entrusted to determine how to best measure and prioritize risk, and how to work with the other business units to drive change. The good news was that the board sponsored my role, so inherently some board risk oversight was established. Check. Naturally, I sought to establish an Information Security Steering Committee, but to my surprise I was strongly discouraged from doing so. The rationale was that the organization was so agile and dynamic, it allegedly did not support committees (although I later learned that project steering committees were commonplace). In either case, I had failed to secure the support of my leadership structure. I decided that without the executive support required, the committee would be an exercise in futility.

In hindsight, I should have pushed hard. I want to advocate that this is so important, if faced with the same decision again I would advise myself to hold firm on establishing the committee, even if it meant getting fired because of insubordination. Regrettably, in my first few days on the job, hoping to build relationships and assimilate into the company culture, I did not recognize the strategic importance of the committee. I did not hold the crucial conversation that was required. I underestimated the importance of this governance lynchpin. This is where I fundamentally failed. I accepted a position that limited my ability to engage the business. At that time, I felt it was possible to change the organizational security culture from the ground up. I was wrong. As a result, I failed to Establish the Operating Structure, I contradicted COSO, and I began a painful lesson. I hope you will learn from my mistake.

Before my arrival, a big, expensive consulting firm conducted a cyber risk assessment and delivered a report. More than half of the report dealt with physical security. While it's true that physical security is a critical aspect of an overall cybersecurity program, there are plenty of other things to consider in concert. Disappointingly, many recommendations were disconnected from the reality of our business. In the end, the report mainly sat on a shelf collecting dust.

Fortunately, one of the suggestions was to hire someone to lead the cybersecurity function. That recommendation was accompanied by guidance to staff an entire team. I eventually learned that our business didn't have an appetite to carry that full cost burden. Hoping to serve as an agent of change, I swiftly encountered the cultural norm "if it isn't broke, don't fix it." With no major incidents at the organization and, at that time, no major incidents across the industry, I quickly fell into a compliance-driven checker of boxes.

Without the support of a steering committee, we were relegated to "fire stompers." We subsumed ourselves with issues-of-the-day rather than strategically assessing and treating risk. Frequently, my team was summoned to advise a broader project team "how to secure 'it'" days before the project go-live.

Although we adopted the NIST Cybersecurity Framework as a guiding document, we simply lacked business context. Without the context, we struggled to develop security champions. You can imagine, constrained by resources and devoid of the champions I needed, cybersecurity was not optimized throughout the organization. We lacked the executive sponsorship needed to lend credibility to our security culture efforts. In a self-perpetuating death spiral, the lack of interaction with the business meant we lacked business context, which then limited the relevance of our cyber risk analysis. Unsurprisingly, these factors led to a misalignment with the organization's ERM program.

Take it from me, and save yourself the trouble by learning these few lessons:

1. Recognize the lack of an information security steering committee as a canary in the coal mine. If you face this prickly challenge, persist with your desire to establish a committee. Don't fall for the fool's choice; instead proceed tactfully using the tools we've covered in other parts of this book. I could have researched case studies of information security program failures, or I could have engaged an external partner (in this case, Gartner) to further push for my cause. Ultimately, I did form a "circle of trust" that I informally used as my security champions, but because it was an informal network, many efforts failed to garner the priority they likely deserved.
2. Perform sufficient due diligence during the interview process. I recommend drafting specific questions to reveal the true state of security culture. Take the time to ensure you understand what the expected investment in your program will look like. Prepare to navigate around the standard "We don't know yet, that's why we're hiring you" reply. Get clear about who controls your budget dollars, and be certain that you understand if your funding is independent or beholden to IT's budget. All this information can be used to ensure aligned expectations, and may also influence other things like how you negotiate your compensation, and what strategy you take in your new role.

Key Insights

- Work with your organization to implement the COSO principle of Establish Board Risk Oversight by first picking a framework. It can be any framework that aligns with your organizational requirements and risk appetite. It will serve as the baseline that you use to evaluate program maturity. Corporate directors want to know that you aligned the security program to established best practices.

- Don't be "Chicken Little." Fear, uncertainty, and doubt (FUD) will get you nowhere. Security operations metrics like "our firewall blocked 1,596,742 attacks last month" or "we have 100,854 critical vulnerabilities on the network" will put the board to sleep in less time than it took to type this sentence. It will also damage your credibility and qualify the need to have you in the room. Don't pigeonhole yourself as the stereotype against which we struggle: that paranoid, antisocial being that still lives in their parents' dark, cold basement hopped up on Mountain Dew and Red Bull (no offense if you do still live in your parents' basement). Use "above the line" metrics (metrics that drive gross profit) or other metrics that matter to your organization.
- Strong security cultures exist when there is strong trust across the organization. Remember that security can be fun, rewarding, and distributed across the organization via an innovative security champions program.
- Attract and retain capable individuals by thinking outside the box and by investing in your people.
- The only constant is change. Internal and external factors are constantly changing. You cannot ensure your cybersecurity strategy aligns with your organization's strategy if you do not ensure you are in sync with the current context of your organization.
- Draw a line in the sand: establish a cybersecurity steering committee. The cybersecurity steering committee is an excellent place to facilitate collaboration across organizational stakeholders.
- Consider how your cyber risk appetite statement cascades throughout the organization. Do you have to create multiple risk statements for various levels within the organization? Will your cyber risk appetite statement require fundamental changes, such as implementing a new multifactor authentication requirement?
- Understand the environment and industry dynamics your organization operates in by referencing the Porter's Five Forces model. For instance, ISO 27001 is costly and resource-intensive to implement, but it is optional for most organizations. PCI DSS may be expensive and resource-intensive to implement but is required for

organizations that store, transmit, or process credit card information. Rationalizing your compliance frameworks is a must. The last thing you want to do is measure your program effectiveness differently based on the framework. That is called "compliance-based security," which quickly turns into "checkbox security," which turns into a data breach. Target had just passed a PCI audit when it had its significant breach back in December 2013. Let the security program produce artifacts that demonstrate compliance to a framework, not the other way around.

- Formulate your cybersecurity business objectives by understanding measurement and reporting resources that are available to allow you to define and gather metrics. This enables you to define metrics that integrate your cyber risk appetite and risk tolerance (derived from your organization's risk appetite and risk tolerance). These should come in the form of lagging indicators (key performance indicators) or leading indicators (key risk indicators). Remember your audience. Different metrics are intended for varying levels of the organization. Operational metrics focus more on data that allows you to manage day-to-day operations and are intended for individual contributors and front-line managers. Executive and board-level metrics concentrate more on information and provide leadership with insight into how the cybersecurity program is performing to allow them to make informed business decisions over time.

Notes

1. Resilient Governance for Boards of Directors, 2019. https://cltc.berkeley.edu/resilient-governance/.
2. Clinton, L., *Cyber-Risk: Director's Handbook Series*, National Association of Corporate Directors, 2020.
3. Gartner, "What Your Board Wants to Know in 2020" (Issue G00716265), 2019.
4. "Powerball," Multi-state Lottery Association. https://www.powerball.com/games/home.

5. COSO, *Enterprise Risk Management – Integrating with Strategy and Performance*, Committee of Sponsoring Organizations of the Treadway Commission (COSO), 2017. All rights reserved. Used with permission.

6. Harvard Law School Forum on Corporate Governance, "U.S. Board Diversity Trends in 2019," 2019. https://Corpgov.Law.Harvard.Edu/. https://corpgov.law.harvard.edu/2019/06/18/u-s-board-diversity-trends-in-2019/.

7. Horowitz, B., *What You Do Is Who You Are: How to Create Your Business Culture*, HarperCollins Publishers, 2019.

8. Covey, S.M.R., *The SPEED of Trust: The One Thing That Changes Everything*, Free Press, 2018.

9. (ISC)², *Strategies for Building and Growing Strong Cybersecurity Teams: (ISC)² Cybersecurity Workforce Study*, 2019, 1–37.

10. "Cybersecurity Talent Crunch to Create 3.5 Million Unfilled Jobs Globally by 2021 (n.d.), *Cybercrime Magazine*. Accessed August 31, 2020. https://cybersecurityventures.com/jobs/.

11. Oltsik, J., "The Life and Times of Cybersecurity Professionals," 2019. https://www.esg-global.com/research/esg-research-report-the-life-and-times-of-cybersecurity-professionals-2020.

12. Pink, D.H., *Drive: The Surprising Truth About What Motivates Us*, Penguin Group, 2011.

13. Porter, M.E., "How Competitive Forces Shape Strategy," *Readings in Strategic Management*, March 1979. https://doi.org/10.1007/978-1-349-20317-8_10.

14. COSO, *Enterprise Risk Management – Integrating with Strategy and Performance*.

15. COSO, *Enterprise Risk Management – Integrating with Strategy and Performance*.

16. COSO, *Enterprise Risk Management – Integrating with Strategy and Performance*.

17. Wong, C., *Security Metrics: A Beginner's Guide*, The McGraw-Hill Companies, 2012.

CHAPTER 7

Translating Cyber Risk into Business Risk

A ship is safe in harbor, but that's not what ships are for.
— John A. Shedd

Opportunity

If anything resonates with the C-suite and the board, it's the Almighty Dollar in both making it (revenue) and saving it (reducing costs/ operational efficiency).

Technology adoption brings about a tremendous growth opportunity for businesses (e.g., revenue). According to the World Economic Council, more than 50% of the world's population is now online, approximately one million people go online for the first time, ever, each day, and two-thirds of the global population own a mobile device.[1] Additionally, technology adoption can reduce costs by automating existing manual processes, enable mobility so that an employee is no longer chained to their desk, and reduce human error.

Now, couple technology adoption by organizations with the rapidly increasing cyber threat landscape. Per IBM, the average cost of a data breach in 2020 is $3.86 million.[2] In their annual *2021 Data Breach and Investigation Report*, Verizon identified that external attackers accounted for about 80% of breaches, which is up from 70% in 2020.[3] This statistic goes against conventional wisdom that the internal threat is the largest cyber threat an organization faces; however, that is not to say that external attackers did not use unknowing internal employees or contractors to help their cause. 2020 will forever be known as the year of the COVID-19 global pandemic. The pandemic forced many companies to shift from a mainly in-the-office work culture to a 100% remote work culture almost overnight. The speed of technology adoption required of many firms to support the new "normal" workforce was mindboggling, leaving cybersecurity teams struggling to keep pace.

The statistics mentioned above are only an appetizer for this chapter's main course, which outlines how to translate technical cyber risk to business-level risk. The good thing is that C-suite executives and the boards of directors are open to that conversation now more than ever before.

Principle

Chapter 6 – Cybersecurity: A Concern of the Business, Not Just IT discussed establishing a cyber risk management program's foundation using the first two risk management components of COSO, *Governance and Culture,* and *Strategy and Objective Setting*. In this chapter, we will expand upon those foundations and focus on the execution of the cyber risk program and how to roll-up cyber risk into a portfolio view of enterprise risk that executive leaders, and the board, can use to make business decisions. To do this, we will align with the final three risk management components of COSO: *Performance, Review and Revision*, and *Information, Communication, and Reporting*. This chapter may be one of the longest of this book, but this topic is a large premise around which we felt the need to write this book.

Foundational to this chapter is an equation you may have seen many times in studying other cybersecurity materials. Still, we will define it here again, so we can set the table stakes. It is the simple risk equation, but this simple, little equation permeates every topic in this chapter:

$$\text{Risk Exposure} = \text{Impact} \times \text{Likelihood}$$

Where:

| Impact | = | the loss expectation if a risk event occurs |
| Likelihood | = | the probability that a risk event occurs |

This equation, which is continuously beaten into our heads from the time we can spell "cybersecurity," is a gross oversimplification of risk (kind of like how $E=mc2$ is a gross oversimplification of Albert Einstein's Theory of Relativity). Still, it does isolate two ways to reduce risk. Either you can reduce the likelihood of a risk event to the business or reduce the impact of a risk event on the business.

Businesses are increasing their dependency on technology, not decreasing it. Digital transformation promises to increase that dependency, more than during any other time in history. As such, the digital threat landscape continues to grow, which means that a cyber incident's potential impact on business also increases. The likelihood that an organization will have a cyber incident also increases as their dependency on technology grows. The rush to adopt new technology often outpaces how cybersecurity teams can put proper security controls in place. All of this amounts to – you guessed it – increased risk exposure to the organization, which means that the responsibility and accountability for implementing appropriate security controls lie across the entire organization rather than only the cybersecurity team. For example, if your organization develops software with one cybersecurity person per 50 developers, it is impractical and inefficient for that single cybersecurity person to ensure the code is secure. Instead, it becomes the cybersecurity team's role to provide assurance that others (in this case, the developers) are doing their job.

Performance

The key to minimizing risk is pulling on the two levers of likelihood and impact by identifying and prioritizing risk events and measuring how risk treatment plans are performing. Just don't forget, if a technology stack fails and it does not (materially) impact the business outcome, nobody in the C-suite cares.

Minimizing cyber risk requires identifying, assessing, and responding to risk that may impact the organization's ability to achieve its business goals. Cyber risks could affect an individual business unit or the organization as a whole, and they may cascade up and down the organization accordingly. Significant investment may be required to mitigate risk. Alternatively, the organization may try to transfer the risk or ultimately accept the risk.

An organization will never be able to "secure all things all the time." More importantly, it should not attempt to do so because that will lead to an ineffective allocation of capital. The organization must ultimately assess the risk and determine the best course of action after factoring in business goals, the criticality of assets, risk appetite, and risk tolerance.

Bubbling up cyber risks to the ERM team (which may just be your Executive Leadership Team in a smaller or privately held company) in a manner that can easily align to other enterprise risks to provide a common view of risk across the organization will:

- Identify conflicting risks
- Highlight, correlate, and aggregate common risks across business units
- Create a risk taxonomy followed across the organization

For instance, the C-Suite will ignore any talk about a CVSS score, which measures the severity of a vulnerability. However, the C-Suite will certainly listen when you can paint a picture of how that vulnerability, along with the likelihood of it being exploited, can lead to a material impact on the company's financials and reputation. Presenting risks in this manner allows executives to evaluate cyber risks alongside other risks that the organization faces.

This component of COSO concentrates on how the organization considers risk while executing on strategy and achieving business goals. The five COSO principles for performance are:[4]

1. Identifies risk
2. Assesses severity of risk
3. Prioritizes risk

4. Implements risk responses
5. Develops portfolio view

Identifies Risk

Oddly enough, minimizing risk starts with first identifying the risk.

Mind-blowing, mic-drop, and end-of-book.

In all seriousness, identifying risk is easier said than done. Much like how an organization identifies new, emerging, and changing risks in achieving its strategic objectives, cybersecurity teams must do the same for cyber risks which can impact those strategic objectives. There is an argument to be made that cyber risks should be evaluated more frequently than traditional enterprise risks due to the fast-changing nature of the cyber threat landscape. Table 7.1 highlights how COSO categorizes when to trigger cyber risk assessments when new, emerging, and changing risks arise and some examples of how assessing cyber risks may apply.

TABLE 7.1 When New, Emerging, or change in risks occur

COSO Statement	Need for Cyber Risk Assessment
Change in business objectives	Digital transformation increases the risk exposure as critical business processes become more dependent on technology and automation.
Change in business context (i.e., changes in consumer preferences lead to the launch of a new product or service.)	New product or service offerings often include new approaches to sales, marketing, operations, and technology that all introduce cyber risk.
New business context	New regulations, such as GDPR or CCPA.
Previously unknown risks	Discovery of new vulnerabilities (or previously unknown assets) that are being exploited by attackers that are directly applicable within your organization's technology environment.
Changes in previously identified risks due to a change in risk appetite, or supporting assumptions	Refer to the beverage company example in Chapter 4. The organization decided to pursue an integrative and diversified growth strategy, in conjunction with cost reduction goals, through the use of new marketing AI and robotic process automation.

It is impossible to identify every possible risk, but it is possible to identify the most likely risks that impact an organization's goal of meeting its objectives. However, paying attention to the items listed in Table 7.1 allows an organization to take a long-term risk approach. It also gives the organization time to assess the potential severity of the risks and develop the necessary treatment plans. For instance, organizations had almost two years from when the General Data Protection Regulation (GDPR) passed the European Parliament until they had to comply.

From a cyber risk perspective, risk identification comprises four primary inputs:

1. Inventory and value of assets
2. Identifying potential threats
3. Identifying successful attack scenarios
4. Evaluating potential consequences

Inventory and Value of Assets

Any risk assessment must first understand your organization's digital and physical assets and their value to the organization. Organizational value always breaks down to dollars and cents, but it is not always easy to translate it to those terms. For instance, risk to revenue may be easy to calculate. If a revenue generating system becomes unavailable, you can assign a value to lost revenue based on prior sales patterns. Assigning a monetary value to the risk to safety or the risk to reputation is much more challenging to accomplish. Cyber risk management is not always about protecting intellectual property and an organization's revenue. Intellectual property and revenue may be the drivers for industries such as financial services and technology, but in the utility industry, the most significant risk to the organization is likely the risk to the safety of employees who are working within the power plant, water treatment facility, or natural-gas plant. In these environments, a networked system such as a *supervisory control and data acquisition* system (SCADA) is connected to the organization's network and can control physical processes such as a valve controlling flow and pressure.

Officially, a *business impact analysis* (BIA) allows you to accomplish the goal of understanding the importance of assets to your organization. The BIA assesses the amount the organization stands to lose when there is business disruption. The BIA assumes worst-case scenarios and involves understanding the type and rate of expected loss under fixed conditions. BIA is used to recognize the magnitude of financial and operational impacts derived from disruptions, failed legal compliance, or failed regulatory compliance. The BIA should produce the following:

- Impact types and criteria relevant to the organization
- Activities that support the provision of products and services
- Assessment of the impacts over time resulting from the disruption of these activities by using the impact types and criteria identified above
- The time frame within which the impacts of not resuming activities would become unacceptable to the organization (maximum tolerable period of disruption)
- Prioritized time frames within the maximum tolerable period of disruption for resuming disrupted activities at a specified minimum acceptable capacity (recovery time objective)
- Prioritized activities based on the analysis above
- Resources that are needed to support prioritized activities
- Dependencies, including partners and suppliers, and interdependencies of prioritized activities

Assessing digital and physical assets' business impact is necessary to differentiate between critical (urgent) and noncritical (nonurgent) services, technologies, or processes. A service, application, or process may be considered critical if the implications resulting from loss or disruption are regarded as unacceptable. For this reason, an organization cannot conduct the BIA in a vacuum. *It must be undertaken and driven by senior management throughout the organization*.

Ironically, determining the criticality of assets is often "the missing link." There are many resources available for determining the criticality of assets, but they largely have to do with the discipline of reliability engineering of physical processes (e.g., a manufacturing plant floor). These models are difficult to adapt to information assets, but NIST published "NISTIR 8179 Criticality Analysis Process Model: Prioritizing Systems and Components," which specifically addresses analyzing the criticality of information assets. The goal of the model is to provide a structured method of prioritizing programs, systems, and components based on their importance to the organization's mission and the risk that their ineffective or unsatisfactory operation or loss may present to the mission. The model is structured to logically follow how organizations typically design and implement projects and systems and can be adapted to fit organizations' unique practices.

The Model consists of five main processes:[5]

1. Define Criticality Analysis Procedure(s) where the organization develops or adopts a set of procedures for performing a criticality analysis.
2. Conduct Program-Level Criticality Analysis where the program manager defines, reviews, and analyzes the program to identify key activities that are vital to reaching the objectives of the program and for reaching the overall goals of the organization.
3. Conduct System/Subsystem-Level Criticality Analysis where the system designer reviews and analyzes the system or subsystem from the point of view of its criticality to the overall organizational goals.
4. Conduct Component/Subcomponent-Level Criticality Analysis where the system or component engineer reviews and analyzes component or subcomponent from the point of view of its criticality to a specific system or subsystem of which these components and subcomponents are a part.
5. Conduct Detailed Review of Criticality for Processes B, C, and D where the program manager or a collaborative group analyzes baseline criticality analysis results to create final criticality levels for Systems/Subsystems and Components/Subcomponents.

The workflows for the above processes can be found at www. CISOEvolution.com.

There are many resources available for conducting a complete BIA, of which determining asset criticality is a crucial part. Some resources include ISO 22301: Societal security – Business continuity management systems – Requirements and NIST Special Publication 800-34r1: Contingency Planning Guide for Federal Information Systems. There is an example of a completed BIA at www.CISOEvolution.com.

IDENTIFYING POTENTIAL THREATS

Per NIST, a threat is "any circumstance or event with the potential to adversely impact organizational operations (including mission, functions, image, or reputation), organizational assets, or individuals through an information system via unauthorized access, destruction, disclosure, modification of information, and/or denial of service. Also, the potential for a threat-source to successfully exploit a particular information system vulnerability."[6]

If we peel that back a little, we can break this down into two parts. The first and obvious part is that a threat needs to have the ability to harm the organization. The second is that a threat also needs to consider the likelihood that it can exploit a vulnerability. If we reference the risk equation from earlier in the chapter, a threat with zero likelihood of exploiting a vulnerability equates to zero risk.

As mentioned above, threats exploit vulnerabilities. Vulnerabilities can come in the forms of software bugs, flaws in system logic, missing patches, or misconfigurations. Many organizations use automated scanning tools to identify these vulnerabilities, but these only address known vulnerabilities in hardware and software. Cybersecurity goes beyond that. Vulnerabilities may exist in other areas such as business continuity, training, utilities, supply chain, and physical access.

There are numerous sources of available cyber threat information, ranging from paid subscriptions to free sources, such as the Cybersecurity and Infrastructure Agency (CISA). Several threat modeling techniques are available for analyzing these threats. These techniques focus on two approaches: top-down and bottom-up. A top-down approach is an asset view that evaluates critical assets for what could potentially go wrong. A bottom-up approach is a threat view that assesses the potential impact of a given set of defined threat scenarios. Some examples of each type of approach are:

- **Software Engineering Institute (SEI) Operationally Critical Threat, Asset, and Vulnerability Evaluation (OCTAVE®) (top-down):** Helps organizations tie together assets that are critical to achieving organizational objectives. The threats to those assets and the vulnerabilities those threats may exploit.
- **Microsoft STRIDE (bottom-up):** STRIDE stands for Spoofing, Tampering, Repudiation, Information Disclosure, Denial of Service, and Escalation.
- **MITRE's ATT&CK™ (bottom-up):** A globally accessible knowledge base of adversary tactics and techniques based on real-world observations.

An example STRIDE threat model can be found at https://www.logicworks.com/blog/2020/02/security-risks-in-public-cloud/. However, no matter which method you use, it is vital to consider them in the context of the threat actors (e.g., script kiddies versus nation-states) and their impact as the result of their actions.

Identifying Potential Attack Scenarios

Now that we understand how to identify threats, we need to determine how they can exploit our environment's weaknesses. Again, a threat cannot become a risk unless there is a weakness that the threat can exploit. That is where our traditional understanding of vulnerabilities come in. As we mentioned earlier, vulnerabilities may exist in areas such as business continuity, training, utilities, supply chain, and physical access, so it is essential to understand vulnerabilities across more than just the traditional Common Vulnerabilities and Exposures (CVEs) that an automated scanner can identify. On the flipside, a vulnerability is not a risk unless a threat is willing to exploit it.

Here is another example of why understanding business context is essential. Attack scenarios will differ for your type and size of organization. A Fintech startup will have vastly differing attack scenarios than a nuclear power plant. Take the time to identify the attack scenarios that attackers are most likely to use in your environment.

You can use many methods to identify attack scenarios for your organization, but our preferred method is to directly look at the organization. No data is more relevant than looking at yourself in the mirror. The three primary approaches to do so are penetration testing, red teaming, and threat hunting. No matter which method you use, the Mitre ATT&CK™ framework (https://attack.mitre.org) is a great resource for identifying attack scenarios for many environments, including on-premise enterprise, cloud, and industrial control systems. Figure 7.1 highlights the similarities and differences between each.

A penetration test (pentest) "is an authorized simulated cyberattack on a computer system, performed to evaluate the security of the

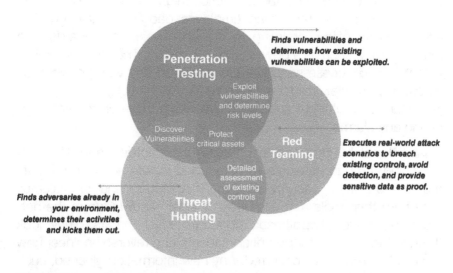

FIGURE 7.1 Penetration Testing, Red Teaming, and Threat Hunting Overlap

system."[7] A penetration test aims to find and exploit as many vulnerabilities as possible that can lead to a compromise. Of the three approaches we describe, this is more of a "spray and pray" approach vs. a more targeted approach. Pentests typically only focus on compromising a vulnerable application or service to gain access to the network. A goal is usually defined, but the pentest team is generally not concerned with remaining hidden. This approach is akin to a burglar testing all of the windows and doors to a home in broad daylight. The organization's security operations team may or may not know the pentest is occurring, so security defenses and controls can be tested, to an extent.

A red team assessment "is similar to a penetration test in many ways but is more targeted."[8] This assessment aims not to find as many vulnerabilities as possible but to test the organization's detection and response capabilities. A red team not only evaluates technology, but it evaluates people and processes, as well. Instead of merely scanning the external network for vulnerabilities and trying to exploit a vulnerable service to gain access to the network, a red team will use a combination of external attacks. Tactics might include a social engineering phone call, replicating employee badges to gain physical access to an office, or trying to breach physical safeguards at a remote facility, such as a power utility substation. The red team will try to get in and access sensitive information in any way possible, as quietly as possible. A red team is more akin to the burglar trying to get into your home at night and doing everything they can to avoid triggering any alarms.

Finally, threat hunting "is the process of proactively and iteratively searching through networks to detect and isolate advanced threats that evade existing security solutions."[9] A security analyst evaluates data from their tools and uses their "insider" knowledge of the network to develop hypotheses about potential threats. They look through the network for potential incidents and reverse engineer how the incident may have occurred. Any new information gleaned, such as indicators of compromise (IOC) or tactics, techniques, and procedures (TTP), is fed back into the organization's capability to prepare or mitigate risks. Threat hunting is an internal effort that is iterative.

EVALUATING POTENTIAL CONSEQUENCES

Now that we understand the potential threats and attack scenarios, we need to evaluate the potential consequences the threats and attacks, or incident scenarios, may have on our identified assets.

A consequence can be loss of effectiveness, adverse operating conditions, loss of business, reputation, damage, etc. that our identified incident scenarios may have on our organization.[10]

The impact of the incident scenarios must consider our business context (refer to Chapter 6 – Cybersecurity: A Concern of the Business, Not Just IT Through the BIA), assets should have assigned values based on their financial cost and business consequences if they are damaged or compromised.

Some consequences to factor in are:

- Health and safety (particularly in operational technology environments)
- Investigation and repair time
- Work time lost
- Opportunity cost
- Costs to bring in outside help for remediation activities
- Image reputation and goodwill

Assesses Severity of Risk

Use the lessons learned from identifying risk to inform the risk register and risk treatment plans (see www.CISOEvolution.com). Once risks are documented in the risk register, it is now time to assess the severity of each risk's potential to disrupt the organization's ability to meet its business objectives and strategic goals. A *risk register* is an inventory of identified risks. A risk register is used to track risk exposure (including likelihood and impact), risk owners, risk treatment decisions, action plans, and residual risk. *Residual risk* is the amount of risk that is left over after the risk treatment is applied. Risk registers can be as simple as a basic spreadsheet, or be incorporated into more complex governance, risk, and compliance software to create and track risk management controls and workflows.

Management cannot address or mitigate all risks due to constraints such as budget and resources; therefore, management decides on how to allocate resources to a given risk based on the assessment of the risk to ensure that the residual risk remains within the organization's risk appetite (see Chapter 6 – Cybersecurity: A Concern of the Business, Not Just IT).

Methods for assessing risk fall into two buckets:

1. **Qualitative:** Qualitative analysis is subjective. You will often see risk scales described as low, medium, or high. Information from international standards, industry best-practices, or prior risk assessments is used to inform a qualitative analysis. Qualitative analysis is helpful when there is not much quantitative data available or intangible risks, and benefits need to be considered. Qualitative analysis techniques include risk factor analysis, the Delphi technique, and SWOT analysis (strengths, weaknesses, opportunities, and threats).
2. **Quantitative:** Quantitative analysis is objective. Numeric data, such as annualized loss expectancy (ALE) and probability, are used to assign impact and likelihood of a risk being realized. The quality of the analysis is only as good as the data that goes into it. The most well-known quantitative analysis technique applied to cybersecurity is Open FAIR™.

Do not pigeon hole yourself into one of these two camps. There is room in our lives for both (much like the *Star Wars* vs. *Star Trek* debate – just stop it). I have witnessed CISOs fail because they only used qualitative analysis with no hard data backing their assessment of risk severity. I have also witnessed CISOs fail because they only used quantitative analysis without considering any qualitative factors, such as an organization's commitment to sustainability or rolling out a new product or service on-time. A complete and defensible risk analysis depends on both qualitative and quantitative considerations.

Both methods have a likelihood and impact component. Likelihood is the probability that a risk will occur. It may be expressed as a set of probabilities assigned to a set of possibilities, "There is a 20% chance that we will experience a data breach in the next five years" (quantitative), or as a scale, "low, medium, high" (qualitative). Impact is usually described as a set of possibilities each with a probability and dollar value (quantitative), "We believe there is a 10% chance that a data breach will result in a legal liability exceeding $10 million," or as a scale (qualitative).[11] Many considerations go into impact, such as the server's criticality, the timing of the risk event (e.g., at the end of a quarter for a financial system), or system redundancy.

Some techniques for estimating the likelihood that a risk will occur include:[12]

- **Decomposition:** A model that breaks large, ambiguous problems into smaller, more digestible subproblems.
- **Bayesian Analysis:** A model that improves upon a prior probability as more evidence or information becomes available. In other words, how we update prior likelihoods with new information.
- **Monte-Carlo:** A simulation model that uses a computer to generate many scenarios based on probabilities for inputs. For each scenario, a specific value is randomly generated for each of the unknown variables, and then the model would generate an output based on these variables. The process is iterative and can go through thousands of rounds.

Tracking risks and their potential consequences in a risk register enables you to integrate these risks in an ERM program more efficiently. Remember, when evaluating the likelihood and impact of risks, it is not only about the controls your organization is missing. You must also consider existing security controls. Do they compensate for the risk? If so, how much? Once a treatment plan for the risk is determined, make sure also to document the residual risk. Be sure to use the same method to calculate residual risk as you did for the original risk to make sure you are comparing apples-to-apples.

Prioritizes Risk

Now that cyber risks have been identified and documented in the risk register, your organization must go about the critical task of prioritizing risks. Again, all risks cannot be fully addressed all the time. That would not be an efficient allocation of capital and resources.

Does the exposure of the cyber risk fall within your organization's risk appetite and risk tolerance? If so, chances are your organization will accept the risk. If the cyber risk falls outside of your organization's risk appetite and risk tolerance, then a decision needs to be made to respond to, or treat, the risk. Suppose the cyber risk is likely to impact the organization's ability to accomplish its strategic goals. In that case, the risk is escalated up to the ERM team to be incorporated in the enterprise risk register in order to be evaluated and prioritized alongside other enterprise risks.

Each organization's ERM team will use different factors to prioritize risk, but these factors will include:

- A determination of overall risk exposure based on impact and likelihood
- A cost/benefit analysis of implementing a given risk response (don't spend a dollar to save a dime)

Given the above, be mindful of biases. Individuals tend to be overconfident in their estimates. Consider "calibration training" to improve subjective estimates.[13]

You have likely seen a version of a likelihood and impact matrix to determine overall risk exposure, as depicted in Table 7.2.

The formula for calculating risk exposure is:

Risk Exposure = Impact x Likelihood

Impact is calculated through the BIA process mentioned earlier in this chapter, and likelihood is the probability that the risk will happen. Table 7.3 shows an example of how I frequently see impact, likelihood, and risk exposure placed into their scales.

TABLE 7.2 Likelihood and Impact Matrix

Likelihood	Impact				
	Very Low	**Low**	**Moderate**	**High**	**Very High**
Very High	Very Low	Low	Moderate	High	Very High
High	Very Low	Low	Moderate	High	Very High
Moderate	Very Low	Low	Moderate	Moderate	High
Low	Very Low	Low	Low	Low	Moderate
Very Low	Very Low	Very Low	Very Low	Low	Low

Source: Ross, R. S., Guide for Conducting Risk Assessments. Special Publication (NIST SP) – 800-30 Rev 1, September 2012, 95. https://doi.org/10.6028/NIST .SP.800-30r1.

It is important to note three things:

1. The monetary values are specific for each organization and are usually set by the board's risk committee or by the executive leadership team at a smaller organization.
2. The likelihood scales may shift according to the organization's risk appetite and may look like a bell curve where most of the range will fall in the "moderate" category.
3. A specific metric often qualifies the impact (e.g. $5 million negative impact to EBITDA, or $2.5 million total cost to recover from the risk event).

TABLE 7.3 Impact, Likelihood, and Risk Exposure Scale

Scale	Impact	Likelihood	Risk Exposure
Very High	> $5M	> 0.8	> $4M
High	$2.5M to $5M	0.6 – 0.8	$1.5M – $4M
Moderate	$1M to $2.5M	0.4 to 0.6	$400K – $1.5M
Low	$500K to $1M	0.2 to 0.4	$100K – $400K
Very Low	< $500K	< 0.2	< $100K

Work with your ERM team to determine the thresholds of your measurement scales, and to ensure they prioritize cyber risks at the business unit level and the enterprise level using the same methodology. The scales may change at the unit level, but the same methodology should always apply.

Calculating risk exposure allows the organization to prioritize risks accordingly. The simplest form is to rank the risks from the highest risk exposure to the lowest. The organization may take other internal and external factors into account, such as regulations, sustainability commitments, and additional corporate social responsibility.

Finally, speaking the same language of risk across the organization and ensuring your cybersecurity team follows suit has four primary benefits:

1. Creates a risk taxonomy across the organization.
2. Enables an aggregated and prioritized enterprise risk register that informs executives and the board of critical risks.
3. Facilitates the cost/benefit analysis of implementing risk responses.
4. Elevates the cybersecurity team's profile within the organization by demonstrating an understanding of cybersecurity's position within the enterprise's entire risk profile.

Implements Risk Responses

After prioritizing the risks, the organization must evaluate and implement treatment for each risk. The organization will strive to ensure that a risk is within its risk appetite and risk tolerance in the most cost-effective way. In other words, the objective in deciding the amount of investment to treat risk is mostly the same as all other organizational investments: to maximize the return on investment (see Chapter 2 – Business Strategy Tools, the section on Measure Business Performance Relative to Risk). A cost/benefit analysis is usually done on various risk treatment options to determine an optimal and effective solution.

The same should be done within individual business units, and in your case, likely the cybersecurity team. The ERM team will likely lean on you to help identify cost-effective yet impactful solutions to treat a risk. This risk treatment not only includes cyber risk, but it will probably include technology risk, in general. More and more, cybersecurity teams are also involved in privacy conversations (have you had your daily dose of GDPR or HIPAA today?). These conversations are yet another opportunity to elevate the cybersecurity team's role within the business. Too often, we, as cybersecurity professionals, love purchasing the shiny new toy without understanding the full context of the risk the toy intends to treat. For example, do you really need the Lamborghini of that bleeding-edge Identity and Access Management (IAM) solution, or will the Honda suffice? Is your organization even ready to invest in a full IAM solution, or does it have to do some data cleanup and implement some foundational processes and standardized workflows first?

There are generally four types of risk responses an organization can take:

1. **Avoid:** Change the strategy to avoid the risk. Avoiding risk is usually considered when there is no cost-effective method for reducing the cybersecurity risk to an acceptable level as defined by the unit's or the organization's risk acceptance and tolerance.
2. **Mitigate:** Apply risk treatment that reduces the threats, vulnerabilities, likelihood, or impact of a given risk so that the residual risk is within the unit's or the organization's risk acceptance and tolerance.
3. **Transfer:** Most organizations consider sharing a part of the risk with another organization in two main scenarios:
   - The organization does not have full control over the implementation of security controls, such as an Infrastructure as a Service or a Software as a Service provider.
   - The organization wants to minimize the financial consequences of a risk, such as in the case of purchasing cyber insurance.
4. **Accept:** Accept the risk as-is because the risk falls within the unit's or the organization's risk acceptance and tolerance but continue to monitor the risk if the risk falls outside of approved tolerance.

There are a variety of security controls that can be applied when deciding to mitigate a risk. A good inventory and taxonomy of controls can be found in standards NIST SP 800-53 (free) and ISO/IEC 27002:2013 (licensed). The controls accomplish one of the following goals:

- **Prevent:** Reduce the likelihood of an incident by mitigating a vulnerability.
- **Deter:** Reduce the threat by discouraging a threat actor from acting upon a vulnerability.
- **Detect:** Identify when an incident is occurring or has occurred.
- **Correct:** Applied after an incident to reduce the likelihood of a similar incident occurring again.
- **Compensate:** Apply one or more controls instead of a primary control because the primary control is not feasible due to technical, resource, or cost constraints.

Once a determination is made of the risk treatment and security controls, the organization should develop a corrective action plan. A *corrective action plan* is a step-by-step plan of action with defined milestones that risk owners will follow to treat the risk. If the risk register represents the "what," a corrective action plan represents the "how and when." Not every risk requires a corrective action plan. There is no reason to write a corrective action plan for an accepted risk. Some companies only write corrective action plans for risks that are deemed "high" or "very high." The development and use of corrective action plans should be part of the organization's risk management strategy and standardized across the organization, but this requires buy-in as it will inevitably generate work for other teams. Get this buy-in by identifying how work is surfaced in other teams' workstreams. If the only projects that get attention are those that get talked about in a weekly scrum meeting, then make sure your initiatives are included there. A completed corrective action plan can be located at www.CISOEvolution.com.

Develops Portfolio View

A portfolio view allows management and the board to consider the type, severity, and interdependencies of risks and how they may affect performance. Using the portfolio view, the organization identifies severe risks at the organizational and business unit level. These may include risks that arise at the organizational level and transactional, processing-type risks that could disrupt the organization as a whole.[14]

Business unit risk registers need to be aggregated and normalized into an enterprise risk register to align enterprise risk. Then risks can be evaluated and prioritized across business units into an enterprise risk profile. It is important to remember that there are other risk inputs across the organization than cybersecurity. Assessing cyber risks alongside other risk inputs and overall business objectives enables a proactive and mission-oriented view of risk and allows effective risk decisions by company leadership. Figure 7.2 depicts a process by which risk decisions and decision flows at each level of an organization roll up into an enterprise portfolio view of risk.

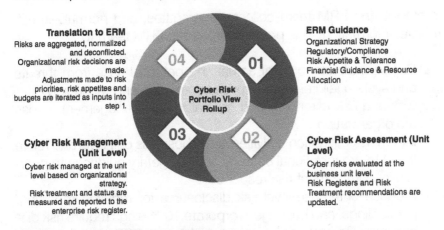

Translation to ERM
Risks are aggregated, normalized and deconflicted.
Organizational risk decisions are made.
Adjustments made to risk priorities, risk appetites and budgets are iterated as inputs into step 1.

ERM Guidance
Organizational Strategy
Regulatory/Compliance
Risk Appetite & Tolerance
Financial Guidance & Resource Allocation

Cyber Risk Management (Unit Level)
Cyber risk managed at the unit level based on organizational strategy.
Risk treatment and status are measured and reported to the enterprise risk register.

Cyber Risk Assessment (Unit Level)
Cyber risks evaluated at the business unit level.
Risk Registers and Risk Treatment recommendations are updated.

04 01
03 02

Cyber Risk Portfolio View Rollup

FIGURE 7.2 Cyber Risk Portfolio View Rollup

Step 1, ERM Guidance, involves risk direction from the top of the organization. Corporate boards and executive leadership teams consider the relative importance of various external and internal factors alongside its strategy and business context, as discussed throughout this and the previous chapter. Organizational leaders can use these factors to determine risk acceptance levels and balance resource allocations for risk treatment across the organization. Operational leaders pass down the resulting resource and financial guidance to the business unit level.

In step 2, cyber risk assessments are conducted at the business unit level. Understanding the guidance from step 1 allows cybersecurity teams to help operational managers frame, assess, manage, respond to, and report cyber risks within the business unit and in alignment with organizational strategy. Security controls can then be selected for the desired cybersecurity risk treatment outcomes to ensure cyber risk is operating within the approved risk appetite and risk tolerance.

In step 3, risk treatment and monitoring results are reported to organization stakeholders. The risk determinations, decisions, and status are conveyed through the enterprise risk register and adjusted as necessary.

In step 4, the ERM team collects, aggregates, and normalizes risk register information. This process allows the ERM team to:

- Report understanding of actual and potential risks from threats and system failures to enterprise information and technology.
- Create a risk taxonomy and normalize risk management across the organization.
- Inform risk mitigation activities at the business unit level and relate these to organizational strategy and budgetary guidance to prioritize and implement risk responses.
- Produce enterprise-level risk disclosures for required reporting, public filings, and hearings. Corporate 10-K filings require risk disclosures. Regulations, such as HIPAA and CCPA, have defined reporting requirements in the event of a data breach. Major security incidents, such as the one that affected Equifax and its customers, have led to Congressional subpoenas and testimonies.

Adjustments made to risk priorities, risk appetites, and budgets are iterated as inputs back into step 1.

Review and Revision

After a football game, a football team will review its game film and performance and make any adjustments they need to ensure success before their next game. A cybersecurity team must do the same for all of its processes, but especially for risk management. An organization reassesses its ERM program over time as its business objectives change. In conjunction with a constantly evolving technology and threat landscape, this reassessing requires cybersecurity teams to reassess and revise their risk management practices continuously. This includes removing security controls, if necessary (the horror). Our experience suggests that it's rare to see security teams remove controls – even when they become outdated. Signature-based detection, anyone?

Managing enterprise risk is a balancing act between organizational strategy, the costs and impacts of a risk, and its benefits. As an input into ERM, cybersecurity risk must be continuously monitored to help organizations evaluate the right formula to maintain the optimal mix of strategy/cost/benefit. Continually reassessing cyber risk management practices ensures cybersecurity teams remain aligned to organizational objectives and can continue to identify and manage risks associated with new threats and vulnerabilities. Our challenge as cybersecurity leaders is to do this faster and more efficiently to keep up with the pace of innovation and digital transformation throughout our organizations. The three COSO principles for Review and Revision are:[15]

1. Assesses Substantial Change
2. Reviews Risk and Performance
3. Pursues Improvement in Enterprise Risk Management

Assesses Substantial Change

The cybersecurity threat landscape is constantly changing; therefore, cybersecurity risks need to be continuously monitored to ensure they remain within the organization's risk acceptance and tolerance. Stay aware of the changing cybersecurity risk landscape through sources such as subscriptions to free community alerts. Some examples include:

- CISA Automated Indicator Sharing (https://www.cisa.gov/automated-indicator-sharing-ais)
- InfraGard (https://www.infragard.org/)
- SANS Internet Storm Center (https://isc.sans.edu/)
- National Council of ISACS: Member ISACS (https://www.national-alisacs.org/member-isacs)

By establishing a methodology to monitor risk continuously, a new risk assessment, or at a minimum, the review of an individual risk, can be triggered to determine if risk priorities have changed. Keep in mind that it is also important to monitor risks that were previously accepted. This measurement is done using *key risk indicators*, which we will review in the next section (Reviews Risk and Performance). Continuous risk measurement also helps drive a strong security culture throughout the organization.

Why would you continuously monitor risk if there were no assigned accountabilities for risk throughout the organization? Of course, you wouldn't. It would be foolish to waste time and resources if there were no accountability for actually doing anything about the newly identified or reprioritized risks. Doing a one-time risk assessment or an annual risk assessment provides a snapshot of your organization's cyber risk profile. It is easy to get buy-in once a year to "get things fixed." It is much harder to get buy-in to respond to risk throughout the year continuously. This buy-in is another reason why the cybersecurity steering committee, described in Chapter 6, is so essential to establish. The roles and responsibilities for managing and responding to risk can be assigned and communicated at that level with buy-in across all key business units.

The cybersecurity steering committee can discuss necessary resource changes, or schedule changes, as the result of identifying or re-prioritizing a risk before rolling up to ERM. A plan can be determined, with the risk owner agreeing to key performance indicators

(KPIs) for measuring milestones in the progress of treating the risk. By measuring these KPIs, the organization can measure appropriate strides in treating the risk. When the residual risk falls within an acceptable risk acceptance, the resources used in treating that risk can be released and shifted with the focus now moving towards maintenance and measurement.

Reviews Risk and Performance

Key risk indicators (KRIs) are the tactical application of a risk appetite statement.[16] They are used to provide an early indication that a risk is increasing and approaching a risk tolerance threshold.

Many organizations focus heavily on KPIs rather than KRIs. Recall from Chapter 2 – Business Strategy Tools, often KPIs are lagging indicators, KRIs are leading indicators, so in reality, they need to be considered in conjunction and complement each other. An example of a KPI can be "100% of crown jewel critical patch deployments within SLA." If only the KPI is reported, ERM may interpret that risk from vulnerabilities being exploited is reduced by 100%. That is, clearly, a false notion. This metric does not measure actual risk reduction. However, linking a KRI to a KPI, as suggested by the McKinsey & Company whitepaper "The Risk-based Approach to Cybersecurity,"[17] provides ERM with a better picture of risk and risk reduction. In our example, the "crown jewel" assets identified by ERM can be the KRI, and tying the KPI to the percentage of "crown jewel" assets covered will give ERM and executives a better view of how risk is trending towards, or away, from, risk tolerances.

Developing and choosing KRIs requires a solid understanding of organizational goals and risks that impact the achievement of those goals. A useful set of KRIs pinpoint appropriate metrics that call out potential risks that may affect the organization's ability to achieve its goals. There must be a connection of risks to strategic initiatives so that the KRIs capture the most relevant information that can inform you, ERM, and executive leadership when a risk may exceed the organization's risk tolerance. Figure 7.3 highlights the linking of organizational goals to strategies to risks to KRIs.

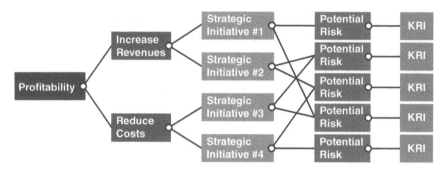

FIGURE 7.3 Linking Objectives to Strategies to Risk to KRIs

Measure both inputs and outputs of the risk processes. The inputs in this case are risk-reduction efforts (e.g., updating antivirus signatures – the KPI). The output is the actual reduction in enterprise risk (e.g., reducing the risk that critical systems will be taken offline or that there will be a data breach due to malware – the KRI). The thresholds set for KRIs and KPIs should be aligned to risk tolerance. One way to think about KRIs and KPIs is to think about the relationship between altitude and trajectory. The McKinsey paper gives a great example of the relationship between KRIs and KPIs:

> A KRI gives the current risk level of the enterprise (the "risk altitude") while the KPI indicates the direction toward or away from the enterprise-risk-appetite level ("risk trajectory"). An enterprise may not yet have arrived at the leadership's KRI target but a strong KPI trajectory would suggest that it will soon. Conversely, an enterprise may have hit the desired KRI threshold, but the KPIs of the run activity may be backsliding and give cause for concern.[17]

When creating KRIs, keep the following tips in mind:

- Link KRIs to specific risk scenarios.
- Ensure they are complete, accurate, and specific.
- Do not have too many KRIs. Select a handful that are specific and applicable for your organization.
- Measuring KRIs is challenging. Ensure you have the appropriate measurement mechanisms in place for the KRIs you develop.
- Aggregate, compare, and systematically interpret KRIs at an enterprise level.

Table 7.4 outlines how organizations can link KRIs, KPIs, and potential business impacts.

TABLE 7.4 Linking KRIs with KPIs Source

KPI (Input)	KRI (Output)	Implication/Business Impact
Number of identified regulations, policy, or process violations	Percentage of incidents involving customer personal data	This indicates a failure to meet compliance obligations and might lead to scrutiny from regulators or media, which can adversely impact the reputation of the organization.
Number of security-related service downtimes	Number of services canceled or delayed as a result of security-related service downtimes	Security incidents impacting critical systems potentially cause service interruption or degradation.
Number of business applications/systems not supported by a backup plan	Percentage of business applications/systems not supported by a backup plan	Lack of data backup for business applications/systems leads to data loss and adversely affects service continuity in case of any interruption.
Percentage of nonconformities detected in security tests/audits, but not resolved within the timeframe planned	Number of nonconformities detected in security tests/audits remaining unresolved beyond the planned time frame	Delay in remediating vulnerabilities detected in security tests/audits makes the organization an easy target for malicious attacks.

(Continued)

TABLE 7.4 Linking KRIs with KPIs Source (*continued*)

KPI (Input)	KRI (Output)	Implication/Business Impact
Inadequate third-party management	Number of security incidents attributed to vulnerabilities in third-party systems/employees	The organization's information can be exposed to risk by third parties with inadequate information security management.
Lack of adequate time frame for scheduled downtime of systems	Number of systems without up-to-date patches	Delay in patching the systems makes the organization an easy target for malicious attacks.
Lack of review of risk management processes	Lack of effective reporting of key risk	In the absence of a review of risk management processes, these processes might continue to be ineffective, resulting in nonidentification of vulnerabilities/risk.

Source: Tammineedi, R.L.S., "Integrating KRIs and KPIs for effective technology risk management," *ISACA Journal 4* (2018): 19–23. All rights reserved. Used with Perimission.

Linking KRIs and KPIs helps bring clarity to the fog of complex and conflicting metrics. Doing so elevates the cybersecurity team's profile by showing that it can engage executives in substantial conversations around which cyber risks are within tolerances, which are not, and why.

Pursues Improvement in Enterprise Risk Management

A robust cybersecurity risk management program must strive for continuous process improvement that reinforces effective processes, identifies ineffective processes, and adjusts accordingly. While all should be responsible and held accountable for any negligent activity, there is value in fostering a community that pursues opportunities within risk appetite levels while also being prepared for and continually thwarting threat actors that would exploit vulnerabilities.

Six Sigma is a recognized process improvement standard in the manufacturing world. Jack Welch, former chairman and CEO of General Electric, is one of the world's most renowned business leaders. He defines Six Sigma as "a quality program that, when all is said and done, improves your customer's experience, lowers your costs, and

builds better leaders." Six Sigma is a data-driven discipline that eliminates defects in any process to improve quality and profitability.[19] We
are not advocating that you run out and get a Six Sigma blackbelt;
however, there are approaches in Six Sigma that can be applied to
improve cybersecurity and cybersecurity risk management, particularly DMAIC (Define, Measure, Analyze, Improve, Control). Villanova
University does a good job at describing each phase of DMAIC, but
we have molded it to fit a cybersecurity project intended to reduce
risk around an immature vulnerability management program.[20]

- **Define:** The main objective of this stage is to outline the borders
  of the project:
  - Stakeholders agree on the parameters that will define maturing
    the vulnerability management program.
  - Scope and budgetary items, as well as organizational goals,
    are aligned with project goals.
  - Team development takes place as the project begins to
    take shape.
- **Measure:** The main objective is to collect data pertinent to the
  scope of the project:
  - Project leaders collect reliable baseline data on the vulnerabil-
    ity management program to compare against future results to
    measure improvement.
    - A vulnerability assessment solution is in place, and scans
      are ad-hoc.
    - System patching is inconsistent.
    - Basic processes.
    - No metrics.
  - Teams create a detailed map of all interrelated business pro-
    cesses to clarify areas of possible improvement.
    - Outline critical systems and data flows.
- **Analyze:** The main objective is to reveal the root cause of pro-
  cess inefficiencies:
  - Analysis of data reveals areas where the implementation of
    change can provide the most effective results.
    - Scheduled vulnerability scanning.
    - Scan-to-patch life cycle.
    - Patching priority is driven by system and vulnerability criticality.
  - Groups discuss ways that the data underscores areas ripe for
    improvement.

- **Improve:** At the end of this stage, the main objective is to complete a test run of a change before it is widely implemented:
  - Teams and stakeholders devise methods to address the process deficiencies uncovered during the data analysis process.
    - Scan-to-patch service level agreements.
    - Allowable windows to scan and patch.
    - Allowable downtime for patching.
    - If downtime is not feasible (e.g., a highly active eCommerce website), develop redundancy for the systems mapped out in the "Measure" phase.
  - Groups finalize and test a change aimed at mitigating the ineffective process.
  - Improvements are ongoing and include feedback analysis and stakeholder participation.
- **Control:** The last stage of the methodology's objective is to develop metrics that help leaders monitor and document continued success:
  - Develop KPIs and KRIs (see Table 7.4).
  - Adjustments and implement new changes as a result of the completion of this first cycle of the process.

DMAIC is an iterative process. Once the improvements are in place, the process owner monitors the KPIs and KRIs and repeats this method as needed to ensure the process is operating efficiently. The ability to improve managing cybersecurity risk supports broad organizational goals as part of ERM.

Information, Communication, and Reporting

The twenty-first century has welcomed exponential growth in technology that has led to a deluge of data. Businesses can use that data to make better and faster business decisions. The volume and velocity of data challenge some organizations and may cause "paralysis-by-analysis."

This data describes stakeholders, products, markets, and competitor actions. Now, we must harness the promise of business intelligence and digital transformation to enrich business decisions with in a risk context. We must prepare to utilize the same data and techniques to help identify risks that could affect business performance. For example, cybersecurity incidents can impact this data's integrity and reliability, eroding the value of an investment intended to give an edge. The impact can be especially damaging if the incident is not detected and resolved quickly.

The three COSO principles for Information, Communication, and Reporting are:[21]

1. Leverages Information and Technology
2. Communicates Risk Information
3. Reports on Risk, Culture, and Performance

Leverages Information and Technology

As mentioned above, organizations leverage data to make better and faster business decisions. Threats, such as ransomware, have become prevalent over the past several years and have significantly impacted an organization's critical data availability and reliability. Threats like ransomware not only have internal repercussions, but also, if customer data is exposed or revenue generating services are taken offline, may result in significant reputational impact or noncompliance (e.g., HIPAA, CCPA, NERC CIP). Organizations may also use internal information systems for critical financial reporting and decision-making support.

Recovering from ransomware, or any cybersecurity incident, for that matter, can be extremely expensive; however, since ransomware has become so prevalent, we will focus on some statistics that should drive the point home:

- Cybersecurity Ventures predicts that a business will fall victim to a ransomware attack every 14 seconds in 2019 and every 11 seconds by 2021.[22]
- The NotPetya ransomware cost FedEx $300 million in Q1 2017.[23]
- The City of Atlanta, Georgia, was affected by the SamSam ransomware in March 2018. The city did not pay out the ransom, but recovery costs are estimated at $17 million.[24]

■ Norsk Hydro was attacked in March 2019 that forced it to fall back to manual processes. The company did not pay out the ransom, but it is estimated that the attack could cost the company up to $75 million in the first half of 2019.[25]

These threats may also impact internal tools used to aid in cyber risk management and reporting, such as governance, risk, and compliance (GRC) systems that track and report risks using automated workflows. SIEMs and SOAR platforms can act on the big data that security tooling generates to facilitate alerting, reporting, and response to security events. Take particular care in protecting the integrity of these systems. Otherwise, a cascading effect may leave executive leadership blind to material threats and risks facing the organization.

Communicates Risk Information

An organization must emphasize its capability to communicate items that can affect cyber risk to internal and external partners. This facilitates the organization's ability to quickly address emerging threats and prevent or mitigate the impact of a cyber incident. Communication channels are often defined in the organization's general information security policy or its incident response plan. They are designed to notify employees when there is the potential of a cyber incident occurring, when a cyber incident is currently occurring, or when a cyber incident has occurred. Efficient communication provides situational awareness throughout the workforce. Such notifications can range from a warning about a phishing email to an alert for employees to not turn on their computers because there is a wide-spread ransomware incident that is ongoing.

Most of the time, the organization will use email to communicate; however, in the case of a wide-spread ransomware event, employees may be greeted with locked doors and paper notes warning them to avoid turning on their computers. This is exactly what Norsk Hydro employees encountered at their headquarters when they arrived for work on March 19, 2019 (Figure 7.4).

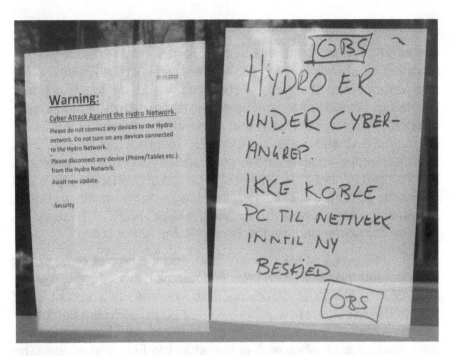

FIGURE 7.4 Notes employees of Norsk Hydro encountered when arriving to work at their HQ in Norway on March 19, 2019

Source: TERJE PEDERSEN / AFP / Getty Images.

The ability to communicate cyber risk concerns with external partners is also vital. Security regulations worldwide have different reporting requirements from HIPAA and CCPA in the United States to GDPR in the European Union. Failure to disclose cyber incidents with appropriate depth, response, and timeliness may result in significant fines from multiple entities. Other external communications include bi-directional communications with third-party service providers, especially when they are hosting critical data and they have encountered a major incident that may put that data at risk. Pre-scripted Public Relations communication plans to support disclosing a major cybersecurity incident to the public are a must.

Reports on Risk, Culture, and Performance

Organizations need to stay abreast of cybersecurity-related regulatory reporting requirements. High profile breaches such as Equifax, Uber, and Verizon, and the privacy concerns raised by the Facebook/Cambridge Analytics scandal, have lawmakers calling for stricter regulations to protect user data and minimize the impact of such incidents. In the United States, as of 2020, Congress has failed to pass any meaningful, comprehensive cybersecurity regulation, so organizations have to contend with a hodge podge of overlapping laws and standards at both the industry and state level. For instance, HIPAA regulates the healthcare industry, and the FERC/NERC CIP standards regulate the power grid (via the Energy Policy Act of 2005).

At the state level, just about every state and the District of Columbia have passed their own data breach notification laws. Finally, there is now GDPR, the legal framework that governs data security and privacy for EU citizens at a global level. Although GDPR is a European-based regulation, every company that collects data from an EU citizen, regardless of whether it is based in the EU, is in scope. The Securities and Exchange Commission has released various regulations and guidance for public organizations. With all of these different laws, regulations, and standards flying around, it is just about impossible for an organization to keep track of them all. Unfortunately, we do not anticipate a consolidation of these laws and regulations soon, so be sure to cozy up with your legal teams to stay in front of it all!

Organizations must implement a process for relevant and timely reporting of pertinent cybersecurity risks at all levels. These levels may include the cybersecurity team, the ERM team, horizontal business units, the executive leadership team, the board of directors, external third parties, and external regulators.

Many crisis communications publications state that crisis communications should contain the "Five W's" (Who, What, When, Where, and Why). Each of the "W's" may not be practical every time. For instance, at the beginning stages of a cyber incident, you may not know exactly "who" is affected, but you want to communicate regardless proactively. The point is to have a communications plan. Having these communications plans in place *before the communication needs to* occur is an important, yet often overlooked, part of an organization's ERM program. Sample communications can be found at www.CISOEvolution.com.

Application

One of my clients services the energy sector. There was a new CIO on-board and mostly new company leadership. The new CIO had three major concerns:

1. Sensitive information leaving the company
2. Inadequately protected industrial control systems
3. Convincing his boss (the CEO) and the board of the risks

After an initial assessment of the situation, we immediately established a cybersecurity steering committee. We developed a charter and had the CEO sign it, which legitimized the steering committee with support from its top executive. It also demonstrated the new leadership's commitment to establishing a strong security culture.

As a result of the CEO's executive endorsement, we swiftly leveraged the CIO's "new guy card" to bring in people from different business units. We were even able to recruit a representative from operations, which was vital to overcome previously fractured organizational collaboration. In this context, the operations team is the team that was responsible for the organization's industrial control systems (ICS). At the first steering committee meeting, we established the NIST Cybersecurity Framework as the foundation of the cybersecurity program. Consequently, we asserted clear expectations for IT, cybersecurity, and the various business units. We expected engagement and input, which we already considered a small victory, given that everyone showed up to the first meeting!

Once we established the ground rules, I launched two efforts in parallel. The first was a security awareness campaign to make people aware of best practices, expectations from a cybersecurity standpoint, and explain the cybersecurity implications in the context of business performance. The second effort was conducting an assessment to benchmark the organization's cybersecurity capabilities. This benchmark was important because it allowed us to eventually establish the measures we would use to track and communicate improvement. Part of this initial benchmarking also included conducting a business impact analysis (BIA) to understand the areas where a cybersecurity incident would have the most significant impact. This process brought clarity to the business units where we should focus our efforts. It also highlighted areas where the organization previously deprioritized for the wrong reasons, including corporate politics. As an unbiased outsider, I was able to elevate this discrepancy to the steering committee and integrate these neglected areas into our efforts.

I then dug into the risk assessment. The organization never completed a cyber risk assessment before now, so I did not have a previous risk inventory upon which to build. My understanding of the industry and the organization's business context allowed me to work with key areas to conduct a threat modeling exercise. The CIO used our initiatives to politically free up some funding for an external red team exercise. This funding was hugely beneficial as the combination of the red team exercise and threat models informed the risk inventory.

After we established the risk inventory, we embarked upon prioritizing the risk based on the resulting risk exposure. Now, we encountered a wrinkle. The organization had never established risk appetite or risk tolerance down to the unit level. There was a general understanding that the organization was not particularly risk averse. Unfortunately, that "gut" feeling did not help us draw the line at which risks to avoid, mitigate, transfer, or accept, so we had to go back to the CEO, who then worked with the board to establish a risk appetite statement with some loose risk tolerances we could use. With these guardrails, we could conduct a cost/benefit analysis to determine the best risk treatment plan for each risk and develop a "right-sized" 24-month roadmap with cybersecurity investment recommendations and associated corrective action plans (CAPs). We then determined the appropriate KRIs and KPIs that we could use to measure the effectiveness of our risk treatment decisions. Eventually we would be able to demonstrate improvements in a measurable way to communicate back to the executive team what they were getting in return for their investment.

We worked with each business unit's representative on the steering committee to frame, assess, and report cyber risk in the context of their unit. We were able to work with the individual business units to normalize cyber risks with their unit-level risks and then report those risks to the higher-level ERM group. Once we did that, the cyber risk trends across the business became apparent, so we were able to work with the ERM group to aggregate and prioritize those risks in the context of the broader enterprise risk register. Before we knew it, we developed a portfolio view of risk for the organization that, for the first time, included cyber risks.

Now, we had to get funding from the board, and we did, for most of the items in the roadmap. Everything is a negotiation, right? Alongside the CIO, we presented our case to the board in terms they could digest – which, by the way, DOES NOT include talking about how the latest zero-day attack can embed itself into the control system firmware to do bad things.

Because we could speak in terms of risk to the business and show that we had the support of every business unit, we received funding and resources to allow the CIO to start executing on the roadmap. It turned out the CIO was right. We were able to demonstrate that, in fact, sensitive information was leaving the organization and that the industrial control systems were inadequately protected. Most importantly, we were able to secure the funding to mitigate both of those risks, among a host of others.

For this organization, we successfully used the COSO framework to enable exponential growth in their cybersecurity capabilities from a people, process, and technology perspective. We were also able to provide a method to measure the effectiveness of cyber risk investments, develop a framework for continuous process improvement, foster better partnerships across IT and other business units, particularly operations, and ingrain a security culture across the organization.

Key Insights

- Understand how and when to trigger the evaluation of risk. The BIA is foundational to a complete evaluation of cyber risk as the valuation of assets and key dependencies are key considerations of the risk assessment.
- Determine the right mix of qualitative and quantitative risk assessment approaches for your organization. Don't get paralyzed by this as you can always add quantitative analysis to a qualitative analysis later. Consider your audience and culture.
  - What does your ERM team already do?
  - Are there opportunities to improve?
  - Do you have the political capital to challenge the status quo?
- Work with your ERM team to prioritize risks but be mindful of biases that may skew your estimates.
- Use the cost-benefit analysis methodology covered in Chapter 5 – Cyber Business Case Development to determine the appropriate risk response, the most cost-effective risk treatment to minimize residual risk, and the appropriate security controls to design and implement to accomplish the desired risk response.
- Work with organizational leadership to get ownership buy-in and accountability for continuous risk management and mitigation.
  - Have small, in-person conversations with potential advocates, explain to them your goals, and work with them to make them feel empowered and part of the process.
  - Score quick wins. What does a minimal viable product look like for continuous risk management within your organization? Is there a specific business-unit, product, or process you can focus on first? Execute your plan successfully to gain broader support.
- Develop KPIs and KRIs that allow you to monitor risks and then leverage the relationships that you build with organizational leadership to communicate those risks with risk owners to ensure risks remain within the organization's acceptable risk appetite.
- Understand your organization's strategic goals and make risks from the risk register that directly impact the ability of your organization to meet those goals.

- Take lessons from well-known process improvement methodologies, such as Six Sigma, to iteratively measure and improve cyber risk management practices.
- Identify how and when to communicate cyber risk information to internal and external stakeholders by understanding cybersecurity regulatory reporting and disclosure requirements for your organization. Develop a tailored crisis communication plan *before* it is needed. Drill your crisis communications plan through designed and scheduled exercises.

Notes

1. World Economic Forum, *The Global Risks Report*, 2019, 1–114. http://wef.ch/risks2019.
2. Ponemom, I., *Cost of a Data Breach Report 2020*, IBM, 2020. https://www.ibm.com/security/digital-assets/cost-data-breach-report/#/pt.
3. Verizon, *2021 Data Breach Investigations Report*, 2021. https://www.verizon.com/business/resources/reports/dbir/.
4. COSO, *Enterprise Risk Management – Integrating with Strategy and Performance*, Committee of Sponsoring Organizations of the Treadway Commission, 2017.
5. Paulson, C., Boyens, J., Bartol, N., and Winkler, K, "NISTIR 8179 Criticality Analysis Process – Model Prioritizing Systems and Components," *NIST Internal Report 8179*, 2018.
6. "Managing Information Security Risk," *NIST Special Publication 800-39*, 2011. https://doi.org/10.1108/k.2011.06740caa.012.
7. "Penetration Test," *Wikipedia*. Accessed October 7, 2020. https://en.wikipedia.org/wiki/Penetration_test.
8. "Red team," *Wikipedia*. Accessed October 7, 2020. https://en.wikipedia.org/wiki/Red_team.
9. "Cyber Threat Hunting," *Wikipedia*. Accessed October 9, 2020. https://en.wikipedia.org/wiki/Cyber_threat_hunting.
10. Sanchez, R., and Enrique, J., *ISO/IEC 27005:2018 Information Technology – Security Techniques – Information Security*, 2018.
11. Hubbard, D.W. and Seiersen, R., *How to Measure Anything in Cybersecurity Risk*, John Wiley & Sons, 2016.

12. Hubbard, D.W. and Seiersen, R., *How to Measure Anything in Cybersecurity Risk*, John Wiley & Sons, 2016.

13. Hubbard, D.W., *Calibrated Probability Assessments: An Introduction*, 2019. http://www.hubbardresearch.com/wp-content/uploads/2019/06/Introduction-to-Calibrating-Probability-Assessments-Hubbard-Decision-Research.pdf.

14. COSO, *Enterprise Risk Management – Integrating with Strategy and Performance*, Committee of Sponsoring Organizations of the Treadway Commission, 2017.

15. COSO, *Enterprise Risk Management – Integrating with Strategy and Performance*, Committee of Sponsoring Organizations of the Treadway Commission, 2017.

16. Bresnahan, E., "Map Your Cyber Risks to Business Outcomes with KRIs," https://www.cybersaint.io/blog/map-your-cyber-risks-to-business-outcomes-with-kris.

17. Boehm, J., Curcio, N., Merrath, P., Shenton, L., and Stähle, T., "The Risk-based Approach to Cybersecurity," *McKinsey Insights*, October 2019. https://www.mckinsey.com/business-functions/risk/our-insights/the-risk-based-approach-to-cybersecurity.

18. Beasley, M.S., Branson, B.C., Hancock, B.V, and Landes, C. (2010), "Developing Key Risk Indicators to Strengthen Enterprise Risk Management," *COSO – Thought Leadership in ERM*, 1–20. papers2://publication/uuid/A17DB7CA-6EC5-4F23-84FE-DB4996794C37.

19. Thomas, J., "The Value of Linking Six Sigma to Your Sales Process – Training Industry," 2017. https://trainingindustry.com/articles/sales/the-value-of-linking-six-sigma-to-your-sales-process/.

20. Villanova University, "What Is DMAIC Methodology and Why Is It Important to Six Sigma?" Accessed October 23, 2020. https://www.villanovau.com/resources/six-sigma/six-sigma-methodology-dmaic/.

21. COSO, *Enterprise Risk Management – Integrating with Strategy and Performance*, Committee of Sponsoring Organizations of the Treadway Commission, 2017.

22. Morgan, S., "Global Cybercrime Damages Predicted to Reach $6 Trillion Annually by 2021," 2017. https://cybersecurityventures.com/cybercrime-damages-6-trillion-by-2021/.

23. Johnson, E.M., "Cyber Attack, Hurricane Weigh on Fedex Quarterly Profit," *Reuters*, 2017. https://www.reuters.com/article/us-fedex-results/cyber-attack-hurricane-weigh-on-fedex-quarterly-profit-idUSKCN1BU2RG.

24. Olenick, D., "Atlanta Ransomware Recovery Cost Now at $17 Million, Reports Say," *SC Media*, 2018. https://www.scmagazine.com/home/security-news/ransomware/atlanta-ransomware-recovery-cost-now-at-17-million-reports-say/.

25. Ashford, W., "Norsk Hydro Cyber Attack Could Cost Up to $75m," 2019. https://www.computerweekly.com/news/252467199/Norsk-Hydro-cyber-attack-could-cost-up-to-75m.

CHAPTER 8

Communication – You Do It Every Day (or Do You?)

The art of communication is the language of leadership.
— James C. Humes

Opportunity

It is far beyond the scope of this book to outline all of the tips and techniques to unlock these benefits or to provide you with a PhD in communications; however, we will review some of the practical concepts that we found, throughout our collective experience, to be the most impactful in a cybersecurity leadership context. Communication skills are as perishable as a golf swing. Use them or lose them, as you will see below.

My parents are Greek immigrants who came to the United States in the 1970s, and they raised my sister and me speaking Greek in our home. I love being bilingual. It has served me very well, from communicating with my parents and family abroad to giving me an advantage in the application and recruiting process of various roles throughout my career. Interestingly, I never needed to use Greek in a professional setting until this year.

My father had a good grasp of English as he was the primary bread-winner for our family and used English every day. My mother, however, was a "stay at home mom" for most of my youth, and as a result she only picked up enough English to understand most of a conversation, but not enough to speak effectively. Ironically, my mother's English was the best during the O.J. Simpson murder trial as she was glued to the TV all day. Shortly after that trial ended, one satellite TV provider started offering a bundle of Greek channels. My parents subscribed, and my mother's English fell off of a cliff, never to return.

On the flipside, since I moved away from the city where my parents live, my Greek has gone downhill because I only use it when I speak with my mother. Today, more than 20 years later, my mother and I communicate through a mix-mashed conversation of "Greenglish," and I am the first to tell you, it is not anywhere near effective. It is unfortunate that, as a result, our phone conversations are usually short and do not have a lot of depth.

It is *my* responsibility to bridge the communications gap. My mother is not bilingual. *I am*. And as a cybersecurity leader, it is *my* responsibility to learn to speak the language of the business instead of the business learning to speak the language of cybersecurity (see Chapter 1 – Financial Principles: The Language of Business).

We communicate every day, so why aren't we connecting with the business? A search for the term "communication" for books on Amazon comes back with over 100,000 results. Searching for "effective communication" narrows down the results to over 16,000. Either way, those numbers are staggering and highlight the importance of communication. Communicating goes well beyond flapping your lips and coherent words coming out of your mouth. Just because you can speak a language does not mean that you can communicate effectively in that language.

The reality is that cybersecurity does not generate revenue in most organizations. As cybersecurity leaders, we are continually battling for visibility and a budget. We have spent this entire century so far pounding our fists and SCREAMING that cybersecurity needs to have a seat at the table. Effective communication is the key to getting that seat. When you scour through many of the popular works in the Amazon search results above, you find many benefits to effective communication in the workplace. The following common themes emerge:

- Forms credibility and trust
- Streamlines the sharing of ideas and problem solving
- Establishes clarity and eliminates confusion
- Promotes employee engagement and teambuilding
- Influences people
- Resolves conflict
- Brings transparency and guidance
- Institutes an understanding of business practices
- Grows career opportunities
- Increases productivity

In this chapter, we will lightly touch upon the elements of communication and point you to several valuable resources that can expand upon the topic if this is an area of growth or focus for you at this stage in your career. Specifically, the sections that follow offer structure to improve communications for the explicit purpose of advancing a cybersecurity program.

Principle

Do you have the courage to listen? Do you have the curiosity to drill down, peel apart, and determine the root cause of the matter at hand? Do you kill them with kindness and are you self-aware enough to understand how your body language makes or breaks a communication? Can you find the "why" and resonate with your audience through the use of stories? Finally, do you create a safe environment for difficult and crucial conversations? We will answer all of these questions throughout this chapter.

Listen

A study that was originally published in 1972 found that we spend up to 80% of our day in some form of communication. The study found that while about 30% of that time was spent speaking, a whopping 45% was spent listening.[1] For those of you doing the math that means that we spend 1.5 times the amount of time listening as we do speaking.

Many, if not most of us, claim to be good listeners. Many, if not most of us, are not. To demonstrate, allow us to walk you through an exercise. Imagine working with a software development manager. Their team frequently promotes code to production riddled with security vulnerabilities. Now imagine this manager becoming defensive every time you try to address this issue. Many of you are probably starting to nod your head in agreement with a visual of this manager's face in your head.

Next, without any self-censorship, jot down some of the adjectives that immediately come to mind for this manager. We are willing to bet they are not very flattering.

Now, imagine that it is the eve of a major production release, and you realize that few, if any, of the vulnerabilities you pointed out in QA are addressed. How many of you just thought of some of those same adjectives to describe this person again? What would you do next? Would you get upset? Would you start yelling at this manager? Would you complain to another manager? Would you claim that you cannot work or reason with this manager? Would you think to yourself, "Why don't they just get it?"

Now, suppose you remain calm and ask the manager, "Why are these vulnerabilities not addressed?" The manager replies, "Look, I want to help you. I understand the importance of security. I really do, but my management insists that functionality trumps security and that we can always go back and fix security later. Our bonuses are tied to innovation, release burndown, return on investment of deployed features, and defect-free code. Nobody has told us how to demonstrate innovation by fixing a security hole or showing a return on investment on security features. Also, our leadership hasn't classified security vulnerabilities as defects. Our performance reviews, and therefore our success at this company, are also tied to these measurements. Put yourself in my shoes. What would you do?"

What *would* you do? Would some of those adjectives change? Would that change how you interact with and respond to this manager?

According to Mark Goulston in his book *Just Listen: Discover the Secret to Getting Through to Absolutely Anyone*, you did not listen. You did what many of us do. You used information gained from your early interactions with this manager, jumped to conclusions, and formed perceptions that became hard-wired with the adjectives that came to your mind during this exercise. Those words became a filter that you heard without truly listening.[2] According to Goulston, the solution is simple. Think about what you are thinking and remove the filters. Easier said than done.

The process of summary may help. Carl Rogers, a renowned psychotherapist, wrote:

The great majority of us cannot listen; we find ourselves compelled to evaluate, because listening is too dangerous. The first requirement is courage, and we do not always have it.[3]

Rogers popularized the process of summary in regard to active listening. The process of summary prevents you from speaking up until you have restated the speaker's idea and feelings accurately and to their satisfaction. There are three primary advantages to this process:[4]

1. It forces you to pause and sincerely understand what a person is saying before replying.
2. It aids in the consolidation and efficacy of memory.
3. It restricts you from formulating a straw man argument when someone opposes you. A widely accepted description of a straw man argument is when one misrepresents a person's argument in a way that distorts the original argument and then refutes the misrepresentation instead of the opponent's actual view.

Ultimately, understanding someone else's point of view allows you to:

- Appreciate those views and learn something new.
- Refine your position against the original argument. In the case of our software development manager, it allows you to have a genuine and unbiased conversation around the issues that are preventing him from addressing security vulnerabilities.

Jordan Peterson does a great job at summing this up:

If you listen, instead, without premature judgment, people will generally tell you everything they are thinking – and with very little deceit.[5]

Ask Questions

Albert Einstein supposedly once said in an interview, "If I had an hour to solve a problem and my life depended on the solution, I would spend the first 55 minutes determining the proper question to ask, for once I know the proper question, I could solve the problem in less than five minutes." Even though we could not find definitive attribution to Einstein, this quote's meaning and intent apply directly to what we should be doing as cybersecurity leaders in every professional conversation.

What do we do when we are evaluating an SaaS provider? Ask questions.

What do we do when asked to define the security requirements for project du jour? Ask questions.

What has every cybersecurity professional ever to grace this planet asked in their head regarding the hypothetical development manager from earlier in this chapter? "What the $%^& did you do that for?" For the record, please do NOT ever say that out loud unless you have a very, very, very good relationship with the person, and it is in private and outside of the office! Even so, we do not recommend going down that road. Instead, take Jordan Peterson's advice and "listen without premature judgment."

Nobody is born with the ability to ask effective questions. It is an ability you must actively develop over time and experience. Your voice, tone, body language, and delivery matter just as much as the question's actual content.

Picture walking through the door at the end of a long, difficult day and asking your spouse or partner, "What's for dinner?"

- Option A: Ask that question in a loving tone and appreciative of whatever may end up on your plate.
- Option B: Ask that question in a gruff, demanding tone, and then complain about what ends up on your plate.

If you wonder which option is the best choice, you probably need to read a different book – one that focuses on relationships and how to treat others. Also, if you happen to be married to a strong Greek, Spartan woman as I am, let me know how Option B works out for you. As ridiculous and evident as this scenario sounds, we seem to forget, at times, how to behave at the office. How many of us have responded to an email from a co-worker that triggered an emotional response and replied with an enraged email? How many of us wish we did not hit the Send button right after we did? I have – more times than I can count.

A better course of action is to first breathe. Second, go ahead and type that enraged email if it makes you feel better, but immediately delete it (do NOT save in "drafts"). Third, and getting back to asking questions, would be to use the *process of summary* to reflect about how you are interpreting the email and asking questions such as "What led you to this conclusion or course of action?" Doing so may even allow you to gain some empathy for the person's position on the other side of the email, and you can use that empathy to foster a more constructive conversation.

There are many benefits of asking questions beyond acquiring a new piece of information. One immense benefit is to persuade, which may be the most critical reason for cybersecurity professionals to ask questions. Since I am Greek, let's talk about the Socratic Method. The Socratic Method is an adaptive strategy of questioning that stimulates personal understanding, but it has been adapted for other purposes, such as persuading.[6] The Socratic Method is named after, you guessed it, the Greek philosopher Socrates. He taught his students by asking a series of questions. The goal was to expose contradictions in the students' thoughts and ideas to guide them to concrete, defensible conclusions.

Let's apply the Socratic method to our software development manager's case from earlier in the chapter. The mileage of the following example may vary based on your personal past experience, but this example is meant to provide you with a framework and to provoke ideas that you can use in your specific situation.

YOU: "Why does your group consistently promote code with security vulnerabilities?"

MANAGER: "Because we don't have the time and resources."

YOU: "Why don't you have the time or resources?"

MANAGER: "Because my management insists that functionality and new features trump security!"

YOU: "Why does your management insist that functionality and new features trump security?"

MANAGER: "Because our bonuses are tied to innovation, release burndown, return on investment of deployed features, and defect-free code."

YOU: "Why are your bonuses tied to those metrics?"

MANAGER: "Because new features generate revenue."

YOU: "However, return on investment is a measure in profitability, not just revenue, correct?"

MANAGER: "Correct."

YOU: "How much more time and effort does it take to fix a critical vulnerability early in the development process vs. after the code is promoted to production?"

MANAGER: "I see where you are going, but salespeople keep promising features we haven't developed yet!"

YOU: "I understand, but let's get back to what impacts your bonus checks, not theirs. I'm sure we have both heard the statistics that it takes ten times the time and effort to fix a code defect early in the development process vs. after promoting the code to production. Does the same hold true for security vulnerabilities in our environment?"

MANAGER: "Yes."

YOU: "Great. So, if a 'traditional' code defect and a security vulnerability have the same impact on profitability due to higher costs and, presumably, longer delays in offering the full functionality of the feature, why wouldn't your management treat them the same?"

MANAGER: "Because feature releases and bugs in the functionality of our application are tangible. Fixing vulnerabilities is not. Besides, it is not likely that vulnerabilities will be exploited, so it is difficult to prove the value in fixing those vulnerabilities ahead of the feature release."

YOU: "Do you remember the data breach that our competitor suffered last year?"

MANAGER: "Yes."

YOU: "The root cause was a cross-site request forgery vulnerability, which is exactly one of the vulnerabilities that is in question here. Various news outlets estimate that it cost them several millions of dollars to recover from the incident, including one year of credit monitoring services for all of their customers that were affected. This does not include the negative press and reputational impact."

MANAGER: "I see your point, but I'm not going to be able to convince management."

YOU: "It is common for management to prioritize metrics that, in reality, lead to not meeting the intent of the business objectives the metrics are supposed to support. I think we can agree that security vulnerabilities in code are closer to being code defects than not, and defect-free code is a metric upon which you are evaluated. Are you willing to set up a meeting with your management to discuss how we can establish KPIs that incorporate fixing security vulnerabilities in the same manner as 'traditional' defects to address real profitability instead of feature releases? You may even come out of the conversation with additional headcount to tackle the challenge."

MANAGER: "Yes. Yes, I am."

We were able to go from vilifying this software development manager (in our heads) and from dreading working with this manager to convincing this manager to work with us in persuading his management to prioritize security vulnerabilities alongside other "bugs." This development manager keeps his bonus, potentially gains more resources, and shows his management that he can raise his head above the weeds and present a business case that improves the return on investment in product features. You get a more robust application security program and reduce risk to the organization. The salespeople, well, the salespeople learn not to write a check they can't cash. It's a win for everyone!

Smile

We have all worked with THAT person. The person who seems never to smile and never has anything positive to say, or do they? Do we truly *listen* to that person to understand the meaning of the words coming out of their mouth, or does the resting scowl on their face prejudice us from respecting their opinion and views? Do they really have *nothing* positive to say? Nothing at all? Doubtful, but we often dismiss these people.

According to Daniel McNeill, author of *The Face: A Natural History*, smiling is innate. Some sort of smile, he writes, first appears two to twelve hours after birth. Those smiles may or may not have any context associated with them, but studies show they are crucial to bonding. McNeill notes that while "courtroom judges are equally likely to find smilers and non-smilers guilty, they give smilers lighter penalties, a phenomenon called the 'smile-leniency effect.'"[7]

Think about yourselves at work and in your lives. To whom do you give the benefit of the doubt? The person who smiles, or the gruff person?

As cybersecurity professionals, we fight the stereotype that we are antisocial, paranoid techno-nerds (even though some of the most social, outgoing people I know are in our profession). Therefore, it is even more vital that we pay attention to how we present ourselves. We will talk about body language later, but smiling will undoubtedly help break that stereotype.

Of course, we don't always feel like smiling. Why is that? First of all, we are humans, and life is not full of rainbows and unicorns all the time. Secondly, from a professional standpoint, we are fighting an uphill battle. We have to be "right" all the time, and the bad guys only need to be right once. We lack budget and resources, leading to increased stress and anxiety from managing an underfunded program. We are burned out.

How do we change that? At the risk of sounding like a hippie, smiling is the way to go. We have heard the term "smiling is contagious," but there is science to back that. Dr. Nicholas A. Christakis (Harvard) and Dr. James H. Fowler (University of San Diego) studied 4,739 people from 1983 to 2003. These individuals were surrounded by a more extensive network of 12,067 people, each having an average of 11 connections to others, and their happiness was measured every few years. Their findings confirmed the impact of a happy person, which smiling represents. A person's happiness is related to the happiness of their friends, their friends' friends, and so on, causing a snowball effect of happiness well beyond their initial interaction.[8]

I am not going to go on a soapbox rant about how the digital age caused us, as humans, to lose the finer points of interpersonal communication, but emojis were created for a reason. What I do know through experience is this: how you speak and how you write, in both the words you choose and the tone in which you deliver those words, can portray any range of emotions, but friendliness often leads to trustworthiness. Trustworthiness often leads to influence. Influence often leads to persuasion. Influence and persuasion will lead to your leadership, viewing you as a strategic partner within the organization vs. a tactical order taker. This can in turn lead to approved requests for budget and resources, and a properly funded cybersecurity program may relieve your stress and anxiety in running your cybersecurity program. Smiling is easy. If there is a small chance that smiling when you speak and write can elevate your team, department, and organization profile, isn't smiling worth the effort?

Body Language

Smiling is only part of the nonverbal communication pie. Body language is the whole pie. Many of us rely on texts, Slack messages, and email to communicate in today's digital age. It's convenient and allows natural introverts to stay in their comfort zone. Every form of communication has a time and place. It's not practical to speak with someone face-to-face, or even verbally, every time we wish to communicate. However, what we lose in not seeing the person as we are speaking with them is potentially critical nonverbal cues, like facial expressions, on top of verbal ones, like voice inflection.

In case you have not picked up on the theme of this chapter so far, let me be explicit about it right now. It is "using various forms of communication to get our way." Getting our way may be getting additional budget for a needed tool, bringing in a consultant to help with a risk assessment, or obtaining additional headcount for your team to keep up with your team's workload.

Body language is fundamental in "getting our way." As cybersecurity leaders, we are often competing with other teams, which generate revenue for the organization while cybersecurity typically does not, for attention and budget. Remember the conversation around "Opportunity Cost" in Chapter 5 – Articulating the Business Case? Developing a business case around cybersecurity spend vs. another value creating activity is one matter. How you deliver and present the business case is another matter. We need every advantage to adequately fund our cybersecurity programs and get the resources we need to maintain the organization's cyber risk appetite.

In their book *The Definitive Book of Body Language* Allan and Barbara Pease state that research convincingly shows that if you change your body language, you can alter your mood before going out, feel more confident at work, become more likable, and be more persuasive or convincing. When you change your body language, you interact differently with people around you, and they in turn will respond differently to you.

At the end of the book, they summarize "The Seven Secrets of Attractive Body Language." They are:

1. **Face:** Have an animated face and make smiling a part of your regular repertoire. Make sure you flash your teeth.
   - In other words, do not have a resting curmudgeon face.

2. **Gestures:** Be expressive but don't overdo it. Keep your fingers closed when you gesture, such as in the form of a hand steeple where the fingertips of both hands are together. Also, keep your hands below chin level, and avoid arm or feet crossing.
   - I am guilty of my hands going all over the place. I am Greek, and we speak with our hands. I continuously and consciously work on this.
3. **Head Movement:** Use triple nods when talking and head tilt when listening. Keep your chin up.
   - I naturally tilt my head when listening because it signals my brain to focus and not worry about what is for lunch. I have also often used a head tilt to signal confusion, but my face usually becomes more expressive in conjunction.
4. **Eye Contact:** Give the amount of eye contact that makes everyone feel comfortable. Unless looking at others is a cultural no-no, lookers gain more credibility than non-lookers.
   - Eye contact is difficult for many because it is so personal in nature. "Eyes are the windows to the soul." It is essential to pick up on social cues that the other person is not comfortable with eye contact. A tell tale sign is when they avoid eye contact. That does not mean that both of you stare off into space. It means that you find a balance between eye contact, quickly looking away, and looking back again during the conversation.
5. **Posture:** Lean forward when listening, stand straight when speaking.
   - Leaning forward signifies to the other person that you intently want to listen to what they are saying. Subconsciously, there is a connection with the physics of traveling sound waves. Being closer to the soundwave source, even by a few inches, allows one to hear better.
   - Standing straight when speaking signals confidence and authority.
6. **Territory:** Stand as close as you feel comfortable. If the other person moves back, don't step forward again.
   - Similar to "Eye Contact." Be sure to pay attention to and respect cultural norms and social cues.
7. **Mirror:** Subtly mirror the body language of others.
   - But don't let this get weird. For instance, both parties of the conversation cannot be listening simultaneously, so both of you leaning forward could violate territorial boundaries.[9]

I have noticed positive differences when minding my body language, whether it was my role as a cybersecurity leader within an organization, with a client now that I am consulting, or with a public speaking engagement. I challenge you to make these small, subtle changes and pay attention to the results.

Explain Why

Pretend that everyone is a two-year-old child who asks "why" to everything that you tell them. Now flashback to communicating to your team and getting them on board with a path forward with a tactical goal, especially when they do not initially agree with the decision. Simple, straightforward, all-around communication, up and down the chain of command, is an essential skill a leader must possess. Everyone must believe in and understand the "why" behind a particular request or management decision and then pursue the "what."

Jocko Willink and Leif Babin outline in their book *Extreme Ownership* that leaders must remove themselves from the immediate tactical objective and understand how it fits into the organization's strategic goals. As a leader, when you receive a directive that you do not understand, it is your duty, to your organization and to your team, to ask "why?"[10]

People generally do not ask you to execute something tactical (e.g., a task or a project) for no reason. Before you can communicate the "why" to your team, you, yourself, must understand it and believe it. Take a step back and analyze the situation and the strategic picture as you understand it. Would you come to a similar decision or "ask" if the roles were reversed? If not, you must ask questions, continuing moving up the chain of command if needed, until you do.

Once you understand "why," you can then communicate "why" to your team. People want to *believe* in what they are doing. Organizational strategies have failed. Heck, WARS were lost because leaders and frontline workers (troops) were misaligned in believing that what they were doing was worth their time, effort, and sacrifice. Just as you sought out understanding "why," you must also make yourself available to your team to answer their questions. Once you and your team are aligned with how the specific tactical objective aligns to the organization's strategic objectives, you can move forward in determining the optimal path ahead in executing the objective (the "what").

There is a rather crude saying that describes "stuff" rolling downhill. Still, it is your duty as a leader to provide feedback uphill on how strategic decisions impact operations and employees "on the ground." The further removed from the top of the corporate ladder, or the strategic decision-maker, employees are, the further removed they are from a clear understanding of the "why," even though the strategic decision-maker believes the reasoning behind the strategy is clear as day. It is this disconnect that leads to a misalignment between strategic and tactical goals. It is this disconnect that often leads to a misalignment of organizational goals and cybersecurity initiatives. Explain why, and don't be afraid of repeating yourself.

Storytelling

Dave Isay, the founder and president of StoryCorps, said in an interview, "A great story is one where you've captured something that feels authentic. That's the gold standard. If you've captured something in your documentary or storytelling work that feels like it's real and hasn't been altered in any way, that's good. In fact, it's a kind of miracle of communications . . . The beauty of an authentic audio story—and I love audio—is that when you're listening in your car or on your headphones, it's as if that person is whispering in your ear. It's very intimate. You're right there. A story authentically told is like an adrenaline shot to the heart. I don't think there's any better way of telling emotional stories."[11]

Do you know what is even more intimate than the audio storytelling Isay describes? It is face-to-face communication. That is the kicker. Face-to-face communication allows you to have visual *and* audio storytelling through your voice, body language, and actions. You have an advantage that Isay typically does not have.

For cybersecurity leaders, our "documentary or storytelling work" is our cybersecurity program. There are many intricate pieces to the story. In Chapter 7 – Translating Cyber Risk into Business Risk, we highlighted the importance of KRIs and KPIs in measuring our programs' performance. That is true, but the delivery of your message is critical. You can choose to tell the story through KPIs, KRIs, threats, vulnerabilities, and incidents; however, that limits your potential audience. As an alternative, you can choose to use those items to inform your story but tell your story through a lens that a wider audience (e.g., the C-Suite or the board) will appreciate and understand. Take a moment and think about it from your own experience. Are you more impressed by a product or service when the salesperson starts spewing off a list of features, or are you more impressed when the salesperson shares a client success story that solved many of your current pain points? Which pitch do you remember first when it comes time for vendor selection? For example, AWS utilizes Case Studies as a primary method of communicating customer success, and their business has grown for many consecutive quarters. As we first discussed in Chapter 4 – Value Creation, either you intentionally control the narrative or simply present facts and let someone else fill in the gaps. As a CISO utilizes storytelling to add value inside a business, it is important to tailor each story for the audience, just as you would highlight unique features of your experience in a job interview.

It is time for another science lesson. Oxytocin is a chemical that is produced by our brains when we are trusted or shown kindness. It is released when you cuddle, hug, or practice skin-to-skin bonding with a newborn. A side-effect of oxytocin production is a greater motivation to cooperate with others. Oxytocin allows us to determine whom to trust. Dr. Paul Zak and his research team discovered this chemical. His lab has been able to hack the creation of oxytocin, and their studies have exposed why stories motivate cooperation. His team realized that to "soften up" others to cooperate, the story needed to sustain attention by developing some tension. If successful in creating that tension, then it is likely that the audience will become empathetic to the storyteller or the individuals in the story and continue to be empathetic long after the story ends. Why do we care? Because Zak's experiments demonstrate that character-driven stories that build tension result in a better understanding of the key points the storyteller wishes to make. Listeners are then able to better recall key points weeks later. As you can imagine, his research also shows that storytelling's effectiveness surpasses the efficacy of a standard PowerPoint.[12]

There are five basic steps in creating a story:[13]

1. Determine whom you are trying to reach (your audience) and find out as much as you can about them. Recall "Stakeholder Analysis" from Chapter 5 – Articulating the Business Case and be sure to invest time to understand their perspective and specific needs.
   - What are their hot buttons? What topics are non-starters? I recently heard of a CEO at a security product company who kicked people out of the room or hung up a call if somebody mentioned the word "COVID."
2. Figure out what you want them to do.
   - Do you want leadership to approve the budget or headcount? Do you need your team to execute on a critical initiative? This is a great opportunity to leverage SCI-PAB® from Chapter 5 – Articulating the Business Case.
3. Think through the challenges that may get in the way of that goal.
   - People, process, technology, or budget? Think about security control friction and cost concepts, such as "Opportunity Cost" and "Cost Avoidance" from Chapter 5 – Articulating the Business Case.
4. Find a character who has overcome that challenge.
   - What is the common ground? Can you blend prevention and promotion to increase your options (Chapter 3 – Business Decisions)? Appeal to risk reduction over cost (only works if risk reduction is greater than cost), cost savings, speed to market, etc. What workarounds are available for the challenges you identified in step 3?
5. Make sure there's a resolution to your story.
   - Everybody loves a happy ending, and nobody loves a story with no end.

In the book *Made to Stick*, Chip Heath, one of the authors, teaches a course at Stanford. During that course, he puts the student through an exercise where he presents them with data regarding crime in the United States. He splits the class 50/50 into two groups. One group is to persuade the class that nonviolent crime is a serious problem in the United States, and the other group is to convince the class of the opposite. The class rates each speaker after each speech on items such as delivery and persuasiveness. After the class thinks the exercise is over, and after Chip kills time by playing a Monty Python clip, he asks them to write down, for each speaker, ideas they remember. Many students completely froze, not being able to recall a thing.

Interestingly, 63% of the students remember the stories within the speeches, and only 5% can recall any single statistic.[14] For cybersecurity leaders, those statistics are analogous to regurgitating KRIs and KPIs. Are you still wondering why the C-Suite and the Board of Directors "just don't get it"?

In short, stories stick. If you want your audience to connect with you, remember you, and most importantly, side with you, learn to use stories.

Crucial Conversations

I venture to guess that many of you reading this book dread and even, on occasion, avoid having difficult conversations. There are three factors that define a crucial conversation:[15]

1. Opinions differ
2. The stakes are high
3. Emotions are high

In cybersecurity leadership, crucial conversations are commonplace. They include a range of scenarios, such as:

- Reporting detected fraud
- Reporting child pornography to authorities
- Disciplining a friend
- Terminating a team member
- Asking for a raise
- Confronting a top executive about how they have personally contributed to policy violations

- Investigating corporate and extramarital scandals
- Negotiating a starting salary
- Asking for an increase in budget
- Closing the sale on a colossal account
- Delivering bad news to your team
- Speaking with congressional committees and public hearings after a major data breach

As you can tell by the non-exhaustive list above, difficult and crucial conversations are a challenge that you must tackle head-on as a cybersecurity leader.

This section will, admittedly, seem like a book report for the book *Crucial Conversations: Tools for Talking When the Stakes Are High,* but we will strive to align it to cybersecurity challenges we all face. It is by far the best and most practical book that I have read on the topic. Like many of you, I do not relish having difficult conversations, and this book helped me navigate some pretty significant minefields after I read it. The book is one tool that I wish I had stumbled across early in my career as it would have saved me much anxiety, but alas, I only came across the second edition around 2015 – a few years after it was published. I will do my best to pull out the key points that have worked for me, but of all the books referenced throughout this book, *Crucial Conversations* is by far the most versatile and powerful.

The authors outline a seven-step model handling crucial conversations derived based on 25 years of research with 20,000 people. The seven steps are:[16]

1. Start with the heart
2. Learn to look
3. Make it safe
4. Master stories
5. STATE your path
6. Explore Others' Paths
7. Move to action

I'll walk through these seven steps and describe how to apply each in our day-to-day interactions as cybersecurity leaders.

Start with the Heart

If you start a crucial conversation with a closed mind and the wrong emotions and mindset, it is probably not going to end up well. Suppose you immediately say "no" to a business unit without fully understanding what is at stake (e.g., speed to market to gain a first-mover advantage) because their request will violate a cybersecurity policy or standard. In that case, you will cause friction within the requested business process, your interpersonal relationship, and your need for the organization to view you as a partner vs. an obstacle. Ask yourself what you want and what is really at stake. If you start the conversation with an open mind and the right emotions and mindset, the conversation is more likely to have a positive outcome. If we cannot maintain an open mind or manage our emotions and mindset during a crucial conversation, how can we expect the other party to do the same? It is imperative to remember that your view may not be the only version of the truth and that you may very well be wrong (gasp)! Check your ego at the door. Let us refer back to our favorite software development manager from earlier in this chapter. Our perception and interactions with him were vastly different before and after we decided to stay calm, keep an open mind, ask questions, and listen.

The first step of having a crucial conversation is to have a crucial conversation with ourselves. We are often quick to play the blame game with the other person, but we also shoulder some of the blame. Have you ever been passive-aggressive? Have you ever tried to change someone's behavior through sarcasm or veiled hints instead of addressing the issue head-on?

Most important, we need to maintain mutual respect. Your authenticity will come through in both your verbal and nonverbal communication. Remember, you do not have to like someone to respect them. Bear in mind that often feelings of disrespect come from focusing on our differing views versus our commonalities. Use those commonalities to build a foundational level of respect and build from there. Everyone brings strengths and weaknesses to the relationship and the crucial conversation. Yes, I said it. Even cybersecurity superheroes have weaknesses!

Learn to Look

Have you ever been so caught up in a crucial conversation that although you know it is going sideways, you cannot seem to break out of it? There are three things you need to look for to help head off potential problems before it becomes too late:[17]

1. Look to spot crucial conversations.
2. Look for safety problems.
3. Look for your style under stress.

LOOK TO SPOT CRUCIAL CONVERSATIONS

Train your brain to look for these three signs:

1. **Physical signs:** It is no secret that stress manifests itself physically, either acutely in the moment or over the long term. Do you feel your face get flush? Can you start to feel your heart race? Do you lose your train of thought and try to get words out faster than your brain can process? Do you feel a tightness in your throat? What was your first reaction to our development manager from earlier in the chapter?
2. **Emotional signs:** Are you feeling scared (I have yet to see a cybersecurity superhero admit this)? Anxious? Nervous? Angry? Hurt?
3. **Behavioral signs:** Do you start raising your voice? Do you get very quiet? Do you point your finger? Do you cross your arms? Do you throw up the universal "talk to the hand"?

There is no universal way to train oneself to pick up on these cues; however, what works for me is pausing, taking a deep breath, and consciously asking myself, "Okay . . . what are you feeling or observing right now?" Did I just give away my tell at the poker table? Maybe . . .

LOOK FOR SAFETY PROBLEMS

Can you spot when the other party of the conversation is exhibiting the signs we mentioned above? In addition to the above, you can spot signs that you, or the other person, are afraid and feel unsafe in the conversation by detecting shifts in the conversation's content.

A safe conversation implies that it is safe to say anything without judgment and fear of the other party blowing up. Free-flowing dialogue is essential in a crucial conversation, and nothing kills a free-flowing dialogue like fear.

Another sign that a conversation may be getting unsafe is when you or the other person seem to lose focus. When emotions kick in, some cognitive brain functions shut down. It is easier to identify losing focus than admitting we are getting emotional. When you recognize you are losing focus, try to detach and react (as Jocko Willink puts it). Relax, look around, and make a call on how to flip the conversation from unsafe to safe. Do something to fix it. As the authors put it, CRIB it to get the conversation back to a safe space and back to a mutual purpose. CRIB stands for:

- **C**ommit to seeking a mutual purpose
- **R**ecognize the purpose behind the strategy
- **I**nvent a mutual purpose
- **B**rainstorm new strategies

LOOK FOR YOUR STYLE UNDER STRESS

The authors outline six styles that we use when we are under stress. It is essential to recognize those patterns so that you can detach and react accordingly to fix the conversation's safety.

The six patterns are lumped into two groups: silence patterns and violence patterns. Silence patterns include actions meant to withhold or omit information from the conversation purposefully. Violence patterns consist of attempts to control, coerce, or punish others.

Silence Patterns

- **Masking:** Understating or selectively showing your genuine opinions. Sarcasm and sugarcoating are both examples. We *never* see this among our cybersecurity peers. Never . . .

- **Avoiding:** Steering entirely away from sensitive topics. I once had a peer steer away from a sensitive topic by sarcastically suggesting that we move to another sensitive topic (masking). The quote was something to the effect of, "Let's stay away from the sensitive topics, and end this meeting with a prayer."
- **Withdrawing:** Pulling out of a conversation altogether by exiting the conversation or leaving the room. I admit I have been guilty of this in the past. The reason was partly frustration and partly to make a point that the conversation was going nowhere. In hindsight, that is not the best way to "reset" the conversation.

Violence Patterns

- **Controlling:** Coercing others into your way of thinking through forcing your views on them or dominating the conversation.
- **Labeling:** Putting a label on people or ideas to dismiss them as a stereotype or category.
- **Attacking:** Moving from winning to making the person suffer.

The authors have a self-scoring test that you can take at www .CrucialConversations.com/exclusive (requires registration).

Make It Safe

We need to make a person feel "safe." Not in the "safe spaces at universities" kind of way, but safe in the way they feel comfortable participating in a two-way, free-flowing dialogue with you. The safer they feel, the more likely they are to open up. The less safe they feel, the more likely they will either close down or fight back.

Sometimes, we focus so much on words and fail to pick up on nonverbal cues. Specifically, we miss nonverbal cues that the other person may no longer feel safe in the conversation. We need to be ever-conscious of the conversation's content, the context of the conversation, and ourselves.

By detaching from the conversation when we sense it is becoming unsafe, we remove ourselves from the conversation's content, which allows us to refocus on the desired result. We can then shift focus to the context of the conversation and clear up any misunderstandings.

How often have we tried to state something positive that was misunderstood or misinterpreted by the other person? This is the time to fix it. We did this earlier in the chapter in our conversation with the software development manager through the following dialogue:

YOU: "How much more time and effort does it take to fix a critical vulnerability early in the development process vs. after the code is promoted to production?"

MANAGER: "I see where you are going, but salespeople keep promising features we haven't developed yet!"

YOU: "I understand, but let's get back to what impacts your bonus checks, not theirs. How much more time and effort does it take to fix a critical vulnerability early in the development process vs. after the code has been promoted to production?"

You sensed that the manager was starting to feel unsafe as he was beginning to get defensive and attempted to shift the focus of the conversation. You were able to detach, evaluate, and reset the conversation by turning the manager's focus on something that he cares about . . . his bonus. You were able to establish mutual purpose by signaling that you wanted to ultimately reduce his workload by addressing vulnerabilities earlier in the software development life cycle (SDLC) rather than later. You were able to demonstrate that you were listening to him openly and respectfully. Doing so led to the manager opening up and sharing more as the conversation progressed until we found ourselves on common ground. Ultimately, you were able to restore.

Master Stories

Crucial conversations involve emotion. Emotions are contagious, and that's where we'll continue to focus. So, how do we stay out of our emotions during the conversation? Essentially, how do we keep a poker face? Make up a story. It is not a story that you will spell out in your actual conversation, but rather a story to yourself that outlines what you are feeling. Stories allow you to explain to yourself what you are feeling and whether it is good or bad.

Stories drive feelings, and feelings drive actions. Therefore, if you can change the story, you can change your actions. The path to action is shown in Figure 8.1.

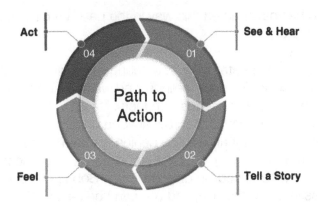

FIGURE 8.1 Path to Action

For example, you may be in a meeting about a project that is going off-track:

- **See/Hear:** Bob just said that he was waiting for a critical piece of information from me that caused him to miss an important deadline.
- **Tell a Story:** This is not true. Bob is trying to throw me under the bus for his ineptitude, and if I speak now, I will look defensive.
- **Feel:** Angry, betrayed
- **Act:** Withdraw, or become snippy

Obviously, this is not a good story, and you have lost control of the conversation. The way to change a story is to retrace your path to action by shifting your mental gear into reverse:

- **Act:** Pay attention to your behavior. Are you exhibiting one of the six Styles Under Stress?
  - Withdrawing from the conversation is a silence pattern.
- **Feel:** What are you feeling? Be precise. Understanding what you feel presents a more accurate picture of what is happening and why. Are you outraged, or are you, in reality, embarrassed? While you will not break out a tool to help you determine how you are feeling in the heat of the moment, you can improve your self-awareness by using a tool like the one Lindsay Braman created at https://lindsaybraman.com/emotion-sensation-feeling-wheel/.

- Bob has never acted this way in the past. I am more surprised than angry.
- **Tell a Story:** Analyze your feelings and original story. Are your feelings appropriate? Are you telling yourself the right story? Remember, stories drive feelings, and we make up the stories. Be sure not to confuse stories with facts.
  - I have never seen Bob throw anyone under the bus before, so there likely is not any malice behind his comments.
- **See/Hear:** Focusing on behavior allows you to separate fact from story. "Bob lied" is different from "Bob is mistaken." "Lied" implies intent to deceive, and you can't be certain of Bob's intent.
  - Bob is mistaken, but why? Where is the communication breakdown?

By taking this approach, we can change the story. We can now proceed with having a conversation about where the communication breakdown occurred and how to prevent it from happening again.

STATE Your Path

To proceed with the above conversation safely requires a few things:

- Confidence in yourself to have the conversation
- Humility and self-awareness to not get worked up so that you can keep the conversation safe
- Skill to maintain the free-flowing dialogue

The STATE method can help in this regard: STATE stands for:[18]
- **S**hare your facts
  - Start the conversation with the observable facts and not the story that is driven by your emotions and assumptions.
  - Facts are the least controversial and provide a safe beginning.
  - Facts are the most persuasive and form the foundation of belief.
  - Facts are the least insulting because your story (assumptions) could surprise and insult others and immediately kill the safety of the conversation.

- **T**ell your story
  - The facts plus your story (assumption) warrants the conversation in the first place.
  - If the person becomes defensive, be mindful of your State Under Stress, detach and bring the conversation back into safety.
- **A**sk for others' paths
  - After you share the facts and tell your story, ask the other person to do the same.
  - Listen actively and be open-minded to rebuild your story as more information is presented.
- **T**alk tentatively
  - Remember that your story is an assumption and not a fact.
  - Share the story as a possibility, not as a certainty.
  - In short, share your story as a story and not as a college lecture of facts.
- **E**ncourage testing
  - Invite opposing views and mean it!
  - Play devil's advocate on your own views.
  - Do it until your motive becomes obvious.
  - The degree to which you encourage testing is a test of whether your motive is to win a debate or to engage in real, free-flowing dialogue.

The first three skills describe what to do, and the final two describe how to do it.

Explore Others' Paths

Exploring others' paths is, effectively, getting the other person to retrace their story. You can accomplish this by:

- Inviting others to share what is on their minds and to be *sincere*. Think about it. How often have you been able to sense the insincerity in others?
- Genuinely be curious.
- Stay curious. It is easy to get wound up as the other person's version of the facts emerge. Staying curious helps keep you grounded.
- Be patient. Give the other person time and space to build safety by recounting their version of the facts.

Easier said than done, you say? Well, fortunately, the authors give us a set of skills to facilitate getting the other person to retrace their story, which uses the acronym AMPP:[19]

- **A**sk to get things rolling. Be mindful of not expressing your biases.
- **M**irror to confirm feelings. Mirroring establishes rapport and safety.
- **P**araphrase to acknowledge the story and to ensure that you understand their story without sarcasm or bias.
- **P**rime the pump. When all else fails, you may share your interpretation so that the other party can steer you to a better interpretation, if needed.

What if, after all of the above, you still disagree? What if the other person's facts are entirely off base and their story (interpretation) does not align with yours? Go back to your ABCs:[20]

- **A**gree: People often disagree on a small minority of the facts and stories. Recognize when do, acknowledge it, and move on.
- **B**uild: Do not create a mountain (an argument) from a molehill (a small disagreement of the facts and stories). Acknowledge the common ground and build from there.
- **C**ompare: Try not to directly call a story "wrong." Try comparing your story with the other person's. Comparisons generate more dialogue rather than emotions.

Move to Action

Now that you have completed the first six steps of managing a crucial conversation, now what? How many plans have you seen, or how many meetings have you attended, where nothing happened as a result? Nobody *did* anything about the plan, meeting ideas and decisions, etc.

Getting stuff done 101 dictates that to get stuff done, you must do two things. First, you must agree on how a decision will be made. Second, you must have a plan with assigned responsibilities and accountability.

Agree with how to decide before making a decision. Several variables may determine how to proceed, such as whether one person can decide or if the decision needs to be made by committee. There are four forms of decision-making:

1. Command
2. Consult
3. Vote
4. Consensus

Many organizations have defaulted to one of the above through the evolution of their culture over time. The culture may be hierarchical, command and control, or the culture may be one to build consensus to the extent where nobody bears any responsibility. Four guiding questions help determine which approach fits best for the given situation:

1. Who cares about the decision?
2. Who knows what is needed?
3. Who must agree on the decision?
4. How many people is it worth involving?

A decision is pointless without a plan. It is critical to establish who does what by when with defined deliverables, assigned ownership of those deliverables, and deadlines. It is also important to lay out follow-up timeframes and methods (e.g., email, meetings, video calls) to ensure that the deliverables are on track and on time. The best-laid plans are challenged once you get punched in the face (Mike Tyson said something similar), but one thing is for certain. Without a plan, the decision will likely fade away.

Application

Presenting a brief on your cybersecurity program to your executive leadership team or board of directors is one of the most *positive* crucial conversations you can have as a cybersecurity leader. These conversations can make or break your cybersecurity program from a visibility, budget, and overall resource perspective.

Let's go back and review the case study from the "Application" section of Chapter 7 – Translating Cyber Risk into Business Risk. To refresh the stage, one of my clients services the energy sector, and there was a new CIO on board and mostly new company leadership. The new CIO had several concerns about the protection of sensitive data and industrial control systems. After the assessment, we went to the board to get funding to mitigate the key risks that we identified. Below is how part of that conversation occurred to the best of my memory and my notes. Particularly sensitive information is omitted.

BOARD MEMBER #1:   "Thank you for the briefing. Admittedly, we have typically seen cybersecurity as 'insurance' with no return on investment, but you certainly raise some valid points. Let's start with the first issue. Why should I care about industrial control systems connected directly to the Internet? Isn't that an Operations issue?"

ROCK: "Sir, thank you for the opportunity. If I understand you correctly, you are asking why we are addressing this issue at the board level? In other words, you would like to understand the impact of the risk better?"

BOARD MEMBER #1:   "Yes, I believe that is a fair representation of my question."

ROCK: "In the world of operational technology, or OT, cybersecurity has a direct impact on safety. That is why we partnered with Operations, HR, and Environmental, Health, and Safety teams to roll out a security awareness plan to highlight cybersecurity risk across the Operations teams. However, awareness is only one part of the puzzle. Operations has a different culture than back-office IT. What is the #1 thing that keeps you up at night regarding operational risks?"

BOARD MEMBER #1:   "Safety to our employees, of course."

ROCK: "Good. This is exactly why safety metrics are part of the organizational KPIs. Since operational technologies control physical processes, a compromise in the OT environment can directly impact employee safety. A cybersecurity compromise within OT has a different impact than within the traditional IT environment. The threats, vulnerability, and risks are different in OT.

The solutions we presented would first prevent access to the OT environment from the internet and segment the operational technology environment from the IT corporate network, where a compromise is more likely to occur and pivot. Our roadmap then matures cybersecurity within the OT environment in a separate phased, yet parallel, path to the IT cybersecurity program."

BOARD MEMBER #2:   "We understand the significance of the problem. Thank you. Now that we've addressed that, let's move to another point. How exactly are we losing sensitive sales information?"

ROCK: "Thank you, ma'am. So that I am clear, I understand that you are concerned with sales information that may materially impact the organization's revenue, leaving the organization and being used by a competitor?"

BOARD MEMBER #2:   "Yes, that is correct."

ROCK: "Thank you. The main issue here is surrounding the 'Bring Your Own Device' policy. The organization decided to allow employees to use their personal devices for work; however, controls such as the proposed mobile device management and data loss prevention solutions were not implemented in conjunction with the policy. As a result, when individuals, such as salespeople, leave the organization, there is nothing in

place to ensure that information such as customer lists, prospective deals, and ongoing projects do not go with them. The risk is that these
individuals can take these lists with them to their
new organization, which is likely a competitor.
Based on my interview with your Chief Financial
Officer, the average deal size in flight is in the millions. What is your risk appetite around losing
these deals, or this type of competitive sales
intelligence landing in the hands of a competitor?"

BOARD MEMBER #2:   "Our risk appetite is very low for this. Depending
on the deal size, even one single deal shifting to
a competitor could be material."

ROCK: "Even one single deal shifting to a competitor
could be material?"

BOARD MEMBER: "Yes."

ROCK: "Thank you. That is very enlightening. The solutions and budget that we have proposed for the
next year cost less than the 12-month average of
a single deal. In that light, should we move on to
discussing exactly how that budget will be allocated and measured?"

BOARD MEMBER #2:   "Your ask is completely reasonable given that
perspective. I fear you may be asking for too little, given the size and scope of the environment.
Yes, let's move on to discussing the budget
request in more detail."

There you have it. As I mentioned in Chapter 7 – Translating Cyber
Risk into Business Risk, we secured the budget. Note that I used
several techniques outlined in this chapter, including AMPP, the process of summary, and some of the Socratic method. You can't see
the smile and confident body language that I made a conscious effort
to maintain, yet still seem genuine. We often think of crucial conversations in a negative light, but with some practice, you can turn them
into a positive for your cybersecurity program!

Key Insights

- Above all else, listen. Summarize the other side of the conversation back to the other person to ensure that you correctly understand their meaning and intent.
- Ask questions. Sometimes, answering a question with a question can get you answers and consensus.
- Smile. Smiles are contagious.
- Be mindful of your body language.
- Ensure your subordinates, peers, and executives understand "why." In the case of subordinates and peers, do they understand your commander's intent? Do you fully understand your leadership's commander's intent?
- Share battle stories. People understand and comprehend stories better than facts.
- Tackle crucial conversations head-on. Practice the seven steps and several techniques we outlined above. Don't be afraid to role-play with a spouse or a trusted colleague.

Notes

1. Klemmer, E.T., and Snyder, F.W., "Measurement of Time Spent Communicating," *Journal of Communication 22*(2) (1972): 142–158. https://doi.org/https://doi.org/10.1111/j.1460-2466.1972.tb00141.x.
2. Goulston, M., *Just Listen: Discover the Secret to Getting Through to Absolutely Anyone*, AMACOM, 2015.
3. Peterson, J.B., Doidge, N., and Van Sciver, E., *12 Rules for Life: An Antidote to Chaos*. Random House Canada, 2018.
4. Peterson, J.B., Doidge, N., and Van Sciver, E., *12 Rules for Life: An Antidote to Chaos*.
5. Peterson, J.B., Doidge, N., and Van Sciver, E., *12 Rules for Life: An Antidote to Chaos*.
6. Wilberding, E.P.D., *Socratic Methods in the Classroom: Encouraging Critical Thinking and Problem Solving Through Dialogue*, Prufrock Press, Inc., 2019.
7. Canegie, D. and Associates and Cole, B., *How to Win Friends & Influence People in the Digital Age*, Simon & Schuster Paperbacks, 2011.

8. Fowler, J.H., and Christakis, N.A., "Dynamic Spread of Happiness in a Large Social Network: Longitudinal Analysis Over 20 Years in the Framingham Heart Study," *BMJ (Online) 338*(7685): 23–26. https://doi.org/10.1136/bmj.a2338.

9. Pease, A., and Pease, B., *The Definitive Book of Body Language*, Bantam Books, 2004.

10. Willink, J., and Babin, L., *Extreme Ownership: How U.S. Navy Seals Lead and Win*, St. Martin's Press, 2017.

11. Black, M., *"Something that Feels Authentic": StoryCorps's Dave Isay on Storytelling*, The Communications Network, n.d.

12. Zak, P.J., *Why Your Brain Loves Good Storytelling*, Harvard Business Review, 2014.

13. Biesenbach, R., *Unleash the Power of Storytelling: Win Hearts, Change Minds, Get Results*, Eastlawn Media, 2018.

14. Heath, C., and Heath, D., *Made to Stick: Why Some Ideas Survive and Others Die*, Random House, 2007.

15. Patterson, K., Grenney, J., McMillan, R., and Switzler, A., *Crucial Conversations: Tools for Talking When the Stakes Are High*, McGraw Hill, 2012.

16. Patterson, K., Grenney, J., McMillan, R., and Switzler, A., *Crucial Conversations: Tools for Talking When the Stakes Are High*.

17. Patterson, K., Grenney, J., McMillan, R., and Switzler, A., *Crucial Conversations: Tools for Talking When the Stakes Are High*.

18. Patterson, K., Grenney, J., McMillan, R., and Switzler, A., *Crucial Conversations: Tools for Talking When the Stakes Are High*.

19. Patterson, K., Grenney, J., McMillan, R., and Switzler, A., *Crucial Conversations: Tools for Talking When the Stakes Are High*.

20. Patterson, K., Grenney, J., McMillan, R., and Switzler, A., *Crucial Conversations: Tools for Talking When the Stakes Are High*.

PART III

Cybersecurity Leadership

CHAPTER 9

Relationship Management

Get closer than ever to your customers. So close to them that you tell them what they need well before they realize it themselves.

— Steve Jobs

Opportunity

In the age where seemingly every company is undergoing a "digital transformation," cybersecurity leaders have a unique opportunity to flip the narrative on cybersecurity. Cybersecurity is one of the few groups within the organization with the tools and capabilities to build visibility into most, if not all, of the organization's critical business processes and data flows. In Chapter 2 – Business Strategy Tools we reviewed this unique vantage point in the context of value stream mapping. Again, this level of visibility allows cybersecurity teams to be a crucial partner in building business resilience, enabling process improvements, and increasing competitive advantage.

The business needs cybersecurity involved early and often in digital transformation initiatives because they need proactive cybersecurity insights and strategies for success. Fostering relationships with the C-suite and other business unit leaders allows cybersecurity leaders to learn about digital transformation initiatives early-on. We described the process of Stakeholder Analysis and Influence Maps in Chapter 5 – Articulating the Business Case. Along with the business acumen we have covered in this book up to this point, cybersecurity can get ahead of potential risks by engaging business unit leaders early regarding the key technologies they rely upon to generate business value. Recall the Beverage Manufacturer Case Study of Chapter 4 – Value Creation. Cybersecurity teams can proactively research these technologies, anticipate the need for new technologies as each business unit embarks on a digital transformation initiative, proactively identify cyber risk, and bring recommended risk mitigation measures to the table. In order to deliver on this promise, you must have solid relationships.

Principle

Like it or not, cybersecurity is a team sport. A wide receiver on a football team cannot catch any balls without a quarterback throwing the ball, and a quarterback cannot throw the ball without an offensive line that blocks for them. The same goes for a cybersecurity team. A cybersecurity team cannot operate in a vacuum, and a robust cybersecurity program relies on individual technical skills *and* interpersonal relationships across cybersecurity, IT, and other business units.

Cybersecurity teams cannot rationally complain that "people are the weakest link," yet isolate themselves from those very people. Unfortunately, this approach is commonplace, which leads to those teams being alienated and the cybersecurity team being marginalized. The most effective cybersecurity leaders develop trusted relationships with other business leaders to foster a culture of security across the organization. As discussed in Chapter 6 – Cybersecurity: A Concern of the Business, Not Just IT, implementing and enforcing security controls is much more effective when cybersecurity is done *with* the business and not *to* the business. To accomplish this, you must develop positive relationships across the organization and at all organizational levels.

Relationships across and up your chain of command with other leaders, executives, and your board members require you to establish an executive presence to ensure you gain support and resources for your cybersecurity program. Relationships with your peers allow you to execute on a cybersecurity strategy. For example, cybersecurity often relies on Audit Committee members, IT teams, and system administrators. We need their critical insights to aid with setting priorities, securely configuring systems, asset management, executing change control, and even applying patches. Finally, relationships down your chain of command ensure that your entire team is aligned and engaged.

Relationships external to your organization are also critical in succeeding in your current role and preparing for your next role. Networking and developing relationships with peers at other organizations and in other industries can facilitate the sharing of information about current and emerging threats and can provide different perspectives on solving challenges you currently face. Networking helps accelerate your growth as a cybersecurity leader. The more you give, the more you gain. Lest we forget, our external interactions include product vendors, service providers, auditors, regulators, and even our customers. People comprise each of these organizations, and strong relationships with these outside parties are necessary for a truly resilient cybersecurity posture. Indeed, whether you are building and improving relationships internal or external to your organization, you cannot do so without trust.

In this chapter, we will focus on building and maintaining relationships through four key traits:

- Establishing and Maintaining Trust
- Indirect Influence
- Managing Through Conflict
- Professional Networking

Establishing and Maintaining Trust

If you were hoping for a conversation on "Zero Trust" or "HITRUST," then I'm sorry, but not sorry, to disappoint. Establishing trust is not an option if you, as a cybersecurity leader, wish to elevate your profile within the organization and be invited to strategy discussions. Your capacity to build trust is a primary predictor of your success. Cybersecurity leaders have to establish trust across a wide variety of stakeholders. So, it is essential that our teams consider the organization's interests first when acting upon cybersecurity risk. Otherwise, we risk reverting to the "Department of No," as a group of paranoid tech guys in the dark corner worried about esoteric improbabilities.

As a leader, you need to establish trust with your employees and peers. Others need to have confidence that you "have their back." In particular, your employees need to know that you have the team's best interest in mind when making decisions. Empire building and personal glory are two ways cybersecurity leaders can leave others feeling betrayed. Thoughtful integrity in vital moments of choice and fervent alignment with your highest values demonstrate your commitment to your team. Even when you execute flawlessly, it is easy for others to misinterpret your actions. Sometimes we face difficult decisions. You must be maniacal in demonstrating loyalty and commitment to shared values.

It is hard to overstate the value of establishing trust across your organization. Trust gets you that coveted seat at the table. Trust brings you an increased budget and resources for your cybersecurity program. Trust allows you to leverage other teams to execute your cybersecurity priorities (e.g., procurement for third-party vendor risk management). Trust enables you to retain employees and reduce the cost of employee turnover. This list is by no means exhaustive, but I'm sure you get the point.

There are numerous books and resources out there about establishing trust. Here, I am going to boil it down into five points that have proven useful while building trust.

1. Say what you do and do what you say.
2. Be authentic and congruent.
3. Be transparent.
4. Shut the hell up and listen.
5. Be humble.

Say What You Do and Do What You Say

There is the old axiom that "trust takes years to build, seconds to break, and forever to repair." In fact, Stephen Covey, a world-renowned leadership expert, says that keeping commitments "is the 'Big Kahuna' of all behaviors. It's the quickest way to build trust in any relationship – be it with an employee, a boss, a team member, a customer, a supplier, a spouse, a child, or the public in general."[1]

Think about a time when someone failed to keep a promise or commitment. Have you ever been promised a promotion only for it to fall through? Have you ever been stood up at a meeting without a courtesy "I need to reschedule" email? How did it feel? The person who failed to keep the promise may not have had control of all of the factors that contributed to your disappointment. I'll bet that didn't stop you from feeling like you misplaced your trust.

Now, let us switch roles. When you tell your boss that you'll have your budget ready by the end of the week, make sure that you do. If you say to a co-worker that you do not have an answer to their question but that you will research it and follow-up with them, make sure that you do. If you tell an employee that you will review a work product and provide feedback, make sure you do. I understand this sounds simple, so why do we have such a hard time keeping promises at work? Nobody is perfect and we have all missed deadlines and broken promises; however, earning a reputation for keeping your promises will establish your reliability and strengthen your working relationships. Making and keeping commitments is the foundation of integrity, one crucial element in establishing trust.

Let's go back to our development manager's story from Chapter 8 – Communication – You Do It Every Day (or Do You?). If you recall, we tell the development manager that if he agreed to set up a meeting with his management to prioritize fixing security vulnerabilities, they might even come out of the conversation with an additional headcount to tackle the challenge. Even though this was not a solid promise, the inference is that you will fight for that headcount. If you go into that meeting caring only about your self-interests (fixing vulnerabilities) vs. theirs (resources), the development manager may likely view that as a broken promise. Integrity is not something to be taken lightly.

Here are some things I have learned throughout my career to help me keep my promises. Some, I learned the hard way:

- **Just say "no":** We all want to be liked. Rather than offering a counterfeit "yes," establish boundaries and know what commitments you can (or want) to accept. When in doubt, politely decline or negotiate (more on this in Chapter 12 – Negotiation). Empathy is key here. Imagine that you promised to send an employee to training and then fail to come through on that promise. Be prepared to lose that employee to an organization that will. Perhaps a downturn in the market resulted in budget constraints, which is clearly entirely out of your control, but that may not matter. In addition to careful negotiation and empathy, language precision can help mitigate the risk of broken promises. For example, you might communicate that "Training is in the budget. Please hurry and submit your training request so that we can pay for it while the budget is still available." In this way your intent is clear, and if your capability to deliver is diminished, there is no confusion.
- **Create a trigger:** First, precisely clarify your commitment. Utilize the "Process of Summary" from Chapter 8 – Communication – You Do It Every Day (or Do You?) to confirm a common understanding with others involved. Then, establish a trigger. I capture my commitments as a task in my calendar, which ensures that I proactively allocate time in my calendar to honor my word. Finally, stay disciplined. It is easy to think, "I have some time to catch up on emails before tackling that task." Ten-minute distractions have a tendency to evolve. When they do, you are placing your integrity at risk.
- **Apologize and take ownership:** It will happen. You will break a promise someday. It is almost as certain as death and taxes. How you handle breaking a promise will impact your ability to mend the relationship and rebuild trust. Priorities shift, emergencies occur, equipment breaks. Often, the circumstances are out of your control. There is a difference between making excuses and being transparent. A sincere apology can make a huge difference. Don't

be a victim. Don't make excuses. Especially do not blame others or cite your "bad luck." People who sincerely apologize and take ownership strive to find a workaround or an alternative solution. They then endeavor to avoid reoccurrence of the transgression. We suggest you follow this pattern.

Be Authentic and Congruent

Consistency builds trust, and results matter. When you need to delegate a critical assignment, to whom do you turn? Do you rely upon the person who is consistent in meeting goals or gamble with someone who may deliver excellent results one week and disappoint the next? Inconsistent results are bad for business and bad for your reputation.

Think back to a person who said one thing and did another. Politicians on both sides of the aisle are notorious for this behavior. An empirical poll of my friends reveals that politicians are less trustworthy than gas station sushi! As leaders, we need to be consistent in our communication, actions, and behavior. Stephen Covey calls this "congruence" when the three come together in a truly authentic fashion.[2] Consistently demonstrating congruence validates that you are trustworthy.

Early in my career, at a Cisco conference, John Chambers, then Cisco CEO, gave the keynote speech. Mr. Chambers spoke for an hour walking throughout the audience and never referenced his slides. His speech was not memorized. The passion, inflection, and charisma he displayed could not be rehearsed. I remember looking around the entire auditorium and noticing that people were mesmerized by his presence. Everyone was entirely focused on him. I could tell that the message was completely genuine. After the keynote, I hunted down some of my colleagues and confirmed that their experience matched my own. Mr. Chambers's congruence drove high-performance at Cisco. His authenticity inspired an entire company to uniformly pursue the mission. When you have this level of congruence, why would you need notes? John Chambers's results speak for themselves and consistency played a major role.

Be Transparent

Usually, when you hear the phrase, "I can see right through you," it means that someone can see your inauthenticity. Well, I want people to see right through me, but not because I am inauthentic. Rather, I strive to be as transparent as a pane of glass on a bright summer day!

However, don't confuse being transparent with being an asshole. You need that filter between your brain and your mouth. What's more, oversharing about your struggles can diminish others' confidence in your skill as a leader. Still, building trust through transparency involves sharing the good, the bad, and the ugly. Further, you need to create an environment where others can feel safe sharing their concerns. Transparency has incredible benefits in establishing trust:

- Transparency expedites trust.
- Transparency creates buy-in.
- Transparency fosters employee empowerment.
- Transparency enables faster negotiations and better decisions.

In a past role leading a cybersecurity program for an energy company, I endeavored to be an open book with my employees. I tried to create a transparent culture when I shared everything necessary with everyone on my team. This transparency led to employee empowerment. Team members could make impactful decisions on projects or other challenges without consulting me continually. This transparency also led to an environment where someone could walk into my office and tell me that I was making a stupid decision (backed with facts) when they felt I was doing so.

However, transparency can have unintended consequences too. When a much larger organization acquired us, I tried to be as transparent as possible. I wanted to minimize the uncertainty that comes with being acquired. My transparency led to information overload. It also fostered endless speculation about post-merger integration, including future organization structures and the potential of terminations. People wanted to know if they were going to have jobs, and if so, who was going to be their boss? As a result of my commitment to transparency we had to spend more time on capturing buy-in, fortifying trust, and confronting a dip in employee morale. It was an unhealthy and a disempowering dynamic I wish I would have avoided. As a leader, you must find a balance between being transparent and being too transparent.

Shut the Hell Up and Listen

We talked about the importance of listening in effective communications in Chapter 8 – Communication – You Do It Every Day (or Do You?) and highlighted some key listening skills; however, listening is just as crucial in establishing trust.

Newsflash: You do not have all of the answers all of the time; therefore, you must listen to ideas and feedback from your employees, peers, and superiors and integrate the information you learn through that feedback into your decisions. Doing so instills trust because those around you, particularly those who may be impacted by the decision, feel what they have to say matters.

I will never forget my first "all-hands" departmental meeting at a new job. The timing of my hire made it so that the meeting happened to be during my first week. I reported directly to the department head, and this meeting was an opportunity to highlight successes, talk through challenges facing the department and the broader organization, and raise any concerns. On that day, I was slapped in the face by the impact listening has on building and maintaining trust. The department head, who was very competent in managing a department and navigating difficult internal and external obstacles to achieve goals, finished the meeting. As he was wrapping up, he asked if there was anything anyone wanted to discuss with his head looking down as he was collecting his things. A couple of people raised their hands, but before he even looked up, he turned around, left the room, and then we all heard the large "thud" of the door slamming shut behind him. Everyone looked at each other. Some stared in disbelief, and others looked as if this was expected. At that instant, I knew this person was a department head by title only and that his team did not have any trust in him. Yes, the department head could allocate resources and navigate challenges, but he had no interest in listening to his employees and receiving suggestions or feedback. That was one of the first impressions I had of the department head at my new job, and he never gained my full trust as a result.

Be Humble

Jim Collins, author of *Good to Great* and *Great by Choice,* once said to a large forum of business leaders that "The x-factor of great leadership is not personality, it's humility."[3] Humility instills trust because humility, by definition, means "freedom of pride or arrogance."[4] A lack of pride or arrogance helps to establish trust because it shows that you are okay with not being the smartest person in the room, that you don't have (at least don't show) an ego, and that you are willing to give others a chance to step up and perform.

In the book *Dichotomy of Leadership*, Leif Babin spells out the importance of humility that Jocko Willink impressed upon his SEAL team, Task Unit Bruiser, during the battle of Ramadi in Iraq. Babin goes on to say:

Being humble also meant understanding that we didn't have it all figured out. We didn't have all the answers. It meant we must learn from other units that had been in Ramadi longer and work with them to support our chain of command and support the mission. It wasn't about how many operations we conducted or how many bad guys we dispatched. . .

. . . Being humble meant understanding the importance of strategic direction from our boss. It meant doing all we could to support the conventional forces we worked with, the Iraqi soldiers we trained and combat advised, and of course our chain of command. Being humble meant we put our heads down and got the job done as directed to the best of our ability.[5]

Do you see a corollary to a cybersecurity team here? Imagine sitting in a security operations center (SOC). I believe that humility ultimately drives a successful SOC. In a typical layout, the tier 1 analysts are the most junior people on the team and are situated in the front, eyes on glass, waiting for an alert to pop from the SIEM to notify them of an anomaly or a possible security event. If, after an initial triage, the potential security event requires further investigation, the tier 1 analyst must first be humble enough to realize that they have reached the end of their capabilities and secondly, to be humble enough to escalate to the tier 2 analysts in a timely fashion. Tier 2 must be humble enough to investigate the incident while sharing their knowledge and experience with tier 1. Tier 2 analysts must also be humble enough to escalate to a focused operations team. By this point, the security event likely is escalated to a security incident, yet the focused operations team must be humble enough to share their knowledge with tier 2 while investigating the incident.

Finally, the focused operations team must be humble enough to engage the critical security incident response team (CSIRT) should the security event escalate into a high priority security incident. In an SOC, it is never about how many alerts pop up in a SIEM or how many events you can triage and investigate by yourself. It is always about having the humility to know that you are part of a broader team that can put your heads down together and get the job done to the best of your ability. At this point, some of you may be saying, "There is no humility here; the SOC playbook is telling them when to escalate." True, the SOC playbook outlines when to escalate from one tier to another, but I challenge you to show me one SOC playbook that says the higher tier in the SOC must take time during what could be a very hectic time investigating an incident to share knowledge with the lower tier. Humility fosters trust throughout this entire ecosystem.

Just as there is a balance in being transparent, there is a balance in being humble. Being humble does not mean being weak and just shutting up and taking orders. It means recognizing there is a broader strategy in place that you or your team support and putting it ahead of your self-interests. Unlike the SEAL teams deployed in foreign conflict, I venture to guess that most of you reading this are working at your organization of your own free will. Therefore, humility also means knowing where your principles are drawn in the stand and fighting like hell not to cross that line, even if it means polishing off your resume.

As a leader, it is vital to press the importance of humility within your team, and it is also important to exhibit humility yourself. One of the most effective ways I have found to do this is to take a "the buck stops here" mentality. In other words, as a leader, you take all of the blame when something goes wrong but redirect all of the praise to your team when things go well. A leader is always responsible for what happens on a team, especially when things go wrong. When you accept the blame for your team, you set an example of ultimate accountability. On the flipside, when a leader deflects praise to his team, he tells his team that all of their individual efforts led to the team's success.

Now that you understand how to lay the foundation of the relationship by establishing and maintaining trust, let us examine how to expand upon relationship management via indirect influence and managing conflicts.

Indirect Influence

As a former CISO and now CEO and consultant, people ask me all the time about how to "manage up." Managing up depends on several factors, including the group you belong in and the individual you report to. There is a great debate among the cybersecurity community of where the chief information security officer should report. Should they report to the CIO, CFO, general counsel, or even the CEO directly? Firms like Gartner, Forrester, and McKinsey publish reports that the CISO is moving out from under the CIO. However, my non-scientific, boots-on-the-ground experience does not support that (although my co-author does report directly to the CEO). My answer? It depends. Many different factors go into determining an optimal reporting structure. I will set an unpopular stake in the ground and say that a cybersecurity leader's reporting structure ***does not matter***.

I think the real question is, "How do you deal with a bad reporting structure?" If you find yourself in a bad reporting structure, focus your efforts on the things you can control. You can control how you deal with it. You can control how you influence others, regardless of reporting structure, including your boss.

Indirect influence means that you keep your objective or goal in mind and take some action other than dealing directly with the person or group whom you wish to influence. Using indirect influence can mean either that you work through other people or use other means to accomplish your objective. For example, you may ask other business units, such as sales teams or procurement, to openly recognize your efforts and signal to leadership the need for allocated resources to the cybersecurity program. You may also. . .wait for it. . .collaborate with auditors and external penetration testers to highlight language in their findings that may tip the scales for securing funding for a new initiative or for hiring new staff. Ensure that you use indirect influence openly, though, so that it is not confused with manipulation, in which you intentionally hide your motivations and agenda.[6]

B. Kim Barnes outlines when indirect influence is more effective:[7]

- You don't have access to the person or group you wish to influence because of political, geographic, language, cultural, or other issues.
  - Imagine being based in the United States and working closely with a group out of Ireland or India, which has a less than cooperative business unit leader, to implement new security controls within their business unit.
- You have not established a good influence relationship with a critical person, and the issue is urgent enough that you do not have the time to build one.
  - Think about being relatively new to an organization that was a victim of the late 2020/early 2021 Solargate breach. Now think about convincing the CFO that your organization should be proactive and rip-and-replace its network monitoring infrastructure at a high cost, even though no tangible negative impact has occurred to your organization yet.
- The other individual does not believe you have the relevant knowledge, expertise, or status that would be the appropriate power sources for this influence issue.
  - You are trying to work with a profitable, revenue-generating business unit to resolve a compliance finding. The business unit

leader brushes you off because, well, in their mind you do not understand their critical business processes, and if it isn't broken, don't fix it. Furthermore, he does not give you the time of day to convince him that this particular process or technology implementation is in fact broken. In this case, you may work through your internal audit team to place emphasis on resolving the issue as the internal audit team typically has the standing and power within the organization to influence change.

- You don't have the power, or political capital, to be effective using direct influence.
  - I recently spoke to a CISO who reported to a CIO that continuously failed to prioritize and allocate budget to cybersecurity to allocate more resources to project that would elevate the CIO's profile within the executive team (until there was a significant cybersecurity incident, of course). The CIO consistently bypassed existing security controls and standards, so the CISO felt an apparent conflict of interest. The CISO felt there needed to be more separation of duties between cybersecurity and IT. The CISO worked through the CFO and the general counsel to affect a reporting change that resulted in the CISO, and their team, reporting to the general counsel. The general counsel had the power and political capital to raise risks to the C-Suite and ensure that cybersecurity was better integrated into IT projects and enterprise risk management.
- You have been trying to influence directly and have hit a snag or are at an impasse.
  - This use case may be similar to the last bullet point. However, the CISO may have a better relationship with the CIO and instead works through business stakeholders to ensure cybersecurity risk and appropriate controls are considered in IT projects.

Exerting indirect influence is a slow, long-term objective that you achieve over time – much like smoking a good brisket. One effective method of indirect influence is called trim-tabbing. In the traditional sense, trim tabs are small surfaces connected to the trailing edge of a larger control surface on a boat or aircraft (e.g., a rudder). Small adjustments to the trim tab can affect the path of the boat or the aircraft over a long distance. The same is true of indirect influence. Effecting many small changes over time can lead to significant changes in the long term. Designer Buckminster Fuller is credited with initially using "trim tabs" as a metaphor for leadership and empowerment. In February 1972, Fuller said:

Something hit me very hard once, thinking about what one little man could do. Think of the Queen Mary – the whole ship goes by and then comes the rudder. And there's a tiny thing at the edge of the rudder called a trim tab.

It's a miniature rudder. Just moving the little trim tab builds a low pressure that pulls the rudder around. Takes almost no effort at all. So I said that the little individual can be a trim tab. Society thinks it's going right by you, that it's left you altogether. But if you're doing dynamic things mentally, the fact is that you can just put your foot out like that and the whole big ship of state is going to go.

So I said, call me Trim Tab.[8]

Stephen Covey (do you see a theme here?) popularized the notion of trim tabbing in his book *The 8th Habit: From Effectiveness to Greatness*. Trim-tab leaders take the initiative to influence their "Circle of Influence"[9] in small ways that eventually lead to indirectly influencing the organization to achieve the leader's goals. Your "Circle of Influence" is smaller than your "Circle of Concern," although your job role will often take you outside of your "Circle of Influence." In other words, focus on things you can control to influence the things that you cannot control.

As cybersecurity leaders, we often have to influence things outside of our control by focusing on things within our control. I once faced a challenge where a business unit leader wanted to use a particular SaaS provider to store and process some of the company's "crown jewels." This SaaS provider happened to be a startup and not very proven within the market, but the business unit leader was so enamored with some of the promised features that they claimed there was nobody else on the market who could provide a similar service. I initiated a third-party cybersecurity risk assessment of the SaaS provider, per our established practices. Since my company would be sharing some of its most confidential and valuable information, the SaaS provider landed in our "high risk" bucket, so they received our most comprehensive set of questions. They were unable to answer almost all of the questions. For instance, when asked about data encryption at rest and transit, along with access controls, they replied, "AWS has a SOC2 and handles that." That is not a satisfactory answer (Google "AWS Shared Responsibility Model" if you don't understand why).

The business unit leader insisted we proceed with the implementation due to various business drivers. I could not directly influence the business leader's desire, nor could I change the business drivers; however, I was responsible for identifying cyber risks to the organization. What I could do was leverage the personal, social, and structural motivations of the Six Sources of Influence that we outlined in Chapter 3 – Business Decisions to influence the situation. I elevated the risk to the enterprise risk management team and objectively outlined the likelihood for significant lost revenue and market share. After considering my analysis, they asked the business unit lead if the new features were so revolutionary and transformative that he could not find another workaround with similar benefits (Harness Peer Pressure – social). They then asked if he would bet his job on that decision (Make the Undesirable Desirable – personal). The answer was a reluctant "no" (Design Rewards and Demand Accountability – structural). Funny how that worked once the leader had to stick his own neck out on the line.

Trim-tab leaders use vision, discipline, passion, principles, and action to grow their "Circle of Influence" regardless of their formal job title, but make sure to pick your battles. Taking initiative that is far beyond your "Circle of Influence" may backfire on you.

Managing Through Conflict

The very nature of our jobs requires us to be able to manage conflict effectively. Conflict may come in the form of varied opinions or in the form of working with a business unit to implement a new security control (as was in the case of our development manager from Chapter 8 – Communication – You Do It Every Day (or Do You?)).

At its core, managing through conflict is just another form of negotiating. As you know, we will cover the topic in Chapter 12 – Negotiations. Nonetheless, I have used the following basic negotiating framework, adapted from *Getting to Yes*,[10] to handle some pretty sticky situations:

- Don't make it personal
- Focus on cause, not effect
- Generate options
- Be objective

Don't Make It Personal

We have all worked with big personalities, some more likable than others. Part of growing as a leader is delivering results despite the circumstances. Sometimes you have to work with people you don't like. The key is to remove the roadblock by counteracting difficult personalities. Conflict is very personal, so making it impersonal is the first step toward resolving conflict.

Human nature compels us to become personally involved in conflict and take a side. When someone challenges our view or position, we may instinctually perceive that challenge as a personal attack. This doesn't have to be the case. The key is to remove the people variable from the problem. Doing so allows individuals to take a step back, be objective, and discuss issues in a safe environment without the fear of losing face or damaging a relationship.

There are three fundamental obstacles to separating people from the problem, namely perception, emotion, and communication. Most conflicts arise because of different interpretations of the facts. You must extend the other party a benefit of the doubt. For example, if the sales team pushes back on multifactor authentication for the CRM system, consider that it is because multifactor authentication creates control friction in the sales process. They are trying to quickly look up a customer record, on the road, with limited connectivity, before a critical meeting. It's not because they are merely reluctant to change.

The second obstacle is emotion. Understanding the other party's viewpoint and demonstrating empathy is crucial. People may react with emotion when they feel their position or character is being challenged (hence, don't take it personally). Dismissing emotions as unreasonable will exacerbate the conflict. Once you acknowledge the other party's emotion, then you can begin to shrink your differences and resolve the conflict.

The third obstacle is communication, and we dedicated an entire chapter to this topic. Instead of playing point/counterpoint, where you anticipate your response while the other party is talking, employ active listening. Give the other party your full attention. When you truly understand the other party's version of the facts along with the emotion that accompanies those facts, you can respond. It's best to formulate a counterpoint that legitimately addresses the other party's concerns rather than invalidating your efforts thus far by forcing your perspective into the dialogue. Of course, many of these obstacles will not come up in the first place if you maintain good relationships and view the other individual as a partner and not an adversary.

Focus on Cause, Not Effect

You must understand the difference between interests and positions. The authors of *Getting to Yes* detail, "Your position is something you have decided upon. Your interests are what caused you to decide." In other words, there is a cause-and-effect relationship between interests and positions. If you focus on the other person's position (the effect), then someone will win and someone will lose in the conflict; however, if you focus on the other person's interests, you can work to find a "win-win" solution that satisfies everyone's interests (the cause).

Identify the interests at hand by asking *why* the other person is standing firm on their chosen position. Ask them "straight-up" and be direct about it. Once the interests are determined, you can then identify a commonality. For example, recall the development manager example from Chapter 8 – Communication – You Do it Every Day (or Do You?) where the security manager used the Socratic method to convince the development manager to work together to get security vulnerabilities the same level of priority and visibility as traditional code defects.

You can see that the security manager and the development manager both wanted fewer code defects (vulnerabilities in this case), and therefore less rework for everyone involved.

After you have identified everyone's interests, you must explain your interests clearly and summarize the other party's interests to ensure a mutual understanding. Doing so also demonstrates respect. You are paying attention and actively concerned with the other party's interests. If everyone can remain open to a third alternative, you will find an innovative solution that satisfies everyone's needs. It is likely to be a new solution that neither party envisioned when you started.

Generate Options

Now, you must develop your options and alternative solutions. Brainstorm and ensure everything is out on the table no matter how outlandish the suggestion or solution may seem. Recall the School of Thought Creative Thinking Cards Deck mentioned in Chapter 5 – Articulating the Business Case. Avoid a "win-lose" scenario because that will derail your conversations and escalate the conflict. Individuals may suggest partial solutions to the problem as a bridge to implementing a more in-depth solution. You should only begin to evaluate suggestions after many suggestions have been made. Considering each idea as it is proposed can be counterproductive. Starting with the most promising suggestions allows you to iteratively refine alternatives until everyone is satisfied. Any low-hanging fruit (low effort/ high value) is a great place to start. Early progress builds momentum and promotes goodwill.

Be Objective

What criteria will you use to resolve the conflict? All parties should agree on objective criteria that removes emotion and ego. Doing so not only allows you to move forward with a solution to resolve the conflict, but it minimizes animosity and preserves your relationships with the other parties moving forward. You can also involve the other party in defining the procedure for resolving the conflict. For instance, if you are implementing a significant security initiative, such as identity and access management (IAM), the cybersecurity team may define the required security controls. Then, you can engage the individual business units to develop their procedures to meet the security controls while minimizing disruption and friction to existing business processes.

Consider the following points when developing objective criteria:

- All parties in the conflict should be involved in defining the objective search criteria.
- Understand everyone's interests and use their reasoning to support your interests.
- All parties must keep an open mind and be willing to evaluate alternative solutions.
- Do not allow yourself to be bullied and give in to pressure or threats.

Professional Networking

Research shows that 70% of all jobs are not published publicly on job sites, and as much as 80% of jobs are filled through personal and professional connections.[11] Networking with humans (instead of computers) is a skill that many cybersecurity professionals struggle to develop. The traits that allow us to focus on solving a challenge, almost to the point of obsession, are some of the same traits that preclude our looking up from our laptops and interacting with others. Networking with peers external to your organization helps accelerate your growth as a cybersecurity leader through exposure to new ideas.

Frankly, many of us are introverts. To this day, I *loathe* the idea of showing up to an event where I do not know anyone and "working the room," but networking has easily had the largest return on investment in my professional career. Networking has benefits inside and outside of your organization. The good news is that there are plenty of opportunities to network with other peers in our industry. There are industry conferences like RSA, Blackhat, Defcon, and the Rocky Mountain Information Security Conference. There are also local chapters of the International Information Systems Security Association (ISSA), the Information Systems Audit and Control Association (ISACA), the Cloud Security Alliance (CSA), and the

Open Web Application Security Project (OWASP). Then, there are vendor-sponsored events and dozens, if not hundreds, of meetup groups and online discussion forums for just about any topic where you can join and contribute. The opportunities to network with your peers are plentiful. You need to take the initiative and do it.

So, how do you go about networking when all you want to do is huddle in a corner? First of all, you have to accept you are going to be uncomfortable. Secondly, realize that the key to successful networking is not to promote yourself and exploit the connection for personal gain but to add value wherever you can to help others succeed. I have used the advice of Dale Carnegie and Keith Ferrazzi, authors of *How to Win Friends and Influence People* and *Never Eat Alone*, respectively, to help develop my networking skills.

Many of the events mentioned above can be a test bed to hone your skills. Let's dig in on Keith and Dale's perspectives on networking. You will notice some commonalities across both author's viewpoints. These can also serve as "Key Activities" for you to consider as you go about networking.

In *How to Win Friends and Influence People in the Digital Age*, Dale Carnegie and Associates takes the concepts from Dale Carnegie's *How to Win Friends and Influence People*, published in 1936, and applies them to today's digital age. The book outlines six key activities that ensure you leave a lasting impression with your connections and interactions:[12]

- **Take an interest in others' interests:** People tend to align and gravitate toward others who share their self-interests. Because of social media's proliferation, it is effortless (and lazy) to engage behind a keyboard. However, the real value comes when you invest time to know people and their challenges or interests personally. That's the only way to lay the foundation for mutual benefit, which also develops indirect influence. Who would have thunk it?
- **Smile:** In Chapter 8 – Communication – You Do it Every Day (or Do You?), we discussed the power of a simple smile. In the digital age, your spoken and written voice and tone translate into a digital smile.

- **Reign with Names:** Your name is your brand. You cannot know someone unless you know their name. When you know someone, you have a relationship, and relationships are your most valuable currency when building your network. To this day, I am terrible with names. Four tips that I use that Carnegie provides for remembering names are:
  - Spell it
  - Create a mental image of the person
  - Say it multiple times
  - Write it down and look at it

  Doing the above helps form the links and associations in your mind that allow for fast recall.

- **Listen Longer:** Think about how frustrated you get when you feel you are not heard. By nature, people desire to be heard and need to know someone is listening. Active listening (Chapter 8 – Communication – You Do it Every Day (or Do You?)) builds strong connections and trust and allows you to leave a lasting impression. Put the damn phone down (again), cut out the distractions from the environment or the event, and focus. Treat the conversation you are engaging in as the most important thing in the universe at that time and pay full attention to what the other has to say.

- **Discuss what matters to them:** This ties to the above point, "Listen Longer." Listening will breed an understanding of what matters to the other person, and it will allow you to focus on what matters to them. Remember, when building your network, it's not about you. . .it's about "them"!

- **Leave others a little better:** Add value. Volunteer information and skills. For instance, if the person you are speaking with expresses frustration around building a business case for a particular initiative, and you happen to be good at building business cases, volunteer to review their business case for them. As you nurture the relationship and the relationship becomes more friendly, if the other person needs help moving, get off your butt and help them move! Psychologists say that a "law of reciprocity" states that people have a deep-rooted psychological need to return favors. By doing something nice for someone, they are very likely to do something nice for you in return.

In *Never Eat Alone*, author Kevin Ferrazzi advocates that building your personal brand and network should be your way of life. Ferrazzi leveraged his relationships to become the Chief Marketing Offer (CMO) at Deloitte & Touche Consulting, the youngest-ever CMO at Starwood Hotel & Resorts, and the CEO at Yaya Media. Finally, he started his own company, Ferrazzi Greenlight.

Many points and tips are outlined throughout the book, but I want to distill the attributes and strategies that resonated with me, and that provided the greatest value.[13]

- **Don't keep score:** Generosity and loyalty are foundational to good networking. This point is analogous to Carnegie's "Leave others a little better." Networking and building relationships is a two-way street. ALWAYS ask how you can help. You give, and you receive, which lays the groundwork later for the "law of reciprocity."
- **Build your network before you need it:** Building relationships is a long-term endeavor. Sorry – there is no Tinder for professional networking. You cannot just swipe left or swipe right. It will be too late to start building a network when you need it. My success as a consultant is 100% attributed to the network that I cultivated over twenty-five years.
- **Do your homework:** Always, always, always prepare for a meeting. If you are targeting networking with a particular person, do some research on the person. Your preparation allows you to focus on touchpoints that you know will pique the individual's interest (Carnegie's "Discuss what matters to them"). You may even start to covertly provide value by sharing insights the other person may not have considered. If you are going to a general networking event, do your homework on the type of people who may be attracted to the event and formulate a small-talk track in your head based on the different personas you may encounter.
- **Be a conference commando:** The most significant value of going to conferences is not in going to all of the talks and sessions. The most significant value lies in the hallway conversations, or as we have coined it in our industry, "Hallway-Con" or "LobbyCon." Get introduced, or introduce yourself, to

like minded people and set up follow-up discussions after the conference. LinkedIn has made connecting, following up, and engaging post-conference extremely easy.

- **Be visible:** It is easy to fill our calendars with every event on the planet, including happy hours, dinners, sporting events, and conferences. When I was leading a cybersecurity program, I could go to a vendor-sponsored event every night, which is not sustainable and would have made for a very disgruntled wife. Be clear about the value you hope to extract from the events you attend.
- **Follow-up:** The money is always in the follow-up. Remember, your currency (money) is your relationships.
- **Leverage super-connectors:** We all know that one person who seems to know everyone. Furthermore, in our field of cybersecurity, it seems that everyone is separated by two degrees of separation rather than the generally accepted six-degrees. Super-connectors have a Rolodex of thousands of contacts upon which they could call, and *the other end of the call answers*. Make friends with these people.

Application

Let's dive into a couple of case studies of how the contents of this chapter has saved my bacon at a couple of points in my career.

Case Study 1 – Humility for Trust's Sake

Sometimes, eating good old-fashioned humble pie actually instills trust. That's right. Own up to your mistakes, admit them as soon as possible, explain why you made the decision you did, and follow up with a plan to correct the error. I speak from experience. When I was working for a federal contractor and running a combined security and network operations center (SNOC) for a US federal government entity, my operations and maintenance team had the responsibility for upgrading the enterprise IT ticketing system over the course of a night. This ticketing system was the backbone for IT support across the organization globally, and it was, shall we say, a very visible upgrade and politically charged. Without it, about 24,000 users across over 125 global field offices could not report IT issues, not receive IT support. I should also mention that our contract was expiring and was coming up for a recompete as mandated by the federal contract, and the success of this upgrade would go a long way to solidify our position as the incumbent.

I got a call at about 11 p.m. that the upgrade was going sideways. After hanging up, I called my boss to inform him of the status to inform the customer (the federal government agency), and then I hopped in the car and drove to the SNOC since I lived only 15 minutes away.

After getting to the SNOC, the system administrators executing the upgrade convinced me that it was better and more time effective if they proceeded to troubleshoot the upgrade versus restoring from a backup since they believed they had narrowed down the issue. Our rules, our playbook, and our approval from the change board all said that if the upgrade was not complete in a specific timeframe, we would roll back the upgrade and restore from backup, but in this case, I let the system administrators sway my decision. One more hour turned to two more hours, and two more hours turned to three more hours. By about 4 a.m., I finally put my foot down and forced a rollback, much to the chagrin of the system administrators who had been troubleshooting the issue all night and were convinced they had almost solved the problem.

Daylight came, and the phones started blowing up. The customer was irate, and they had every right to be. I proactively called my government stakeholders to let them know what had happened. What could have been a 4-hour rollback turned into a 12-hour marathon. Jobs, including my own, were potentially on the line. I could have made excuses, or I could have taken responsibility. I took full responsibility. They appreciated me explaining why I made the decisions that I did and why I believed they were the best decisions based on the information I had. I had to weigh blowing a change window with the risk of corrupting an installation and data by rolling back the upgrade, but the federal government places a lot of weight on processes, and

I didn't follow their process. I understood that, and owning up to that mistake was not only the right thing to do, but in my mind, it was the only thing to do.

I didn't leave the office until after I personally wrote the after-action report. I reviewed all after-action reports from the SNOC before submitting them to the government client, but I rarely wrote them myself. I held myself responsible in the root cause analysis. Unbelievably to me at the time, instead of mandating that I be removed from the contract, which would have likely cost me my job, the government client changed some change management rules due to the after-action report to give the SNOC more decision-making authority during these types of outage windows so that we *could* troubleshoot more during these types of change windows. At the risk of creating an oxymoron and bragging about how humble I was, the humility I exhibited immediately after that event rewarded the SNOC with more trust, not less.

Case Study 2 – Professional Networking

For many of us, our networks begin in college. Many of us can even go as far back as junior high and high school. For instance, my website's latest iteration was developed mainly by a friend I have known since high school. I first learned the real value of networking in college during my first internship. I was an intern at the Bellagio Hotel in Las Vegas, Nevada, before the resort opened. We developed "Leader's Guides," which were "train the trainer" materials used before and after the resort's opening. The nature of our work required that we talk to various department heads about their jobs and critical challenges (discuss what matters to them) and then distill their input into a work product that they would use to train new employees as they onboarded. These Leader's Guides offloaded some of the already tremendous workload and pressure that comes with opening a billion-dollar resort. An added benefit was that some department heads could use the amount of work and training documented in these Leader's Guides to justify additional resources (leave others a little better). The relationships I built as a mere intern with senior director and vice president level roles led to references that spring-boarded my career.

Now, let us fast-forward almost 25 years. I was hired by an energy company to build its cybersecurity program from the ground up, which included traditional IT and Operational Technology (OT). My professional goals were aligned with the organization's goals. I wanted to build and lead the cybersecurity program of an organization whose mission was vital to our nation's critical infrastructure. I was happy and proud of the work we were doing. Then, one July morning I woke up to a text message from a former MBA classmate asking, "Did you guys just get acquired?" He lived two time zones ahead of me and saw the press release via the _Wall Street Journal_. I jumped up, looked at the email on my phone, and replied, "Holy shit – I need to get back to you."

From that point, I was fortunate enough to go on an incredible journey leading security and technology integration efforts between the two companies. I was very proud of the work we had accomplished. Two years later, it became apparent that the acquiring company's corporate headquarters was absorbing more and more of my job function. I was not willing to relocate. In truth, I was also slightly burned out. The previous two years had been a sprint. At the same time, the prospect of job hunting was nauseating. After consulting my wife, I realized that it was a perfect time to start my own business. There were plenty of risks, including the risk of not winning enough business, on a continuing basis, that would lead to me scrambling to dive back into that nausea-causing job hunt without the cushion of an existing paycheck. Together, we decided that while the financial risks were high, the mental health risks of burnout were higher and that launching a consulting business was still the best thing to do. We also decided that it was prudent to slowly build up business. Once the value proposition and business volume reached critical mass I could transition into full-time consulting.

Over the next six months, I reached out to the vast majority of my network to let them know of my plans. I asked for advice and referrals, which led to many one-on-one conversations. The energy company I served was aware of my consulting aspirations, and my boss was very supportive. In the end, the new integrated security team reorganized and eliminated my position before I was ready to exit. It was the perfect incentive, sink or swim. My last day with the company was on a Thursday, and thanks to my fantastic network, I started billing my first full-time client the following Monday.

My network took 25 years to build and 6 months to prime before I was ready to thrive on my own. At the time of this writing, the vast majority of my work as a consultant has come through referrals. *Do not wait* to start building and nurturing your professional relationships. Done right, your network will be there when you need them the most.

Key Insights

- Follow a simple five-step process to establish and build trust:
  - **Say what you do and do what you say:** Keeping promises is a key factor in establishing and maintaining trust. As a leader, how can you expect your employees to get behind you and the organizational mission if your communication and actions are not aligned? Your words and actions must match. Failing to do so will lead to people not trusting you.
  - **Be authentic and congruent:** Authenticity lends to congruency. If you have any level of emotional intelligence, you can usually tell quickly when someone is authentic or not. Sometimes, people contradict themselves and show their inauthenticity. Other times, it's a gut feeling that indicates to you that someone is inauthentic, like when you are buying a new car, and the salesperson is your "best friend" the second you walk onto the car lot.
  - **Be transparent:** Make sure your employees remain informed of key developments and why the organization made certain decisions. Ensure expectations are clear and that every employee has a chance to provide feedback on those expectations. However, be mindful of when sharing too much information, or sharing it at an inappropriate time, can lead to confusion and distrust.

- **Shut the hell up and listen:** When you say you have an open-door policy, have an open-door policy. Don't sit there and wonder why your employees do not open up to you about their concerns during a project, a major company initiative, or even their career growth plan, when you regularly dismiss their concerns or avoid their feedback altogether. Furthermore, don't interrupt! Our parents teach us not to interrupt from childhood, yet we are all still guilty of this. I am particularly guilty of this when I have a point I want to get out before the thought leaves my feeble mind. However, interrupting is rude and implies that what you have to say is more important than what the other person has to say. Nothing instills trust with someone, like suggesting what they have to say doesn't matter, right? Stay present in the conversation. That email or text that comes through during the conversation can wait. Nothing says, "Don't trust me because I don't care about what you are saying," like not paying attention to someone when they are speaking to you.
- **Be humble:** Surrounding myself with people who are smarter than me reminds me that my stuff really does stink. Every day, I remind myself how lucky I am to have a successful consulting business that has grown mainly through referrals. I am thankful that I am in a position every day to learn from people and teach. Remember that it is *okay to admit mistakes*. It's okay to utter the words "I was wrong." Doing so as soon as possible, being candid as to why you made a particular decision, and having a plan of action to rectify the mistake go a long way in building trust.

- **Create indirect influence:**
  - **Establish indirect influence through "trim-tabbing":** Small nudges will have huge effects over time.
  - **Understand the "big picture" direction and destination:** What are your goals? Are they aligned to the organization's goals? Do you understand what is in and out of your "Circle of Influence" and what factors determine your "Circle of Influence"? Can you trim-tab through changing organizational dynamics?
  - **Listen more, speak less:** Review Chapter 8 – Communication – You Do it Every Day (or Do You?).

- **Get people to like you:** Say "please" and "thank you" a lot. Lift up your co-workers. Speak well of people and don't speak negatively about people behind their back (like the development manager from Chapter 8 – Communication – You Do it Every Day (or Do You?). Show genuine interest in how your colleagues are doing, or how they spent their weekend. Don't fake it. People will see right through it.
- **Be supportive:** Volunteer to help someone prepare for a presentation. Get "in the weeds" with your team when troubleshooting an issue. Share knowledge. Allow a stressed colleague to talk to you to vent.
- **Bribe:** Yes, I said that. Coffee, donuts, pizza, and beer (when appropriate) go a very long way.

- **Remember these keys to managing through conflict:**
  - **Don't make it personal:** There are three fundamental obstacles to separating people from the problem, namely perception, emotion, and communication. Most conflicts arise because of different interpretations of the facts. You must extend the other party a benefit of the doubt.
  - **Focus on cause, not effect:** Interests are the cause. Positions are the effect.
  - **Generate options:** At the risk of sounding like a cliche, focus on "win-win" scenarios even though "win-lose" scenarios may seem rewarding.
  - **Be objective:** Agree on objective criteria to resolve the conflict. All parties in the conflict need to be involved in determining this criteria.
- **Cultivate your professional network:**
  - **Get comfortable:** They key to networking is to get comfortable with being uncomfortable, particularly if you are an introvert.
  - **It's not about you:** Do not promote yourself and exploit the connection for personal gain, but add value to where you can without any expectation of "quid-pro-quo."
  - **Do your homework and remember names:** Always prepare for meetings. How can you expect others to remember positively when you show up "winging it" and you when you can't remember their name?

- **Build your network before you need it:** Don't wait. Start now.
- **Get out there:** Participate in "HallwayCons," and be focused on the types of events you want to attend.
- **Follow-up:** The money is always in the follow-up. Remember, your currency (money) is your relationships.
- **Super-connect:** Find the super-connectors in your network and get introduced to them. Then, figure out how you can help them.

Notes

1. Covey, S.M.R., *The SPEED of Trust: The One Thing That Changes Everything*, Free Press, 2018.
2. Covey, S.M.R., *The SPEED of Trust: The One Thing That Changes Everything*.
3. Davis, K., "Jim Collins on Creative Discipline, Paranoia and Other Marks of a Great Leader," 2012. Accessed January 30, 2021. https://www.entrepreneur.com/article/224568.
4. "Humility," Merriam-Webster. Accessed January 30, 2021. https://www.merriam-webster.com/dictionary/humility.
5. Willink, J., and Babin L, *The Dichotomy of Leadership: Balancing the Challenges of Extreme Ownership to Lead and Win*, St. Martin's Press, 2018.
6. Barnes, B.K., *Exercising Influence: A Guide for Making Things Happen at Work, at Home, and in Your Community*, John Wiley & Sons, 2015.
7. Barnes, B.K., *Exercising Influence: A Guide for Making Things Happen at Work, at Home, and in Your Community*.
8. "Playboy Interview: R. Buckminster Fuller – Candid Conversations," *Playboy*, February 1972.
9. Covey, S.M.R., *The 8th Habit: From Effectiveness to Greatness*, Free Press, 2004.
10. Fisher, R., and Ury, W., *Getting to Yes: Negotiating Agreement Without Giving In*, 2nd ed., Penguin Group (USA) Inc., 1991.
11. Freeland Fisher, J., "How to Get a Job Often Comes Down to One Elite Personal Asset," Accessed February 4, 2021. https://www.cnbc.com/2019/12/27/how-to-get-a-job-often-comes-down-to-one-elite-personal-asset.html.

12. Dale Carnegie and Associates, and Cole, B., *How to Win Friends & Influence People in the Digital Age*, Simon & Schuster Paperbacks, 2011.
13. Farazzi, K., and Raz, T., *Never Eat Alone: Expanded and Updated – And Other Secrets to Success, One Relationship at a Time*, Currency, 2014.

CHAPTER 10

Recruiting and Leading High Performing Teams

If you want to lift yourself up, lift up someone else.
— Booker T. Washington

Opportunity

In Chapter 6 – Cybersecurity: A Concern of the Business, Not Just IT, we briefly discuss addressing the cybersecurity skills gap in the context of the COSO principle of "Attract, Develop, and Retain Capable Individuals." Cybersecurity professionals have specialized skills that are in short supply. Think about the following (in your best internal Liam Neeson voice) when dealing with an adversary that is holding your organization's technology environment for ransom:

I don't know who you are. I don't know what you want. If you're looking for ransom, I can tell you I don't have bit-coin. . .but what I do have are a *very particular set of skills*. Skills I have acquired over a very long career. Skills that make me a nightmare for people like you. If you let my server go now, that will be the end of it. I will not look for you, I will not

> pursue you. . .but if you don't, I will look for you, I will find
> you. . .and I will do whatever I can to work with the authorities
> to squash you.

I've always dreamed of doing that; however, let's get back to reality.
The skills gap has driven a vigorous competition for talent, which
forces organizations to tailor how they approach their cybersecurity
staffing. They must ensure they have the right people in the right roles
at the right time. Recruiting and developing cybersecurity professionals is an investment in time and money, and turnover is costly for any
organization. Each employee departure costs about one-third of that
employee's annual earnings, including expenses such as recruiter
fees, temporary replacement workers, and lost productivity.[1]
Therefore, you must also focus on retaining capable individuals. It is
often said that people leave managers, not companies. This chapter
will dive into how to recruit "A-Players" by reviewing best practices for
candidate screening and reference checks. This chapter will then
review various leadership styles, such as transformational, servant,
and adaptive leadership, to enable you to lead and retain a high-
performing team to keep you from falling into the "people leave managers" category.

Principle

Cybersecurity leaders should assert that cybersecurity deserves to be
on the same playing field as other departments such as operations,
finance, or even general IT. Doing so involves retaining and leading a
high-performance team. In this context, leadership refers to motivating others to achieve a common goal irrespective of reporting structure. Recruiting and developing high-performing teams is increasingly
difficult and even more imperative now with the substantially remote
workforce. Leadership is an art and not a hard skill like analyzing a
PCAP or implementing a new SASE solution. I believe this is why
leadership tends to be difficult for cybersecurity professionals.
Cybersecurity often requires logical, analytical skill sets, but leadership is not always logical and analytical.

The reality is that the "'soft stuff' is what makes the 'hard stuff' possible."[2] Cybersecurity is only successful when people work as a team to enable the organization to achieve its strategic goals. Innovation only happens when people feel safe enough to risk vulnerability as they fail and learn. If people don't feel like they can contribute or are afraid to speak up, they lose their incentive to perform. Instead, they fail to apply their passion, talent, and intelligence until they can find another opportunity. Few things drag on team morale and performance more than dead weight. Leadership involves:

- Establishing a clear strategy
- Sharing the strategy
- Clearly communicating the "why" behind the strategy so that others follow willingly rather than simply comply with your formal authority
- Guiding, motivating, and enabling employees to achieve the goals of the strategy
- Persistence with the mundane, everyday tactics required to realize the strategy

Good leadership yields intrinsically motivated, engaged, loyal, and happy employees that consistently produce great results. To have a high-performing team, you must first recruit the right employees. Demonstrating leadership during the recruiting and interviewing process will increase your chances of finding the right employee for your organization. Effective leadership then allows you to keep those employees by elevating them, guiding them, investing in them in ways that are aligned with company outcomes, or creating room for work-life integration.

Honor people as whole individuals with a life outside the boundary of work. Take an active interest in their desires, wants, priorities, and personal lives. You may even frequently put their interests ahead of your own. We will explore several leadership styles throughout this chapter, but it is up to you to determine which is the best fit for you.

Recruiting High-Performing Teams – Topgrading

Recruiting and interviewing can be "noisy" if you do not know what your ideal candidate looks like, or if you cannot remove as much bias as possible from the hiring process. Daniel Kahneman, who if you remember we first referenced in Chapter 3 – Business Decisions when introducing decision science, says, "A general property of noise is that you can recognize and measure it while knowing nothing about the target or bias."[3] He and his co-authors go on to say that if all you know about a set of candidates is how they interviewed compared to each other, the chances that the top candidate will perform better are about 56 to 61%. A little better than flipping a coin, but would you leave an important hiring decision to chance? What if there was a way to identify through the core competencies and eliminate much of the bias? Kahneman advocates for structure, and we believe Dr. Brad Smart provides a framework that provides a structure that delivers results.

Brad Smart, who has a PhD in Organizational Psychology, observed early in his career that the standard one-hour interview process and aptitude tests only produced high performers 30% of the time. He developed a methodology called "Topgrading" that focuses on a more dynamic interview process than the standard question-and-answer formality to provide a comprehensive profile of a candidate's background and personality.

Topgrading involves a 12-step process, so consider it a rehab program for your recruiting and hiring practices. Important undertakings in this process include extensive interviews, detailed job scorecards, and having the candidate arrange reference interviews. Candidates are then categorized as "A-Players," "B Players," or "C Players."[4] An independent doctoral thesis at Georgia State University evaluated six different companies that employed Topgrading. The study evaluated six companies that made a total of about 1,000 new hires between them. Results of the study showed that the average "mis-hire" rate before Topgrading was 69.3%. After implementing Topgrading, however, the average mis-hire rate plummeted to 10.5%.[5]

Smart has written several books dedicated to Topgrading, and countless others reference it. I first learned about Topgrading while reading *Scaling Up: How a Few Companies Make it. . .and Why the Rest Don't (Rockefeller Habits 2.0)* by Verne Harnish. I will try to give Topgrading justice here by summarizing the 12 hiring steps. Suffice it to say, you should more thoroughly examine these references for a complete understanding.

Be forewarned, instituting this type of hiring methodology is not for those with a weak stomach. You don't need to be a Fortune 100 organization to institute some of the methodologies mentioned below, but you will need to partner with your HR and recruiting teams. Many of you reading this are already working with your HR teams to right-size cybersecurity job classifications and salaries for your respective markets. Leverage this same partnership to adjust recruiting practices.

Even if you cannot immediately establish a partnership with HR to adjust the organization's hiring practices, you can still implement many of the steps outlined below. You can create a job scorecard to share with candidates (step #2), seek out and encourage individuals from your networks to apply for your open positions (step #3), screen candidates against that job scorecard (step #4), and streamline the rest of the steps to fit the size and capacity of your team.

Before undertaking this endeavor, make sure it is right for your organization. For example, in today's market (2020/2021), a cloud security role is most likely to be filled by a millennial and our experience is that the average tenure of someone in that role is 18 to 24 months. That might just be the "cost of doing business" in the current market conditions. Topgrading is not a fast process, so you need to consider the lost opportunity of a vacant role for perhaps several months. How would this compare to a mis-hire in your organization? In a growth business with a ticking clock on the value, that cost of a mis-hire may be less than the cost of a no-hire. Our point? Topgrading is one perspective on hiring. Consider other perspectives on hiring and ensure that whatever approach you take aligns with your organization's overall strategic goals.

Step #1: Measure Your Baseline Success Hiring and Promoting People and Your Cost of Mis-Hires

We often focus on measuring metrics such as mean-time-to-detect, mean-time-to-recover, and adhering to patching SLAs, but have you measured your success in one of the most critical things you will ever do for your organization, which is selecting people? Many organizations only track the time and cost to fill jobs but do not measure the cost of a mis-hire. There are four key measures that you need to calculate and track:

- **Baseline Hiring Success**
  - Baselining hiring success is a relatively straightforward calculation. Rate each hire over the past three years as of one year after their hire date. Write down the number that you believed were high performers, which in this case is defined as "are they performing at or above expectations when you hired them." That number divided by the total hires is your baseline hiring success rate.
- **Talent Projection**
  - This calculation may sound a little brutal but necessary to achieve 90% hiring success, where hiring success is defined as hiring "A-Players." Talent projection will outline how many people you will have to hire and fire to achieve a 90% success rate given your current success rate.
    - "A-Players" are the top 10% of talent available for any job, at any given salary level.
  - The ratio of the number of people you will need to hire to anyone when they leave will improve as your hiring success rate improves.
    - On average, you will need to hire about four individuals to replace one underperformer if your baseline hiring success rate is 25%. This ratio moves closer to 1:1 as you approach a 90% hiring success rate. Remember, the Topgrading method calibrates at 90% because the reality is that you will never reach a 100% baseline hiring success rate. If you do, we need to have a conversation!

■ **Cost of Mis-Hires**

- You have to determine the parameters of a mis-hire within your organization. Are they an underperformer, do they not fit with your team's culture, or do they simply leave within two years? Determining the parameters of a mis-hire is crucial.
- Interestingly the cost of mis-hires includes costs to retain, as well as the cost of mistakes, disruption, morale, and opportunity costs for time spent coaching, etc.
- You can take advantage of the online calculator, https://topgrading.com/resources/mis-hire-calculator/, which requires providing your email address.

■ **Organizational Cost of Mis-Hires**

- Assume you have 15 mis-hires in a given year, and you estimate the average cost of a mis-hire is $250,000. Replacing all 15 with "A-players" with 25% hiring success rate would involve three mis-hires for every good hire. You would have to hire 60 people, mis-hiring 45, to end up with 15 "A-Players." The 45 mis-hires would each cost you $500,000, for a total of $11.25 million. *Staggering!!!*
- Notice that this does not include the cost of typical turnover. This only represents the mis-hires. As much as we will explain later in this chapter how good leadership drives retention, we recognize that you will never be able to retain everyone!

Step #2: Create a Clear Job Scorecard (Not a Vague Job Description)

Get rid of the traditional templated and ambiguous job descriptions. These traditional job descriptions do not set clear expectations to hiring managers about what they are hiring someone to do. In turn, this leads to confusion with candidates that leads to a "fake it 'till you make it" attitude with the job resulting in costly mis-hires.

Instead, create a job scorecard that defines metrics for the hiring team and candidate metrics and sets what "A-Players" look like for the job. Most organizations write job descriptions such that "C-Players" can execute the items, almost like a checklist. These job scorecards layout precise expectations on how to perform the job, influence hiring decisions, steer the recruiting process, and allow you and the candidates to home-in on the most critical performance objectives before making a job offer. Solidify what the candidate will be accountable for in the first year, ensure the goals are measurable, and include the ratings to be achieved on each goal for the new hire to be considered a high performer. All scorecards should consist of:

- Job role mission and strategy
- Measurable job accountabilities
- Competencies linked to accountabilities

Additionally, ensure the following when developing the job scorecard:

- All stakeholders agree on how "A/B/C Players" will be objectively differentiated.
- The competencies spell out the fit for the specific job.
- Competencies are measurable.

A sample job scorecard for a cybersecurity engineer role is included at www.CISOEvolution.com.

Step #3: Recruit from Your Networks

Simply put, "A-Players" want to work with other "A-Players." "B/C Players" want to work with other "B/C Players." Reach out to your networks and take advantage of your current employees to find other "A-Players." Also, reach out to your super-connectors (Chapter 9 – Relationship Management) if your employees or existing network cannot produce "A-Player" candidates. Your super-connectors know a ton of people (by their very nature), and given that the super-connector is already in your network, you presumably trust their judgment. Some Topgrading strategies include:

- Make recruiting through networks a job scorecard accountability for managers, but this may be a double-edged sword. Make sure that managers do not lower their hiring standards to meet this goal.

- Create a bonus or referral program.
- Encourage the use of professional social networks, like LinkedIn.
- Ask new hires to highlight "A-Players" in their networks. Doing so is relatively easy, because as you will find out in step #7, you already asked them for names of "A-Players" they inherited, hired, or developed.
- Don't hide behind email. Use personal communication methods to stay in touch with people. Pick up the phone and have a conversation (the horror)!
- Invest in your public-facing websites. Nothing says "It's boring as hell to work here" as a dull, early 2000s looking website.

Step #4: Screen Candidates

Resumes are often ambiguous and include a lot of inflated information. In many cultures, lying on resumes is even encouraged, so it is difficult to identify the "A-Players." Using a career history form with the promise of a reference check pulls more truth out of candidates. As you will learn in step #10, the key is to communicate to candidates early and often that they will have to arrange reference check calls with former bosses. That's right. That puts a lot more of their skin in the game.

A career history form is part application form, part threat of reference check (TORC), but all, "Let's pull out all of the information that we wish candidates put on their resume, but don't." The career history form should include items like reasons for leaving jobs, what they love and hate about their job, estimates on how their bosses (the same ones they are arranging reference check calls with) would rate them, and how they would rate themselves. The benefit is that non-"A-Players" quickly stop the application process once they realize they can't hide behind words on a resume. Even something as simple as forcing a candidate to reveal that they were "fired" and not "laid-off" can pay huge dividends down the road.

Furthermore, you can take the essential information from the career history forms and create dashboards or "snapshots" (as Topgrading calls it) to screen candidates quickly. Most applicant tracking systems

(ATS) have similar capabilities, but some simple spreadsheet hacks can get you some similar results. Even if your ATS can weed out 90% of the applicants, that final 10% can still be significant, and streamlining the time and effort required to screen those applicants before getting deep into the interview process is an excellent investment.

An example career history form and example dashboard are located at www.CISOEvolution.com. You can use these to integrate with your ATS to allow applicants to apply with a click of a button using their LinkedIn profile to auto-populate fields in the career history form. The applicant will only have to complete missing information. The cybersecurity team likely does not have control over the ATS, but taking the initiative and working with your HR team streamlines the process for both you and the candidate. This integration can then also be leveraged for other teams, and thus, improving the hiring process as a whole.

Step #5: Conduct Telephone Screening Interviews

If you can recruit from your networks, then you may be able to skip this step and go straight to in-person interviews. Otherwise, utilize phone screens that incorporate the career history form to provide laser focus to the interview and help ensure that when you invest in the time and money to interview candidates in-person, you interview only the top candidates. After you have studied the career history form, the telephone screening interview should include:

- What will happen on the call, along with informing them that, before a final job offer, you will ask them to arrange personal reference calls with former bosses
- Describing the organization and the job role
- Allowing the candidate to ask any questions up front
- Evaluating the following for the previous two jobs:
  - What they are most proud of
  - Their biggest mistakes, the impact of those mistakes, and how they overcame them
  - How their boss would rate their strengths, weaknesses, and performance

- What they loved/hated most about the job
- Reason for leaving
- Questions from the various job competencies you outlined on the job scorecard from step #2.

At this point, you should have enough knowledge about the candidates to invite only the candidates who are most likely to be "A-Players" for in-person interviews.

Step #6: Conduct Competency Interviews

This is the first step in conducting in-person interviews. Some methods may leave this step out and go straight to step #7, but I believe this is critical for crucial cybersecurity roles. This step allows the candidate to meet with more people they would be working with, and it allows for a deep dive to investigate how their skills line up to the job competencies. True, you can always teach hard skills, but the candidate has to hit the ground running in some roles.

For example, when I started working for eBay in the mid-2000s, I did not have any experience with Checkpoint firewalls and Provider-1, but managing those firewalls and overall network security were the crux of my job. What I did bring to the table were soft skills and a solid foundation in network security and with other specific firewall technologies. If my hiring manager and team were adamant about hiring someone with years of experience with Checkpoint, I would have never landed that job. I know for sure that I would not have some of the friendships I cherish to this day (thank you, eBay crew. . .you know who you are). It is certainly plausible that without their faith and support I might not have the experience and tenacity to co-author this book! Who knows?

It is important to continue to allow the candidate to ask questions in this step. Questions from the candidate, and the types of questions they ask, demonstrate that they are engaged and not merely looking for a paycheck. Allowing a candidate to ask questions and qualify the opportunity is just as important as your need to qualify their fit for the role.

Standardizing the competency interviews using interview guides allows you to compare apples-to-apples and provides top-cover should the question of "why did you hire candidate 'X' over candidate 'Y'" ever arise. The following outlines areas you should consider when creating the competency interview guides:

- Pick five or six key competencies to focus on.
- Create four to six questions for each competency.
  - Half of them should focus on when the candidate showed the competency, and the other half should focus on when the candidate did not show them, yet should have.
- Have each interviewer focus on one culture-fit type of question.
  - For example, if a competency requires working with a global team, one interviewer can focus on frequency and types of communications, and another can focus on patience and flexibility.
- Choose the competency interviewers.
  - Ideally, the competency viewers should be a 360-degree perspective of the hiring manager's peers, the candidate's peers, and subordinates (if any).
    - Note: the hiring manager will interview the candidate in the next step.

An example of a competency interview guide for a cybersecurity engineer role can be found at www.CISOEvolution.com.

Step #7: Conduct Tandem Interviews

This step is likely the most critical step of the Topgrading interview process. If the competency interview is a script-kiddie attacker, then the tandem interviews are an advanced nation-state attacker. The sophistication and depth of the former cannot be compared with that of the latter.

The tandem interview is an interview that begins with the candidate's experience in college (if applicable) and then progresses through a series of questions about every job along the candidate's career timeline (the tandem interview guide). The tandem interview also includes questions about the candidate's career plan and goals, intrinsic and extrinsic motivations, and self-assessment. These interviews should put the candidate "on-the-spot." Anything high-lighted in their resume, career history form, or during the competency interview is fair game. The tandem interview should dig into all accomplishments, failures, critical decisions, and essential relationships (particularly the relationships with the prior bosses that the candidate will arrange the personal references checks with).

As the name implies, the tandem interview involves using two inter-viewers (one being the hiring manager) and is most effectively learned in two phases. For our purposes, we will focus on the first phase, which is the starter phase. The second phase is much more in-depth. I encourage you to read more about it in Chapter 2 of *Topgrading: The Proven Hiring and Promoting Method That Turbocharges Company Performance.*

- Ask someone you trust, whether it be a peer or someone above you, to be your tandem interviewer.
- Both interviewers should ask all of the questions in the tandem interview guide, ask follow-up questions, and take copious notes.
- Ask the candidates to arrange the personal reference calls with former bosses that they chose and other references that you selected (you have already primed them to do this in step #4).
- Make the reference calls.
  - We will discuss this more in step #10, but you and your tandem interview partner can split these.
- Decide upon next steps (job offer, pass the candidate to another role in the organization for which they would be a better fit, or pass completely).

The tandem interview can be a long process, ranging from one-to-four-hours long, but it allows a hiring manager to genuinely get to know a candidate and identify if the candidate is an "A-Player." The payoff is worth it. Think of all the hours (and money) wasted with mis-hiring that we discussed in step #1.

Step #8: Interviewers Give Each Other Feedback

Another crucial benefit of the tandem interview process is that it allows interviewers to provide immediate feedback to each other. Frankly, many of the personalities that we come across in cybersecurity do not engender good interviewing techniques. Providing each other with constructive feedback will greatly improve each other's interviewing techniques.

For example, one interviewer might ask questions that do not adequately probe the candidate, or one interviewer may be so busy taking notes that they seem disinterested and callous.

Step #9: Write an Executive Summary

Skipping this step seems easy, but I encourage you not to. Leverage all of your notes from all of the interviews to create an executive summary of the candidates that will allow you to compare candidates and facilitate your hiring decision vs. using "gut feeling." You may be asking yourself, "Why not just compare notes?" The answer is twofold. First, it forces you to analyze all the data you now have on the candidate and identify noteworthy patterns and trends about the candidate throughout their career. Secondly, it allows you to prepare for the reference calls in step #10.

An example of an executive summary for the cybersecurity engineer role can be found at www.CISOEvolution.com.

Step #10: Conduct Candidate-Arranged Reference Calls

Now it is time to come through on your promise of conducting a reference check. Remember, the candidate is the one who is responsible for setting up reference check calls. Put the onus on them as they (presumably) have direct contact with their previous employers to help eliminate phone tag and the time it takes for you to conduct the reference check. "A-Players" should be eager to do this as "A-Players" do not typically leave companies on bad terms.

Provide the candidate with the list of people you selected. You should plan to hear back from the candidate within 48 hours with their reference's availability and mobile number. After four or five days, if the candidate cannot arrange for you to talk with the people you requested, consider that the reason may be that the candidate decided to "call your bluff" and now realized that you are not bluffing.

Take these reference checks seriously. Prepare your questions carefully based on the information you learned from developing the executive summary in step #9. Are there any specifics that jump out that you want to probe about during the reference check?

Step #11: Coach Your Newly Hired "A-Player"

Congratulations! You have made a hiring decision, and the candidate is no longer a candidate. They are an employee! Start coaching immediately. Let the new employee know how they can improve (based on your interactions with them) and areas you feel they excel in that pushed them over the top in your hiring decision. Even the most astounding "A-Players" can get frustrated and leave when they are left to fend for themselves in their early days and months at the company. Also, imagine all the lost productivity by allowing the new hire to flounder!

Review your executive summary with the employee and have them append an Individual Development Plan (IDP) that they create for themselves. Then, you and the employee can sit down, review, and discuss together. Be sure their IDP includes SMART goals and what, why, when, and how they will be measured. When you and the employee settle on the IDP, be sure to inject at least quarterly, informal reviews to review progress and solicit employee feedback.

Step #12: Annually Measure Success

Finally, it is time to reassess your hiring success. Close the Topgrading hiring feedback loop and continually measure your success (at least annually) in hiring "A-Players." Conduct the talent projection and cost of mis-hires calculations from step #1 and check for improvements in hiring success percentages. Annually evaluating your hiring success provides accountability for the quality of hires, highlights success pre-Topgrading and post-Topgrading, and promotes the continued use of

Topgrading. Topgrading recruiting and hiring practices are a lot of work, but the investment pays off, and you tangibly demonstrate it by continuous measurement.

Leadership

Companies require business leadership from their CISOs now more than ever. That means possessing the skills and knowledge to participate in strategic conversations, such as new product or service development, digital transformation, and merger and acquisition diligence. Of course, participating in strategy doesn't alleviate the CISO's need to execute operationally.

To succeed in today's global economy, CISOs must influence business leaders up and across the entire organization to implement security controls, while leading their teams to execute on tactical objectives that meet strategic goals. They must secure commitments to continuously evaluate and respond to evolving risks while keeping their teams motivated and engaged to maintain high performance. Doing so requires leadership. As cybersecurity leaders, we will always be expected to retain some technical competence such as a fundamental knowledge of network security, endpoint security, and incident response. However, our greatest calling is to serve as choice architects that skillfully guide our organizations through enterprise risk management.

In the Leadership section of this chapter, I will introduce emotional intelligence, and then examine four leadership methodologies (transformational, authentic, servant, and adaptive) to indicate when each may apply. As you read further, consider how you fall into one of these leadership styles. Perhaps you exhibit multiple leadership styles. This awareness will help you honor yourself as an individual and release your greatest leadership potential.

Emotional Intelligence

Emotional Intelligence (EQ) is a concept that has been around for over 50 years. Daniel Goleman popularized the concept in 1995 and defined it as the array of skills and characteristics that drive leadership performance.[6] EQ is the capability of individuals to recognize their own emotions and those of others, discern between different feelings, label them appropriately, use emotional information to guide thinking and behavior, and adjust emotions to adapt to environments.[7]

Yes, EQ deals with feelings and all of the soft, squishy topics many cybersecurity professionals avoid. Firewalls, network packets, SIEM alerts, and the latest artificial intelligence silver bullets do not have feelings. However, people do. Leading and influencing people requires you to be emotionally aware of yourself and others. EQ is the foundation upon which we build trusted relationships, forge partnerships, and engage in genuine conversations. Efforts to align employees, peers, and the C-Suite in cybersecurity strategy require us to leverage these relationships. And we have to go further; we must courageously engage in honest and forthright dialogue while putting risks into perspective. We need to inspire with compelling stories, and sometimes it's best to allow our audiences to reach their own conclusions. By doing so, people engage, allowing you to ultimately add meaning to your relationships. Whether speaking to the board to secure a budget or coaching an employee through a rough patch, EQ allows you to tailor the perfect message for a given scenario.

Goleman breaks down EQ into five domains:

- **Knowing One's Emotions:** This deals with self-awareness. How can you navigate others' emotions if you cannot navigate your own? People who have a better handle on their feelings are more confident about decisions they make and how to lead people to achieve that goal.
- **Managing Emotions:** Builds on self-awareness by appropriately handling feelings. Has your boss ever made you want to rage-quit? Don't lie to yourself. The answer is "yes" even with the best of bosses. The ability to "shake it off" allows you to plow through setbacks.
- **Motivating Oneself:** Appropriately suppressing your feelings in the pursuit of a goal is critical for self-motivation. The ability to "go with the flow" and have emotional self-control tends to lead to greater productivity.

- **Recognizing Emotions in Others**: This is empathy. Empathy is the ability to understand other people's emotional composition and treat people according to their emotional reactions. People frequently confuse empathy with compassion, but empathy can also be used to foster negative behavior, such as manipulation.
- **Handling Relationships:** Managing relationships and building your networks requires finding common ground to build rapport. Building rapport builds trust, and trust allows your audience to be more receptive to your "storytelling."

Don't fret. It is possible to improve your EQ. A study conducted by Harvard Business Review Analytic Services concludes that organizations that highlight EQ have higher employee engagement and customer loyalty.[8] The study found that the most effective form of EQ development starts with conversation and interaction intended to increase self-awareness. Self-exploration and in-depth discussions lead to greater levels of self-awareness, empathy, and the ability to understand others' viewpoints. This in turn leads to better relationships.

Here are some steps you can take to improve EQ. I encourage you to focus on yourself first and then extend this activity to your teams:

- **Identify and name your emotions:** Dig deep and ask yourself what you are feeling. Are you happy and excited about an opportunity? Are you angry and upset with a co-worker? Why? You become more mindful of how you speak to yourself and others as you become more cognizant of your emotions. Have you ever beat yourself up over something that happened at the office? Have you ever wished you could take back a heated conversation with a co-worker? Of course, you have.
- **Pay attention to how you talk to yourself and how you talk to others:** Focus on strengthening your communication skills. People with high EQ tend to invest in more specific language to identify shortfalls, and then they immediately strive to tackle those shortfalls. Are you having a hard time getting a particular business unit to buy into approved security controls? Why? What can you do to communicate the benefits of the security control better?

Don't dwell on the problem. Pinpoint the barrier and knock it out of the way!

- **Ask for feedback:** I understand this may be awkward, but ask managers, colleagues, friends, or family how they would rate your EQ. How do you handle difficult situations? Do you remain calm, or do you let your stress show? How flexible are you to change? How empathetic are you? How do you deal with conflict? It may not always be what you want to hear, but it will often be what you need to hear. Extend the same, sometimes harsh, courtesy and honesty, to those who ask you for feedback.
- **Learn from prior experience:** How have you successfully navigated similar feelings in the past? Learn from that experience and reuse it. Much like incident response, make sure you close the feedback loop to be better prepared to deal with similar situations in the future.
- **Practice empathy:** Pick up on verbal and nonverbal cues to gain insight into your colleagues' feelings. Refer to our review of Crucial Conversations in Chapter 8 – Communication – You Do It Every Day (or Do You?), where we covered the skills of Learn to Look and Make it Safe. Practice "putting yourself in their shoes," to understand both content and feelings.
- **Know what triggers you and others you influence:** What stresses you out? Do what you can to avoid the stress while acknowledging that stress is inevitable. Sleep is an excellent stress reliever. Conversely, lack of sleep can elevate your emotional volatility. If you don't like horror movies, don't watch one immediately before bedtime. Emails are the equivalent of horror movies for me. I try to avoid them at all costs just before bedtime; otherwise, I will toil with mental gymnastics all night long.
- **Be resilient:** Suck it up, buttercup. Stuff happens. Everyone encounters challenges. Just like Rocky Balboa said, "It ain't about how hard you hit. It's about how hard you can get hit and keep moving forward; how much you can take and keep moving forward. That's how winning is done!" Positive thinking and continuous improvement will take you far. Consider what you can learn, what will make you better, and how you can be more resilient in the future.

- **Celebrate successes:** Building your own EQ is one challenge but convincing a team to do it is an entirely different challenge. You have to set the standard. Define how people disagree with each other. Mandate that disagreement be cordial and constructive. Also, recognize and celebrate those who demonstrate EQ. Reward not only your high-performers but also those who help the high-performers be high-performers.

Transformational Leadership

Transformational leadership is a relatively new approach to leadership where a leader inspires others to rise above their self-interests to benefit the entire organization. Imagine Mr. Spock when he proclaims, "Logic clearly dictates that the needs of the many outweigh the needs of the few," with Captain Kirk replying, "Or the one." Transformational leaders encourage and inspire employees to innovate and create change that will help grow and shape the organization's future success. This leadership style enhances employee motivation, morale, and job performance through various methods such as connecting employees' sense of self and identity to a project and fostering a collective identity to the organization. Cybersecurity leaders of today need to be mentors and lead by example. They must encourage innovation that aligns with the organization's values and strategic objectives and recognize individuals for their contributions and for going above and beyond what is expected of them.

Transformational leadership contrasts with transactional leadership styles that focus on a carrot and stick to get teams to do what they want. I don't call this leadership at all. I call it bad management. According to James M. Burns, whom many consider to be the father of transformational leadership, transformational leadership aims to create a significant positive change in people. It changes the perceptions, values, expectations, and aspirations of employees. Transformational leadership is not based on a carrot and stick, give and take relationship, like transactional leadership. Instead, transformational leadership is based on the leader's charisma, traits, and ability to set an example that others can follow. Transformational leaders strive to paint a vision of the future to inspire people to drive progress and accomplish goals. Transactional leaders lean toward maintaining the status quo and attempting to get results from their teams through strictly their authority.[9]

In 1985, scholar Bernard M. Bass identified four basic elements for transformational leadership that are crucial if a leader needs to encourage and inspire others. These elements create an open, forthcoming, and diverse culture that empowers individuals by enabling them to share ideas freely. The four elements are often referred to as the "Four I's":[10]

- **Idealized influence:** Refers to the way a leader exerts influence on others. Teams tend to highly respect these leaders because they set an example, and they consistently demonstrate that they prioritize the needs of their team above their own. Individuals tend to follow this leader because they are relatable.
- **Inspirational motivation:** Fundamentally, leaders must inspire their teams to achieve. This leader sets high yet attainable goals, and they inspire commitment by creating a shared vision for the team or organization and articulating their expectations clearly. Inspirational motivation leverages both extrinsic and intrinsic factors and requires a high level of charisma. Charisma inspires a sense of authority and could be considered both inspirational and visionary by the team.
- **Intellectual stimulation:** Refers to creating a diverse and open environment that encourages individuals to think for themselves and safely express their ideas. These leaders tend to promote the concept of "fail fast, fail often," as often associated with agile methodologies because doing so fosters growth and improvement.
- **Individualized consideration:** Refers to establishing a strong relationship with the team and acting as a caring, supportive resource. These leaders mentor their team and allocate their time to developing individual and team potential.

Much like EQ, there are things you can do to strive towards becoming a transformational leader. Transformational leadership may align better with those who have charismatic personalities, but here are some things Bass identifies that will allow you to move the needle.

- **Create an inspiring vision of the future.**
  - If you want to lead, not merely manage, your team, you need to create and clearly communicate an inspiring vision of what the team should strive toward.
  - The vision establishes your team's purpose. The vision needs to consider:
    - The values of the people on your team
    - The capabilities and resources of your organization
    - The context of your organization
    - How you plan to move forward, given those considerations
  - Start with your organization's mission and align your vision so that your team can drive toward it.
- **Get people buy-in and deliver the vision.**
  - As alluded to above, you need to appeal to your people's values and motivate them with where you are going to lead them, and clearly communicate why.
  - Consider building a story around your vision to help your team appreciate and emotionally feel the positive direction of your vision and how it will help the team and the organization.
    - It is all the better if you can pull from your personal life experiences.
  - Link your vision to individual and team goals so that people see how they specifically support the vision.
  - Communicate every significant business decision in terms of your vision.
- **Manage delivery of the vision.**
  - Now it is time to make your vision a reality, which will likely involve hard and tedious work.
  - You will need to combine practical project management with organizational change management.
    - Chris Laping's book *People Before Things* is an excellent book to read more on this topic.
  - Ensure that everyone understands what part of the vision they are responsible for.
    - Establish SMART goals.
    - Identify some quick wins that can start achieving momentum toward your vision.

- Be visible and present.
  - Do not hide in your office or cubicle all day.
  - Walk around and check in with your team regularly.
  - Always practice what you preach.
- **Build ever-stronger, trust-based relationships.**
  - Focus on providing your people with the tools and resources they need to achieve their goals.
  - Leadership is a long-term play, so relationship building, earning trust, and helping your people grow is a continuous process.
  - Have regular one-on-one meetings with your people to stay in touch with how you can continue to help them achieve their goals.
    - Dictate a frequency that is practical for the size of team you have.
  - Be open, honest, and transparent and demonstrate some vulnerability, albeit safely, through sharing personal stories and anecdotes.
  - Coach and mentor your people.

Servant Leadership

Servant leadership is often related to transformational leadership. Robert K. Greenleaf was one of the first to write about servant leadership. He defines the classical definition as "[Servant leadership] begins with the natural feeling that one wants to serve, to serve first. Then conscious choice brings one to aspire to lead. . .The difference manifests itself in the care taken by the servant – first to make sure that other people's highest priority needs are being served. The best test . . . is: do those served grow as persons; do they, while being served, become healthier, wiser, freer, more autonomous, more likely themselves to become servants? And, what is the effect on the least privileged in society; will they benefit, or, at least, will they not be further deprived?"[11]

I prefer the definition that Mark Schlereth, former Denver Broncos offensive lineman, articulated on the radio during one of my morning drives to work where he stated, "True leadership is when you care about what happens to others more than caring about what happens to you."

The primary difference between transformational leadership and servant leadership is the focus of the leader. The transformational leader directs their focus toward the organization, and his or her behavior builds follower commitment toward organizational objectives, while the servant leader's focus is on the followers. The achievement of organizational objectives is a secondary outcome. The extent to which the leader can shift the primary focus of leadership from the organization to the follower is the distinguishing factor in which of these two leadership types the person is executing.[12]

However, being a transformational leader or a servant leader is not a "one or the other" decision. Servant leadership aligns with developing individual team members, encouraging innovation within the team's context, and mentoring a team to exhibit empathy with business units who are just trying to get their job done, which in turn motivates the business units to adopt adequate security controls. Transformational leadership aligns with motivating a team when there are significant external pressures, such as after an acquisition, a significant decline in economic outlook, or booming growth. Transformational leaders encourage intellectual risk, innovation, and creativity to effectively develop team members to be successful within the current, stressful context of the organization. You should evaluate which leadership style aligns the current business environment with your team's needs and your individual skill set.

There are 10 characteristics of a servant leader that you can work on with countless resources available to delve into each one.[13] You will notice that many of these characteristics are similar to those found in transformational leadership. Commit to incremental improvements in an area or two every day.

- **Listening:** Communication between leaders and their team is an interactive process that includes sending and receiving messages (e.g., verbal, written, body language). Servant leaders listen first and speak second. To listen, you must be receptive to what others have to say. Through listening, servant leaders acknowledge the viewpoint and perspective of the other person.

- **Empathy:** As mentioned previously, when reviewing EQ, empathy is the ability to understand the emotional composition of other people and to treat people according to their emotional reactions. In other words, you put yourself "in their shoes" to try and understand the other person's point of view. Empathetic servant leaders confirm and validate what the other individual is thinking and feeling, making the other person feel empowered and heard.
- **Healing:** Servant leaders care about the personal well-being of individuals on their team and demonstrate it by helping them overcome personal and professional problems.
- **Awareness:** Servant leaders understand themselves and the impact they have on others. With awareness, servant leaders can step back, disconnect, and view themselves within the context of the greater picture.
- **Persuasion:** Persuasion is clear and persistent communication that convinces others to see your perspective and change. As opposed to coercion, which utilizes the authority granted by position and title to force change, persuasion creates change through gentle, nonjudgmental argument.
- **Conceptualization:** Conceptualization is the ability to be a visionary for your team by providing a clear sense of its goals and direction. Conceptualization goes beyond day-to-day operations and focuses on the greater picture and long-term strategy.
- **Foresight:** Foresight is a servant leader's ability to connect dots and predict the future. This ability does not mean that they are psychic. It means that the servant leader can predict what will happen based on what is currently happening or what has happened in the past.
- **Stewardship:** Stewardship is about taking responsibility for the leadership role entrusted to you. Servant leaders accept the responsibility to lead, manage, mentor, and motivate their team.
- **Commitment to the growth of people:** Servant leaders focus on intrinsic motivations for each individual that go beyond "what's in it for me?" Servant leaders are committed to helping each individual in their team grow personally and professionally. Some

ways to help enable growth are providing career development opportunities, assisting individuals in developing new work skills through formal or on-the-job training, or empowering them by listening to their ideas and involving them in decisions.

- **Building community:** Servant leadership fosters the development of community. A community is a collection of individuals who have shared interests, relate to each other, and feel a sense of unity, which allows them to identify with the greater good of the organization.

Adaptive Leadership

Working in cybersecurity means living and breathing tough challenges and change. Attackers are seemingly always one step ahead of defenders, so adapting and dealing with difficult situations is critical. A common definition of adaptive leadership is "the practice of mobilizing people to tackle tough challenges and thrive."[14] Adaptive leadership often focuses on change, but it can be applied to many challenges, including managing conflict across different business units, acquiring and integrating another company, or being acquired (Table 10.1 highlights how adaptive leadership may be applied to these challenges). The key differentiator with adaptive leadership is that this leadership style focuses less on the leaders themselves and more on their behaviors and activities in relation to their teams and business context. Adaptive leadership is just that, adaptive, and it is mainly about enabling your teams to adapt and overcome challenges no matter the circumstances. Adaptive leaders engage in the following five activities:[15]

- **Mobilize:** Engaging in activities that move your team to move toward needed change
- **Motivate:** Coaching your team in the ideals they need to feel like they can change
- **Organize:** Identifying the opportunity for change and determining what to provide to the team to ensure the team succeeds
- **Orient:** Helping teams to recognize the starting line, the finish line, and how to get from "A" to "B"
- **Focus the attention of others:** Clearly explaining the goal and how the change will help them, individually

TABLE 10.1 Adaptive Leadership Examples

Situation	Example
Managing conflict across different business units	Bringing together people affected by conflict to be part of the solution and creating a process where everyone can be part of the solution (reference the story of the development manager from Chapter 8)
Acquiring and integrating companies	You are working for a large telecommunications company, and your company acquires a smaller competitor. Tensions between you and your competitor ran high before the acquisition, and now you must help integrate employees and systems to ensure the synergies promised by the acquisition are realized.
Being acquired	Similar to above, but as the acquired company, you must clearly articulate and convince your team that the acquisition is best for the company and that a successful integration is beneficial to them professionally and personally.

Adaptive leadership requires that leaders handle three types of situational challenges. Identifying these situational challenges allows us to put into better context the six key leadership behaviors that follow. The three types of situational challenges are:

- **Technical challenges:** Problems that are clearly defined (e.g., implementing a firewall rule)
- **Technical and adaptive challenges:** Challenges that are clearly defined where there is no clear solution (e.g., integrating two identity and access management programs)
- **Adaptive challenges:** Challenges that are not easily identified (e.g., situations with many variables, such as integrating two companies)

Six leader behaviors exemplify adaptive leadership. Think of these behaviors as individual elements of a concoction, such as your favorite cocktail or a magic potion from Hogwarts given to leaders allowing them to help their teams tackle difficult challenges and the inescapable resulting changes. Much like ingredients in your favorite cocktail, there is a general order to the mixing of behaviors in the adaptive leadership process. Many of these behaviors overlap with each other and should be demonstrated by leaders at the same time. These leader behaviors suggest a kind of recipe for being an adaptive leader.[16]

- **Get on the balcony:** This is like a prerequisite to the aforementioned potions course. It requires an adaptive leader to step out and find perspective in the middle of a challenging situation, which allows them to see the bigger picture and what is really happening.
- **Identify adaptive challenges:** Identify and diagnose the situational challenge correctly.
- **Regulate distress:** Distress during change is inevitable and even beneficial, but too much distress can bring individuals and teams to their knees. Adaptive leaders need to help others recognize the need for change but not become overwhelmed by the need for the change itself.
- **Maintain disciplined attention:** Get people to focus on the tough work they need to do.
- **Give the work back to the people:** Adaptive leaders provide enough direction to allow their teams to perform and troubleshoot work themselves. Think of the proverbial, "Give a man a fish, and you feed him for a day; teach a man to fish, and you feed him for a lifetime."
- **Protect leadership voices from below:** Adaptive leaders listen and are receptive to ideas from *everyone* on the team, no matter how junior, outlandish, or marginalized the individual is.

Application

This is a challenging Application section for me to write because one leadership trait alluded to but not deeply discussed in the various leadership styles outlined in this chapter is humility. You see, I have a fundamental belief that if you need to go around saying "I'm a leader," then you are very likely not a leader. Think about that for a second in the context of the leadership styles highlighted in this chapter, and you will understand why I cringe at writing this section.

I managed a rather large security and network operations center (SNOC), and I ran into many of the challenges highlighted in this chapter almost daily. Hiring and retaining "A-Players" was critical to our mission, yet it was absolutely, without a doubt, the most challenging part of the job. A requirement for working in our SNOC was a secret-level government clearance and an additional "entry on duty" (EOD) by the agency we were supporting. While someone leaving the organization typically provided two weeks of notice, the hiring process to replace them, end-to-end, took at least six months if the candidate did not have an active clearance. Finding candidates with an active clearance made matters that much more difficult, so we had to keep our options open. We did not implement a Topgrading strategy because we were already losing candidates to the hiring process bureaucracy. We were having problems keeping the talent pipeline full due to the high demand for cybersecurity talent. Many "A-Player" cybersecurity analysts and engineers found other opportunities and fell out of the hiring process during that six-month (often longer) time-frame. Frankly, we struggled as a result sometimes, but we still persevered and performed at a high level *because of the handful of "A-Players" that we did have*. The "A-Players" were patient and worked with the non-"A-Players." That solid foundation elevated the performance of the entire team.

During my tenure, the client announced they would move the SNOC out of state before the end of the contract. The announcement led to a lot of distress, and it was my role as a leader to navigate this team through the transition. Most of the team members did not want to, or could not, relocate; however, we had to maintain operations through the transition. My role was to first deliver on the organization's mission, but priority 1A was to the individuals on my team. I was baptized by fire in servant leadership.

To be successful, I had to be adept at many of the traits of servant leadership. I had to *listen* to the concerns of the individuals regarding the uncertainty of their futures. I had to show *empathy* as every single individual of my 35-person team faced a unique challenge. I had to show *healing* in helping them tackle their unique challenges. There were many difficult conversations, and while my advice was always, "You have to consider what is best for you and your family," when pressed, sometimes my advice was, "You should be proactive and look for another opportunity if you don't want to relocate." I also had to temper this advice with the *persuasion* of having the individual stay long enough to ensure a successful transition. I had to convince people who did not want to relocate that if they wanted our SOC to win more work, we could not be known as the SOC that failed to meet its responsibilities. I also had to do all of this while continuing the *commitment to the growth of people and maintaining our community*. I did this knowing in the back of my mind that I would not take an offer to relocate and that I would be likely leaving the organization when the right opportunity presented itself.

The right opportunity did present itself, and I left the organization, but I left the SOC in good hands as I was able to coach and mentor my deputy so that he could seamlessly take over if I did leave or get hit by a bus (you will always be my #2). In the end, there was a successful and smooth transition, along with the SOC winning more work in the process, so while there was a reduction in staff through attrition, there were no mandatory reductions in force.

Key Insights

- **Topgrading:** Recruiting and retaining high-performing teams is a challenge for any cybersecurity leader. Calculate your hiring success rate and your cost of mis-hires. The cost will astound you. Consider using the Topgrading method to attract and select "A-players" to your team and watch your hiring success rate soar, and your cost of mis-hires plummet.
- **Emotional Intelligence:** A high EQ improves communication, conflict resolution, and relationship. EQ also helps to build resiliency when faced with tough challenges.
- **Leadership Types:** There are many leadership types. We evaluated transformational, servant, and adaptive leadership in this chapter, but there are many more. It is important to be authentic with any leadership type you choose to exhibit. Additionally, you may choose to apply a different leadership type depending on the type of challenge or situation you are facing.

Notes

1. Agovino, T., "To Have and to Hold," Society for Human Resource Management, 2019. Accessed February 13, 2021. https://www.shrm.org/hr-today/news/all-things-work/pages/to-have-and-to-hold.aspx.

2. Boss. J., "Leaders Only Need to Do This to Retain Top Talent," Entrepreneur.com, 2018. Accessed February 13, 2021. https://www.entrepreneur.com/article/318102.

3. Kahneman, D., Sibony, O., and Sunstein C.R., *Noise: A Flaw in Human Judgement*, Little, Brown Spark, 2021.

4. Smart, B.D.P., *Topgrading: The Proven Hiring and Promoting Method That Turbocharges Company Performance*, 3rd ed., Penguin Group (USA) Inc., 2012.

5. Lorence, M.S., *The Impact of Systematically Hiring Top Talent: A Study of Topgrading as a Rigorous Employee Selection Bundle*, 2014. https://scholarworks.gsu.edu/bus_admin_diss/38/

6. Goleman, D., *Emotional Intelligence: Why It Can Matter More than IQ*, 25th anniv., Bantam Books, 1995.

7. Coleman, A., *A Dictionary of Psychology*, 3rd ed., Oxford University Press, 2008.

8. Harvard Business Review Analytic Services, *The EI Advantage: Driving Innovation and Business Success through the Power of Emotional Intelligence*. *Harvard Business Review*, 2019. https://hbr.org/resources/pdfs/comm/fourseasons/TheEIAdvantage.pdf.

9. Burns, J.M., *Leadership*, Harper & Row, 1978.

10. Bass, B.M., *Leadership and Performance Beyond Expectations*, New York Free Press, 1985.

11. Greenleaf, R.K., *The Servant as Leader*, Greenleaf Center for Servant Leadership, 1970.

12. Gregory Stone, A., Russell, R.F., Patterson, K., "Transformational versus Servant Leadership: A Difference in Leader Focus," *Leadership & Organization Development Journal*, 25(4) (2004): 349–361. doi:10.1108/01437730410538671.

13. Heifetz, R., Frasho, A., and Linsky, M., *The Practice of Adaptive Leadership: Tools and Tactics for Changing Your Organization and the World*, Cambridge Leadership Associates, 2009.

14. Northouse, P.G., *Leadership: Theory and Practice*, 8th ed., Sage Publications, Inc., 2019.

15. Heifetz, R., Frasho, A., and Linsky, M., *The Practice of Adaptive Leadership: Tools and Tactics for Changing Your Organization and the World*.
16. Heifetz, R., Frasho, A., and Linsky, M., *The Practice of Adaptive Leadership: Tools and Tactics for Changing Your Organization and the World*.

CHAPTER 11

Managing Human Capital

When people are financially invested, they want a return. When people are emotionally invested, they want to contribute.

– Simon Sinek

Opportunity

There is a fundamental difference between leadership and management. Leadership is about getting individuals bought into your strategy and vision so that they are willing to work with you to achieve your goals. Management is more about managing the day-to-day activities required to march toward those goals. Leadership and management are intertwined. Strong leadership without strong management ensures a vision remains a vision and nothing else. Strong management without strong leadership leads to a "master/slave" mentality with low employee buy-in and morale and high employee turnover.

Globalization and digital transformation foster an astonishing pace of change in how businesses operate. Today's workforce puts intrinsic factors, such as personal and professional development and flexibility, above extrinsic factors such as salary and benefits. In other words, a manager is no longer just a supervisor. A Gallup poll finds that managers influence 70% of a team's engagement, and the traditional command-and-control structure is not effective with today's work-force.[1] Managers are expected to be more of a coach rather than a boss.

Human Capital Management is a set of practices related to people resource management. These practices are focused on the organizational need to provide specific competencies and are implemented in three categories: workforce acquisition, workforce management, and workforce optimization.[2] We covered workforce acquisition in Chapter 10 – Recruiting and Leading High Performing Teams. We tied recruiting and leading together because, without effective recruiting, there is nobody to lead. As Paul Russell, formerly of Google, put it, "Development can help great people be even better – but if I had a dollar to spend, I'd spend 70 cents getting the right person in the door." In other words, teaching the technology side of cybersecurity is much easier than finding the "A-Players" we described in the previous chapter.

We discuss the importance of Stephen Covey's 8th habit of "Find your voice and inspire others to find theirs" and influence in Chapter 9 – Relationship Management. Exercising the 8th habit requires an understanding of how to lead your workforce by understanding their motivations, strengths, and weaknesses so that you can leverage their skills in an optimized manner to create a high-performing team that meets your organization's goals.

Principle

This chapter will not be an education on traditional human resources and their function. Instead, in this chapter, we will focus on managing and optimizing your workforce through strengths-based leadership, managing a multigenerational workforce, training, and diversity of thought.

Strengths-Based Leadership

Managers are instrumental in maximizing the use of employees' strengths to optimize team performance. Study after study has found that doubling down on employee strengths is more effective than minimizing employee weaknesses. According to Gallup, people who use their strengths every day are six times more likely to be engaged on the job, which leads to more employee engagement, better performance, and lower employee turnover.[3]

First, as a manager, you must identify strengths. Outside of evaluating an employee's hard skills, determine how they instinctively think, feel, respond to stressful situations, and work within a team. Is the employee a collaborator, or do they prefer to work alone? Does the employee lash out when under stress, or do they defuse stress with an appropriate sense of humor? Several tools are available to help you identify employee strengths and effectively connect your team's work to individual strengths. By the way, these tools are not only for your employees. There should not be any "do as I say, not as I do" attitudes in cybersecurity, so be sure to take some of these tests yourself and openly share the results with your employees *and* leadership so that you can best understand and leverage your strengths. We will highlight these tools in the following sections, and they include the Kolbe A/B/C Indices, The CliftonStrengths Assessment (StrengthsFinder 2.0), LPI: Leadership Practices Inventory, and Myers-Briggs.

Kolbe A/B/C Indices

(www.kolbe.com)

Kathy Kolbe's father developed the first cognitive assessment used extensively by business and government. Kathy built upon the original assessment and developed the Kolbe indices to understand further the drivers of human performance and built upon her father's research.

The Kolbe A Index aims to reveal natural strengths and intrinsic abilities. Many organizations use it to hire, retain, and organize highly effective teams. It is based on the premise that your mind comprises three distinct parts.

- **Affective:** Accounts for things like your personality, likes, and dislikes. Other assessments, such as Myers-Briggs (which we will discuss later), also measure this part of the mind.

- **Cognitive:** The part of your mind responsible for what you know and how you learn. SAT, ACT, or IQ tests attempt to measure your cognitive mind. (If you ever meet Rock, ask him about his ACT story.)
- **Conative:** This part of your mind is responsible for your human nature and how you naturally solve challenges if you have no constraints. The Kolbe A Index attempts to measure this part of your mind.

The Kolbe A index then divides the results into four action modes:

- **Fact Finding:** The instinctive need to prove and the way you gather and share information. Do you require a lot of detail and low amounts of uncertainty to start a project, or can you get rolling with minimal details and a high amount of uncertainty? Do you dig into the details, or do you focus more on the big picture?
- **Follow Thru:** The instinctive need to pattern and the way to organize and design. Are you rigid and structured? How well can you adapt to change in a plan? Can you remain focused while executing the entirety of a project?
- **QuickStart:** The instinctive need to improvise and the way you deal with risk and uncertainty. Do you like to experiment and "fail fast, fail often"? or would you rather minimize change and the risk that comes with it?
- **Implementor:** The instinctive need to demonstrate and the way you handle space and tangibles. Do you like to get your hands dirty on a keyboard or dig into the contents of a PCAP, or do you prefer to envision a long-term strategy?

The Kolbe B and C indices are both comparisons against the Kolbe A, so everyone, including you, must take Kolbe A before the others to have an efficient measurement. Kolbe B measures your perception of your own job responsibilities. Comparing Kolbe A and Kolbe B results helps you recognize when you are trying to perform contrary to your natural strengths and abilities.

Kolbe C measures the functional expectations of a specific position (e.g., the supervisor's expectations of a particular job function).

Comparing Kolbe A and Kolbe C results helps supervisors and employees see how the employee's strengths line up with the demands and requirements of the job and identify areas of conative stress.

When personal expectations don't match natural abilities, you can adjust the team by redirecting talent and leveraging underutilized talent. The worst and most stressful scenario is when the supervisor's requirements don't match the employee's natural abilities, and employees must work against their natural tendencies. In this case, consider redefining the job requirements or redirecting underutilized talent to fulfill the job requirement.

The CliftonStrengths Assessment

(https://www.gallup.com/cliftonstrengths/en/252137/home.aspx)

Donald C. Clifton invented the CliftonStrengths Assessment, which about 25 million people have completed at the date of this writing.[4] After earning the Distinguished Flying Cross in World War II, Clifton taught and researched educational psychology at the University of Nebraska–Lincoln. While there, he studied tutors at the university to determine what differentiated the truly talented ones. Clifton wondered why psychologists traditionally looked at what was wrong with people (e.g., their weaknesses and challenges) and not why they excelled (e.g., their strengths). Through this research, he identified common attributes that successful people had that allowed them to excel at their work. Clifton created the CliftonStrengths Assessment in 1999 as an online tool in the early days of the Internet. CliftonStrengths focuses on 34 themes, grouped into 4 domains, that make up a person's personality (see Figure 11.1).

CliftonStrengths asserts that individuals do not necessarily need to be well-rounded, but teams need to be. Well-rounded teams that include talent from all of the themes often lead to high levels of performance. By understanding our strengths, we can understand the kind of duties in which we are likely to excel and provide the most significant contribution to the team.

As managers, we can use the understanding of strengths within the individuals of our team to match the best person for the task at hand. We can also use this understanding to hire people to fill-in-the gaps in

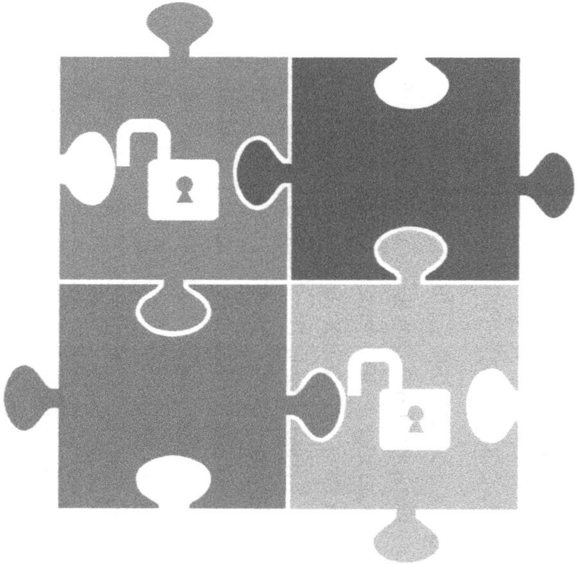

STRATEGIC THINKING

Analytical	Context
Futuristic	Ideation
Input	Intellection
Learner	Strategic

INFLUENCING

Activator	Command
Communication	Competition
Maximizer	Self-Assurance
Significance	Woo

RELATIONSHIP BUILDING

Adaptability	Connectedness
Developer	Empathy
Harmony	Includer
Individualization	Positivity
Relator	

EXECUTING

Achiever	Arranger
Belief	Consistency
Deliberative	Discipline
Focus	Responsibility
Restorative	

FIGURE 11.1 CliftonStrengths Themes

themes where our team is lacking. Understanding our strengths pro- vides insight into working within our given teams and whether we impose too much of our strengths onto how we view and work with others. For instance, are you very logical and analytical and expect all of your security analysts to act in the same way when in reality, abstract thinking can provide complementary benefits in that role? When a person's strengths are particularly dominant in a given domain, it means that an individual's most significant contributions to the team will come from performing the tasks aligned with that domain. Allowing individuals to execute duties aligned to their strengths increases their sense of value to the team and drives employee engagement.

LPI: Leadership Practices Inventory

(https://www.leadershipchallenge.com/)

The Leadership Practices Inventory (LPI® 360) is based on The Five Practices of Exemplary Leadership created by James M. Kouzes and Barry Z. Posner and highlighted in their book *The Leadership Challenge.*[5] They approach leadership behaviors as measurable, learnable, and teachable. The LPI® 360 involves leaders and observ- ers where observers are anyone who has direct or indirect interac- tions with the leader, such as a manager, direct report, peer, or other coworkers. The leader takes a self-assessment where the leader records, on a 10-point scale, the frequency they believe they exhibit 30 different behaviors. The leader then moves on to answer a few open-ended essay questions. Observers then do the same for the leader undergoing the assessment.

Kouzes and Posner collected thousands of case studies and inter- views to discover traits common to effective leaders. The consistent themes from this initial research now comprise The Five Practices of Exemplary Leadership:

1. **Model the Way**
   - Establish principles concerning the way people should be treated and the way they should pursue goals.
   - Create standards of excellence and send an example for others to follow.

- Put up signposts when people feel unsure of where to go or how to get there.
- Leaders create opportunities for victory.

2. **Inspire a Shared Vision**
   - Leaders believe they can make a difference.
   - They envision the future and create an ideal and unique image of what the organization can become.
   - Through their magnetism and persuasion, leaders enlist others in their dreams.
   - They breathe life into their visions and get people to see exciting possibilities for the future.

3. **Challenge the Process**
   - Search for Opportunities to change the status quo.
   - Look for innovative ways to improve the organization.
   - Experiment and take risks.
   - Set interim goals so that people can achieve small wins as they work toward larger objectives.
   - Unravel bureaucracy when it impedes action.
   - Accept occasional disappointments as opportunities to learn.

4. **Enable Others to Act**
   - Foster collaboration and build spirited teams.
   - Actively involve others.
   - Understand that mutual respect sustains extraordinary efforts.
   - Strive to create an atmosphere of trust and dignity.
   - Strengthen others, making each person feel capable and powerful.

5. **Encourage the Heart**
   - Recognize the contributions that individuals make.
   - Celebrate accomplishments and make people feel like heroes.

The LPI® 360 offers three (3) types of reports:

1. Individual Feedback Reports
2. Reassessment Reports
3. Group Reports

The Individual Feedback Report is particular to the assessed leader and contains the leader's self-assessment data and feedback from the observers who participated in the assessment. The report breaks down the results through the lens of The Five Practices of Exemplary Leadership, the 30 behavioral statements, a percentile ranking against millions of other respondents, and includes responses for the open-ended essay questions.

The Reassessment Report compares the leader's reassessment with the initial assessment results, where the reassessment is usually completed in 6-to-12-month increments. The reassessment allows the leader to measure their progress and make any needed adjustments to their improvement efforts.

The Group Report presents the entire group's aggregated data (e.g., team, department, or organization) and includes both self-assessment and observer results. This report highlights potential large-scale gaps across the group and allows leaders to focus improvement efforts accordingly.

Myers-Briggs

(http://www.myersbriggs.org)

The Myers-Briggs Personality Type Indicator (MBTI) is a self-assessment to identify personality types, strengths, and preferences. The questions were originally developed during World War II by the daughter-mother duo of Isabel Myers and Katherine Briggs. They wanted to build upon Swiss psychiatrist Carl Jung's persona theory after realizing that understanding individual differences could have real-world applications. They found that a critical real-world application was to help people select occupations best suited to their personality types, leading to increased happiness and satisfaction.

After the assessment, people are identified as having one of 16 personality types. The MBTI's goal is to allow individuals to understand their personalities by evaluating their likes, dislikes, strengths, weaknesses, career preferences, and how they get along with others. The assessment comprises four scales:

- **Extraversion (E) – Introversion (I):** Describes how people respond and interact with the world around them

- Extraverts tend to be action-oriented and enjoy more frequent social interaction.
- Introverts tend to be thought-oriented and enjoy deep, meaningful, and less-frequent social interactions.
- **Sensing (S) – Intuition (N):** Evaluates how people gather information from the world around them.
  - Sensing individuals tend to focus on reality, facts, and details and enjoy getting hands-on experience and learning from their senses (seeing, hearing, touching, smelling).
  - Intuitive individuals tend to enjoy thinking about possibilities, the future, and abstract theories.
- **Thinking (T) – Feeling (F):** Homes in on how people make decisions based on the information that they gathered from sensing or intuition.
  - Thinkers place more value on facts and objective data and tend to be consistent, logical, and detached when weighing a decision.
  - Feelers are more likely to consider people and emotions when weighing a decision.
- **Judging (J) – Perceiving (P):** Describes how people tend to deal with the outside world.
  - Judging individuals prefer structure and firm decisions.
  - Perceiving individuals prefer more flexibility and adaptability.

Each type is then identified by its four-letter code. Interestingly, the Myers-Briggs company published a study in 2019 that examined the relationship between cybersecurity behavior and personality type, as measured by the MBTI, to develop personality-based cybersecurity guidelines.[6] Figure 11.2 outlines each four-letter coded personality type and the percentage of the study respondents classified into each type.

You can probably immediately recognize some of these tendencies in yourself before even taking a formal assessment. It is important to note that these are scales and not a "this or that" evaluation. For example, an individual can exhibit extraversion and introversion,

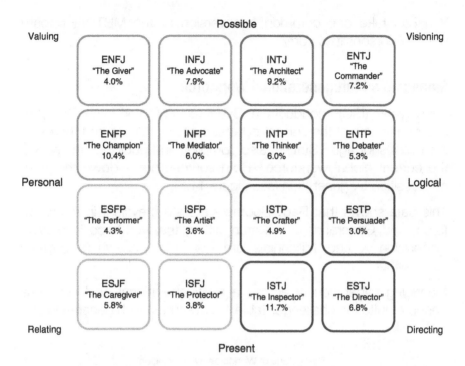

FIGURE 11.2 Myers-Briggs and Cybersecurity Personality Types

judging and perceiving, etc. The MBTI tries to evaluate one's tendency and preference towards one side of the scale over the other.

When working within a team (a group of your peers or a team that you supervise), it is critical to recognize your strengths and understand others' strengths. Doing so allows you to carve up the work based on the individuals' strengths within the group. In case you haven't noticed, allocating tasks based on strengths is a common goal of all of the assessments we have described.

MBTI does differ from the other assessments in that your results are standalone and not compared against any database of other assessment results. The MBTI's goal is not to compare you against others but rather to provide a deeper understanding of your personality and strengths.

You can take one common free version of the MBTI at https:// www.16personalities.com/.

Managing a Multigenerational Workforce

Every year, (ISC)² conducts a Cybersecurity Workforce Study to assess the size of the current cybersecurity workforce and the existing talent shortage.[7] Statista also compiles and publishes the size of the current global workforce.[8] Both sources break down the labor composition by generation (see Figure 11.3).

This data shows that Baby Boomers are still prevalent in the workforce, and Generation Z will start hitting the workforce in droves. Generation X and Millennials are not going anywhere anytime soon, either.

Managing cybersecurity across a multigenerational workforce has become quite the challenge. Table 11.1 outlines each generation and

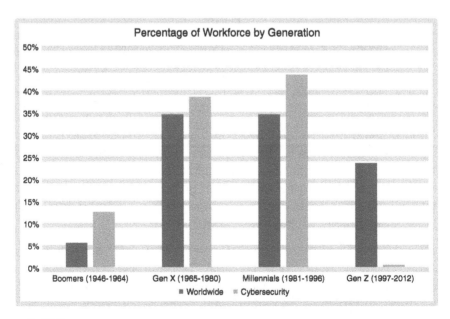

FIGURE 11.3 Global Cybersecurity Workforce Compared to Global Total Workforce

TABLE 11.1 Managing Across Generations. Data sourced from Purdue Global "Generational Differences in Workplace Content"

	Baby Boomers	Generation X	Millennials	Generation Z
Born:	1946–1964	1965–1980	1981–1996	1997–2012
Characteristics:	▪ Optimistic ▪ Competitive ▪ Workaholic ▪ Team-oriented	▪ Flexible ▪ Informal ▪ Skeptical ▪ Independent ▪ Resistant to change	▪ Competitive ▪ Civic-minded ▪ Value Diversity ▪ Achievement-oriented	▪ Global ▪ Entrepreneurial ▪ Progressive ▪ Less-focused
Shaped by:	▪ The Vietnam War ▪ Civil Rights Movement ▪ Watergate	▪ AIDS ▪ Fall of the Berlin Wall ▪ Dot-Com Boom	▪ Columbine ▪ 9/11 ▪ The Internet	▪ Life post 9/11 ▪ The Great Recession ▪ Access to technology from a young age
Motivated by:	▪ Company loyalty ▪ Teamwork ▪ Duty	▪ Responsibility ▪ Quality of their manager ▪ Unique work experiences	▪ Responsibility ▪ The quality of their manager ▪ Unique work experiences	▪ Diversity ▪ Personalization ▪ Individuality ▪ Creativity
Communication Style:	▪ Phone calls ▪ Face-to-face	▪ Phone calls ▪ Face-to-face	▪ IMs ▪ Texts ▪ Email	▪ IMs ▪ Texts ▪ Social Media

(Continued)

TABLE 11.1 (Continued)

	Baby Boomers	Generation X	Millennials	Generation Z
Worldview:	▪ Pay your dues and sacrifice for success	▪ Value diversity, and quick to move on if their employer fails to meet their needs; resistant to change at work if it affects their personal lives	▪ Continue to challenge oneself to grow and develop with an emphasis on work-life balance	▪ Self-identify as digital device addicts, valuing independence and individuality ▪ Prefer to work with Millennial managers, innovative coworkers, and new technologies
Key Activities:	▪ Do not micromanage, and provide specific goals and deadlines ▪ Coach vs. direct ▪ Want to leave a legacy – consider establishing a formal mentorship program where they can volunteer to mentor less experienced team members ▪ Patience on your part will lead to exceptional results on their part	▪ Be as flexible with schedules as possible – if they are producing results, don't watch the timeclock ▪ Provide opportunities for professional and personal development ▪ Emphasize work-life balance, incentivize taking paid time-off	▪ Provide diversity of work and feedback often ▪ Evaluate based on results, not based on time clocked in ▪ Provide immediate feedback ▪ Offer mentoring opportunities ▪ Explain "why"	▪ Provide diversity of work and feedback often ▪ Encourage ▪ Do not micromanage; provide direction and get out of the way ▪ Let them lead innovation initiatives

their worldview, motivations, and key activities I have learned along the way to interact with each generation. Credit goes to Purdue Global for condensing the attributes for each generation.[9]

Managing human capital is not only about managing your direct reports. It is about managing the people around you. We talk throughout this book about influencing others around you, directly or indirectly. Security awareness training, establishing security champions, and building a successful business case all involve "managing" others somehow. NTT conducted a study outlining how different generations approach cybersecurity.[10] The NTT study shows what we have inherently known. There are no "one-size-fits-all" answers when it comes to implementing a sticky security culture across your workforce. The type and age of worker goes a long way toward how they influence cyber risk.

One may think that younger generations being digital natives correlates to increased cyber awareness and hygiene. I often joke that my nieces (Generation Z) do not know a world before smartphones. On the other hand, I do remember a world before music CDs and with 5.25" floppy disks! However, it is wrong to assume that my nieces are natively more "secure." In fact, they "get" cybersecurity concepts, but they also expect cybersecurity and privacy to be baked into the technology they use with minimal friction (like their iPhones). However, they are naïve to the fact that social media platforms have led our younger generations to believe that sharing tons of private information will have no long-term consequences, but it will, and it has.

In fact, employees over 30 are more likely to be cyber-aware. They have better cybersecurity practices than their younger counterparts who grew up with smartphones, tablets, and the ability to access the entire knowledge base of the human race through a simple web browser, a few keystrokes, and a couple of clicks. Conversely, employees under 30 take a more laissez-faire approach toward cybersecurity. They expect cybersecurity to be flexible, adaptive, and built into their work processes to enhance productivity. This expectation includes the ability to use their own devices, which is why you have seen the enterprise mobility management market take off over the past several years. Considering these multigenerational requirements is paramount when designing and implementing cybersecurity controls.

The study lays out several statistics, but three jump out at me. The first statistic is 39% of employees under 30 are more likely to pay a ransom to recover from a ransomware attack vs. 30% of employees over 30. As the workforce grows younger, it is important to entertain the thought of establishing bitcoin escrow accounts to have in such a "break glass in case of emergency" scenario, but the ultimate decision should be left to organizational leadership. Many cybersecurity insurance providers are now offering this service, along with professional negotiators to help negotiate down the final ransom payment.

The second statistic is 71% of employees under 30, and 79% of employees over 30 believe that using personal devices for work is a potential security risk. While those under 30 are more risk acceptant of using personal devices, the numbers for both groups are still high at above 70%, which is why you will continue to see the proliferation and growth of enterprise mobility management solutions.

The third, and a significant reason we chose to write this book, is that 81% of employees under 30, and 85% of employees over 30 believe cybersecurity is a concern that the boardroom must address.

Training

Do not be the pointy-haired boss from *Dilbert*! (See Figure 11.4.) Training is often the first to go when budgets get tight. This is the exact wrong thing to do, and we argue that when money is tight and projects are on hold, that is the best time to double down on upskilling

FIGURE 11.4 DILBERT

Source: DILBERT (2009) Scott Adams, Inc. / with permission from Andrews McMeel Syndication

your workforce. First of all, they have the time due to a reduced work-load. If there is never time due to the number of fires to put out daily, it is likely time to reevaluate and do a complete reset of your cyberse-curity program. Second, a downturn in the market usually leads to uncertainty, and uncertainty leads to your employees looking for other opportunities. Training is an excellent way to help retain your best people.

An ESG and ISSA research report concluded that most cybersecurity professionals do not believe their organization provides the right level of cybersecurity training to keep their skills effective and relevant. Based on four years of research, training seems to be perpetually inadequate.[11] If cybersecurity professionals are receiving inadequate cybersecurity training, we can conclude that the rest of the workforce is in far worse shape. Attackers like to kick organizations when they are down. Hence, it is more important than ever to ensure that employees' cybersecurity skills remain up to date to deal with the ever-evolving and complex threat landscape.

At the risk of beating a dead horse, cybersecurity is everyone's job; therefore, extend cybersecurity training to everyone in the organiza-tion. Upgrade your entire workforce by upgrading your cybersecu-rity training and tailoring training to each job role. You are likely not going to send an accountant to a training course on penetration testing, but the accountant certainly needs to be aware of how they can help prevent a data breach, how to recognize when they are the target of a cyber-attack, and what to do if they do suspect a data breach. Cybersecurity skills, both hard skills that we learn as cyber-security professionals and softer skills that we teach to the rest of the organization, are perishable and can become stale if we are not constantly learning and practicing. Doing so improves productivity, reduces the impact and likelihood of a cybersecurity incident, and boosts employee confidence and morale.

Humans are usually the weakest link in your organization's cyberse-curity defenses. We can no more go around blaming employees for not noticing a business email compromise attempt or recognizing a threat actor moving laterally throughout the network than a neurosur-geon can blame us for not knowing how to remove a brain tumor. Most employees understand the importance of cybersecurity, regardless of their role, and appreciate the organization's effort to maintain cyber vigilance. Continuing to put in the effort to train employees up-front will help combat issues in the future.

Cybersecurity professionals have a hard time staying abreast of the latest tactics, techniques, and procedures that attackers use, much less the rest of IT and then the rest of the organization. It is crucial that you, as leaders, emphasize the importance of training and outline the appropriate actions employees should take to recognize and react to potential cyber incidents. All employees must realize how important it is to remain knowledgeable and diligent when maintaining the confidentiality, integrity, availability, and sometimes safety of their organization's data and people.

In the Application section of this chapter, we will walk through building a business case for role-based cybersecurity training for the entire workforce.

Diversity of Thought

There is an entire budding movement and industry around diversity, equity, and inclusion (DEI) in technology fields. We do not claim to be DEI experts, but we can certainly agree that there is a DEI gap in our industry, and it must be acknowledged. Neither of us have robust experience within this area, so we will not virtue signal by claiming that you should take some sort of action that we ourselves have not lived and breathed. Books such as *Athena Rising: How and Why Men Should Mentor Women* by W. Brad Johnson and David Smith, and *I Think, You Think, We All Think Differently: Leadership Skills for Millennials & Gen Z* by Greg Buschman approach the DEI issue from a perspective of allyship, the ability to acknowledge differences and to promote those differences from the perspective of inclusion versus the perspective of "yeah, but." Karen Worstell, former CISO for companies such as Microsoft and AT&T Wireless, is doing some excellent work in promoting diversity and allyship in her podcast series, *MOJO Maker for Women in Tech Podcast*. Other incredible individuals, like Naomi Buckwalter and Tazin Khan Norelius, have written extensively on LinkedIn about DEI and have formed non profits around the importance of diversity efforts in technology and cybersecurity (www.cybersecuritygatebreakers.org and www.cybercollective.org, respectively).

We are writing this book in 2020–2021, just as the global COVID-19 pandemic escalated, eased up, and started escalating again due to the delta variant. Some things as innocuous as perspectives on going to a party or going back to the office have become extremely polarized. The debates around DEI are exponentially heated. While we are not going to claim we have the answers to these challenging questions, we understand that it is critically important to respect the diversity of thought. Even boards of directors are striving to incorporate more diversity in boards by intentionally trying to fill vacancies outside of their networks. The State of California even enacted a law, effective January 1, 2020, that all locally headquartered publicly traded companies must have at least one female director by 2020.[13] Diversity is not achieved strictly through gender equality, but it is at least a start.

However, diversity of thought *is* something we have both strived to build in teams that we have led, so we will focus on diversity in that context in this section. It is vital that the demographics within our teams more closely reflect the demographics in society. Many organizations benchmark their DEI efforts around gender, age, and ethnic diversity. Women and minorities are more prevalent in the workplace today than ever before in our society. We outlined the multigenerational nature of our workforce in a prior section of this chapter. A diverse team brings diverse perspectives to the table. There is always more than one way to tackle a problem, and your way may not be the best. Diversity in brainstorming solutions to problems as complex as gathering cyber intelligence or tracking an attacker's actions is critical in staying ahead of today's threats.

Each of us has cognitive biases. A cognitive bias is a systematic error in thinking that occurs when people are processing and interpreting information in the world around them. Cognitive biases affect the decisions and judgments we make.[12] As cybersecurity professionals, we are processing information all day, every day – none more so than our security analysts working the front lines, who are required to make quick decisions while immersed in a deluge of security data, logs, and alerts. We briefly touched upon cognitive bias in Chapter 3 – Business Decisions in the context of decision processes and widening your options, but let's dive into more specifics and investigate how each type of cognitive bias appears in our daily cybersecurity lives. There are 13 primary cognitive biases that we should all be aware of and understand where they may creep up in our jobs (see Table 11.2).[14] I have been guilty of every one of these biases at some point in my career.

Bringing together people with multiple backgrounds and life experiences to build your cybersecurity teams and providing the psychological safety that we discussed with enabling crucial conversations in Chapter 8: Communication – You Do It Every Day (Or Do You?) leads to many benefits, including:

- Minimized impact of the biases listed above
- Increased candor
- Encouraged debate of different ideas
- Minimized groupthink
- Safe risk-taking
- Increased candor
- Improved decision-making capabilities of the team

TABLE 11.2 Cognitive Bias in Cybersecurity

Cognitive Bias	Definition	When it may be found in Cybersecurity
Correspondence Bias	The tendency to draw conclusions on someone's personality based on their behaviors, even when the given situation can explain these behaviors. In other words, when we see someone behaving in a certain way, we think it is because they are "just that kind of person" instead of taking into account factors of why they are exhibiting such behaviors.	Conclusion: "Our offshore SOC analysts cannot think beyond the checklist-style playbooks we provide. This is always the case when we deal with individuals from that country!" Situation: The offshore SOC analyst is at risk of losing their job if they deviate from the exact checklist YOU provided because of liability and scope-creep concerns.
Unconscious Bias	An inherent assignment of positive or negative traits to a person or group.	"Millennials are lazy." or "Boomers can't keep up." (see Managing a Multigenerational Workforce)

Cognitive Bias	Definition	When it may be found in Cybersecurity
Priming Bias	The tendency to be influenced by what someone else has said, creating a preconceived idea.	Security analyst 1: "Our crappy webserver crashed again. What a joke! It happens every time it gets a little busy!" Security analyst 2: Ignores evidence of a DDoS attack against said webserver.
Confirmation Bias	The tendency to search for or interpret information in a way that confirms your preconceptions or discrediting information that does not support your views.	Leaning too much on past root causes and experience when troubleshooting a connectivity issue and not considering other possible root causes.
Affinity Bias	The tendency to be favorably biased toward people like ourselves.	Leaning toward hiring someone with a similar background to you.
Self-Serving Bias	The tendency to claim more responsibility for successes than failures or to evaluate ambiguous information in a way beneficial to your interests.	Individuals who take all of the credit when things go well, or none of the blame when things go sideways. "Spinning" information to side with your point of view or stance.
Belief Bias	Allowing your belief in the premise of an argument to bias your evaluation of the strengths of the logic of the argument.	You believe that your organization should invest in detective vs. preventative security measures. You hear at a conference, "It's not *if*, but *when*, your organization will suffer a breach." You interpret that statement to mean that no matter what measures are used to prevent a breach, they are futile, and all efforts should be focused on detecting a breach while ignoring any premise that preventative measures can help minimize the impact of a breach should it occur.

(Continued)

TABLE 11.2 (Continued)

Cognitive Bias	Definition	When it may be found in Cybersecurity
Framing	Making decisions based on the way information is presented instead of merely evaluating the facts themselves.	Promoting framing bias is the job of just about every marketer (in this case, cybersecurity marketer) that exists.
Hindsight Bias	"Hindsight is 20/20." The tendency to see past events as predictable, although they were likely not predictable when the event occurred.	"I knew the incident was caused by a zero-day attack against the SMB protocol."
Embodied Cognition	A tendency to make conclusions and decisions based on the biological state of the body.	All of us are guilty (especially this author) of passing judgment or snapping at someone when we are not feeling well or have not had enough coffee.
Anchoring	The tendency to focus too much on an initial piece of information for subsequent decisions. It is the inability to pivot from an initial impression as new information presents itself.	Missing a multi-vectored attack by focusing too much on the first attack. A classic example is focusing on a DDoS while ignoring or missing the mass exfiltration of data occurring while the attack has the team distracted.
Status Quo	The tendency to select an option because it is the default option or less likely to cause friction.	Not pointing out an affinity bias with your manager because you feel you are in a weak position to do so.
Overconfidence	Trusting your ability to make correct decisions too much and overrating your skills as a decision-maker.	Employees who do not understand the full impact of cyber risks to the organization yet are overconfident in their own understanding and their ability to make cyber risk treatment decisions.

Application

Earlier in this chapter, we promised to build a business case around justifying training up your cybersecurity workforce instead of suffering the consequences of employee turnover, even during a down market. Let's examine a general use case of a cybersecurity architect making around $150K per year. We will use a simple cost-benefit analysis to analyze this use case by analyzing both quantitative and qualitative costs. Cost, in this case, is the cost of employee turnover. The benefit, in this case, is the cost of training. In this case, we want the benefit to be savings to the organization, so we expect the dollar value of the benefit to be less than the dollar value of the cost (see Table 11.3).

Based on this simple analysis, no CFO on the planet would disagree that investing $25,780 to save $280,780 over two years is a good investment. There are other intangible benefits to consider, such as the loss of institutional knowledge when an employee departs, which we tried to capture in "Lost Productivity." Positive cash flow might be tight in your organization, which may still lead to a "no" for training. Again, understanding business context is key.

Assumptions and Risks

Several assumptions and risks regarding this business case include the following. As with any business case, you may identify other issues or factors to address as you learn more information:

- **Salary:** For this simple case, we assume that the departing employee and the new employee make the same salary at $150,000/year
- **Hiring and onboarding:** In my last role, the cost to post a job, advertise, interview, screen, and hire candidates was about 20% of their annual salary. The cost to train them once they were onboarded so that they were self-sufficient was an additional 30% of their salary when we account for their salary and lost productivity from one or more other employees on the team due to the "new employee tax."

TABLE 11.3 Cost-Benefit Analysis of Employee Training

EMPLOYEE TURNOVER (COSTS)	YEAR 1	YEAR 2	TOTAL
NON-RECURRING COSTS			
Job Posting, Advertising, Interviewing, Screening, Hiring	$ 30,000		$ 30,000
Onboarding & Initial Training	$ 50,000		$ 50,000
TOTAL NON-RECURRING COSTS	$ 80,000	$ -	$ 80,000
RECURRING COSTS			
Lost productivity	$ 75,000	$ 25,000	$100,000
Lost employee engagement (high turnover disengaging other employees – assuming one other employee leaves)	$ 50,000	$ 25,000	$ 75,000
Training costs (training invested in departing employee)	$ 12,890	$ 12,890	$ 25,780
TOTAL RECURRING COSTS	$137,890	$ 62,890	$200,780
TOTAL COSTS	$217,890	$ 62,890	$280,780
TRAINING (BENEFITS)	**YEAR 1**	**YEAR 2**	**TOTAL**
COST OF TRAINING			
Training	$ 7,500	$ 7,500	$ 15,000
Travel/Hotel	$ 2,000	$ 2,000	$ 4,000
Food	$ 500	$ 500	$ 1,000
Loss of productivity from 1 week of training	$ 2,890	$ 2,890	$ 5,780
TOTAL TRAINING COSTS	$ 12,890	$ 12,890	$ 25,780
TOTAL TRAINING COSTS	$ 12,890	$ 12,890	$ 25,780

- **Lost productivity:** Per Deloitte, a new employee may take one to two years to reach the productivity of an existing employee. This fact is more evident in highly skilled roles such as a cybersecurity architect.[15]
- **Training Costs:** I have strived to invest 5% to 10% of the employee's salary on training every year before travel, lodging, and food.
- **Market Conditions:** It is important to consider market conditions. While on paper, investing in training seems like a no-brainer, a cash-strapped organization during a downturn in the market may decide to hold on to cash to ensure it survives. Cash is king!

Key Insights

- Leverage tools, such as the Kolbe A/B/C Indices, The Clifton-Strengths Assessment (StrengthsFinder 2.0), LPI: Leadership Practices Inventory, and Myers-Briggs to identify your strengths and the strengths of the individuals of your team. Use this knowledge to effectively connect your team's work to individual strengths.
- Organizations must engage all generations when establishing and maintaining security culture. Here are some best practices when engaging your multigenerational workforce:
  - Ensure your security champions are diverse, including in age.
  - Solicit feedback from your security champions frequently surrounding their views on cybersecurity.
  - Be the "Department of How" vs. the "Department of No" by ensuring business adaptability, flexibility, and productivity are foundational to your security strategy.
  - Almost everyone hates compliance-based security training, so strive to make security awareness fun for all generations through gamification and small prizes.
- Understand how to identify the 13 types of cognitive biases, and identify if any of them creep up into your hiring and management practices.

- Evaluate your leadership style. Do you include and treat individuals fairly no matter your personal like or dislike towards them?
- Ask yourself if your team welcomes and listens to differences of opinion. Do they evaluate new information as it comes in, whether or not it aligns with a previous decision or the status quo?

Notes

1. Ratanjee, V., "Why Managers Need Leadership Development Too," January 15, 2021. Accessed March 20, 2021. https://www.gallup.com/workplace/328460/why-managers-need-leadership-development.aspx.
2. Definition of Human Capital Management (HCM), Gartner Information Technology Glossary. Accessed March 16, 2021. https://www.gartner.com/en/information-technology/glossary/hcm-human-capital-management.
3. Sorenson, S., "How Employees' Strengths Make Your Company Stronger." Accessed March 20, 2021. https://www.gallup.com/workplace/231605/employees-strengths-company-stronger.aspx
4. Gallup, "The History of CliftonStrengths." Accessed April 3, 2021. https://www.gallup.com/cliftonstrengths/en/253754/history-cliftonstrengths.aspx.
5. Kouzes, J.M., and Posner, B.Z, *The Leadership Challenge: How to Make Extraordinary Things Happen in Organizations*, 6th ed., John Wiley & Sons, 2017.
6. Myers-Briggs, *Type and Cyber-Security: A Research Study from the Myers-Briggs Company*, 2019.
7. (ISC)², *(ISC)² Cybersecurity Workforce Study, 2020: Cybersecurity Professionals Stand Up to a Pandemic*, 2020.
8. Statista, "Employment Worldwide by 2020, by Generation," December 31, 2016. Accessed April 8, 2021. https://www.statista.com/statistics/829705/global-employment-by-generation/.
9. Purdue Global, "Generational Differences in the Workplace Content." Accessed April 8, 2021. https://www.purdueglobal.edu/education-partnerships/generational-workforce-differences-infographic/.
10. NTT Ltd., *Meeting the Expectations of a New Generation: How the Under 30s Expect New Approaches to Cybersecurity*, 2019.
11. Oltsik, J., *The Life and Times of Cybersecurity Professionals*. https://www.esg-global.com/research/esg-research-report-the-life-and-times-of-cybersecurity-professionals-2020.

12. Cherry, K., "What Is Cognitive Bias?" Accessed April 19, 2021. https://www.verywellmind.com/what-is-a-cognitive-bias-2794963.

13. Creary, S.J., McDonnell, M-H, Ghai, S., and Scruggs, J., "When and Why Diversity Improves Your Board's Performance," *Harvard Business Review*, March 27, 2019. Accessed July 14, 2021. https://hbr.org/2019/03/when-and-why-diversity-improves-your-boards-performance.

14. Wikipedia, "Cognitive Bias." Accessed April 19, 2021. https://en.wikipedia.org/wiki/Cognitive_bias.

15. "Employee Retention Now a Big Issue: Why the Tide Has Turned." Accessed April 21, 2021. https://www.linkedin.com/pulse/20130816 200159-131079-employee-retention-now-a-big-issue-why-the-tide-has-turned/2021.

CHAPTER 12

Negotiation

Negotiation is <u>not</u> an act of battle; it's a process of discovery.
— Chris Voss

Opportunity

In my experience, all leaders expect to leave an imprint on the organizations they serve. Every attempt to change the status quo is a negotiation. The concepts we have described throughout the book equip you to understand, empathize, and communicate with your colleagues *in their terms*. This chapter covers the art of letting others have your way. Like Harry S. Truman, 33rd President of the United States, once said, "It is amazing what you can accomplish if you do not care who gets the credit."

The average tenure of a CISO has been estimated at 18 to 26 months by various sources in recent years.[1] Indeed, some of the reason that CISO tenures are so short is that the role is one of influence, not control. Cynthia James estimates that CISOs only have control of 60% of what might get them fired.[2] I posit, therefore, you must be a trim tab. You must hold difficult conversations with uncertainty abound, and you must obtain results through others. Usually, all this happens without formal authority. You must build your circle of influence through moral authority so that people want to follow your leadership. You must be prepared to scale your impact by empowering others in your team to hold the same conversations successfully. Often requests from cybersecurity departments appear at odds with the primary goals of the business. After all, there are only so many hours in a day. Every minute your company spends on cybersecurity is a minute that the business could spend elsewhere.

Now, before we go on further, it's worth clarifying that negotiation isn't about taking the most for yourself and leaving the scraps for others. If you favor an abundance mindset rather than playing a zero-sum game, you can relax and enjoy the journey. You can appreciate the relationships you build and relish the business value you protect. You can avoid the burnout and moral dilemmas that have driven many cybersecurity leaders out of the field entirely.

The opportunity to negotiate is ever-present. It's not just about getting what you want. It's about getting what you want *and having the other party feel good about it*. In my first CISO role, I neglected to recognize how important it was to make sure the other party felt good about the work we accomplished. In my first 90 days, we achieved an enormous feat, narrowly avoiding fines for recurring PCI failures. I paid the price every day after, in the form of malicious compliance and an undercurrent of resistance. My greatest lesson from that experience was that I needed stronger relationships if my legacy was to survive beyond my time with an organization. Indeed, short-term gain can cause long-term pain.

Eventually, I left that role and took a year to travel. I invested the time to think and learn new skills. Finally, when I surfaced in the job market in pursuit of a new role, I positioned and promoted myself with this catchphrase:

I am an organizational change catalyst laser-focused on enterprise cyber resilience. I inspire change through piercing insights and profound relationships. Notably, my success as a security professional comes at the heels of dogged persistence and intense discipline.

When you look closer, what I'm saying is that it is essential to bring both intellect and heart to the role. I didn't realize it at the time, but negotiation is the confluence of piercing insights and profound relationships. So, in this chapter, I'll adapt techniques from Chris Voss's book *Never Split The Difference: Negotiating As If Your Life Depended on It* to the CISO role. I'll show how consistent application of these concepts can add up over time to produce a rising tide, in essence, the virtuous cycle of a cultural shift. That shift is the most powerful tool in your arsenal, and it happens slowly. Despite what you might think, there's no bolt of lightning. Culture shift does not happen overnight. Instead, the persistent presence of influence gradually saturates the culture. Like filling a bucket one drip at a time, applying these techniques will help you cultivate and nurture that cultural change one conversation at a time.

Principle

In this section, I will provide some techniques I have adopted to avoid being the department of "No" without succumbing to wimp-win negotiations. Here, we'll explore tactical empathy, which fuels both piercing insights and profound relationships. Additionally, we'll cover forced empathy to ensure that your colleagues reciprocate the compassion you meticulously cultivate.

The Department of "No"

For years, businesses have become accustomed to cybersecurity teams that function as the department of "No." In my career as a consultant, I saw businesses struggle to adopt wireless technologies. Those that did successfully adopt Wi-Fi first had significant cultural and performance advantages. Then I saw the onslaught of mobile technologies that transformed into the various forms of shadow IT that we live with today. The battle of bring your own device (BYOD) eventually gave way to cloud workloads deployed on expense cards. Every few weeks, I participate in conversations with cybersecurity departments uncertain about adapting to enable digital business strategies that leverage hyper-scale public clouds.

While one strategy is to be the force of innovation, it is unrealistic to expect that the cybersecurity department can be the source of all innovation. By observation, often, businesses evolve in the space beyond their cybersecurity capabilities. And as they do, cybersecurity leaders and their teams either absorb the progress as a personal assault or recognize that it's not about them – it's about agility, growth, cost containment, and in some cases, survival.

Even so, it's very tempting to lead with "No."

A look at the psychology behind "no" reveals that you feel safe and protected once you have said no. You have made no commitment. And the great thing about "no" is that anything you say while exploring the potential paths of implementation after you have said "no," flows more easily. There's no risk of confusion or unknowns, or ambiguity. Simply, "no" is safe. "No" is comfortable.

However, we cannot reside in the cozy cocoon of "No." If we want a seat at the table, we must find ways to facilitate calibrated risks and informed decisions. So, there are a few great alternatives to a simple "no" answer in the heat of conversation. Tactfully navigating pressure situations is a skill every successful executive should master. If you find yourself in one of these situations, stay calm and create room to maneuver with any of these responses:

- I'm not sure that I fully agree.
- This makes me feel uncomfortable.
- I don't understand.
- I'd like more information.
- I don't think we have adequate resources to support that safely.
- I believe we'd be better off considering an alternative.
- Let me check in my peer slack channels or CISO forums to see how others think about this challenge.
- I'd like to have an SME from [*my team, a consulting partner, etc.*] participate in making sure I'm considering all the angles.

Then, you can immediately follow with a solution-based question or simply observe your colleague's emotional response.

For example:

- It seems like you are not satisfied with this approach.
- What about this doesn't work for you?
- What would you need to make it work?

Using this strategy avoids a hard no, avoids offering approval to proceed, and indicates you are engaged in finding a solution that works for everyone. Then, focusing on the solution and offering your colleague an opportunity to explain more about their goals, approach, or strategy will help you identify new pieces of information that often permit you to divorce the goal and the strategy. More times than I can count, through this discovery process, I have separated the outcome from the steps to obtain it. Doing so frequently results in solutions that neither side was considering when the conversation started. Steven Covey refers to this as the third alternative. It is not your way, nor is it mine, but instead we agree to find a new way. Both parties should expect an outcome that is better than either party imagined in the first place.

More interestingly, if you use these alternatives in conversation, you are not cornered to make difficult decisions. You end up recruiting the most talented resources in the room to identify what is acceptable as an alternative and build buy-in for the solution. In the end, you won't carry the stress of a controversial decision or feel trapped if the chosen path blows up.

You eliminate that layer of stress, which helps you avoid burnout. When we, together, collaboratively design what we feel is the best solution, there is buy-in. Of course, let's be pragmatic. In some cases, you simply cannot get aligned. As a last option, push for a Risk Acceptance Form (RAF) signed by the department executive. Make sure you have a structured approach to communicating the risk. Don't forget to review the techniques covered in Chapter 7 – Translating Cyber Risk into Business Risk. Take time to purposefully articulate the risk so that business leaders know what risk they are accepting. Consider the 5-point finding format provided in the Risk Acceptance Form template available online at www.CISOEvolution.com.

"Yes" Is NOT the Goal

Just like there is safety in "No," you are likely to encounter hesitation in "Yes." More than one cybersecurity leader I know is challenged by operating in a culture that lacks accountability. The negotiations that take place on the internal battlefield include both the support you require from your business counterparts, as well as the security diligence you can offer to them. I mean that sooner or later, you will need a change in process, support to implement a technology, or even just access to a new system. Sometimes you will have to negotiate to get your way.

However, yes is not simply yes. Chris Voss has identified three styles of "Yes." They include:

- Counterfeit – this is one in which your counterpart plans on saying "no" but either feels "yes" is an easier escape route or just wants to disingenuously keep the conversation going to obtain more information or some other kind of edge.
- Confirmation – is generally innocent, a reflexive response to a black-or-white question; sometimes a confirmation "yes" is used to lay a trap, but mostly it's just simple affirmation with no promise of action.
- Commitment – a commitment "yes" is the real deal; it's an actual agreement that leads to action, a "yes" at the table that ends with a signature on the contract. The commitment "yes" is what you want, but the three types sound almost the same, so you must learn how to recognize the differences.[3]

Chris argues that since "yes" is so tricky, you are seeking "That's right." The way you get there is by labeling feelings to pull them out. Once you get to an emotional and intellectual alignment, you can pursue the strategy. Although my style is to think big, start small, and move fast. I continue to learn that it's essential to take the time to obtain emotional alignment and ensure that the subsequent steps are clear. As a finishing touch, you can create accountability with the simple script:

Who, does what, by when, and how will we follow-up?[4]

Forced Empathy

First, what is empathy? In its purest form, it is understanding both content and feelings.

You don't have to agree with someone to empathize with them. However, once you have demonstrated empathy, you must be exceptionally careful to honor other people's feelings. If you don't, you can quickly reverse all the goodwill that stems from empathy.

Here we are going to use "how" questions to engage your counterpart. In particular, "How am I supposed to do that?" Remember, your tone will make or break this technique. How questions can alter the conversation in a way that improves relationships and enhances security culture. Here's the typical dialogue:

Sales: "We want to sub-contract application development with this very innovative boutique consultancy. We want to carry them on our paper. They don't feel like it's necessary to perform the third-party diligence process since they already serve large healthcare customers. We need to move quickly, so we don't lose this deal. I just need your approval to proceed. Will you approve this?"

Me: "No. We can't do that and maintain our compliance."

As an alternative, you can leverage forced empathy via a "how" question. Here's what that might sound like:

Me: "It seems like this relationship has the potential to be a game-changer. And this deal is important. Assuming that's true, my concern is that we're going to sign a contract today, and eventually, the nature of the relationship may change over time. If that happens, the small risk we have today evolves subtly, and soon we're taking on much greater liability than anyone anticipated. How could we mitigate the risk of a compliance failure and elevated liability over time if we don't perform third-party diligence as the standards require?"

Sales: "Well, the deal is average in size, so it's not a game-changer, but to answer your question – these guys aren't going to have any access to sensitive information. And we're only working with noncompliance customers."

Me: "Hmm. Okay. It strikes me that less than 15% of our customers have no compliance requirements. So, 15% doesn't sound like a needle mover. I wonder, is all the effort for a partnership worth it? I mean, that essentially excludes them from doing business with most of our clients. It also really feels like a heavy qualifier as we try to include them in pre-sales efforts. Is our lead flow deep enough and qualification process streamlined to justify a partnership that at best can help us with 15% of deals?"

Sales: "I suppose we want them working on customers with more sensitive data eventually. Certainly, for the relationship to matter, they are going to have to."

Me: "If that's true, it seems like a hassle to track all this in a way that will satisfy our auditors until they are ready. It would be a disaster to have audit findings that might trigger exit clauses with our existing customers. This potential for disaster raises a few more questions for me. For example, are you prepared to manage client communications if that happens? Are our CRO and CFO bought into this already? *How* do you think that notifications should work? *How* can we ensure that other key executives are included to help make this strategic decision?"

Sales: "Well, I wanted to focus on this first deal. But if this partnership is going to function, we're going to need them to step up and do the assessment."

Me: "That's easier for our team since we have a whole platform and dedicated staff trained to facilitate the process."

Sales: "Let's go that route. I'm going to push a little harder to have them complete the process. Otherwise, we can find another vendor to partner with."

> Me: *"Okay, let me know, and we can press for more broad-based executive support if you think the risks and additional process are worth it."*

You can see that calibrated "how" questions caused the sales rep to consider the additional challenges he was introducing. In other words, forced empathy. In this case, maybe he realized the impact on his existing customers, and the energy to push the deal forward with the other executives might not be worth the time. Either way, he qualified the actual value of the relationship and ultimately decided that the path of least resistance was a more persistent pursuit of the security diligence process. In the dialogue, he also learned how our compliance program works and gained a further appreciation for the interconnected processes inside our business.

Now imagine the cumulative effect of this type of dialogue taking place repeatedly throughout your team and the many touchpoints in your business. With forced empathy, you gradually start to bend the culture in a direction that favors effective cybersecurity. You avoid being a department of "no," and others can feel good about the collaborative outcomes you achieve.

Influencing Those Behind the Table

In Chapter 5 – Articulating the Business Case, we reviewed a case study on utilizing *SCIPAB® to Present a Business Case for Password Management* and then we examined a case study to present the *Cost-Benefit Analysis* performed for that same initiative. Combined, the messaging and cost-benefit analysis provided enough for us to obtain executive approval and funding to execute the roll-out. However, in that chapter we also described *Stakeholder Analysis* and *Influence Mapping*, two activities that influence the execution of a project after it has been funded. In this case, I failed to do both.

For better or for worse, I did a great job presenting the business case, but in the process of execution, I intentionally suppressed the voice of others whom I figured might have concerns. I thought that it was better to just push forward without building consensus. That was too slow. Years later, we achieved only a partial roll-out of the solution despite having tried on three separate occasions.

At the onset, I anticipated the project would be entirely uncontroversial. So, following such an extensive effort to get full executive buy-in, there was no way I was going to give anyone outside the executive team further opportunities to find obstacles. If you recall, my thinking on the effort was:

As the first CISO, I was naturally working to establish a positive presence in the business. I wanted to dispel the false narrative that security is always inconvenient. I was also working to highlight the difference between security-driven culture and compliance-driven culture.

I thoroughly regret the damage to relationships I inflicted in the process of failing to stop for red lights. So much for a quick win that enhances the overall sentiment of the InfoSec department. In hindsight, I wish I had taken just a moment to ask a few questions to influence those behind the table:

- How does this affect the rest of your team?
- Who are the other key players here? Will they have objections we should consider further?
- What do your colleagues see as primary concerns for this project?

I believe that if I had improved my negotiation approach, we would have saved a lot of effort, learned about better alternatives, and built stronger relationships in the process.

Application

This section will present how tactical empathy and intellectual curiosity helped elevate our application security program systematically over time. To set the stage, in early 2017, I joined Logicworks following a recapitalization event. This enabled opportunities for growth and the introduction of several changes in the business, including the formalization of a product team, reorganization of our service delivery functions, modification of our pricing strategy, refinement of our target markets, and the evolution of our revenue model.

Case Study – Security Culture and Application Security

As the company sustained hypergrowth over several years, there was limited software development life cycle (SDLC) documentation, and the ground was shifting beneath our feet.

The product team was challenged with a healthy volume of change – structurally with new leadership and team members, new agile development processes to adopt, and the fluidity of staffing up quickly. The product roadmap was aggressive given the pace of change and natural evolution of the industry. Needless to say, there were a lot of competing priorities to work through in addition to addressing the need for additional code security measures.

As you will see below, we were neither the source of innovation nor the killer of ideas or inspiration. Of course, I was concerned with the trailblazing appetite to integrate new cloud-native features. I prefer much more definition in our processes and made mention of that on several occasions. I simply communicated that I don't understand, and I'd like more information. Eventually, we all agreed that we needed additional resources to support the goals of our business.

Nevertheless, we started with awareness. We met for three hours. In the first hour, I provided an overview of the common frameworks and standards, including Building Security In Maturity Model (BSIMM), and how leveraging The Open Web Application Security Project (OWASP) Top 10 was essential to maintain PCI compliance. Then we conducted a threat model using Microsoft STRIDE. Just under 90 days on the job, I walked away from the conversation, happy that the code didn't perform anything critical yet. I learned that we were coding in Python on Django. The team mentioned that all the concepts we touched upon were not new to them. We ended the session with three enhancement opportunities for the sprint schedule:

- Password Complexity
- Dual Factor Auth Support
- Logging of State Changes

Recognizing that the vulnerabilities we identified were not exactly groundbreaking, I probably underappreciated the primary outcomes of this conversation. I was now a customer, and we established that vulnerability budgets, similar to SRE error budgets, would be burned down timely.[5] The other thing that happened is that we had a shared understanding of all the things that make up a software security initiative. The team gained exposure to the full suite of practices we would consider. They knew we would add capabilities incrementally. This interaction happened very near the instantiation of the Product department.

In our subsequent conversations, I pushed forward with tactical empathy. Only, my questions were genuine in that I had quite a bit of learning to do myself. I inquired, "How can we validate, in addition to understanding threat modeling and OWASP Top 10, that we are proactive in identifying and mitigating vulnerabilities in our code? How can we be confident that the software we expose to the internet is safe? And how would you like to add the security touchpoints we've discussed incrementally?"

After burning down the findings we identified in our threat model, we committed to conducting a grey-box (credentialed, code-assisted) penetration test of our client portal web application. So, with outside consulting help, we conducted an informal threat model to reinforce the process and centered our assessment on evaluating our performance against the OWASP Top 10. The test revealed a few findings, but overall we faired much stronger than I anticipated.

We fixed those issues, and later that year, around the time of AWS re:Invent, a release of new features on the AWS WAF product prompted conversations for us to experiment with an OWASP aligned AWS CloudFormation Template. As Amazon and Microsoft release new features and services that get integrated or offered to our customers, it is important to ask additional questions on limitations or areas of concern.

In different meetings throughout the business I asked, "How can we be prepared to support the AWS WAF if we aren't familiar with the technology? How can we be advocates for the solution if we don't have experience deploying and operating it ourselves?" So, we implemented the WAF internally in a low-maintenance way. Later we also established a WAF responsibility matrix and supported the WAF as a solution in our managed cloud operations. We found that it helped us overcome some limitations in manually blocking IP addresses, and it also automated remediation for several repeat findings that were flooding our NOC. So, we augmented revenue opportunities and rationalized our operating costs.

Meanwhile, we evaluated several security partners in search of a cloud-native, forward-thinking partner that would help us address a comprehensive attack surface. Internally, we experimented with containers, and we were already deploying them with a variety of container orchestration engines for our customers. We knew that we wanted visibility into the containers we leveraged in our applications. As we integrated Threat Stack, Inc. into our security program, we took the opportunity to implement the runtime application self-protection (RASP) features. I asked, "What would prevent us from adding these features, especially as we augment our defenses and help clients consider leveraging the full solution?" After all, they were already licensed, and it was easy to integrate.

At some point along the way, we discussed the need to ensure our software didn't include any problematic open-source licensing issues, so we acquired a software composition analysis tool that we eventually integrated into our evolving continuous integration (CI) pipeline. Our CFO was pleased knowing we didn't have any software packages that could disrupt our valuation or sale should a future investor make an offer.

As we have continued to align our offerings to be congruent with Site Reliability Engineering (SRE) and the value software drives in our business has continued to grow, tactical empathy has been a very productive tool. Incrementally, with some humility, a lot of "how" questions, a bit of luck, and some patience, we've enhanced a defensible software security program. I believe we have a positive relationship with most of our development team. We even integrated an infrastructure as code (IaC) scanner that the development team identified for us!

We now leverage open-source libraries inside our Image Factory (a multi-level image bakery) to ensure image hardening. Soon enough, we'll add staff to support a team that already views nonfunctional security requirements as a critical part of developing a quality code. It's through their support in requesting additional DevSecOps resources that we've secured the budget in the first place. We'll be conducting an independent third-party review of our CI/CD maturity on the same timeline. I'm confident we'll continue to mature our practices, and I'm happy with both the relationships and the progress we've made to date.

Key Insights

- When negotiating you should honor your relationships over your immediate priorities. In other words, prioritize people first.
- You should rehearse scripted responses that offer you a means to retreat during high pressure negotiations. Then follow up with a solution-based question. This pattern is an effective way to stay engaged without caving-in or becoming the department of "no."
- Calibrated "how" questions can help you achieve forced empathy. Further, persistent application of forced empathy techniques can lead to culture shift over time.
- It's never too early to predetermine successful execution by starting to influence behind the table. Ensure those not present in the room have a voice.
- There are three types of "yes," and you want to obtain the commitment "yes," which comes in the form of "that's right." To get there you need to ensure *emotional* alignment.

Notes

1. Morgan, S., "24 Percent of Fortune 500 CISOs on the Job for Just One Year," *Cybercrime Magazine*, 2020. Accessed May 24, 2021. https://cybersecurityventures.com/24-percent-of-fortune-500-cisos-on-the-job-for-just-one-year/.
2. James, C., "Why Are CISOs (Chief Information Security Officers) so Cranky?!?" *LinkedIn*, 2021. Accessed May 24, 2021. https://www.linkedin.com/pulse/why-cisos-chief-information-security-officers-so-cranky-cynthia-james/.
3. Voss, C., *Never Split The Difference: Negotiating As If Your Life Depended on It*, Harper Business, 2016.
4. Patterson, K. et al., *Crucial Conversations*, McGraw Hill, 2013, 245.
5. Thomson, J., and Laing, D., "Extending the Error Budget Model to Security and Feature Freshness," Usenix Association, 2019. https://www.usenix.org/conference/srecon19americas/presentation/thomson.

Conclusion

*The only metrics that will truly matter to my life
are the individuals whom I have been able to help,
one by one, to become better people.*

— Clayton M. Christensen

When Rock and I first sat down to discuss this book, it was immediately following a Birds of a Feather roundtable on *Security Budgets and Planning in a Cloud Consumption Era* at the RSA Conference 2020. The roundtable discussion turned out to be a one-on-one chat.

I was incredulous that this complex topic wasn't a stronger draw. I was also thoroughly embarrassed that at a conference with nearly 40,000 people in attendance, my roundtable attracted just a single attendee. At first, we waited patiently for others to join us. Eventually, we began to consider reasons why we were there alone, just the pair of us. Our hypotheses included things like, I'm not a famous industry personality, I did a poor job promoting the session, I was in direct competition with other more exciting events at the conference, it was late in the day and the conference, many people are just not far enough along in their cloud adoption efforts, people have this all figured out already, etc.

Although I'll never know exactly why my session was poorly attended, I have since spoken with several CISOs at some of the most cloud-forward successful organizations in the world. I learned that they still don't have great answers for the questions we were slated to discuss. I also came to understand that as cybersecurity leaders we all experience imposter syndrome. Even the most notorious and well credentialed experts confront this experience. As people, we grapple with ethical dilemmas that are complex and multifaceted. Our stresses, frustration, and burnout are real. And the reasons we avoid sharing or share only with a small intimate group of trusted peers are endless. Sometimes we only feel safe enough to propagate frivolous cliches; even when our most genuine desire is noble.

Each of us have strengths and weaknesses, as well as a unique set of circumstances that affect our lives. Whether you are a charismatic leader with room to grow your business acumen or a technologist who needs to elevate your emotional intelligence; we hope that the frameworks, resources, and case studies offered within this book expand your capabilities.

Throughout the book we endeavored to share our successes and failures as they relate to the experiences many cybersecurity leaders are likely to encounter. We hope that the theories we reviewed offer predictive value in terms of the outcomes you achieve. We aspire to help you avoid the pain and mistakes we experienced in our journeys and savor the victories of your own.

We hope that the time you invested reading this book helped provide at least one resource or insight that consoled your heart, emboldened your courage, sharpened your mind, or enriched your career and family. Finally, we look forward to building solidarity within the cybersecurity community, and we eagerly anticipate the conversations with individuals we will cherish, one by one.

Engage us online at www.CISOEvolution.com.

Index

Page numbers followed by *f* and *t* refer to
figures and tables, respectively.

A

AAMP method, 266
ABC method, 266
Ability, 69, 70*f*
Accelerating revenue, 13
Accept (risk response), 215
Access Control Policy, 187
Accrual accounting, and cash flow, 19–20
Accumulated Depreciation, 22
Active listening, 296
Adaptive challenges, 333, 334
Adaptive leadership, 332–334, 333*t*
Affective mind, 341
Affinity bias, 359*t*
Agile methodologies, 327
ALE (annualized loss expectancy), 210
Altegrity Risk International, 21
Amazon, 73
Amazon Athena, 50
Amazon Machine Images (AMIs), 26
Amazon QuickSight, 50
Amazon Web Services (AWS), 50–51, 182,
    254, 290, 378–379
Amortization, on income statement, 16
Anchoring, 360*t*
Andon, 144
Andreessen Horowitz, 177
Annualized loss expectancy (ALE), 210
Annual measures of hiring success, 321–322
"A-players," 313–315, 317,
    319–321, 335, 340
Apologizing, for broken promises, 280–281
Appetite for risk, *see* Risk appetite
Applicant tracking systems (ATSs), 315–316

Asking questions, 244–248
Assets, valuation of, 202–205
Asset-based valuation, 100
*Athena Rising: How and Why Men Should
    Mentor Women* (Johnson and
    Smith), 356
Atlanta, Ga., 227
ATT&CK™, 206, 207
Attacking others, 261
Attack scenarios, identifying potential,
    206–208
Attain Distance Before Deciding (in WRAP
    mnemonic), 61, 65–66
AT&T Wireless, 356
Authentic, being, 281
Automation:
    of code checks, 183–184
    warehouse and distribution center,
        117–118, 122
Avoid (risk response), 215
Avoiding (silence pattern), 261
Awareness:
    security, 177–178, 183
    in servant leaders, 331
AWS, *see* Amazon Web Services

B

Babin, Leif, 252, 284
Baby Boomers, 350, 351*t*–352*t*
Balance sheet, 17–19
"Balcony, getting on the," 334
Bankruptcy:
    cybersecurity failures leading to, 21
    insolvency vs., 21
Barnes, B. Kim, 287–288
Baseline hiring success (measure), 312
Bass, Bernard M., 327–329

Bayesian analysis, 211
Belief bias, 359*t*
Benefits, costs vs., *see* Cost-benefit
    analysis (CBA)
Berra, Yogi, on theory and practice, 58
BIA, *see* Business impact analysis
Bias:
    cognitive, 357–358, 358*t*–360*t*
    confirmation, 64, 359*t*
    status-quo, 66, 360*t*
Blackhat, 294
Boards of directors, 33, 170–173. *See also*
    Corporate governance
    and diversity, 357
    diversity of, 174–175
    and risk oversight, 174–175
Body language, 249–252, 330
Bonuses, referral, 315
Boundaries, establishing, 280
"B-players," 314
Brainstorming, 143–144
Briggs, Katherine, 347
Buckwalter, Naomi, 356
Building Security in Maturity Model
    (BSIMM), 183, 377
Burns, James M., 326
Buschman, Greg, 356
Business case articulation, 129–165
    case studies, 153–165
    cost concepts in, 131–137
    financial analysis in, 143–153
    messaging in, 138–143
    as opportunity, 129–131
Business context, 180–184
Business impact analysis (BIA), 203–205,
    209, 212, 232
Business model canvas, 40, 41*f*, 42–46
Business models, 31, 32*f*, 33
Business objectives, 189–190
Buy-in, getting, 328

C

Calibration training, 212
California, 357
California Consumer Privacy Act (CCPA),
    170, 184, 218, 227, 229
Cambridge Analytics, 230
CAPs (corrective action plans), 216, 233
Capital appreciation, 99
Capital Expenditures (CapEx), 18–19, 22
Career history forms, 315

Carnegie, Dale, 295, 297
Case studies:
    beverage manufacturer with competing
        priorities, 110–125
    business model canvas, cybersecurity via,
        40, 41*f*, 42–46
    choice architecture, 82–87
    coordination, competitive advantage
        via, 49–51
    cost-benefit analysis (CBA), 156–157,
        157*f*, 158*t*–159*t*, 159–160
    decision science, 78–82
    failure to govern, 190–194
    gaming the financial statements, 24–25
    humility for trust sake, 298–300
    negotiation, 377–380
    Net Present Value (NPV),
        160–161,162*t*–164*t*
    optimization, competitive advantage via,
        46–47, 48*f*
    professional networking, 300–302
    SCI-PAB® Thinking & Messaging Tool,
        153–156, 154*f*
    value creation through property team
        structure and tooling, 25–27
Cash flow, and profit, 19–20, 24
Cash flow statement, *see* Statement
    of cash flows
Cause, focusing on the, 292–293
CBA, *see* Cost-benefit analysis
CCPA, *see* California Consumer Privacy Act
Center for Internet Security (CIS), 73
CEO (Chief Executive Officer), 186, 286
Certification bootcamps, 179
CFO, *see* Chief Financial Officer
Challenge the Process (LPI® 360), 346
Chambers, John, 281
Champions, cybersecurity, 178
Change, assessment of substantial,
    219–221
Charisma, 327
Checkpoint, 317
Chief Executive Officer (CEO), 186, 286
Chief Financial Officer (CFO), 18, 42, 172,
    186, 286, 288
Chief Information Officer (CIO), 24, 27,
    233, 286, 288
Chief Information Security Officer (CISO):
    average tenure of, 367–368
    in gaming the financial statements case
        study, 24–25
    in team structure and tooling
        case study, 25–27

Chief Revenue Officer (CRO), 42
Chief Technology Officer (CTO), 25–26, 42
Choices, structuring complex, 77, 86, 87
Choice architecture, 68–69
Christakis, Nicholas A., 249
Christensen, Clayton M., on metrics, 383
Churchill, Winston, 64
Cialdini, Robert, 72
CI/CD (continuous integration/continuous
    deployment), 38, 74, 380
CIO, *see* Chief Information Officer
Circle of Concern, 289
Circle of Influence, 289–290
CIS (Center for Internet Security), 73
CISA (Cybersecurity and Infrastructure
    Agency), 205
CISA Automated Indicator Sharing, 220
Cisco, 281
CISO, *see* Chief Information Security Officer
CISSP certification, 178
Clifton, Donald C., 343
CliftonStrengths Assessment, 343,
    344f, 345
Cloud-based applications, 171
Cloud Security Alliance (CSA), 294
Coaching, 321
Coalfire, 46–47, 48f
Code Space, 21
Cofense Phishing Detection and Response
    Platform, 87, 87f
Cognitive bias, 357–358, 358t–360t
Cognitive mind, 342
COGS, *see* Costs of goods sold
Collins, Jim, 284
Colonial Pipeline, 170
Colorado Timberline, 21
Commitments, 67, 279, 280
Commitment yes, 372
Committee of Sponsoring Organizations
    (COSO), 172–173, 180, 184,
    187, 188, 198
Common Vulnerabilities and Exposures
    (CVEs), 206
Communication, 239–271
    and asking questions, 244–248
    and body language, 249–252
    in crucial conversations, 256–267
    and Emotional Intelligence, 324–325
    and explaining why, 252–253
    and hiring, 315
    and listening, 241–244
    of risk information, 228–231
    and smiling, 248–249
    and storytelling, 253–256, 262–264
    of vision, 328
Community, building, 332
Company culture, 176–178, 369
Company performance measures,
    33–34
Competency interviews, 317–318
Competitive Advantage (Porter), 34–36, 35f
Complex choices, structuring, 77
Compliance Assessment, 42–43
Conative mind, 342
Conceptualization, by servant leaders, 331
Confirmation bias, 64, 359t
Confirmation yes, 372
Conflict, managing through, 290–294
Congruence, 281
Consequences of data attacks, identifying
    potential, 209
Consistency, and trust, 281
Continuous improvement, 184, 223,
    225–226, 325
Continuous integration/continuous
    deployment (CI/CD), 38, 74, 380
Contract termination, lost revenue from, 21
Controlling others, 261
Core priorities, clarifying your, 66
Core values, 176–178
Corporate governance, 173–180. *See also*
    Boards of directors
    board oversight, 174–175
    capable individuals in, 178–180
    case study in failure of, 190–194
    and core values, 176–178
    and operating structures, 175–176
Corrective action plans (CAPs), 216, 233
Correspondence bias, 358t
COSO, *see* Committee of Sponsoring
    Organizations
Costs, 131–137
    of data breaches, 197
    incremental, 131–132, 132f
    opportunity, 62, 133–135, 134f
    sunk, 135–136
    training, 363
Cost avoidance, cost savings vs.,
    136–137
Cost-benefit analysis (CBA), 143–146
    assigning monetary values in, 144–145
    brainstorming in, 143–144
    case study, 156–157, 157f,
        158t–159t, 159–160
    comparing costs and benefits in, 145
    flaws of, 145–146

Cost center, cybersecurity as, 15
Costs of goods sold (COGS):
  and EBITDA, 15
  on income statement, 13–14
Cost of mis-hires (measure), 313
Cost of revenue, on income statement,
  13–14
Cost savings, cost avoidance vs., 136–137
Counterfeit yes, 372
Covey, Stephen R., 129, 177, 279,
  281, 289, 340
COVID-19 pandemic, 44, 198, 357
"C-players," 313, 314
Creative Thinking Cards Deck, 144, 293
Credibility, 177
CRIB, 260
CRO (Chief Revenue Officer), 42
Crowdstrike, 181
Crucial conversations, 180, 256–267
  exploring others' paths in, 265–266
  learning to look in, 259–261
  making it safe in, 261–262
  moving to action in, 266–267
  starting with the heart in, 258
  STATEing your path in, 264–265
  storytelling in, 262–264
Crucial Conversations: Tools for Talking
  When the Stakes are High
  (Patterson et al.), 257
Cryptocurrency, 21
CSA (Cloud Security Alliance), 294
CSO Online, 26–27
CTO (Chief Technology Officer),
  25–26, 42
Customer relationship management
  (CRM), 176
CVEs (Common Vulnerabilities and
  Exposures), 206
CVE-2021-3156, 130–132
CVSS score, 200
Cyber risk, managing, see Risk
  management
Cybersecurity:
  as business issue, 170
  as cost center, 15
  as part of value chain, 34–37
  and personality type, 348, 349f
Cybersecurity and Infrastructure Agency
  (CISA), 205
Cybersecurity and Resiliency
  Observations, 170

Cybersecurity goals, and organizational
  mission, 9–10
Cybersecurity steering committees,
  175–176, 186
Cybersecurity strategy, 180–190
  business context of, 180–184
  and evaluation of alternative
    strategies, 188–189
  and formulation of business
    objectives, 189–190
  and risk appetite, 184–188
Cybersecurity Ventures, 179, 227
Cybersecurity Workforce Study
  ((ISC)²), 350, 350f
Cyber unit (SEC), 170
Cybint, 179
Cybrary, 179

D

Dalio, Ray, 9, 58
Dashboards, hiring, 315–316
DAST (Dynamic Application Security
  Testing), 63, 184
Data Breach and Investigation
  Report, 197–198
Data breaches, average cost of, 197
Data Classification and Protection Policy, 187
Data Loss Prevention (DLP), 43
DCF (discounted cash flow), 100, 107
Deaton, Angus, 56
Debt repayment plans, 21
Debt-to-Equity (D/E) ratio, 18
Decision making, 58, 60–68
Decision science, 60
Decisive (Heath and Heath), 60–61
Decomposition, 211
Defaults (in NUDGES framework),
  73–74, 85–86
Defcon, 294
The Definitive Book of Body Language
  (Pease and Pease), 250–251
DEI (diversity, equity, and inclusion), 356–358
Deloitte, 25, 363
Deloitte & Touche Consulting, 297
Deming, W. Edwards, 34
Denver Broncos, 329
Department of "no," cybersecurity teams
  as, 369–371
Depreciation, on income statement, 16, 22

DevOps teams, 26
Dichotomy of Leadership (Babin), 284
Digital Certificates, 43
Digital transformation, 199, 339–340
Dilbert, 354, 354*f*
Diligence questionnaires, 13
Direction, providing, 334
Direct labor costs, 13
Direct-to-consumer strategies, 118–119, 123
Disagreements, 326
Disciplined attention, maintaining, 334
Discounted cash flow (DCF), 100, 107
Distress, regulating, 334
Distribution center automation, 117–118, 122
Diversification, 116–117, 121–122
Diversity, equity, and inclusion (DEI), 356–358
Diversity, of corporate boards, 174–175
Dividends, 99, 100
DLP (Data Loss Prevention), 43
DMAIC process, 225–226
Docker Images, 26, 66
Drive (Pink), 72
Drucker, Peter, 176
Dynamic Application Security Testing
    (DAST), 63, 184

E

Earnings Before Interest, Taxes, Depreciation,
    and Amortization (EBITDA), 22,
    25, 102, 113
  on income statement, 15–16
  risk impact on, 213
Earnings Before Interest and Taxes (EBIT), 16
eBay, 317
*The 8th Habit: From Effectiveness to
    Greatness* (Covey), 289
80/20 rule, 40
Einstein, Albert, 199, 244
Eisenhower, Dwight D., 64
Email, 325
Embodied cognition, 360*t*
Emotional Intelligence (EQ), 322–326
  definition of, 322–323
  domains of, 323–324
  steps for improving, 324–326
Empathy, 76, 325, 331, 335, 373–375
Enable Others to Act (LPI® 360), 346
Encourage the Heart (LPI® 360), 346
Energy Policy Act (2005), 230
Engagement, 178

Enterprise risk management (ERM),
    171–174, 185*f*, 188, 200. *See also*
    Risk management
  continuous improvement in,
    223, 225–226
  and development of portfolio view, 218
  and risk/performance review, 221
  and risk prioritization, 212–214
  and risk response, 215
Enterprise Strategy Group, 179
Enterprise Value (EV), 18–19
EQ, *see* Emotional Intelligence
Equifax, 169, 230
Equity value drivers, 108*f*
ERM, *see* Enterprise risk management
Error, expecting, 76, 86
ESG, 355
EternalBlue, 50
European Union (EU), 184, 202, 230
EV (Enterprise Value), 18–19
Executive summaries, 320
Executive support, gaining, 178, 197, 198
Expect Error (in NUDGES framework), 76, 86
Expedited learning, 58
Experiments, conducting small, 65
Explaining why, 252–253
Extortion, 21
Extraversion (E) – Introversion (I) scale
    (MBTI), 347–348
Extreme Ownership (Willink and Babin), 252
Eye contact, 251

F

Face, in body language, 250
The Face: A Natural History (McNeill), 248
Facebook, 230
Fact Finding (Kolbe A Index), 342
"Fail fast, fail often," 58, 327
"Failing intelligently," 39
FAIR Institute, 67
FAIR technique, 189
Faux options, avoiding, 62
Favors, returning, 296
FCFF (future cash flow to the firm), 107
FedEx, 227
FedRAMP certification, 181
Feedback:
  and Emotional Intelligence, 325
  giving, 74–76, 86
  from interviewers, 320

Feelings, dealing with others', 323
FERC, 230
Ferrazzi, Keith, 295, 297–298
Ferrazzi Greenlight, 297
Financial analysis, 143–153
   cost-benefit analysis, 143–146
   Net Present Value, 146–153
Financial buyers, 96–97
Financial Planning and Analysis (FP&A) team,
   14, 25, 42, 109
Financial statements, 12–24
   balance sheet, 17–19
   connections between, 21–22, 23f, 24
   gaming the (case study), 24–25
   income statement, 12–17
   statement of cash flows, 19–21
   visibility of, 29
Firewalls, 317
Firm infrastructure, cybersecurity as, 35
The Five Practices of Exemplary
   Leadership, 345–347
"Five W's," 230–231
Focusing, by adaptive leaders, 332
Follow Thru (Kolbe A Index), 342
Follow-up, importance of, 298
Forced empathy, 373–375
Foresight, of servant leaders, 331
Forrester, 286
Fowler, James H., 249
FP&A team, see Financial Planning and
   Analysis team
Framing, 360t
Fraud, 21
Free Cash Flow, 22
FUD (Fear, Uncertainty, and Doubt), 27
Fuller, Buckminster, 289
Future cash flow to the firm (FCFF), 107
Future Value, 149

G

Gains, realization of, 101–102
Gallup, 339–341
Gamification, 71
Gartner, 40, 114, 286
General Data Protection Regulation (GDPR),
   170, 202, 229, 230
General Electric, 223
Generation X, 350, 351t–352t
Generation Z, 350, 351t–352t, 353

Georgia State University, 310
Gestures, 251
getAbstract, 11
"Getting on the balcony," 334
Getting to Yes (Fisher and Ury), 291, 292
Give Feedback (in NUDGES framework),
   74–76, 86
Global Data Protection Regulation, 184
Globalization, 339–340
Goals:
   of business, 31
   cybersecurity, 9–10
Goleman, Daniel, 322–323
Google, 340
Goulston, Mark, 243
Governance, see Corporate governance
Governance, risk, and compliance (GRC)
   functions, 179, 228
Governance and Culture (COSO framework),
   173–180, 198
Greenleaf, Robert K., 329
Gross margin, 14
Gross profit (GP), on income statement, 14
Group Report (LPI® 360), 347

H

Hallway conversations, 297–298
"Happiness is Love – and $75,000" (Deaton
   and Kahneman), 56
Harkins, Malcolm, 9–10, 37
Harnish, Verne, 311
Harvard Business Review Analytic
   Services, 324
Harvard University, 249
Head movement, 251
Healing, and servant leadership, 331
Healthcare industry, 230
Heath, Chip, 60–61, 255–256
Heath, Dan, 60–61
Hedge funds, 98
Helping others, commitment to, 331–332
High performing teams, 307–336
   case application, 334–336
   coaching new members of, 321
   interviewing for, 316–320
   job scorecard for, 313–314
   leading, 322–334 (See also Leadership)
   measuring success of, 321–322
   networks as source for, 314–315

recruiting, 310–322
  screening candidates for, 315–317
Hindsight, prospective, 67
Hindsight bias, 360*t*
HIPAA, 218, 227, 229, 230
Hiring, 310–311, 361. *See also* Topgrading
Home Depot, 169
Horowitz, Ben, on company culture, 177
How to Read a Financial Report (Tracy),
  21, 23*f*, 24
How to Win Friends and Influence People
  (Carnegie), 295
*How to Win Friends and Influence
  People in the Digital Age* (Carnegie
  Associates), 295–296
Hubbard Decision Research, 67
Human capital management, 339–364
  case application, 362*t*, 363
  and diversity, 356–358, 358*t*–360*t*
  with multigenerational workforce, 350,
    350*t*–352*t*, 353–354
  as opportunity, 339–340
  strengths-based leadership for, 340–350
  and training, 354–356, 361, 362*t*
Humble, being, 284–286
Humes, James C., on communication, 239

I

IaC (Infrastructure as Code), 49
IASTS (interactive application security
  testing), 184
IBM, 197
Idealized influence, as element of
  transformational leadership, 327
Identity and Access Management (IAM),
  215, 293–294
Identity Governance and Administration
  (IGA), 67
IDP (Individual Development Plan), 321
Impact, risk, 211, 213*t*
Implementor (Kolbe A Index), 342
iNcentives (in NUDGES framework),
  69–72, 82–85
Income statement, 12–17
  costs of goods sold/cost of
    revenue on, 13–14
  depreciation and amortization on, 16
  EBITDA on, 15–16
  EBIT on, 16
  gross profit on, 14
  income tax expense on, 17
  interest expense on, 16–17
  net income on, 17
  revenue on, 12–13
  sales, general, and administrative
    expenses on, 15
  top line of, 12
Income tax expense, on income
  statement, 17
Incremental costs, 131–132, 132*f*
Independent software vendors (ISVs), 26
Indicators of compromise (IOC), 208
Individual Development Plan (IDP), 321
Individual Feedback Report (LPI®
  360), 346–347
Individualized consideration, as element of
  transformational leadership, 327
Influence, idealized, 327
Influence mapping, 139–140, 141*f*, 375
Influencer, 72
Information, Communication, and Reporting
  (COSO framework), 226–231
Information security management system
  (ISMS), 189
Information Security Systems Association
  (ISSA), 179, 294, 355
Information Sharing and Analysis Centers
  (ISACs), 63
Information Systems Audit and Control
  Association (ISACA), 294
InfraGard, 220
Infrastructure as Code (IaC), 49
Injunctive norming, 71
Insolvency, 20, 21
Inspirational motivation, as element of
  transformational leadership, 327
Inspire a Shared Vision (LPI® 360), 346
Insurance, cybersecurity, 354
Intangible assets, 16, 19
Intellectual property, 19, 21, 202
Intellectual property rights, 16
Intellectual stimulation, as element of
  transformational leadership, 327
Interactive application security testing
  (IASTS), 184
Interest expense, on income state-
  ment, 16–17
Internal Rate of Return (IRR), 151–153
International Organization for Standardization
  (ISO), 189

Internet, 171
Interviews:
    competency, 317–318
    tandem, 318–320
    telephone screening, 316–317
Introverts, 294, 347–348
Inventory, 202–205
IOC (indicators of compromise), 208
Iraq War, 284
IRR (Internal Rate of Return), 151–153
ISACs (Information Sharing and Analysis
    Centers), 63
ISACA (Information Systems Audit and
    Control Association), 294
Isay, Dave, on great stories, 253
(ISC)², 178, 350
ISMS (information security management
    system), 189
ISO (International Organization for
    Standardization), 189
ISO 22301: Societal Security – Business
    continuity management
    systems – Requirements, 205
ISO27001 certification, 44, 175, 181, 189
ISO/IEC 27002:2013, 216
ISSA, see Information Security Systems
    Association
ISVs (independent software vendors), 26
I Think, You Think, We All Think Differently
    (Buschman), 356

J

James, Cynthia, 367
Job history forms, 315
Jobs, Steve:
    on getting close to your customers, 275
    on influencing the world around you, 29
Job scorecards, 313–314
Johnson, Brad, 356
Johnson, Mike, 154*f*
Judging (J) – Perceiving (P) scale (MBTI), 348
Jung, Carl, 347
*Just Listen: Discover the Secret to
    Getting Through to Absolutely Anyone*
    (Goulston), 243

K

Kahneman, Daniel, 56, 60, 61, 310
Kahneman, Daniel, on courage vs.
    overconfidence, 55

Kaizen, 144
Kaseya, 170
Kaufman, Josh, 11
Key performance indicators (KPIs), 33,
    40, 185–186, 221–223, 222*f*, 224*t*,
    225–226, 254
Key risk indicators (KRIs), 185–186,
    220–223, 224*t*, 225–226, 254, 256
Kickstarter, 65
Kolbe, Kathy, 341
Kolbe A/B/C Indices, 341–343
Kouzes, James M., 345
KPIs, see Key performance indicators
KRIs, see Key risk indicators
Kubernetes (k8s) Clusters, 26, 66

L

Labeling, 261
Labor costs, direct, 13
Lag measures, 34, 40
Language, injunctive norming with, 71
Laping, Chris, 133, 328
Law of reciprocity, 296
Leadership, 322–334
    adaptive, 332–334, 333*t*
    case application, 334–336
    elements of, 309
    and Emotional Intelligence, 322–326
    servant, 329–332
    strengths-based, 340–343, 344*f*,
        345–350, 349*f*
    transformational, 326–329
    value of effective, 309
Leadership Practices Inventory (LPI®
    360), 345–347
Leadership voices, protecting, 334
Lead measures, 34
The Lean Startup (Reis), 58
Learning:
    from emotional experience, 325
    expedited, 58
    proprietary, 36
Learning to look, in crucial conversations,
    259–261
Leveraging, and D/E ratio, 18
*The Life and Times of Cybersecurity
    Professionals 2020* (report), 179
Likelihood, risk, 210–211, 213*t*
Limit test, 67
Linkages, in value chain, 35–36
LinkedIn, 298, 315, 356

Listening, 241–244, 283–284, 296, 330–331
Little and King, LLC, 21
Logicworks, 41*f*, 43
LPI® 360 (Leadership Practices
    Inventory), 345–347

M

McAfee, 181
McKinsey & Company, 221, 222, 286
McNeill, Daniel, 248
Made to Stick (Heath and Heath), 255–256
Madison, James, on knowledge, 169
Making it safe, in crucial conversations,
    261–262
MAM (mobile application management), 176
Mappings, 72–73, 85
Market-based valuation, 100
Marketing, 115–116, 120–121
Masking, 260
MBTI (Myers-Briggs Personality Type
    Indicator), 347–350, 349*f*
Measure(s):
    baseline hiring success as, 312
    of company performance, 33–34
    cost of mis-hires as, 313
    lag, 34, 40
    lead, 34
    organizational cost of mis-hires as, 313
    of success of high performing
        teams, 321–322
    talent projection as, 312
"Mere-measurement" effect, 71–72
Microsoft Azure, 73, 356
Microsoft STRIDE, 206, 378–379
Millennials, 350, 351*t*–352*t*
Mirroring (body language), 251
"Mis-hires," 310, 313
Mitigate (risk response), 215
MITRE, 206, 207
Mobile application management (MAM), 176
Mobile devices, global ownership of, 197
Mobilization, by adaptive leaders, 332
Model the Way (LPI® 360), 345–346
Modern Portfolio Theory (MPT), 39
*MOJO Maker for Womxn in Tech
    Podcast*, 356
Monte-Carlo analysis, 211
Motivation, 69, 70*f*, 323
    by adaptive leaders, 332
    as element of transformational
        leadership, 327

Mt. Gox, 21
MPT (Modern Portfolio Theory), 39
Multi-factor Authentication, 43
Multigenerational workforce, managing a,
    350, 350*t*–352*t*, 353–354
Multiples valuation model, 105–107
Myers, Isabel, 347
Myers-Briggs (company), 348
Myers-Briggs Personality Type Indicator
    (MBTI), 347–350, 349*f*

N

Names, remembering, 296
National Association of Corporate Directors
    (NACD), 170–171
National Council of ISACS, 220
National Security Agency (NSA), 50
Negotiation, 367–380
    case study, 377–380
    and cybersecurity teams as department
        of "no," 369–371
    empathy in, 373–375
    as opportunity, 367–369
    as a team, 375–376
    and varying types of "yes," 372
NERC CIP, 227, 230
Net 30 payment terms, 20
Net 45 payment terms, 20
Net income:
    and EBIT, 16
    and EBITDA, 15
    on income statement, 17
    and retained earnings, 22
Net Present Value (NPV), 146–153, 160–164
Net revenue, 13, 15, 16
Networking:
    for job candidates, 315
    professional, 294–298
Never Eat Alone (Ferrazzi), 295, 297–298
*Never Split the Difference: Negotiating As If
    Your Life Depended on It* (Voss), 369
9 Box of Controls, 133–134, 134*f*
NIST, 204, 205
NIST Cybersecurity Framework, 188, 191
"NISTIR 8179 Criticality Analysis Process
    Model: Prioritizing Systems and
    Components," 204–205
NIST SP 800-53, 216
NIST Special Publication 800-34r1:
    Contingency Planning Guide for
    Federal Information Systems, 205

Nonoperating expense, interest as, 16–17
NopSec, 74, 75f
Norelius, Tazin Khan, 356
Norsk Hydro, 228, 229f
Nortel Networks, 21
North Korea, 50
"No," saying, 280
NotPetya, 227
NPV (Net Present Value), 146–153, 160–164
NSA (National Security Agency), 50
NTT, 353
Nudges, 68–69
NUDGES framework, 69, 82
NYDFS, 175

O

Objective, being, 293–294
Objectives, business, 189–190
OCTAVE® (Operationally Critical Threat,
        Asset, and Vulnerability
        Evaluation), 206
ODM (outcome-driven metrics), 40
Office of Compliance Inspections and
        Examinations (OCIE), 170
The Open Group, 189
Open Web Application Security Project
        (OWASP), 183, 295, 377, 378
Operating activities, 19
Operating expenses, 15
Operating profit, 16
Operating structures, establishing, 175–176
Operationally Critical Threat, Asset, and
        Vulnerability Evaluation (OCTAVE®), 206
Opportunity costs, 62, 133–135, 134f
Opposite, considering the, 65
Options:
    faux, 62
    generating, 293
    removing, 62
Orca Side Scanning, 182
Organizational cost of mis-hires (measure), 313
Organizational mission, and cybersecurity
        goals, 9–10
Organizing, by adaptive leaders, 332
Orienting, by adaptive leaders, 332
Others:
    feelings of, 323
    recognizing emotions in, 324
    taking an interest in, 295, 296, 329–332

Outcome-driven metrics (ODM), 40
Overconfidence, 67, 77, 360t
OWASP, see Open Web Application
        Security Project
Ownership, taking, 280–281
Oxytocin, 254–255

P

PAIR (Productive Asset Investment Ratio), 19
Parallel, exploring multiple options in,
        62–63
Pareto Principle, 40
Passwordless initiatives, 136
Patents, 16
Payment Card Industry Data Security
        Standard (PCI DSS), 189
Payment terms, 20
Pease, Allan, 250–251
Pease, Barbara, 250–251
Peer pressure, 71–72
Penetration (pen) testers, 29–30
Penetration tests (pentests), 207, 207f, 208
People, as weakest link in cybersecurity
        programs, 176–178
People Before Things (Laping), 328
PER (price-to-earnings ratio), 105–106
Performance (COSO framework), 198–218
Performance measures, company, 33–34
Personal attacks, avoiding, 291–292
Personal incentives, 70–71
The Personal MBA (Kaufman), 11
Personal motivation, 69
Persona theory, 347
Perspective, shifting your, 66
Persuasion, by servant leaders, 331
Peterson, Jordan, on listening, 244
PE (private equity) transactions, 33
Phishing defense, 83, 83t, 84, 87f
Phoenix Project, 144
Pink, Daniel, 72, 179
Pluralsight, 179
Politicians, 281
Porter, Michael, 34–36, 35f, 46, 49, 181
Porter's Five Forces, 106, 181
Portfolio view (risk management),
        217, 217f, 218
Positive injunctive norming, 71
Positive reinforcement, 178
Positive thinking, 325

Posner, Barry Z., 345
Posture, 251
Power grid, 230
PPE (Property, Plant, and Equipment), 19
Premortems, 67
Prepare to be Wrong (in WRAP
    mnemonic), 61, 66–68
Pre-scripted Public Relations communication
    plans, 229
Present Value, 146–149
Presidential Executive Order 14028, 170
Prevention focus, 61–62
Price-to-earnings ratio (PER), 105–106
Priming bias, 359*t*
Priorities, clarifying your core, 66
Prioritization, risk, 212–214
Privacy by Design, 184
Private equity firms, 98
Private equity (PE) transactions, 33
Prizes, monthly, 178
Problem, separating people from
    the, 291–292
Processes, systems and, 37–38
Process of summary, 245
Proctor, Paul, 40
Productive Asset Investment Ratio (PAIR), 19
Professional networking, 294–298
Profit:
    and cash flow, 19–20, 24
    operating, 16
Project managers, 183
Promises, keeping, 279
Promotion focus, 61–62
Property, Plant, and Equipment (PPE), 19
Proprietary learning, 36
Prospective hindsight, 67
Provider-1, 317
Purdue Global, 353
Python for Managers, 180

Q

Qualitative analysis, 210
Quantitative analysis, 210
Questions:
    asking, 244–248
    interview, 317–318
Questionnaires, diligence, 13
QuickStart (Kolbe A Index), 342
Quick wins, 328

R

RAF (Risk Acceptance Form), 371
Ramadi, battle of, 284
Ransomware, 21, 227–228
Raw materials, 13
Reality-Test Your Assumptions (in WRAP
    mnemonic), 61, 64–65
Reassessment Report (LPI® 360), 347
Recruitment, 310–311. *See also*
    Topgrading
Redemptions, 99
Red team assessments, 208
Reference calls, candidate-arranged,
    320–321
Reference checks, 315
Referral programs, 315
Regulatory environment, 230
Reis, Eric, 58
Relationship management, 275–305
    case studies in, 298–302
    and conflict, 290–294
    and Emotional Intelligence, 324
    indirect influence in, 286–290
    as opportunity, 275–276
    and professional networking,
        294–298, 300–302
    and trust, 277–286
Removing options, 62
Requests for Proposal (RFPs), 63
Residual risk, 209
Resilient, being, 325
Resumes, 315
Retained earnings, 22
Revenue:
    accelerating, 13
    cost of, 13–14
    definition of, 12–13
    on income statement, 12–13
    net, 13, 15, 16
Review and Revision (COSO
    framework), 219–226
Reviews, 221–223, 224*t*
RFPs (Requests for Proposal), 63
Risk, value, cost (RVC) maps, 40, 114
Risk Acceptance Form (RAF), 371
Risk-adjusted Value Model (RVM),
    40, 73
Risk appetite, 184–189
"The Risk-based Approach to Cybersecurity"
    (whitepaper), 221, 222

Risk identification, 201–209, 201*t*
    attack scenarios, potential, 206–208
    consequences, potential, 209
    and inventory/value of assets, 202–205
    threats, potential, 205–206
Risk information, communication of, 228–231
Risk management, 197–235. *See also*
        Enterprise risk management (ERM)
    assessment of risk severity, 209–211
    assessment of substantial
        change, 219–221
    case application, 231–233
    and communication of risk
        information, 228–231
    continuous improvement in,
        223, 225–226
    identification of risk, 201–209
    leveraging technology in, 227–228
    portfolio view in, 217–218
    prioritization of risks, 212–214
    and regulatory environment, 230
    reviews, 221–223, 224*t*
    and risk responses, 214–216
    third-party, 13, 20
    vulnerability, 24
Risk registers, 209
Risk responses, 214–216
Risk tolerance, 174, 180, 185–187, 188*f*
Rocky Mountain Information Security
        Conference, 294
Rogers, Carl, on listening, 243
RSA, 294, 383
Russell, Paul, 340
RVC (risk, value, cost) maps, 40, 114
RVM (Risk-adjusted Value Model), 40, 73

S

Sales, General, and Administrative (SG&A)
        expenses, 15, 25
Sales commissions, 13
SamSam ransomware, 227
SANS Institute, 179
SANS Internet Storm Center, 220
Sarcasm, 258, 260, 266
SAST (Static Application Security Testing),
        63, 183–184
"Say what you do and do what you
        say," 279–281
SbD (Security by Design), 182–184

SCADA (supervisory control and data
        acquisition system), 202–203
*Scaling Up: How a Few Companies Make It
        . . .and Why the Rest Don't (Rockefeller
        Habits 2.0)* (Harnish), 311
Schleen, DJ, 39
Schlereth, Mark, 329–330
School of Thought, 144, 293
Scientific method, 58–59, 59*f*, 65
SCI-PAB® Thinking & Messaging Tool,
        140–143, 153–156
Screening job candidates, 315–317.
        See also Interviews
SDLC (software development life cycle), 262
Securities and Exchange Commission (SEC),
        169–170, 230
Security by Design (SbD), 182–184
Security Culture Index, 75–76
Security Performance Management
        (SPM), 37–39
SEI (Software Engineering Institute), 206
Self-serving bias, 359*t*
Sensing (S) – Intuition (N) scale (MBTI), 348
SentinelOne, 181
Serial, exploring multiple options in, 62–63
Servant leadership, 329–332
SG&A (Sales, General, and Administrative)
        expenses, 15, 25
Shared vision, 327–329, 346
Sharpe Ratio, 39
Shedd, John A., 197
Shifting your perspective, 66
Shipping costs, 13
SIEMs, 228, 284
Silence patterns, 260–261
Sinek, Simon, on being emotionally
        invested, 339
Single Sign-on, 43
Site Reliability Engineering (SRE), 379
Six Sigma, 223, 225
Sleep, getting enough, 325
Small experiments, conducting, 65
Smart, Brad, 310–311
SMART goals, 189, 321, 328
Smartphones, 353
"Smile-leniency effect," 248
Smiling, 248–249, 295
Smith, David, 356
"Snapshots," hiring, 315
SOAR platforms, 228
SOC2 certification, 175, 181

Social incentives, 71–72
Social media, 295
Social motivation, 69
Social networks, 315
Socrates, 245
Socratic Method, 245–247
Software development life cycle
    (SDLC), 262
Software Engineering Institute (SEI), 206
Solargate, 287
Solarwinds, 170
SolarWorld, 21
SRE (Site Reliability Engineering), 379
Stakeholder analysis, 138, 139, 139f, 375
Standardized Work, 144
Starting with the heart, in crucial
    conversations, 258
Statement of cash flows, 19–21
STATE method, 264–265
Static Application Security Testing (SAST),
    63, 183–184
Statista, 350
Status-quo bias, 66, 360t
Steering committees, cybersecurity,
    175–176
Stewardship, by servant leaders, 331
StoryCorps, 253
Storytelling, 71, 253–256, 262–264, 328
Strategic buyers, 97
Strategy, cybersecurity, *see* Cybersecurity
    strategy
Strategy and Objective Setting (COSO
    framework), 180–190, 198
Straw man arguments, 243
Strengths-based leadership, 340–343, 344f,
    345–350, 349f
Stress:
    avoiding, 325
    communicating under, 260
Structural incentives, 72
Structural motivation, 69
Structure of Complex Choices (in NUDGES
    framework), 77, 86, 87
Successes, celebrating, 326
Sugarcoating, 260
Summary, process of, 245
Sunk costs, 135–136
Sunstein, Cass R., 68
Super-connectors, leveraging, 298
Supervisory control and data acquisition
    system (SCADA), 202–203

Symantec, 181
Systems, processes and, 37–38
Systems theory, 46

T

Tactics, techniques, and procedures
    (TTP), 30, 208
Taking ownership, 280–281
Talent projection (measure), 312
Tandem interviews, 318–320
Tangible assets, 16
Target, 169
Team(s):
    high performing (*see* High
        performing teams)
    negotiating as a, 375–376
Technical challenges, 333
Technology:
    integration of, 171
    leveraging, in risk management, 227–228
Telephone screening interviews, 316–317
10/10/10 strategy, 65–66
Territory (body language), 251
Thaler, Richard H., 68
Theory of Constraints, 144
Theory of Relativity, 199
Thinking, Fast and Slow (Kahneman), 60
Thinking (T) – Feeling (F) scale (MBTI), 348
Third-party risk management (TPRM), 13,
    20, 116–117
"This AND that," vs. "this or that," 63
Threats, identifying potential, 205–206
Threat and vulnerability management (TVM)
    programs, 24
Threat of reference check (TORC), 315
The Three Ways, 39
Topgrading, 310–322
    and coaching new hires, 321
    executive summaries in, 320
    and interviewing, 316–320
    job scorecards for, 313–314
    and measuring success annually,
        321–322
    and measuring your baseline success
        with hiring/promotion, 312–313
    and recruiting from your
        networks, 314–315
    reference calls in, 320–321
    and screening candidates, 315–317

TORC (threat of reference check), 315
TPRM, *see* Third-party risk management
Tracy, John A., 21, 23*f*, 24
Training, 354–356, 361, 362*t*
Transfer (risk response), 215
Transformational leadership, 326–330
Transparency, 282–283
Treadway Commission, 172
Trigger(s):
   knowing your, 325
   setting a, 67, 280
Trim-tabbing, 288–289
Truman, Harry S., on getting credit, 367
Trust:
   and company culture, 177
   establishing and maintaining, 277–286
   oxytocin and, 254–255
   and transformational leadership, 329
TTP (tactics, techniques, and
    procedures), 30, 208
Tversky, Amos, 60
TVM (threat and vulnerability management)
    programs, 24
Twitter, 171

U

Uber, 230
Unconscious bias, 358*t*
Understanding Mappings (in NUDGES
    framework), 72–73, 85
Unified Endpoint Management, 43, 64
University of California Berkeley, 170
University of Nebraska Lincoln, 343
University of San Diego, 249

V

Valuation, asset- vs. market-based, 100
Value, 91–126
   adding, to others, 296
   and audience, 95–99
   as black box, 29–30
   case study, 110–125
   determination of, 103–110
   in discounted cash flow model, 107–109
   importance of, 101–102
   for investors, 99
   investors and, 96–99, 98*t*
   locales for creation of, 100
   in multiples valuation model, 105–107

   as opportunity, 91–95
   and realization of gains, 100–101
Values (ethical), 176–178
Value chain, cybersecurity as part of, 34–37
Venture capital firms, 97
Verizon, 197–198, 230
Visible, being, 298
Vision, shared, 327–329, 346
Vital Behaviors, 40
Vital Smarts, 69–71
Voss, Chris, 367, 369, 372
VRM (Vulnerability Risk Management), 24
Vulnerability Management Index, 74, 75, 75*f*
Vulnerability reporting, 38
Vulnerability Risk Management (VRM), 24

W

Warehouse automation, 117–118, 122
Washington, Booker T., 307
Waterfall thinking, 65
Website, upgrading your, 315
Welch, Jack, 223
Welch, Suzy, 65
Westinghouse Nuclear, 21
"Whether or not" decisions, 62
Why, explaining, 252–253
Widen Your Options (in WRAP
    mnemonic), 61–64
Wilde, Oscar, 91
Willink, Jocko, 252, 284
Win Wire, 44
Wire transfer fraud, 21
Withdrawing (silence pattern), 261
World Economic Council, 197
World War II, 64
Worstell, Karen, 356
WRAP mnemonic, 60–61
Wrong, preparing to be, 66–68

Y

"Yes," in negotiations, 372
YouBit, 21

Z

Zak, Paul, 254–255
Zero Trust model, 43
Ziegler, Ken, 106